Does Multiculturalism Work in Europe?

An investigation of Turkish labour migration to Germany, the integration of Turkish immigrants into Germany, and the impacts of this on bilateral relations between Turkey and Germany

Osman Delialioğlu

Pichu Press

A catalogue record for this book is available from the British Library

ISBN: 978-1-907962-22-6

Published by Pichu Press

This book is dedicated to the memory of my mother Zeliha Őzer Delialioğlu who passed away at the age of 28 when I was a little boy. It is also dedicated to former PM of Turkey Mustafa Bülent Ecevit (1925-2006) and to my wife Eva Ersoy Delialioğlu.

February 2012

Contents

1 Germany's immigration policy from 1960 to 2007   1

2 Germany's integration policy   42

3 Methodology, implied methods on integration of
   Turkish immigrants   80

4 Primary data analysis survey conducted on Turkish
   immigrants' integration, analysis of 30 survey questions   114

5 Analysis of specific grouped questions with secondary
   Data derived from German sources on Turkish integration
   process by using graphs and tables   203

6 Employed a series of statistical models such as
   chi-square Bivariate), Pearson's correlation, linear
   regression and the Ordered logit to test and analyse   246

7 Comparing primary and secondary data of German public
   opinion reflecting the German attitudes towards the
   integration of Turkish immigrants and evaluating the
   results comparatively. Conclusion, recommendations and
   lessons from the research   259

Chapter 1

1.1 Chapter Introduction: Research objectives, research field and research question

This chapter deals with the background of the book and explores the migratory situation in Europe after World War II. I explore the background to Turkish migration by giving an explanation of why Turks migrated to Europe, and especially to Germany. I then consider Germany's encouraging immigration entry policy, guest workers recruitment stop, migration through family unification, and the formation of Turkish communities in German industrial areas. I outline general migration theories and compare the German case with other European countries' and their immigration policies within the EU context by using empirical approaches to (former guest-workers who are currently long-term residents) immigrants' economics, political and socio-cultural integration problems with limited access to social, civil and political rights.

Although immigration has been a long debated subject, many countries have economically benefited by the contribution of immigrants. For example, 17% of the economic growth in the UK in 2004 and 2005 can be attributed to the direct effect of immigration (Home Office, UK, 2007). This benefit can be exploited more if immigrants are well integrated in the host country. This requires a scientific examination of the problems that arise in the integration process. The deeper understanding of this problem will enable to design proper public policy on immigration. This thesis investigates this issue considering integration of Turkish immigrants into German society.

This study carries special importance for a number of reasons. Turkish immigrants are the largest minority group in Germany comprising 2.4 million people and the Turkish population alone constitutes more than 5% of Germany's inhabitants. A large entry of these labour workers occurred when West Germany suffered from labour shortage after the Second World War and subsequently during the economic boom in 1970s. Turks worked in the factories and places which were considered harmful and unsafe for German workers.[1] Despite their considerable contribution, even the third generation of these workers remained as foreigners, although they were born and raised in Germany still living there as "second class", excluded and deprived of their socio-economic and political rights have not been recognized yet by host authorities.[2]

---

[1] Wallraff, Günter: 'The Lowest of the Low' (*Ganz Unten* or "*Ich Ali*"), [Translated into Turkish by Osman Okkan], Kiepenheuser & Witsch, Köln, 1986, p. 104-105
(documented Wallraff's posing as a Turkish guest worker, and the mistreatment he received in that role at the hands of employers, landlords and the German government).

[2] Ulrich, Ralf: German Socio-economic Panel Study, "A Positive Approach to Migrants", Sarah Spencer (ed.), Rivers Oram Press 1994.Chapter 4, (p.65).
Guardian 1 September 1993, 'Old Germans need young migrants' pay'.

This has caused two major problems: neither Germany is being benefitted fully by exploiting their economic potential nor are the Turkish immigrants being suitably placed into greater German society.

This research aims at giving an explanation for their economic, politic and socio-cultural integration problems within the European integration and citizenship policies by investigating the factors which are facilitating or hindering the process of Turkish immigrants' integration into host society.

Studies of immigration and integration of legal resident immigrants in their host countries is a new emerging interdisciplinary field in Europe. Integration models from Canada, America and Australia can be applied by European countries. Classical immigration countries such as Australia, Canada, and America have developed multicultural integration policies based on point system, whereby highly skilled and educated immigrants gained automatic host country's resident permit and citizenship. Alternatively, European cases can be treated as a subfield of European integration, which deals with the adaptation of immigrants into host European countries, economically, politically, socially and culturally. Germany, France and Britain as the three major "host" countries should have a common European immigration and integration policy at least.

Previous studies indicate that Turkish immigrants have been a great economic asset to their host country (Germany). Ralf Ulrich argues that immigrants contribute more to the public purse than they receive from it. In 1989, immigrants paid 7.8% of all contribution to the pension fund but received only 1.9% of pension payments because of the young age structure of the immigrant population.[34] Faruk Şen claims that there is the need for immigrants to feel secure in German society and to have rights which incorporate them economically, socially, and politically as productive members of society. However, the German population needs to recognise and accept the contribution which Turks make. There are also allegations that Turks exclude themselves from German society, politics and culture. Then they are unwilling to be integrated sufficiently into German society and the German way of life.[5]

An investigation of Germany's immigration and integration policies and an empirical study on the integration of Turkish immigrants in Germany within European immigration and integration policies is the subject matter of this research.

In this research the following question has been addressed and investigated in seven chapters.

'Have Turkish immigrants integrated into Germany (during 1961-2007) and has their integration any impact on bilateral relations, either positively or negatively?

---

[3] Şen, Faruk: 'Identity Crises and Integration Constraints of Turkish Migrants in the Federal Republic of Germany'; German Socio-economic Panel Study, ILO, Geneva, 1989 (p.2).
Spencer, Sarah (Ed): 'Immigration as an Economic Asset', German Experience, "A Positive Approach to Migrants" Rivers Oram Press 1994, Chapter 5, p.93-103.
[4] Şen, Faruk: "The Historical Situation of Turkish Migrants in Germany". Published in:*Immigrants and Minorities,* Volume 22, Issue , July 2003 , pp. 208 - 227
[5] "The Turks live in parallel societies, urban areas where Turkish grocers, Turkish satellite television, and Turkish newspapers ease self-isolation. Between 10 percent and 15 percent of the immigrant population is "unwilling" to be part of German society", says Interior Minister Thomas de Maiziere, whose department is responsible for immigration affairs.

The aim of this thesis is to investigate Turkish immigrants' integration level into Germany and impact of their integration on bilateral relations by giving an explanation of the factors which facilitate or hinder the integration process of Turkish immigrants, and aims at contributing to the creation of a public understanding of social, economic and political questions related to the integration of Turkish immigrants living in Germany. Since mutual recognition of both sides (Turkish immigrants and host countries) cultural distinctiveness of that each group brings to interaction partly plays a role in the immigrants' integration process. In addition, similarities between many previous integration policies will lead to a more successful long term integration policy and contribute to public understanding of social, economic and political questions related to integration of immigrants. The mutual lack of understanding between Turkish immigrants and German nationals deepens the existing problems of integration, even cause to disintegration, isolation, ghettoisation by creating parallel societies. Therefore, integration of immigrants into their host country is necessary to secure democracy, prosperity, and peaceful co-existence across Europe. In 1960s, immigration was considered to be a purely economic and temporary nature, thus having no social, political integration problems. However, by the mid 1970s economic recession and the rising unemployment rates resulted in politicisation of immigration and the introduction of restrictive immigration policies in most Western European countries.

The 'Europeanization' of the issue of immigration has given it a higher political importance. Two top leaders of the EU (French president Nicolay Sarkozy and German chancellor Angela Merkel's common plan on immigration) opened up a new field of research into the process of European integration. In fact, integration of Turks in Europe is not only German problem, it interests all the European countries which houses immigrants.

The specific challenges faced in Germany are formed in part by the historical notion of nationhood and the ungrounded threats perceived by a German population unaware of the positive aspect of multiculturalism.

This research can be a model for integration of immigrants from distinct language, social, cultural, political and religious background into host societies. Obviously, Turks and Germans are not indistinctive people like Austrians in Germany and Britons in Australia. However, as long as the host and immigrants have interaction, common interest such as in sportive activities, and some common goals their integration is possible into majority languages, cultures, social and political systems.

This thesis will not only contribute to the improvement of mutual understanding of the process of immigrants' integration into host countries, but will also improve bilateral relations between the nations.

1.1.2 The concept of migration

Migration is defined as a permanent or semi-permanent change of residence. It is a socio-economic and political phenomenon, which involves an origin and destination and includes in- or out migration. There is always a change in geographic region of residence which exposes migrants to a set of obstacles (including distance, new language and different environment) from known to unknown that are always present.[6]

---

[6] Evcil, Ayşe Nilay: An internal Conference on Globalism and Urban Change "People's Propensities on the Internal Migration: The Case of Turkey", City Futures 2009, PhD Thesis, Beykent University, Istanbul., 2009, p. 4

A *migrant* leaves one social environment for another at the cost of some socio-economic and political deprivations (such as voting rights) at home. Migration is population movement between two places or two nations. The movement of migrants is not random. These people have an intention to move from one place to another the reasons for which can be economic, politic or social. In the Turkish case *a guest worker* is actually attracted by the prospect of better socio-economic and political status abroad to earn money.[7] By this he hopes to achieve an income in his socio-economic and political status at home, and plans to return there at a later date.

From a capitalist point of view, migration (including migration forced by natural catastrophes, political persecution and wars) means a change of industrial production, marketing and consumption.[8]

Migration brings changes to the sending and receiving societies, and shapes the relationships between both states as well.

Movement Table 1.1

Motives or reasons for migrating

⇧

Origin or sender country---------------------------------→Host or receiver country

I   I

Return Migration<---------------------------------------Choosing a specific country

This movement is from an origin which is called 'sender country' to a certain destination that is called 'receiver country' and a distribution of migrant population occurs according to requirement of the chosen or receiver country.

Research on migration and ethnic relations is interdisciplinary: political science, sociology, history, economics, geography, psychology and law are all relevant. Immigration has appeared as a separate field of research dominated by historians, political scientists, economists and lawyers. Migration can change demographic and social structures, and bring a new cultural diversity. However, international migration does not always create diversity. For example, migrants such as Britons in Australia or Austrians in Germany are almost impossible to differentiate from the receiving populations.

---

[7] Siegfried Berninghaus and Hans Günther Seifert-Vogt: Journal of Economic Dynamics and Control (The role of the target saving motive in guest worker migration: A theoretical study) Volume 17, Issues 1-2, January-March 1993, Published by Elsevier B.V. (p. 181-205)

[8] Meçin, Mansur: The Question of Urban Integration and Forced Migration from East and Southeast Anatolian Regions after 1980: The Case of Mersin, PhD Thesis, Middle East Technical University, May 2004, p. 8-9

1.1.3 Historical role of migration in European socio-economic and political system

This section deals with the role of migration in international politics from ancient times to the present. Migration has been part of human history from the earliest times. It contributed to the development of world politics, legal and social institutions and formation of European political systems from ancient times to the present. Even current European citizenship law originated from classical times.

In classical times, migration played an important role in the rise and fall of empires such as the Greek and Roman empires, the relative power and interaction of Greek city-states as well as the transformation of Athens into a multi-ethnic empire and in the development of Roman citizenship and its role in the political incorporation of non-Romans.

Machiavelli argues that migration contributed to the rise of Roman Empire and its fall as well. [9] Morgenthau agrees that migration has also contributed to the United States and Russia becoming great powers in the 19th century.[10] Robert O. Keohane claims that labour migration contributed to shape international economic, politic, and social institutions as well as citizenship law of European nations. [11]

McNeill argues that "through migrations and borrowings, grain cultivation spread into Europe and India, China, and port of Africa."[12]

The history of migration, formation of city-states' political system in ancient Greece and Rome are useful contributions that indirectly affected the nation-state model on the pre-modern past as well as IR scholars' summons of Thucydides to prove the historical reach of their state-centric theories.[13] The multi-ethnicity of European societies and migration among these societies that spread that multi-ethnicity, informed the organisation of politics among European states up until the French revolution. The common conceptualization of world politics as a system of interacting states and state-centric IR theories based on it are probably useful for understanding world politics in the 19th and parts of the 18th and 20th centuries.

1.1.4 Migration Types and migratory situation in Europe since 1945

Migration types were classified as follows:

---

[9] Niccollo Machiavelli: The Prince, First Published 1515, Translated by W.K. Marriott "...even Machiavelli warned princes to take good note of the public's view" [tr. by George Bull], Penguin, 2006, (p.24).

[10] Hans J. Morgenthau, Politics Among Nations, Revised by Kenneth W. Thompson & David Clinton, Morgenthau "recognized the importance of migration to the US as he argued that immigration fuelled the development of American power and the international power vis-à-vis Western Europe", Published by McGraw Hill, 2005, p. 25, 131, 179-209

[11] Keohane O. Robert: Migration and Western Europe, Cambridge MIT Press, 1999 (p.188-92).

[12] McNeill, John Robert: A World History, The University Press of Kentucky, 2005, p 130-132)

[13] Rood, Tim: Thucydides and Athenian Imperialism, Oxford: Basil Blackwell (1963), ISNB 6-88143-072-2.

- Mass migration to U.S.A. in early 1900s, and then in wars; there was mass migration within Europe between 500 BC and c. 1100 A.D. and from the 1990 again.

- Second wave of mass migration occurred in Europe after World War II (1945)

- Seasonal migration: In 1956, 95 percent of recruited workers in Germany were such migrants.

- Pull migration: During the 1960-1973 there was a demand for labour power in host countries.- Push migration: 1973-1983 continued to encouraged foreign workers to go back home

- Return migration: those who return home and face re-integration problems

- Step migration: Some who passed to another country and settled down there

- Illegal migration: exists all the time

The German recruitment system of the 1960s was characteristically pull migration and British immigration expert Stephen Castles argued that "Post-Second World War Western European guest-worker policies created a riddle when unplanned, unforeseen mass settlement occurred. The guest-workers and their families could not be excluded from Western European democracies without grievous damage to the fabric of democracy".[14]

The migratory situation across Europe after World War II was multifaceted. About 12 million Germans had left Eastern Europe and about 6 million of them went to West Germany in the 1950s. The construction of the Berlin Wall in 1961 was necessitated by the flight of 2.6 million Germans moving from East to West German within which period of time (Once the wall was up, they would no longer migrate!). Belgium, France, the Netherlands and the United Kingdom were affected by return migration from their colonies during the process of decolonisation. More than 1 million French residents of Algeria resettled in France during 1954-1962 because of civil and anti-colonial war in Algeria.

1.1.5 Theories of emigration and immigration

Emigration of highly skilled migrants from less developed countries to post-industrial countries causes 'brain drain'. The *'brain drain'* suffered by eastern and south-eastern Europe delays its economic progress. Gunnar Myrdal argued that migration could make rich countries richer and the poor countries poorer. Most empirical studies confirm that immigration is mostly beneficial for the receiving countries.[15] Migration affects not only the migrants themselves, but the sending and receiving societies as a whole.

---

[14] Castles, Stephen and Mark, Miller: 'The Age of Migration', Third Edition, University of Oxford, 2003 (p.180)

[15] Sarah Spencer (ed.): 'Immigration is a great economic asset',), Rivers Oram Press, 1994, in Sarah Spencer, The German Experience, Strangers and Citizens, a positive approach to Migrants and Refugees, Rivers Oram Press, 1994, Myrdal, Gunnar, Ch. 2, (p. 34).

The emigration concentrates on younger and better qualified workforce. Emigration countries lose considerable investments they have made in education and training. The 'Brain drain' is not the case for the 1st generation Turkish guest workers. Even they have been selected by German recruitment officials according to their age, education level, and employment records in 1960s; mostly they have been employed in industrial sector. However, among second and third generation Turks have emerged an elite group including scientists. Turks in Germany have become German-Turks. Their language draws on both cultures, although they are treated as strangers in both Turkey and Germany. Over the years, among the younger generations, some writers, journalists, academics and politicians have begun to communicate (in German) between the two cultures and contribute to a new cross-cultural identity in German society.[16] However after 1973, German migration policy began to be less welcome, mainly because of oil crises and economic recession in the Western European countries but partly because these countries had completed their industrial revolution. Beside these, there was no need for additional man-power anymore because of mechanization which reduced the demand for unskilled migrant labour; all these resulted in turning pull-migration into push-migration.

"Push-pull" theories (1945-1973): The causes of migration are push-factors, impelling people to leave the areas of origin, and 'pull factors' attracting people to receiving countries. Pull factor has been attracted by a strong economy and sometimes active governmental encouragement. Internal and external factors affect supply. Push all internal factors affect demand. 'Push factors' include demographic growth, low living standards, lack of economic opportunities and political repression. Push migration increases unemployment and prices, while 'pull-factors' are demand for labour, availability of land, good economic opportunities and political freedoms. [17]

According to Petersen (1958), "Migration is not unitary; it differs from fertility and mortality in that cannot be analyzed, even primarily in terms of supra cultural, physiological factors but must be differentiated even at the most abstract level with the social conditions obtaining. This means that (the most general statement) that one can make concerning migration is in the form of a typology, rather than a law"[18]. His typology divided migration into 5 classes: primitive, impelled, forced, free, and mass. Each class was subdivided into two types; conservative migration, in which the mover changes residence to maintain his present standard of living, and innovative migration where the move is made in order to improve the living standards.

Geographer E. G. Ravenstein formulated "Statistical Laws of Migration" in the nineteenth-century. His theory explains the movement of people without regard to any particular temporal situation or location. Labour is not only caused to move but also desire to achieve a better

---

[16] 'Unhappy Turkish Academics emigrate to English speaking countries from Germany', Der Spiegel, 19 May 2008

A recent opinion poll shows a part of Turkish descent academics have a feeling as if they are unwelcome or unwanted in Germany, or they do not feel comfortable. Therefore, some consider returning Turkey (their country of origin) and some of them emigrate to English speaking countries Australia, Canada or America. The same poll suggests that 38 percent of academics of Turkish descent believe that they will be given more chance there if they return Turkey or emigrate to English speaking countries. 42 percent of them feel that they have been deprived of feeling at home in Germany. Every 4 in 5 academics believe that Germany does not have serious integration policy for its immigrants. [TRANSLATION]
Source: Der Spiegel, (19 May 2008)

[17] Zimmermann Klaus F.: European Migration, Push-pull theories, Proceeding of the World Bank Annual Conference on Development Economics, Munich, 1994 (p.313).

[18] Petersen's Typology of Migration, Petersen, Amer. Sociology Rev., Vol. 23, 1958, (p.229, 286).

material respects and find well-paid occupation.[19] Ravenstein argues under normal conditions the migratory movement will be a gradual from town to cities. Short distance movements like in America, where the conditions are exceptional. Second type, most moves from rural areas into towns, cities and metropolis. According to Ravenstein, '*Migration means life and progresses*'.[20] George Borjas suggests an 'immigration market' model.[21] Borjas claims that this approach leads to an empirically testable categorization of the types of immigrant flows.[22] According to his theory only disadvantaged people move from poor countries to richer areas and equalise wages and conditions in underdeveloped and developed regions. His theories have been criticised by Saskia Sassen as simplistic and unable of explaining real activities or predicting future ones.[23] An alternative economic approach is provided by the new 'economics of labour migration' suggested by Oded Stark. Stark argues that migration cannot simply be explained by income differences between two countries, but also by factors such as chances of secure employment.[24]

According to Aristide R. Zolberg labour migration is a "movement of workers required by the dynamics of the trans-national capitalist economy, which simultaneously determines both the push and pull."[25] This implies that migrations are collective phenomena, which should be examined as sub-systems of an increasingly global economic and political system.[26] An alternative explanation of international migration was provided from the 1970s called 'historical-structural approach'. This has its intellectual roots in Marxist political economy, and stresses the unequal distribution of economic and political power in the world economy. From a Marxist point of view migration is seen mainly as a way of mobilising cheap labour for capital.

Most empirical studies confirm that immigration is mostly beneficial for the receiving countries. Previous studies demonstrate that the economic growth of the 1960s and 1970s would not have been possible without immigrant labour.[27] Mehrländer also says that for many Germans integration means adopting German customs and traditions, but now German attitudes are much more positive: presence of immigrants 'is considered an enrichment of our society'. The social health and security systems like compulsory health and pension insurance have profited greatly from the contributions of immigrant workers. For example, in 1989 immigrant workers contributed 12.8 billion DM to the state pensions fund, 7.8 % of the total payments (164 billion

---

[19] Ravenstein, E.G.: The Laws of Migration, Journal of the Statistical Society of London, 1885-1989, Volume 48, Nr. 2, pp.167-235

[20] Ibid., (p. 28, 286)

[21] Borjas, George J.: *Friends or Strangers*, the impact of immigration on the U.S. Economy, New York Basic Books, 1990

[22] Borjas, George J.: Ethnic Capital and Intergenerational Mobility, *Quarterly Journal of Economics*, Vol. 107, No. 1, 1992, p. 123-150

[23] Saskia, Sassen: Columbia University 1988, Boyd, Alejandro Portes and Ruben G. Rumbaut, 1990

[24] Stark, Oded: The Migration of Labour, Basil Blackwell, Oxford, 1991 (pp. 406).

[25] Aristide R. Zolberg: Immigration and Multiculturalism in the Industrial Society, European Centre Vienna Averbury, 1989, (p. 401-7)

[26] Bauböck, Reiner; Heller, Agnes and Zolberg, Aristide R.: The Challenge of Diversity, Integration and Pluralism in Societies of Immigration, Aldershot (UK), 1996, 'Public Policy and Social Welfare', Volume 21, pp. 401-9

[27] Mehrländer, Ursula: 'Immigration as an Economic Asset', in: Chapter 1 Sarah Spencer (ed.), The German Experience, Strangers and Citizens, a positive approach to Migrants and Refugees, Rivers Oram Press, 1994, (p. 13-27)

DM); but only 3.43 billion DM (1.9 %) of the total pension was paid out to immigrant workers in 1992).

Hof argued that the economic impact of immigration was gainful until 1991.[28] Given anticipated developments mean that Germany will be even more dependent on immigrants in the future. According to Eva Kolinsky the economic impact of labour migration to German economy has been contributed to German welfare state. Germans have been especially proud of their economic achievement. Economic success, rising living standards and improved social opportunities were of vital importance for the acceptance of political democracy by the German population, for the social and political integration of its immigrants, and for the development of the contemporary welfare state and social policy.[29] Ralf Ulrich argues that the SOEP macro-data analysis suggest that immigrants contribute more to the public purse than they receive from[30]. In 1989, immigrants paid 7.8% of all contribution to the pension fund but received only 1.9% of pension payments because of the young age of structure of the immigrant population. According to Faruk Sen, each German worker would have to spend about 40% of his/her income on pension contributions without the presence of young migrant population.[31] Turks are showing an increasing interest in participating in the mainstream political parties. Sen argues also that the need for immigrants to feel secure in German society and to have rights which incorporate them economically, socially, and politically as productive members of society. However, the Germans need to recognise and accept the contribution which immigrants make.[32]

The push-pull model cannot explain why a certain group of migrants goes to one country rather than another: for example, why have most Algerians migrated to France and not Germany, while the opposite applies to Turks? West Germany was a major pull-migration receiving country in the 1960s, with pull-migration dominating until 1973. Perception of guest workers by German authorities was a temporary project until 1973. 1973 was a turning point as to whether Turkish immigrants would return home or stay permanently in the host country. However, circumstances such as the oil-shock and economic recession since 1973 have changed dramatically.

Parallel with Germany the EC member states' pull-migration policy turned into push factors in 1973, because of global changes and worldwide economic recession affected by rising oil prices and economic recession. Although the German authorities encouraged immigrants to return home at the beginning of 1980s, many Turks could not return home due to following reasons: they could not return home, even though some financial incentives were offered in 1983.The economic, social and political prospects in their countries of origin were not too bright. There was also political instability because of military coup in 1980 in Turkey.

The ending of recruitment contributed to clarifying the intention of foreign workers in Germany, many of whom then decided to stay with family members from their country of origin.

---

[28] Hof, B.: Arbeitskraftebedarft der Wirtschaft. Arbeitsmarktchancen fur Zuwandrer,in:Friedrich-Ebert-Stiftung (Hrsg.),Zuwanderungspolitik der Zukunft, Reihe Gesprachskreis Arbeit und Soziales, Nr.3,S.7-22, Bonn, 1992

[29] Horrocks, David and Kolinsky, Eva (eds.): Migrants or Citizens? 'Turks in Germany between Exclusion and Acceptance', "Non-German Minorities in Contemporary German Society" Berghahn Books, 1995, (p.78).

[30] Ulrich, Ralf: German Socio-economic Panel Study,"A Positive Approach to Migrants", Sarah Spencer (ed.), Rivers Oram Press 1994.Chapter 4, p.65.

[31] Şen, Faruk, 1994, 'Immigration as an Economic Asset', Chapter 5 in Sarah Spencer (ed.), The German Experience, Strangers and Citizens, a positive approach to Migrants and Refugees, Rivers Oram Press, 1994, (p. 93)

[32] Guardian 1 September 1993, 'Old Germans need young migrants' pay'.

1. Turkish guest workers could not have saved enough money to rebuild a new life again in their home country after being absent for 15-20 years. The Economic recession has affected both countries as well as themselves.

2. Their children attended German schools.

3. Some of the first generation guest-workers who returned to Turkey faced unpleasant experiences such as re-integration problems. Their German-born children were frustrated because of social and cultural alienation. [33]

4. Technological and communicative developments which abolished the existing deprivation of Turkish 1st and 2nd generation immigrants in Germany. Thanks to Satellite TV channels in late 1980s, Turkish immigrants could watch the same TV channel in Germany at the same time with their relatives in Turkey. In this way, deprivations such as longing, homesickness weakened the intention of 1st and 2nd generation Turks to return home.

5. Another important factor which made the return of Turks unnecessary in the eyes of many is the size of Turkish population in Germany. [34] Due to their high population rate, Turks created a new homeland similar to Turkey in the middle of the Germany. [35]

6. Compared with Turkey, the Turkish community in Germany has better economic, social, political, cultural and educational facilities for their children. They have their own social, cultural and religious organisations. [36] They have also their newspapers, their discos and commercial organisations. [37] They have even established their own airline companies which operate between Germany and Turkey with reduced prices. Many established their own businesses.

Turkish immigrants brought their Turkish life-style with them to Germany. They were sending money home until 1990; now they do not send money to Turkey any more. What they earn now they invest in Germany to establish their businesses, to building grounds, to buy houses and other real estate. Turkish immigrants in Germany own 220,000 properties in Germany. In this way, they became rooted in Germany. [38] Respond to these, foreigners in Turkey have bought 65,000

---

[33] Returned Turks and their German-born children in Turkey face re-integration problems. They are given a new name (*Alamanyali*) 'Turks from Germany' or (*Alamanci*) 'Germanised Turks'. Their children are victims of 'culture differences'. For many of them it is first contact with Turkey and face problems with Turkish language, education system, socialisation, and making new friendships in a new environment.

[34] Since an agreement between two states signed in 1961, there were only 225, 000 Turkish guest workers in Germany. Now by year 2008 this number has increased to over 2 million. These numbers are higher than some of the EU members such as Estonia, Lithonia, Malta and Cyprus.

[35] In 1980s Berlin, for example, a quart of Turkish immigrants lived in seven of the city's 75 districts. In Cologne, the situation is the same, a heavy concentration of Turks in private housing in the centre (Altstadt Nord) and in a northern industrial suburb (Fühlingen). This ghetto-style settlement is both a sign and cause of the immigrants' isolation from society at large.

[36] In 1982 the Turkish Islamic Union (DITIB) was founded as the German branch of the Turkish government's Directorate of Religious Affairs (Diyanet). By 1987, more than 50 per cent of the 1.7 Muslims in Germany were practising this form of Islam that conformed with the ideology of Atatürk's Secular state (Amiraux, 2000).
Turkish Islamic organisations became dominant and in 1995, more than 2.000 Turkish Islamic organisations were established. Most of these organisations are affiliated with the DITIB mosques controlled by the Turkish state, the Islamist Milli Gorus (AMTG) represent only a tiny fraction of the Turkish Muslims in Germany.

[37] Top-selling Turkish newspaper Hurriyet has a printing plant in Morfelden-Wattdorf which sells 50.000 copies a day in Germany.

[38] Turkish Ministry of Housing and Public Works' Report, Ankara, 16 June 2008. *Turkish parliament allow property sell to foreigners.* The Turkish parliament approved late Wednesday a government bill that allows sale of property to foreigners following the annulment of a similar law by the Constitutional Court. According to the bill, foreigners will be not allowed o

properties (**14%** of them are Germans who own houses in Turkey). As a result, the most important problem for Turks in Germany is their integration problems such as 'integration efforts of Turks and their acceptance by German society as new members'. German ambassador Eckhart Kuntz says the Turkish community in Germany is a component (a part of a whole) of the German society.[39]

As mentioned earlier, after 1973 pull migration lost its importance and encouraging the return migration became a government policy in West Germany. As the German recruitment policy ended in the economic crisis in 1973, family migration which is also called 'family reunification' became important and the German Government concentrated on active integration programs. At the same time return migration was encouraged by financial measures until 1983. In the same year a new conservative government came into power in Germany with an active push-migration policy. Foreigners from those countries which had a recruitment treaty with Germany were eligible to receive money, on condition that they returned to their home countries, if they were employed or performed short-term work in West Germany. Financial support was 10, 500 Deutsch Marks plus 1, 500 Deutsch Marks for each child leaving the country. About 17, 000 applicants were received (19, 000 were expected) and about 14,000 were accepted, but this policy was not continued.

As a consequence, it is evident that the majority of the Turkish population in Germany intends to settle and stay there permanently. Due to the negative economic conditions, unemployment and the dissatisfaction of the Turkish returnees back home have influenced many Turks in Germany and decreased the tendency to return. According to a representative nationwide survey in 1980, 40% of Turks living in the Federal Republic of Germany had no intention of going back to Turkey at the time of the survey. It also revealed that Greeks, Yugoslavs, Italians and Portuguese migrants were more likely to return to their home countries. Another survey concluded by TAM (Centre for Turkish studies) in 1985 suggested that almost 40% of Turks had no plans to return to Turkey, 21% considered the possibility of returning in 10 years at the earliest. Thus 61% of Turks in Germany hoped to stay in the country for more than 10 years or permanently.[40]

Migration in the post-war period challenged earlier concepts of the nation state, it is re-defined and opened a discussion as to whether the nation states would be preserved or would be allowed to become multi-cultural states with ethnic diversities. Bhikhu Parekh argues that most of the immigration countries follow three different immigration policies. These are: (1) liberal, (2) communitarian and (3) ethnic.[41]

(1) According to the liberal view, the state is simply a civil society, like a club. To be a member, individuals ought to participate in its collective affairs and obey its laws. In the view of some

---

purchase property in irrigation, agricultural, religious, cultural, archaeological, strategic and specially protected areas, as well as areas protected for their unique characteristics such as energy resources and mines, and flora and fauna reserves.

The bill authorises the Council of Ministers to change the percentage not more than 10 percent taking into consideration the significance of towns in terms of infrastructure, economy, energy, environment, culture, agriculture and the like. Housing Minister Faruk Nafiz Özak said Turkish people own 220.000 properties in Germany; however, the number of properties sold to foreigners was 65.000 in Turkey at the parliamentary session held for the bill. The Ministry of Public Works and Settlement temporarily halted Turkish property sales to foreigners at the beginning of April incline with a Constitutional Court ruling three months prior.

[39] German Embassy's report, Ankara, February 18 2008.

[40] Şen, Faruk: 'Problems and Integration Constraints of Turkish Migrants in Germany', ILO, Geneva, 1989 (p. 12).

[41] Spencer, Sarah (Ed.): Stranger and Citizens, A positive approach to migrants and refugees, River Oram Press, 1994, in Chapter 3, Bhikhu Parekh: Three Theories of Immigration, p. 91

liberals like Henry Sidgwick there is no need to restrict immigration and favour an unrestricted movement of labour, goods and capital. [42] However, the required membership of the state has been interpreted differently over years by some contemporary liberals and neo-liberals. Until recently most liberals have chosen to exclude only convicted criminals and politically rebellious activists. But in recent years many immigration countries which implies the liberal view in Europe as well as America have changed their view towards more restrictive view like the ethnic view against their Muslim immigrants after the rise of Muslim 'fundamentalism' in Iran, Afghanistan and Pakistan especially after 11 September attack. [43]

(2) The Communitarian view is similar to the ethnic view but they are not the same; it regards the state as "a group of people united by shared understandings, meanings, and common interests" like participating in sportive and political activities, "values, sentiments, loyalties, affections and collective pride. It is distinguished by a common ethical life, a body of ideals and moral self-understanding." [44] Individuals have obligation and loyalty to each other and "a common history, a shared understanding of their past, common collective memories, shared ceremonies and rituals." [45] The state is an integral part of their shared way of life and is not like a club or a voluntary association as it is in the liberal view. The communitarian view obviously requires a distinct conception of who can be a member of a state, but that conception has not so far been clearly stated by its supporters. Being a distinct ethnic-cultural unit, every state wishes and is entitled to preserve, its identity. However, Michael Walzer argues that such rights can only be acquired after a long residence of immigrants in the host country. [46]

(3) The ethnic or nationalist view: Although the ethnic or nationalist view is sometimes indistinguishable from the communitarian view, it is basically quite distinct. It describes the state as a 'legacy' group members of which have come to be related to one another by 'ties of blood' or kinship, very similar to former German citizenship law of 1913. The unity of the state is based on the unity of people, shared collective feeling of loyalty to members of a common kind. In the ethnic view, the state is a family, a relative group, and not just a community let alone a society. Although the ethnic view is similar to the racist view, it is quite different.

Another category similar to the ethnic view but which is more radical is the racist view. This view divides mankind into distinct races, and considers them unchangeable. It resembles fascist regimes of Hitler's Nazi-Germany and Mussolini's Italy in the early 1990s. These views are not static. Immigration countries introduce changes depending on their country's needs and economic situation. For example, in Germany's case, because of shortage of labour in the 1960s and the economic boom, politicians implied liberal views. With economic recession since the

---

[42] Sidgwick, Henry: The Elements of Politics, (4th ed.), London, Longmans, Green & Co, 1919, (pp. 166, 298–9)

[43] Modood, Tariq; Anna Trandafyllidou and Ricard Zapata-Barrero, (eds.): Multiculturalism, Muslims and Citizenship, A European Approach, Published by Routhledge, 2006, Ch.10 'Europe, Liberalism and Muslim question' by Bhikhu Parekh, (p. 179-203)

[44] Spencer, Sarah (Ed.): Stranger and Citizens, A positive approach to migrants and refugees, River Oram Press, 1994, in Chapter 3, Bhikhu Parekh: Three Theories of Immigration, p. 94

[45] Ibid.

[46] Article by Michael Walzer: 'The Communitarian Critique of Liberalism', Political Theory, Vol. 18, No. 1, 1990 (pp. 6-23)

mid 1980s, their view turned into ethnic or nationalist. European countries who favour ethnic or nationalist view, implies assimilation policy or encourage their immigrants to return their country of origin. Arthur Lermer claims that "assimilation is anti-democratic; while allegedly solving problems arising from differences, it actually undermines some of the basic tenets of Democracy."[47]

Immigrants either remain as guest workers of their host countries or embrace the culture of the host country, like the Polish immigrants since the late 1900s, or the Italians since the 1960s. At best they become full members of the *state* and enjoy all the rights of citizenship, but they remain marginal to the *nation* and its collective life. They are ethical and cultural outsiders whose values, sensibilities and deepest emotions find no expression in the ethical life of the host country. However, if immigrants already settled can not be repatriated (the Turks' situation in Germany showed that only 17,000 Turks returned to Turkey in 1984, and most of them refused the DM 10,500 per person to leave, preferring to stay in Germany as guest workers by retroactive laws or through assimilation policy into the German national life). Due to this, the German government's (Helmut Kohl) assimilation (meant simply being absorbed by German's social values) and repatriation policy ended up in failure, just as the French assimilation policy (Nicolas Sarkozy, Former Interior Minister of France) for the North African Muslim immigrant population in December 2005, which provoked the Paris Riots.[48]

In the ethnic view, Bhikhu Parekh argues "all outsiders who happen to be related to state by ties of kinship."[49] The boundaries of a state do not, and need not, always coincide with those of ethnic groups. Not all German citizens living in Germany are ethnic Germans. In fact they can not be deprived of their claim to the unrestricted hospitality of their 'ethnic' or 'national' home or both.[50]

In conclusion, three influential ways of understanding the nature of the state and the criteria of admission to its membership suggest that all three views have been a part of Western self-understanding at least since the Second World War. Michael Walzer as a communitarian does not appreciate if the state is a long-established and cohesive community bound by strong ties (not necessarily blood ties), its citizens may not leave it as easily as they leave an association. The members of the communitarian view need to remember that they have obligations and loyalties to their fellow citizens without important reasons (in the case of brain-drain). In this aspect,

---

[47] Lermer, Arthur: The Evolution of Canadian Policy towards cultural pluralism, Information and Comment Papers, No. 16, Canadian Jews Congress, 1955, (p. 1)

[48] African Immigration Rebel 'Like French Revolution', Vatan Gazetesi, November 5 2005 +
Former French Interior Minister Nicolas Sarkozy, the son of a Hungarian father, became president of France, is known with his anti-immigrant policy. Mr. Sarkozy's slogan was during the presidential election campaign, "There is no place for an immigrant in France who does not speak French; who does not accept 'Gender Equality'; republic and secularism. One, who beats his wife, has polygamy and girls who wear head-scarf or enter in classroom with head-scarf."
An Academie Francaise, Helene Carrere d'Encausse, said. "Many of these Africans in France are polygamous. In an apartment, there are three or four wives and 25 children."

[49] Spencer, Sarah (Ed.): Stranger and Citizens, A positive approach to migrants and refugees, River Oram Press, 1994, in Chapter 3, Bhikhu Parekh: Three Theories of Immigration, p. 96

[50] Frank Selbmann, the Drafting of a Law against Discrimination on the Grounds of Racial or Ethnic Origin in Germany' – Constraints in Constitutional and European Community Law, it is available on the European Centre for Minority Issues, Flensburg, Germany, and Issue 3/2002.

Walzer sometimes favours the liberal view when the emigration (brain-drain) issue is concerned. He encourages people from high density population countries such as East Asia with little economic resources to move to Australia and America or Canada where there are huge empty areas. So the communitarian view easily turns into the ethnic view.

According to the communitarian view, a state needs to be re-defined. The state is not only a piece of land and a random collection of people; it is also an expression of common like a national family. In times of trouble, the state's values and boundaries need to be defended by its members or fellow citizens. In this situation, if the state is ruled by a majority group in anti-democratic way, the communitarian view goes back to ethnic view or the state turns into an ethnic homeland of the majority. Furthermore, ethnic minorities sometimes face troubles like forced migration and ethnic cleansing between neighbouring countries. For example, although the two states agreed on the population exchange in 1923 after the Turkish Republic proclamation, Turks driven from Greece and Greeks from Turkey, after the wars and revolutions of the early twentieth century, had to be taken in the states that bore their collective names.[51] Even in 1984-6, Bulgaria's government forced the ethnic Turks to change their names to Bulgarian names.[52] In case of Germany, the non-ethnic citizens including Germans of Turkish descent become second class citizens and are denied an equal right to participate in and reshape the socio-political life of Germany.

After comparing the three views are applied by classical immigration countries such as the USA, Canada and Australia which were recently made up of emigrant people from different part of the world. The liberal view seems more satisfactory, the ethnic view is the least satisfactory. Although the ethnic view seems to contradict the liberal or multicultural societies of contemporary European states when three major European countries (Germany, France and Britain) claim that they are homogenous.

In general, among the three views of the nature of state, the ethnic view is the least satisfactory. In a contemporary definition, some states are the product of considerable recent ethnic intermingling and cannot pretend to be of a single ethnic stock such as the USA, Canada and Australia which were recently made up of immigrants drawn from different part of the world. The ethnic view contradicts that the European states (Germany, France and Britain) are supposedly homogenous. Each of these three in turn is a product of much ethnic mixture only the mix took place 1000 year ago. If a state identified itself as a 'political expression' of a specific ethnic group, then it would necessarily discriminate against those not belonging to that group and end up with violating the principle of equal citizenship that lies at its basis. If Germany were a state of the ethnic Germans, then its non-ethnically German but German citizens including Turkish descent Germans would become cultural and ethnical outsiders. So they can not become bearers of equal rights and subjected to equal obligations (like George Orwell's political satire 'Animal Farm'. "All animals are equal, but some animals are more equal".[53] It means that ethnic or native Germans are more equal than non-ethnic Germans and Germans of Turkish descent. Thanks to the influence of the ethnic view of the state in Germany, non-ethnic Germans are virtually excluded from citizenship and the worst in Belgian non-ethnic Belgians can not join the

---

[51] Lewis, Bernard: The Multiple Identities of the Middle East, Published by Phoenix, London, 1999, p. 9-10

[52] Central Europe Tinderboxes: Old Border Disputes, 'Minorities in Eastern Europe', *International Herald Tribune,* January 1 1990, p. 5

[53] Orwell, George: Animal Farm, Random House, London, 1945, (p.188).

armed forces and occupy certain offices of the state even after becoming its naturalised citizens. [54] If a state accepts only the ethnic view it cannot extend equal citizenship to all its citizens. As in the case of Germany, German politicians stress integration of Turkish youths into the German society. For instance the German defence minister in 1998 proposed citizenship to youths of German-born Turkish descent resident in Germany, if they are willing to serve their military duty in the German army instead of the Turkish army. Similarly in 1920 hired Anzacs-soldiers from Zealand and Australia fought at the Dardanelles in Turkey and in 1982 the current Nepali soldiers in the British army fought at Falkland Island. So citizenship does not always play a key factor as long as it is in the interest of the host country. The idea was refused by his Turkish counterpart. [55] Turkish citizenship law is not based on blood ties like former German citizenship law, neither on birth-place like British, American and Australian nationality law. Children who are born to a Turkish national mother or father, in or outside of the country, is regarded a Turkish citizen. Gaining Turkish citizenship is possible by submitting a petition to ministry of interior in Turkey or to Turkish consulates abroad. Dual citizenship means having two citizenships at the same time. Individuals may have dual citizenship by choice, if individual has a good reason for such as possessing property and inheritance in the country of origin; even it sometimes conflicts laws. [56]

Contrary to the ethnic view, the communitarian view contains many valuable insights. Every well-established community has different way of life and a recognisable character. Its members define themselves and relate to each other in specific ways, share in common a body of practices and goals, characteristic of temperament, interest, and institutions. Although members of the state share a sense of collective identity, there is less agreement on what the collective identity means. For example, British identity has changed considerably over the centuries. British society has become almost multi-cultural. [57]

According to Jim Jordan, "The idea of multiculturalism is a product of liberal democracies which ring fence the rights of the individuals within a self-declared secular society". [58] The communitarian view also emphasis shared understandings, values, interests, attachments, affections and loyalties. In the case of values, every modern society is characterised by moral pluralism and diversity, and its members enjoy different beliefs. They, who favour the communitarian view, widen the range of life styles open to all its citizens, enabling them to borrow from others whatever enriches their way of life. They also bring different traditions into a mutually beneficial dialogue and stimulate new ideas and experiments. A creative interplay between the ethnic minority musical, literary and artistic traditions on the one hand (See Turkish

---

[54] According to 'Belgian Ministry for Foreign Affairs and Information on Belgian nationality', Belgian nationality or naturalization is only granted by the House of Representatives. Individuals ought to have had their main place of residence in Belgium for three years (Stateless persons for two years) in order to be naturalized. Individuals can either apply for naturalization directly to the House of Representatives, or through the Registrar in the municipality where they have their main place of residence. If their main place of residence is abroad, they must submit your application to the Belgian Embassy or Consulate. Dual citizenship is allowed since 28 April 2008 Belgian law permits all Belgian nationals to obtain any other nationality without losing their Belgian nationality.

[55] Geddes, Andrew and Favell, Adrian: Politics of Belonging, Ashgate, 1999, p. 176-191

[56] Adem Sözüer , H. Nuri Yasar, Turgut Tarhanli, Nilufer Narli (April 2005). "Türkiye'nin Ulusal Kimlik Meselesi" (in Turkish). *Hukuki Perspektif Dergisi* 3: 137–166.

[57] The British immigration policy was at first the liberal and later in the ethnic view of the state. Thanks to the influence of the liberal view, every immigrant from Commonwealth countries had a right to enter Britain and gained the citizenship on arrival until the British Nationality Law of 1981, later on it was redefined.

[58] Jordan, Jim: Migrants in German speaking countries, Published by CILT, 2004, (p.100).

immigrants' cultural activities in Germany-Chapter 2), and those of the host (British, German and French) society on the other, has led to many exciting developments and enriched both (for example, the Frankfurt International Book Fair on 14 October 2008 was opened by German Foreign Minister Frank Walter Steinmeier, German Culture Minister Alte Oper, Cem Özdemir Turkish descent Politician from the Green Party, and Turkish Nobel Prize Winner Orhan Pamuk joined to cultural activities at the fair). New ways of life also bring with them new talents, skills, sensitivities and ways of looking at things, different kinds of imagination, new psychological and moral resources, new sources of spiritual energy (as former Czech President Havel Vaclav once urged that "Europe Needs a Spiritual Dimension") and give the receiving society a cultural diversity.

As a result the liberal view is a kind of description of a modern state. The modern state therefore does not require unity of race, ethnicity, religious, and even language to maintain itself in existence. Though, there are only modern European states where multiple national languages exist and do not create any ethnic tension such as Switzerland and Belgium.

A modern state is not a family, a national home of a specific group, or based on the unity of ethnicity. No immigrant therefore is denied admission on the grounds that his/her life is different from the host society members. The immigration policy of a state must be seen not in narrowly economic terms, but also as a means of enriching the cultural diversity of the host country such as multiculturalism.[59]

Dairan Smith's definition of multicultural society is as "Multiculturalism based on equality diversity as key concepts; the practice of tolerance, equal opportunities and tolerate others' views points".[60] The *Concept* of multiculturalism as a term first emerged in an American periodical (NEXIS) in 1981. Then it appeared in Western European countries, especially in welfare states such as Netherlands, Sweden and in the UK as a central theme of identity regarding ethnic diversity. Immigration in the US goes to the heart of the common understanding of the nature of the American people. The 1990 census showed that the great majority of those living in America who was born abroad are citizens of the US now. Henry Kissinger is also technically a German immigrant, and was a prominent political figure in US politics.[61] Joe L. Kincheloe describes the concept of multiculturalism as "Multiculturalism means everything and at the same times nothing".[62] In fact, the idea of multiculturalism derives from the Frankfurt school of Social Research in Germany in the 1920s (Society for Social Research, 1925:12).

The immigration policy of a country is interrelated with and shapes the way its citizens treat the immigrants already settled among them. However, it does not mean that Turks in Germany will enrich themselves and will keep well away from the host nation's culture. Or, when there are only two well-known full integrated persons of Turkish origin. A Turkish proverb says, '*Exceptio probat regulam*' (Exception proves no rule). The majority of Turkish immigrants are still not integrated into German society as much as Italian and Greek immigrants did. If the

---

[59] Modood, Tariq; Anna Trandafyllidou and Ricard Zapata-Barrero (eds.): Multiculturalism, Muslims and Citizenship, A European Approach, Published by Routhledge, 2006, Ch.10 'Europe, Liberalism and Muslim question' by Bhikhu Parekh, (p. 179-203).

[60] Dairan, Smith: Multiculturalism, 1999, Berkeley, University of California Press (p. 97).

[61] Kissinger, as a successfully integrated immigrant and former foreign secretary of the US, he shaped his (host) country's foreign policy. In addition, he is one of the international politic theorist, realist, and the author of the book 'Diplomacy'.

[62] Kissinger, as a successfully integrated immigrant and former foreign secretary of the US, he shaped his (host) country's foreign policy. In addition, he is one of the international politic theorist, realist, and the author of the book 'Diplomacy'.

policy discriminates against, or places strict restrictions on, specific ethnic, cultural or religious groups, as seen in the Turkish case, a group of Turks feel that they have been excluded by German society.[63] This gives them a negative impression and encourages the majority to believe that it would not be acting wrongly if it ill-treated or discriminated against them even after they become their fellow citizens.[64]

The right to marry and have children is universally recognised as a basic human right. Hence to admit individuals is also but the family is the unit of immigration. This means that no state may deny the immigrant admitted to its membership the right to marry wherever s/he pleases and to bring in her or his spouse. The new German law (2007) practice of making Turkish immigrants wait for years before uniting them with their spouses and families, and making them annoyed all manner of obstinate bureaucratic obstacles, is applicable neither in law nor morality.

W.R. Böhning describes historical phases the migrants have been through in the four stage model as following: a guest worker migration flow matures in four stages. In the first phase, males come from the industrialized, urbanized areas or more developed part the sending country were likely to be employed in the most marginal of positions.[65]
In the second phase, the first emigrants return home and they talk to friends and neighbours about their experience; so more emigrate from smaller town with a lower level of skills and socio-economic status.[66]

In the third phase, duration of stay increases, wives and younger children join the parents abroad. Family unification would put an end to their separation and remove the expense of maintaining two separate households. Their children would surely receive a better education in the receiving country than at home. By this time, there appears a demand for labour such as teachers, secular religious leaders which results in importing additional workers.[67] On the contrary, expenses increases and saving of money becomes slower than they had planned and they find themselves at the bottom of the socio-economic ladder. Turkish governments send some professionals such as teachers, secular religious leaders to Germany every year, not because Turkish education is better than the German, but with an intention to protect its compatriots from German assimilation and maintain their ties with Turkey. As matter of fact, Turkish authorities make the integration impossible or place poorly educated Turks in a situation of isolation or ghettoisation.[68]

In the final phase, as the psychological comfort afforded by the company of their fellow countrymen leads the immigrant workers and families to settle in groups, then slowly arises a demand for ethnic shops and places of worship such as mosques, schools and other facilities.[69]

---

[63] R. Zegers de Beijl: 'Discrimination of Migrant Workers in Western Europe', World Employment Programme Discussion Paper, no.49, Geneva, ILO, 1990.
60 Joe L. Kincheloe and Shirley R. Steinberg: Changing Multiculturalism, Open Univ. Press, 1990
[65] Böhning,W.R. and Zegers de Beijl, R.: *The integration of migrant workers in the labour market: Policies and their impact,* International Migration Papers, No.: 8, International Labour Office Geneva (Geneva: ILO, 1995)
[66] Ibid.
[67] Ibid.
[68] During a 2008 visit to Germany, Turkish Prime Minister Recep Tayyip Erdogan told a Turkish audience, "Nobody can expect you to submit to assimilation. Assimilation is a crime against humanity."
[69] Turkish authorities (Turkish Ministry of Education sent to Germany in 2008, 400 mother-tongue teachers) have tried to preserve their Turkishness, German authorities tried to assimilate or germanise

1.1.6 Background of Turkish labour migration to Germany in the framework bilateral relations

Just as in-migration out-migration started with agricultural workers, farmers with limited fields and shopkeepers followed them. No matter whether in- or out the main reason for Turkish migration is always economic. First agreement between Turkey and West European countries is signed with West Germany in 1961, with Austria, the Netherlands and Belgian in 1964, with France 1965 and with Sweden in 1967. Turkish migrations to Germany have been discussed from two perspectives namely German labour needs and Turkish economic needs. Among other reasons economic causes of the decision to migrate are co-determinates for the success of migration. Then an integration or assimilation process should be followed: From the migrant's point of view various factors may influence his/her decision to migrate,

a) the choice of the country of immigration, the future of the children; money earning, wage problems, taxes in the homeland;

b) the attitude of the wife and the comments of his friends on emigration plans, other factors may be difficulties with family at home, desire for adventure, an exceptional position in the home country as a stimulus to emigrate, and the wife as a driving force

c) the influence of parents{or in-laws} on the decision to migrate;

d) the employment situation at home; problems concerning the work in the homeland, e.g. the labour market situation; knowledge of a certain language; housing problems at home, the possibility of becoming a house owner abroad;

e) information about the immigration country via migrated acquaintances or family members, and via literature dealing with the country of destination, emigration offices, government migration services and non-governmental migration organisations;

f) the desire for social advancement and eventual self-employment; essential factors may be:

---

them. In fact they could neither stay as Turks in Germany, nor could they become assimilated Germans, maybe half Turk, half German identity or hoping not to lose from both sides.

Table 1.1.1 Unequal income distribution pyramid in 1960s before labour migration in Turkey:

Upper Layer

= 8.7% of population, 44% of total income

M i d d l e L a y e r

L o w e r   L a y e r   **= 54% of population, 4.9% of total income**

Source: Unequal income distribution pyramid in Turkey in 1960s, Urbanisation, migration and poverty, 2002 (p.61-62)

Income distribution in Turkey: unequal income distribution among Turkish population is one of the in- and out-migration reasons in 1960s.

Internal migration in Turkey started in 1950s from small central Anatolian villages to large cities. They worked in the village fields and lived in village houses with garden before they moved to flats in the suburbs of large cities like Ankara, Istanbul, Izmir, Bursa and Mersin. Before moving they worked in agriculture. Then they became factory workers in the cities. They were deprived of the opportunities of the country side where they used to have additional income. As factory workers they had to manage with their minimum wages. Mübeccel Kıray explains reasons for in-migration from villages to cities 52 % shortage of field, 22 % unemployment in the rural areas.[70]

According to 'unequal income distribution' pyramid at the top of the page, low layer consisted 54 % of total Turkish population but they receive only 14, 9 % of total income as annually TL 499. Middle and upper layers together is 8, 7 % of total population but they receive 44 % of total income approximately TL 15, 135 annually.[71] A survey on 587 Turkish workers and their reasons for emigration to Germany (1972-1977 in the below table) is ranking as follows:

---

[70] Kıray, Mübeccel, B.: "Reconstructing of agricultural Enterprises Affected by Migration in Turkey" in C.A.O. von Nieuwenhuijze: Mouton, *Emigration and Agricultural in the Mediterranean Basin*, Institute of Social Studies, The Hague, 1972

[71] Dikmen, Ahmet Alpay (Ed.): Kentleşme, Göç ve Yoksulluk (Urbanisation, migration and poverty) Imaj Yayınevi, Ankara, 2002, p. 73

Table 1.1.2 Background of Turkish Labour migration to Germany

Reasons for emigration	Number of workers	Proportion of total sampling
Poverty	368	62.4
Employment shortage	67	11.4
Dept payment	5	8
Saving money	79	13.4
Education & other reasons	60	10.2

Source: Urbanisation, migration and poverty, 2002 (p.62)

As seen above table main reason for Turkish labour migration is poverty, labour shortage, dept payment, education and other reasons. 71.2 % of total sampling 587 workers stated also they worked in Turkey as workers, service men, small businessmen before they migrated to Germany.[72] The table indicates also out-migration by Turks is considered to be as a last resort to overcome their poverty, unemployment and unequal income distribution in Turkey.

They dreamed of establishing their own businesses in cities and become their own bosses upon their return. Besides these, labour workers aimed at industrialising their hometowns by founding similar factories they worked in Germany. In general, emigration makes receiving countries richer, sending countries poorer.[73] Sending countries should improve their citizens' living and working conditions to avoid 'brain-drain'. Furthermore, the sending countries should take action together under the ILO auspices to stop the brain-drain. Such an aim could only be successful if all sending countries reach an agreement to determine a common policy with the ILO to protect their workers' social and legal rights in the host countries. Such a solution can free migrant workers from being dependent on host countries.

According to Nermin Abadan Unat, large wave out-migration causes people to lose their traditional occupation, status and respect among their countrymen. Thus, before they went to Germany, ¾ of them were working with small business and in service sector, ½ constructing sector, while in Germany they all became manufacturing workers.[74] As happened in-migration, unemployment is also one of the main reasons for the Turkish workers' emigration to Germany. Even if people want to work and are active job seekers they are unable to find a paid job in their country. Unemployment makes people hopeless and insecure in society.[75] In addition, high unemployment spoils rhythmic daily activities, family relations negatively and threatens social peace as well. Employment and occupation gives people self-confidence, self-respect and

---

[72] Ibid. p. (57-75)

[73] Ibid., p. 76

[74] Abadan-Unat, Nermin: A case Study, Turkish Workers in West Germany – Immigrant and Migrant Labour – The Citizenship Debates; Minneapolis; University of Minnesota Press, 1998 (pp.131-167)

[75] Ekin, Nusret: "The Problem on the Agenda: Turkish Migrant Workers"; *Economic and Touristic Bazaar International*; 1982; Vol. 1; No: 2; p. 3-4.

strengthen their social belonging. Opposite to these values ruin family structure/ life and cause psycho-social behaviours.[76] Even like a social time-bomb took place in France 2005.[77]

The demographic structure of host country, immigration and integration policy, impact of unemployment on native workers and illegal migrants cause to low wage, discrimination, exclusion and poor social and housing conditions.[78] During the period of economic crisis presence of Turkish workers in Germany have been seen as a threat by many Germans and foreign workers became scapegoats. Illegal workers worsened the legal workers' situations. Even many Developed Capitalist Countries (İleri Kapitalist Ülkeler-İKÜ) like Germany do not regard labour workers as humans just 'work force' but slaves. Max Frisch citation as follows: "We invited labour force, but humans came (*Wir haben Arbeittskrafte geholdt, aber Menschen sind gekommen*)" [79]

Samuel Pisar explains the situation of Turkish workers with the following citation. "Yesterday guest, today burden (*Gestern Gast, heute Last*)" [80]

According to The Economist of 13 January 2001, Turkey was awarded as 'the best indebted country' by The Financial Review, since Turkey pays back its debt on time.

According to a survey by Cevdet Yilmaz of 423 persons, entitled 'Citizen to what extent' the outcome of Turks emigration is the following:

Turkish labour migrants have left two things in Turkey after leaving for Germany.

i)   Village development cooperatives
ii) Companies established by workers in Germany

The aim of the first establishments was to send Turkish peasants to Germany as guest workers systematically.

The village cooperatives' aim was to invest the remittances of workers in Turkey through these small scale entrepreneurs. These companies were establishing by intellectuals who completed their education in Germany. The first one was established in 1964. In fact, preconditions of these factories were prepared by Labour minister Bulent Ecevit, Finance minister Zeyyat Baykara, German educated Necati Telger and Ömer Yilmaz.[81] Besides those investments in Germany, Turkish workers continued to invest in purchasing houses, building grounds, fields and shops in Turkey resent years. Between the year 2002 - 2010, 17,271 German nationals bought real estates in Turkey and paid $ 14.4 billion in return. [82]

---

[76] Ekin, Nusret: "Turkey's and the World's Most Pressing Problem: Unemployment"; Article by Nusret Ekin, *Anka Review*; Dec. 20, 1983.

[77] Vatan Gazetesi, October 19 2010

[78] Dikmen, Ahmet Alpay (Ed.): Kentleşme, Göç ve Yoksulluk (Urbanisation, migration and poverty) Imaj Yayınevi, Ankara, 2002, (p. 43)

[79] Dikmen, Ahmet Alpay (Ed.): Kentleşme, Göç ve Yoksulluk (Urbanisation, Migration and poverty) Imaj Yayinevi, Ankara, 2002 (p. 81)

[81] Birsen Ersel: *'Worker Companies in Turkey'* Unpublished PhD Thesis, Ankara 1985, (p. 47).

[82] Posta Gazetesi, 14th July 2010, foreign nationals purchase real estate from Turkey, estimated $14.4 b.

1.1.7 Germany's encouraging immigration/entry policy (1955-1973)

In the 1950s labour shortages in some the West European countries have already encouraged openness to labour immigration and even active recruitment. Germany's migration history is different from other European countries. For example, British and French immigrants were from their former colonies whereas West Germany established a *'Guest worker system'* through recruitment treaties with (Southern Europe countries) such as Italy in 1955, Spain and Greece in 1960, Turkey in 1961, Portugal in 1964, and former Yugoslavia in 1968. Several nations including Turkey signed treaties allowing Germany to set up recruiting offices in their cities for use by German firms. About 400 recruitment officials of the German Federal Labour Office operated in these countries on behalf of German firms. These officers selected workers on the basis of qualifications, health, age, and employment records. Turks began to immigrate to Western Europe (Germany), simply as a response to a growing shortage of labour in Europe. In the 1960s and 1970s came the so-called guest-workers from Turkey and other southern countries, welcomed in by the German government to provide needed labour for a rapidly growing economy.

The period of Pull-migration to Western Europe lasted until 1973 and ended with the recession following the first oil price shock. The chain migration process changed with the halt in recruitment in the 1970s.The migration policies became more restrictive. Since 1973, emigration from Turkey to Western Europe has slowed but it did not stop. (West) Germany became the biggest importer of the Turkish work force. Although the German official sources show that the first Turkish guest workers arrived in Germany in 1961, the Turkish and British sources show that the first Turkish guest workers arrival was in 1956, 150 Turkish people as an experimental project initiated by West Germany and later in 1961 turned out to be the beginning of large scale migration. In fact, this is important evidence that first Turkish guest workers migrated to Germany 5 years before the bilateral Recruitment Treaty is signed between Turkey and Germany in 1961.[83]

Comparing Germany with other major European immigration countries, such as France and Britain, Germany represents all the EU member states in regard to Turkish immigrants.
The construction of the Berlin Wall in August 1961 ended movement from East Germany and West Germany placed greater reliance on foreign labour to fuel economic growth. Additional recruitment agreements were signed with Portugal (1964), Tunisia (1965), and Morocco (1966).
In April 1965 a new Foreigner's Law was introduced to replace the 1938 Alien Regulations.

Almost all opinion surveys show that Turkish guest-workers migrated increasingly for economic reasons. Then they chose to live in Germany, and their present integration problems emerged. After the war, the German economy needed labour; in 1950s this supply had become inadequate. (In 1961 there were some 500,000 unfilled job vacancies); so the Federal Government began to look abroad, to the poorer countries of Southern Europe. European migratory movements have sometimes been interrupted and sometimes accelerated by historical events (world wars, economic crises, and political division of Europe; economic deprivation, political-instability and ethnic violence were the reasons to migrate).Western Europe's foreign

---

[83] Eight bilateral contracts have been signed (with Italy, 1955; Spain and Greece, 1960; Turkey, 1961; Portugal, 1964; Tunisia and Morocco, 1965; and Yugoslavia 1968).

resident population reflects three migratory geographic patterns: South-North migration: from Southern Europe, Middle East, and North Africa to Western Europe;

1. East-West Migration: from East and Central Europe (Poland, Romania, and former Soviet-mainly ethnic Germans;
   Migration linked by cultural, economic and political affinities rooted in history.
2. Europe's three major migrant receiving countries (Germany, France and Britain) characterised the following patterns:

Since 1945 Germany has a long history of both foreigners and foreign-born people. People of 'German-origin' living abroad are not regarded as migrants. Although more than 20 million people have come to the country since 1945, Germany insists on defining itself as a non-immigrant country. Until 1945 Europe's migration history was predominantly marked by emigration. The historical background of immigration has three period of migration to Western Europe since 1945: Germany, since 1945 with the largest immigrant population, is home for the large majority of immigrants from Central and Eastern Europe. [84]

Table1.1.3: First labour emigration from Turkey to West Germany

Years	Total
1961-67	**225,000**
1968-73	733,000
1974-78	70,000
Total	1,028,000

Source: Is ve Isci Bulma Kurumu-Turkish Labour and Employee Institute (I.I.B.K., 1976, p.6); Devlet Planlama Teskilati-State Planning Organisation (D.P.T., 1979, p.64).

Table 1.1.3a: Approximate distribution of Turkish immigration in Western Europe (1979)

Country	Total
West Germany	**1,096,000**
Holland	73,000
France	69,000
UK	52,000
Belgium	40,500
Austria	37,000
Switzerland	29,000
Scandinavian Countries (Sweden, Denmark, Norway)	28,000
Total	1,425,000

Source: Devlet Planlama Teskilati-DPT (State Planning Organization), 1979, p. 64, İş ve İşçi Bulma Kurumu-IIBK (Turkish Labour and Employee Institute) p. 6.

---

[84] Germany's migrants are (i) labour migrants-Guest workers; (ii) ethnic migrants-Germans; (iii) illegal migrants: as tourists, asylum seekers, refugees or entering Germany through different ways.

Table 1.1.3a indicates the distribution of first generation Turkish immigrants in Western Europe as a proportion of the total population of their European host countries and the Turkish labour migrants as a percentage of the total labour force. Comparing the concentration of Turkish labour force in Germany with other European countries (such as in the Netherlands, Belgium, Austria and Switzerland, West Germany represents Western Europe as a highest Turkish worker receiving country; the number of the Turkish workers in France, Britain and Scandinavian countries (Denmark, Sweden and Norway) was not so many in 1975

Table 1.1.4: **Immigrant workers in the EEC states by nationality, 1976 (as percentage)**

Country of origin	EEC	(West) Germany	France
Italy	11.6	14.3	12.1
Other EU	14.8	6.6	3.7
Spain	7.8	6.1	13.9
Greece	4.3	9.6	0.3
Portugal	9.4	3.3	25.0
Turkey	10.0	**26.6**	1.3
(Former)Yugoslavia	8.0	20.4	2.6
N.Afr.(Alger,Mor.Tun.)	11.8	1.4	**33.6**
Other non-EU	22.3	11.7	7.5
Total	100.0	100.0	100.0

Source: CCE (Commission des Communautes Europeenes, Direction Generale des Affaires Sociales (Commission of the European Communites, General Directorate of Social Affairs), 1976, (p.7)

In Table 1.1.4 is displayed the distribution of Turkish workers as compared with guest workers from other south-eastern countries such Italy, Spain and Portugal. In 1976, the number of Turkish workers in Germany is placed as the second biggest national group after Italy. However, the following years Turks became the largest national group in West Germany. In France, this applies to former French colonies such as Algeria, Morocco and Tunisia in 1976. The same is valid for Britain, whereas most of the British immigrants are Asian and African origin. There are not so many Turks, just a tiny proportion from Turkey and Cyprus.

Table 1.1.5: Immigrant workers in (West) Germany, by nationality, 1965-75 (per cent)

	From year (in %)	To year (in %)
Country of origin	1965	1975
Italy	**29.4**	14.3
Spain	15.3	6.1
Greece	16.0	9.6
Portugal	1.0	3.3
Turkey	10.5	**26.6**
(Former)Yugoslavia	27.7	40.1

Source: CCE (Commission des Communautes Europeenes, Direction Generale des Affaires Sociales (Commission of the European Communites, General Directorate of Social Affairs), 1976, (p.7), 1976, p.7., Bundesanstalt fur Arbeit-BA (West German Labour Office), 1970, p. 96

Table 1.1.6: Total work force in (West) Germany, and Turkish immigrant workers, by branch of Economical activity, 1973-4 (per cent)

Turkish immigrant workers	(In %)	Total workforce (%)
Agriculture and fisheries	0.8	6.6
Mining and quarrying	6.1	1.2
Manufacturing, power and water	67.3	40.1
Construction	14.2	7.5
Transport	2.2	5.7
Other services	0.3	38.9

Source: Bundesanstalt fur Arbeit-BA (West German Labour Office), 1970, p. 96, 1974, pp.84-7; ILO (International Labour Organization), 1975, pp.130-1

Although many Turks worked as farmers in agricultural jobs before their migration to Germany, in Germany they were mostly employed in factories, mining, manufacturing and construction rather than agricultural jobs. Table 1.1.6 shows that they have a tendency to do less desirable, heavy, noisy and boring jobs. Rather than to be working in an office, probably the latest arrivals were forced to take the jobs which were left by the more well-established migrants from southern Europe, as well as by the native German workers. Nor did most Turkish immigrants have the skills to take a better-paid white collar jobs, as most did not speak German where they arrived in. The number of guest workers in Germany peaked at 1.3 million in 1966, but the recession of 1966-7 appeared to validate the expectation of return migration by the 'guests' because between 1966 and 1967 the number of guest workers fell from 1.3 million to 0.9 million. The numbers picked up as the economy recovered between 1967 and 1973, but the ethnic composition of guest workers population changed. There were fewer beginning of the 1970, 13% of the foreign population were Turks; by 1980 33% were Turks.[85]

Table 1.1.7: The foreign population of the Federal Republic of Germany 1973-80

Guest workers	Total foreign population
1973 2,595,000	3,966,000
1980 2,070,000	4,450,000

Source: Esser H., p. 172

There were four main sources of post war migration to Germany: First, between 1945 and 1955 amounted to around 12 million people fleeing persecution in Soviet bloc countries. Article 116 of the 1949 Basic Law gave automatic German citizenship to people possessing 'German nationality or who as a refugee or as an expellee of German descent or as their spouse or descendant has found residence in the territory of the German Reich in its borders of 31 December 1931'. They were seen as part of the German 'community of fate' even if they were geographically distant. By 1950, refugees and expellees accounted for 16% of the FRG's population. The second source was the recruitment of 'guest workers': Between 1945 and 1955 ethnic Germans had initially filled labour market gaps, but their numbers were insufficient. Guest

---

[85] Esser, H.: Aspects of migration sociology, Darmstadt and Neuwied, 1980, p. 127, 146, 172

workers' recruitment was requested first by agriculture and then by industry. The first formal agreement was signed with Italy in 1955.

The third major source of post war movement to Germany was by the family members of guest workers. As seen In France and Britain, the end of labour migration did not mean the end of immigration. After so-called immigration-stop the foreign population actually increased in Germany, as Table 1.1.7 shows. The fourth main source was asylum seekers whose rights were protected by the comparatively liberal provisions of Article 16 of the German constitution that recognised the right of the asylum applicant to make a claim rather than the obligation of the state to consider a claim made.

Table 1.1.8: Population of Turks in selected European countries

Germany	1,851,000
Netherlands	214,000
France	240,000
Belgium	85,000
Denmark	30,000
Austria	117,000
Switzerland	70,000
Britain	20,000
Total	2,542,000

Source: Statistisches Bundesamt, Wiesbaden, 1992; Ministry of labour and Social Security, department of services for workers Abroad , 1991 report, Ankara,1992.

The recruitment of guest workers was subjugated to the economic interests of the Federal Republic of Germany. Article 2(1) of the 1965 Law stated that a residence permit 'may be issued *if the presence of the foreigners does not harm the interests of the FRG'*. Conditions for these residence permits were all dependent on executive discretion. Residence permits were lined to work permits and both these types of permit were subordinated to West Germany's *economic interests.*

Turkish migrant workers who opted to live in German society for a variety of economic, social, personal and political reasons, have not been accepted as 'immigrants' until 2001, but as residents. As residents they are 'social citizens' entitled to the personal protection and liberties as human beings which the German Basic Law guarantees to all inhabitants of post-war Germany. Two aspects of the 1965 legislation were particularly significant. First, the issuing of residence permits was a matter for the States (*Länder*) and dependent to a considerable extend on the political complexion of these 11 regional governments. Conservative Bavaria and Baden-Württemberg were, for instance, more restrictive than liberal Hesse. Second, the 1965 legislation made no provision for family reunification. Such legislation was not put in place until 1981.

Perhaps a sense of moral obligation to the guest workers could explain continued openness to immigration. In 1982, Interior Minister Gerhard Baum stated that: "We have brought them to this country since 1955. Even if they are without jobs we have obligations towards

26

them".[86] But how could this vague commitment is given legal or political effect to guest workers? Christian Joppke identifies the role of law and the courts utilising two of the FRG's basic constitutional principles, the subordination of state power to the rights of the individual and the granting of the rights have enshrined in German Basic Law to all irrespective of their nationality. In practical terms, this meant that resident foreigners were able to access formal legal and social rights and enjoys equal protection of the law. These rights increased with the duration of their residence because of the 'legal fate of dependency': long term resident foreigners had nowhere else to go and therefore should be formally treated in the same way as other Germans.[87]

In December 1981, measures concerning guest workers' family reunification were introduced by the Federal government, to allow family reunification; although with an eight year residence qualification for the spouse and a one- year outside the FRG for the partner (ultra restrictive Bavaria imposed a 3 years wait for partners). This appeared to conflict with Article 6 of the Basic Law, which guaranteed the rights of the family, and a challenge was made to these family reunification measures on this basis. The Constitutional court upheld the 8-year / 1-year rule, but disallowed the Bavarian stringency The Constitutional Court confirmed the state's sovereign power to control access to the state territory, but at the same time reduced the capacity of the state to control family migration in the sense that as automatic right (though restrictive) to family migration was established. (See Table: 1.1.4). Seven out eight Greeks, three quarters of former Yugoslavs and Turks has resided in Germany. Italians, Spaniards and Greeks have declined sharply by 1975.The reason was a surge of immigration from Turkey, former Yugoslavia and other European and non-European Countries. Poland, Romania, and Iran also had some impact. The Turks' share among all foreigners remained stable between 1980 (about 33%) and 1989 (32.2%), those of other nationalities declined: Yugoslavs from 14% in 1980 to 12.5% in 1989 and Italians from 13.9% to 10.7 in the same period.[88]

In 1993 the number of foreign nationals living in Germany was 6.8 million (8.4% of the total population), in 1994 some 20% of Germany's population including population born in the GDR was foreign-born. In comparison the largest single group of foreigners in Europe, the 1.5 million Turkish nationals (1993), accounted for only 2.3% of Germany's resident population. Germany's immigrants originated mainly from Eastern, Central and southern Europe and Germany's immigrants are white people. Germany differs from France and the UK in this aspect. France is Europe's second most important country of immigration, French-speaking residents of former colonies (Algeria, Tunisia and Morocco) were encouraged to come to France and emigration from Italy, Spain, and Portugal was also welcomed. Similar patterns prevail in Britain, regarding English-speaking Pakistanis, Bangladeshis and Indians. In 1992 about 60% of the UK's 1.9 million foreign residents were immigrants from African or Asian countries (all of them are from the former colonies). However, the proportion of the foreign-born population is about 7 % of total population.

---

[86] Karapin, Roger: Politics of Immigration Control in Britain and Germany; Comparative Politics, Vol. 31, No. 4, July 1999, pp. 423 - 444.

[87] Joppke, Christian: Immigration and the Nation-state, the United states, Germany and the Great Britain, 1999, (p. 69-70)

[88] Bade, Klaus J.: Germans abroad – foreigners in Germany. Migration in Geschichte und Gegenwart, Munich, 1992, p. 395

- Labour migration between 1950s-1973, West European economic reconstruction,
- Family reunion became a form of immigration to Europe; [89]
- The third wave of migration emerged in the end of the Cold war in 1989-1990 as asylum seekers, refugees (or as a tourist), this type migration is defined by state policies as illegal, especially neighbouring countries affected by this type when people: (i) enter legally on a tourist visa and overstay; (ii) cross state borders without documentation;(iii) are legally resident but work illegally.

1.1.8 German migration stop and reunification of Turkish families (1973-83)

Although Germany had officially declared the intention to end the recruitment of migrant workers in 1973, the FRG continued to accept immigration after the migration stop. Between 1955 and 1973 economic interests and labour market pressures underpinned the policy of expansiveness. After 1973 economic conditions did not favour the large-scale recruitment of migrant workers. There was some fluctuation in business attitudes to immigration. Employers and industrialists hesitated between their conservative leanings, ideas that immigration is an economic necessity in a time of demographic change, and interests in a cheap and motivated labour force. Economic interests were central to the period of large scale recruitment, but are less helpful in explaining why immigration continued during the economic slowdown after the recruitment stop.

The percentage of immigrant women increased greatly in late 1970s because of the family reunion process. A recent survey of female immigrant workers in North-Rhine-Westphalia has shown that the employment rate among Turkish women (3%) has more or less reached the level of German women. It is also important to emphasise that 44 % of the immigrant residents are women.[90]

---

[89] The term family reunion applies to family members (spouses and children) and to new family creation when settled migrants bring in a marriage partner from the 1970s onwards (Castles and Miller, 1998).
[90] Schültze, Günter: Soziale Situationen ausländischer Mädchen und Frauen in Nordrhein-Westfalen, Düsseldorf, 1987

Table 1.1.9 Comparing Turkish Migration with other nations to Germany

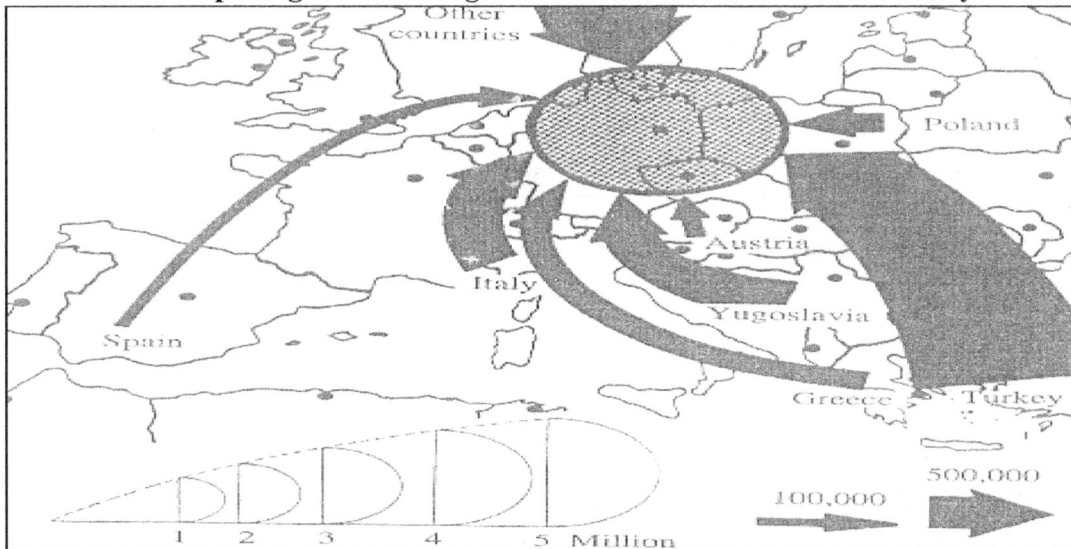

Source: David Horrocks and Eva Kolinsky 1996: Migrants and Citizens, (p. 71-101). Adapted from Eva Kolinsky, Chapter 5, Table 5.5 Non-German population in Germany by Country of Origin, 1992 p. 84.
Original Source: Der Spiegel, 23, 1993, p. 1

Table 1.2.1: Non-German population in Germany by Country of Origin, 1992

Country of Origin	Population (in 1,000)	% of non-German Population
Turkey	1,855	41
Ex - Yugoslavia	916	21
Italy	558	12
Greece	346	8
Poland	286	6
Romania	167	4
Spain	134	3
Portugal	99	2
Iran	99	2
Morocco	80	1
Total	4,540	100

Source: David Horrocks and Eva Kolinsky 1996: Migrants and Citizens, (p. 71-101). Adapted from Eva Kolinsky, Chapter 5, Table 5.5 Non-German population in Germany by Country of Origin, 1992 p. 84.
Original Source: Der Spiegel, 23, 1993, p. 19.

The Migration phenomenon has constantly been developing Germany's economy as a receiving country. In the time of economic downturns, migrant workers were affected more than citizens of the host country. Host country authorities force long term unemployed migrant workers to return to their home country. The Host's attitudes towards immigrant workers change dramatically, the hospitality in the beginning turns into jealousy and discrimination. The host becomes more unwilling to accepting well-established long term immigrants as a part of host society.

Table 1.2.2: Non-German population and Turkish Minority in the German (Länder) States

Land (in 1,000)	Non-German Population	Turkish Minority	as % of German Population
Baden-Württemberg	1,190.8	324.5	27
Bavaria	995.9	224.4	25
Berlin	382.8	129.8	34
Bremen	75.7	29.7	39
Hamburg	235.5	60.3	26
Hesse	745.9	184.4	25
Nord-Rhine Westfälin	1,812.3	639.1	35
Lower Saxony	425.8	121.4	29
Rhineland Palatinate	258.9	68.0	25
Saarland	68.2	12.6	18
Schleswig Holstein	125.9	38.6	31
New Länder (East German Federal States)[91]			
Brandenburg	55.0	0.6	1.1
Merklenburg-Pomerania	22.5	0.2	1.0
Saxony	50.8	0.5	1.0
Saxony-Anhalt	33.9	0.4	1.0
Thuringia	20.3	0.3	1.4

Source: David Horrocks and Eva Kolinsky 1996: Migrants and Citizens, (p. 71-101). Adapted from Eva Kolinsky, Chapter 5, Table 5.6 Non-German population in Germany by Country of Origin, 1992 p. 85.
Original Source: Calculated from data in *Statistisches Jahrbuch für die Bundesrepublik Deutschland*, 1994.

Table1.2.3: Percentage of foreigners in the German cities (1991)

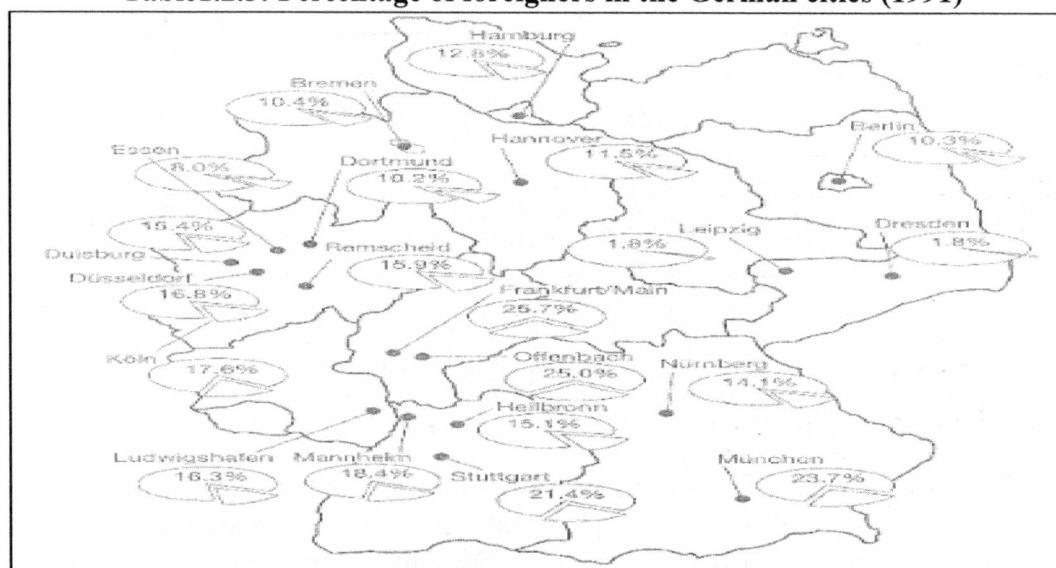

Source: German Federal Statistical Institute, 1991 and 1996

---

[91] Since (New Länder) these five states were a part of East Germany before the reunification, there was just few Turkish immigrants in those states.

Table 1.2.3: Percentages of Foreigners in German Federal States in 1996

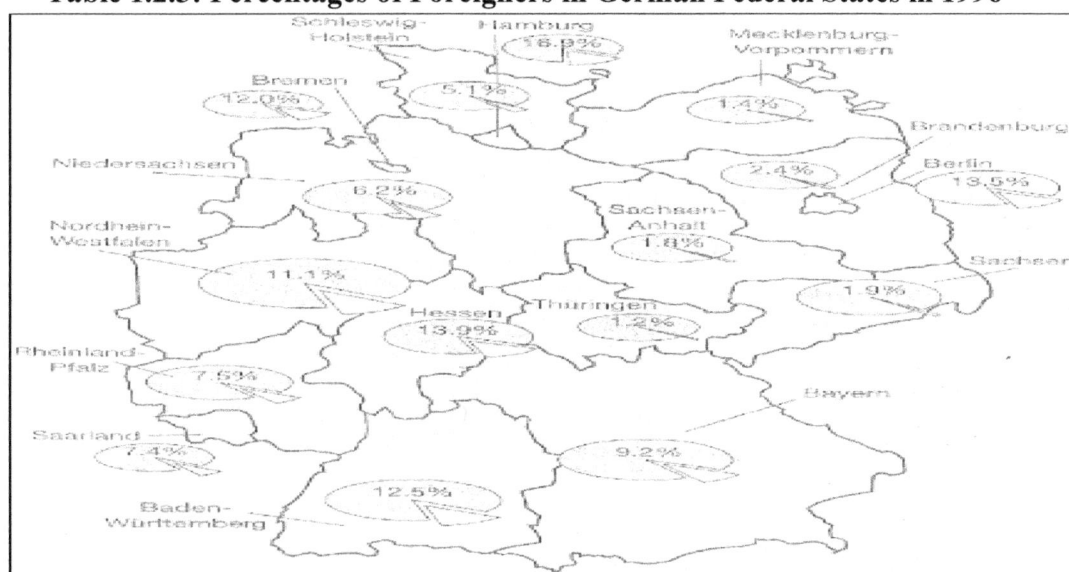

Source: German Federal Statistical Institute, 1991 and 1996

As can be seen, about 80 per cent of the Turkish immigrants have settled in West Germany, a pattern which has persisted throughout the main period of migration. Within West Germany, there is a heavy concentration of Turks in the most industrialized regions of North Rhine-Westphalia and Baden-Wurttemberg; in fact almost 40 per cent of all the Turkish workers in Western Europe live in these two German states. In view of West Germany's numerical dominance, conditions of life and employment for Turkish immigrants as a whole are overwhelmingly influenced by those in a single country, and much of the information which follows related primarily to (West) Germany.

Table 1.2.5 Turkish populations in European cities in 2002 (excluded naturalised)

Host country	Population (000s)	Percentage	Percentages in main city	
Germany	2,014.0	66.4	Berlin	7.0
France	261.0	8.6	Paris	25.0
The Netherlands	260.1	8.6	Amsterdam	20.0
Austria	143.2	4.7	Vienna	32.0
Belgien	119.0	3.9	Brüssels	33.0
Switzerland	79.4	2.6	Zürich	21.0
UK	58.2	1.9	London	80.0
Sweden	35.7	1.2	Stockholm	50.0
Denmark	35.7	1.2	Copenhagen	50.0

Source: Manco (2004, pp.4-5). London from Struder (2003a p.21)

Table 1.2.6 Turkish population in the European Union: by status (in '000s) in 2002

Country	Turkish origin	Turkish nationals	Naturalised number	Percentage
Austria	200	120	80	40
Belgium	110	67	43	39
Denmark	53	39	14	26

31

France	370	196	176	47
Germany	2,642	1,912	730	28
The Netherlands	270	96	174	64
Sweden	37	14	23	62
UK	70	37	33	47
Other EU	20	19	1	5
Total EU	3,772	2,500	1,272	34

Source: Tumbas (2003, p.2)

Table 1.2.7: Turkish enterprises in the EU: indicators (1995-2002)

Indicators -Years	1996	1998	2000	2002
Number	56,500	67,400	80,600	82,300
Total number of employees	232,000	323,000	419,000	411,000
Average number of employees	4.1	4.8	5.2	5.0
Average investment by enterprise (Euro)	98,500	104,800	110,400	112.000
Total investment (Euro, billions)	5.6	7.0	8.9	9.2
Total annual turnover (Euro, billions)	21.8	28.7	34.8	36.0

Source: Tumbas (2003, p. 4)

The Table 1.14 indicates that Turkish immigrant enterprises are growing to an economic power year by year across Europe in spite of the lack of citizenship of the host country.

Table 1.2.8 Immigrant entrepreneurs in the Netherlands in 2003 Sectoral concentration (%)

Immigrant group	Number of enterprises	First		Second		Third	
Turkey	7,478	Catering	22	Retail	17	Wholesale	15
Surinam	5,690	Personal	14	Wholesale	14	Retail services	17
Chine	2,297	Catering	79	Wholesale	10	Retail	4
Morocco	2,883	Retail	26	Catering	23	Personal services	10
Hong Kong	1,113	Catering	75	Wholesale	8	Retail	6

Source: Rath and Kloosterman (2003, pp.131, 133)

Table 1.17 displays immigrants of foreign origin entrepreneurs in the Netherlands in 2003. Different distribution of the sectoral concentration is showed in percentage. The table also indicates that the Turkish immigrant entrepreneurs in the Netherlands are the largest group among other groups.

Table 1.2.9: The chances of immigrants for employment in European countries (2005)

Country	%
France	22
Spain	18
Austria	12
Germany	8
Employment probability is less than for the native born in (by %)	
Denmark	25
France	23
Germany	12
Austria, Spain and Finland	9

Source: Herault (2006, pp.2, 3-4)

Table 1.3.1: Where are the migrants' new homes (2005)? The world's migrants reached an annual displacement of 191 million in 2005. The migrants distributed regionally as follows:

Europe	34 (percentage)
Asia-Pacific	28
North America	23
Africa	9
Latin America-Caribbean	4

Sources: UN, Centre d'Analyse Stratégiques, Paris, 2005

Table 1.19, displays that the highest percentage (34 per cent) of migrants preferred 'Europe', as new homes in 2005 in spite of strict EU policy and high unemployment rates in European countries.

Number of Turkish population in Germany has sometimes been exaggerated. According to the latest sources, the number of Turkish population is shown in the following tables:

Table 1.3.2: Turks in Germany with Migration Background, 2007

Detailed migration status	Total	Share of total population
Turkey	2,527,000	16.4

Source: Adapted from Germany's 2007 micro-census, Germany

Table 1.3.3: Turks in Germany by Nationality and Gender, 2008

Citizenship	Total	Share of total (percent)	Men	Women	Percent women
Turkey	1,688,370	25.1	889,003	799,367	47.3

Source: Adapted from German Federal Statistical Office and the Central Register of Foreigners, 2006 to 2008

According to Germany's 2007 micro-census, the population with migration background which includes Aussiedler and their children as well as the German-citizen descendants of immigrants totalled 15.4 million, or 18.7 percent of Germany's population (see Table 21). Of these 15.4 million, 16.4 percent were of Turkish origin.

1.1.9 Ethnic Germans

The perseverance of Germany's ethno-cultural conception is closely related to migratory developments after World War II. Almost ten million refugees fled Eastern Europe to Germany between the years 1945-1950, and another 1.6 million followed between the years 1951-1988. During the cold war these repatriates sustained the legitimacy of West Germany's claim to embody German unity, despite its actual division. Ethnic Germans were actually the legacy of the war, their private memories structured public memory. The Soviet aggression and the advantages and superiority of a free west triggered Ethnic German migration. Anti-communism was not only a response to communist aggression, but it was also a widely shared ideology that unified Germans and helped integrate their co-ethnics. This common ideology contributed also to European integration and the gradual reformation of Germany's national self-understanding. These refugees played a role for the reassertion of nationhood was also evidenced in strong legislative measures on their behalf. Between 1945 and 1949 the legal situation of Germany remained unclear and divided into different zones. All these changed with the formation of the FRG and the passing of the Basic Law in 1949. The Basic Law refers explicitly to ethnic Germans in three articles. The most important of them is Article 116. According to paragraph one of article 116.German citizenship was granted to those who had either held German citizenship (*Staatsangehörigkeit*) or had lived in the borders of the German Reich on or before 31 December 1937 as members of German ethnic origin (*Volkszugehörigkeit*). This law conferred legal status upon both native Germans and ethnic Germans. The distinction between these two categories-citizens of the FRG (*Staatsangehöriger*) and those who did not possess German citizenship but belonged to the community by virtue of descent constituted the foundation for the continuous migration of ethnic German resettlers ever since. Article 116 thus solidified the citizenship status of ethnic Germans coming to the FRG and ensured that they would enjoy full legal equality.

The central law that governs the integration of ethnic German repatriates is the Federal Expellee Law of 1953.Germany's division and the ethno-cultural idiom served as a sole foundation for Germanness. Nearly one-fifth of the West German population consisted of refugees and the majority of people shared some sense of community of destiny (*Schicksalsgemeinschaft*) based on similar experience during the war years. By the early 1960s, the incorporation of ethnic Germans was accomplished. After reunification, public resentment towards ethnic German immigrants from the East often expressed itself of questioning whether they were really Germans. Aussiedler have become the target of public controversy and previous distinctions between co-ethnics, guest-workers and asylum seekers became unclear. However, the government continued to treat ethnic Germans as an integral part of the nation (with a slogan such as: '*Ethnic Germans are not foreigners*', and the pre-unification slogan of 'two states, one nation' gave way to the view of 'two nations, one state' which helped revive the tension between *Staats-und Kulturnation*. Frederick Nietzsche once asked himself, 'It distinguishes the Germans that they never get tired of asking who they are' (Nietzsche, 1978, p.13).

In most European countries nationality or citizenship is the decisive criterion for distinguishing between 'locals' and immigrants. Most countries try to distinguish between EU national and 'other' foreign residents. Between 1945 and 1992 West Germany accepted 24 million displaced persons, ethnic Germans, and labour migrants (so-called guest-workers) from central and Eastern Europe because of economic deterioration, political instability, rising nationalism, unemployment. Others are victims of the wars and ethnic cleansing in Croatia and Bosnia-Herzegovina or political repression against ethnic or religious minorities in other parts of the Balkans. In 1991-3 the war in Croatia and Bosnia created the largest single wave of European emigration since the end of World War II.5 million people were forced to leave their home town and villages to Western Europe where they were tolerated there. Geographic closeness also played a role. Germany and Austria were the two most affected countries. Partly, their historical, ethnic and geographic links with these countries also played a role.
They seek to safeguard themselves against immigration by means of compulsory visas, more stringent border controls, very restrictive asylum regulations, and troop deployment along the common borders with East-Central Europe.

As a result, with the inflow of the Ethnic Germans Germany became an immigration country without migration policy. Germany, which had already lost its overseas colonies in 1914, has been playing an analogous role by serving as destination of immigration for millions of ethnic Germans from Eastern Europe, the Balkans and Central Asia. Ever since Germany's first unification in 1871, its identity has been problematic, reflecting recurrent tensions between ethnic and civic understandings of nationhood.[92] In its formative phase, the German concept of *nation-centred* on the *Volk,* signifying organic relationship among a people rather than a political organisation; the emphasis on cultural cohesion responded to the fragmentation of the German states between 1815 and 1871. After the unification of Germany in 1871 a new, *state-centred* conception of nationhood was introduced. Ever since, German politics has been shaped by tensions between ethno-national and state-national conception remained unclear between the *Kulturnation* and the *Staatnation.* Tensions between ethnic and civic conceptions are constitutive for the national conjunctures in which these aspects of nationhood came into conflict. Its national identity was reshaped as these defining tensions reappear in varying contexts.[93]

1.2.1 Immigrants' rights in European countries

Those immigrants arrived in Europe from former European colonies, holding the passport of host and nationality of the country to which they moved, and thus with same formal rights as other citizens (France, the UK and the Netherlands all seem in this respect). The German case is different, thus all non –national migrants such as guest workers in Germany were granted legal rights and welfare state membership in accordance with what Thomas Hammar (1990) calls 'denizenship'. This status can be understood as legal and social rights linked to legal incomplete membership status denizen-ship into full citizenship would then depend upon naturalization laws, as France and Germany demonstrate.

For almost three decades these migrants were not regarded as 'real immigrants', but as a kind of transferable and temporarily transferred work force. It was expected that these migrants would return home after a limited period of employment, no integration was intended, as the name 'guest-workers' suggested.[94] In fact the majority of migrants wanted to stay for long periods and often for the rest of their lives. In this way so-called 'guest-workers' became permanent residents or immigrants.

The receiving countries had to face the problems of family reunions, integration of foreign-born children into their educational systems, and finally the demands for suffrage and citizenship by immigrant workers and their relatives.[95] Thus the challenge of integration has become even more acute in the 1990s than it was before. Meanwhile, closed borders led to rising numbers of illegal immigrants since 1973. The control of the labour supply by administrative means (work permits, residence permits, etc.) had only limited success. The existing of informal networks and the opportunity to enter the receiving country as a tourist became as essential basis for illegal immigration. No precise data on illegal immigrants are available, so we can only

---

[92] Brubaker, Rogers: 'Immigration, Citizenship, and the Nation-State in France and Germany': Shafir, Gershon ed., *the Citizenship Debates*; Minneapolis; University of Minnesota Press, 1998 (pp.131-167)

[93] Ibid., p. 168-173

[94] Bade, Klaus J.: Germans abroad – foreigners in Germany. Migration in Geschichte und Gegenwart, Munich, 1993, p. 395

speculate about the magnitude of this stream. Changes during the 1980s new patterns of migration have also developed. Most southern European (emigration) countries became countries of immigration (Italy, Spain, Portugal and Greece).

1.2.2 Changing concepts of the guest-workers

As consequence of exclusion of the immigrants (including Turkish guest workers) by German authorities caused to be emerged new terms such as a 'foreigner', since they are regarded as non-Germans. The concept of 'foreigners', that is, a person who can claim only limited civil rights and whose right to stay and access to gainful employment are restricted.[96] Foreign born children who joined their immigrant parents at a later stage of the family life cycle and second generation immigrants, that is, children born to foreigners in the country of immigration, children are not foreign-born but remain foreign citizens.

The main aspects of the weaker status for foreigners are: (i) the principle of priority for Germans over foreigners concerning access to the labour market as 2nd or 3rd class citizens; (ii) temporary limited employment permits for foreigners; (iii) restricted regional mobility for foreigners. For decades, the German labour market authorities took advantage of this work force which had to accept a marginal status as it is characterized by these restriction. One-third of them are women, not even regarded as migrants, but foreign women until 2001. One of the reasons to recruit labour force was for reconstruction of war devastated post war West Germany after 1945. The recruitment of foreign workers operated quite selectively, the most important criteria used by the officials were productivity, health, age and political clearance.

As a rule a permit to work and stay in Germany was granted for one year only and restricted to a specific job and local community. The administration had considerable powers of discretion on whether or not to extend a permit. Because of increased flexibility, time limits were gradually relaxed: the principle of forced rotation after two years' stay (included in the contract with Turkey) was abandoned in 1964.[97]

1.2.3 Comparing German Turkish communities within other EU countries'

This section aims to show socio-economic status of Turkish immigrants and their economic contribution in Germany vis-à-vis in other European host countries. European countries need immigrants not only for their declining demographic rates and ageing population, but also due to immigrants' economic contribution to their host country's economic growth, and immigrants' contribution to the host social security fund, public budget and tax office. Although their nature of need differs from country to country European countries are still dependants on immigrants in future. Previous studies indicate that European countries have benefited greatly from their

---

[96] Abadan-Unat, Nermin: A case Study, Turkish Workers in West Germany – Immigrant and Migrant Labour – The resulting tensions in affluent countries 109th Wilton Park Conference, Steyning Sussex. Faculty of Political Science University of Ankara, Ankara, 1969, (p. 30-34)
[97] Ibid

immigrants economically. Immigrants have also benefited from the host's immigration and integration policy as well as economically. Former West Germany has become an economic giant of Europe thanks to its guest worker system. In new Germany German-born younger Turkish immigrants replace the local workforce and keep German social security system operating. Therefore, Turkish immigrants' contribution to German public purse carries a great importance. This section provides statistically significant evidence that Turkish immigrants added an economic, politics and socio-cultural dimension not only to Germany but also to other European countries.

Table 1.2.7 Turkish enterprises in the EU (1995-2002) indicates that Turkish immigrant enterprises are growing to an economic power year by year across Europe in spite of the lack of citizenship of the host country.[98] Table 1.2.8 Turkish population in the European Union: by status (in '000s) in 2002 indicates that the number naturalised Turkish immigrants in Sweden are 62% thanks to Swedish immigration and integration policy. The same table shows that the number of naturalised Turkish immigrants in the Netherlands is even higher than Sweden, 64% of Turkish immigrants have become Dutch citizens. Table 1.2.9 Immigrant entrepreneurs in the Netherlands in 2003-Sectoral concentration show that Turkish immigrant entrepreneurs in the Netherlands with 7,478 enterprises are the largest group among other immigrants groups thanks to Dutch immigration/integration policy. Even in Britain and France the percentage of naturalised Turkish immigrants are higher (with 47% for both countries, see Table 1.1.3) than Germany (only 32% of Turks are German citizens in Germany) in spite of lack of a good integration policy of Germany.

Table 1.1.4 Turkish populations in the European gateway cities in 2002, indicates that Turkish entrepreneurs are growing economic force in Europe. According to Manco during 1996 an estimated 58.000 businessmen employed a total of 186,000 workers throughout Europe.[99] The vast bulk of the firms (42,000) were in Germany, with The Netherlands, France and Austria making up the reminder. Recent data on self-employed Turkish immigrants from the Turkish Research Centre (TRC) at the University of Essen suggest that during 2002 an estimated 82,300 firms employed 411,000 people. As the above indicates, during the five-year period 1996-2002 nearly 25,000 more self-employed businesses were added to the total, representing a 41.8% rate of increase. Employment during the same period increased by 225,000, a rate of increase of 82.6 per cent TRC, 2003). According to Panayiotopoulos something like 77% of Turkish businessmen in Germany have German suppliers and an increasing number are relying on German consumers. About 17% of employees in firms are Germans and 9% are from other nationalities. One estimate of the total contribution made by Turkish immigrant entrepreneurs to the European economy is that it is equivalent to one fifth of Denmark's GDP- gross domestic product and 51 equivalents to 51% of Greek GDP.[100]

---

[98] Turkish Immigrant entrepreneurs in the EU, By Prodromos Ioannous Panayiotopoulos, Emerald, Journal of Entrepreneural Research, 2008, Volume 14, Issue 6, pp. 395-413

[99] Manco U.: Turks in Western Europe, Centrum for Islam in Europe, University of Ghent, 2004, (pp.6-7) In: Turkish Immigrant entrepreneurs in the EU, By Prodromos Ioannous Panayiotopoulos, Emerald, Journal of Entrepreneural Research, 2008, Volume 14, Issue 6, pp. 395-413

[100] Türkiye Araştirmalari Merkezi, Turkish Research Centre- TRC, University of Essen, 2000, (p. 3).

The number of (non-national) immigrants living in the EU is 25 million which make up, 5.5 per cent of the total population[101]. There are also 15 million immigrants who are Muslims. A great number of these people live in EU countries where nearly 4.3 millions of them are Turkish immigrants. [102] The largest numbers of foreign citizens reside in Germany, France and the UK.

Turkey has a population of 70 million, 6.2 million of Turks live abroad, 5.2 million of them live in Europe (2.4 million of them can vote) and 80 percent of all Turks in EU countries are living in Germany. Approximately 450,000 Turks live in France, two in three of them have received French citizenship and can vote; about 120,000 Turks live in Britain and more than 50.000 received British citizenship and can vote. There are 300,000 Turkish immigrants in Austria; one in three (100,000) of them is an Austrian citizen, and naturally they have voting rights as political right.

The proportion of foreign-born population in Germany is 20% of the total population (including ethnic Germans); 8.9% of those are non-Germans. This means that Germany has become an immigration country, as France and Britain, despite German denial of being an immigration country until 2000. The proportion of foreign-born population in France is 9% of total population, and French immigrants come mainly from French speaking colonies. Foreign-born people in Britain make up 7% of the total population. Germany, which is absolute numbers hosts the largest foreign population in the EU, experiences a remarkably stable order of the five largest non-national populations; Turks, (ex-) Yugoslavs, Italians, Greeks and Poles. A review of the cynical sensitivity of migration to West Germany from the key recruitment countries before and after the halt in recruiting shows that, contrary to expectation, cynical variability did not decline for West European countries with the tightest restriction on mobility. New data shows that relative economic conditions in the receiving countries have affected the flow of asylum seekers in Europe. In the initial period, migration was directed to the industrialized countries of the Western Europe, but after the enlargement of the numbers of the EU member states (in 1995 joined 5 new members, in 2004 joined 10 new East European countries) the tide turned to even the new member countries.

1.2.4 Conclusion of Chapter One

In general, German guest-worker recruitment system, in other words, German immigration policy has been successful so far, but it is not easy to say the same for 'integration policy' which is the research topic of the thesis. At first glance, Germany may not seem an obvious model from which other European countries can learn positive lessons about immigration from German experience.

In the meantime, 'immigration policy' is often used synonymously with active labour recruitment .West European governments traditionally denied such a policy's existence. Even they applied measures to control the inflow of non-natives. Before the 1970s, several West European countries that once actively recruited labour migrants turned to restrictive policies in the 1970s.

---

[101] Euro-stat 8/2006
[102] Source: Euro-stat July, 1998 and December, 2006

The existence of a cheap work force from abroad kept the German wage levels fairly low and reduced the necessity to rearrange the structure of wages, foreign labour allowed the continuation of poor working condition. Zimmerman explains the impact of migration on host society as long term immigrants have been a great contribution to host economy, but illegal and low skilled migration flow caused higher inflation and putting wages down. [103]

As to the impact of Turkish migration to Europe specifically Germany, it had a positive effect on Turkish economic growth as manifested in the increase of national savings, investment and foreign currency reserves (i.e. 3.70% in 1967-70, 5.79% in 1971-74 and 8.49% in 1975-78). [104] Since 1980, Turkish export, tourism and entrepreneurship became more important contributors to the country's economic growth as well as the remittances of Turkish workers in Germany. [105]

Turkish labour migration has been an economic asset in Germany since they were recruited as labour force and in time their migration caused socio-economic and political changes including demographic changes i.e. industrial society becomes a post industrial and a multi-cultural society.

Germany tried to continue with nation state and non-immigration country policy until unification in 1990. But it was already on the way to become an immigration country despite official denying. Britain, Sweden, Netherlands and Switzerland have already become multi-cultural states with ethnic diversities. The first Turkish migrants came to Europe with the intention of returning home. In fact, some of them returned. Some of them have settled down, married and had children. The second and third generation are reluctant to uproot their families in order to return home. In addition, they have become accustomed to the German way of life. Although they believe that integration and not assimilation by the host society is their best hope. Turkish immigrants make their own considerable contribution to their new home country. Immigrants have been a politically salient and important aspect of population change in many European countries. Without immigration, Germany, France and Britain would already have registered a population loss in 2000s. In the context of an ageing population and a need for certain skills, migrants make an important economic contribution.

Prime Ministers and other politicians of the two countries have also had an impact on Turkish immigrants' integration and bilateral relations. For example, during a 2008 visit to Germany, Turkish Prime Minister Recep Tayyip Erdogan told a Turkish audience, "Nobody can expect you to submit to assimilation. Assimilation is a crime against humanity." German chancellor Angela Merkel said during a speech in Potsdam on 16 October 2010 to youth members of her Christian Democratic Union party, "attempts to create a multicultural society utterly failed, and the concept of different cultures can live happily side by side does not work". She also stressed that immigrants need to do more to integrate, including learning to speak German. [106]

---

[103] Zimmermann Klaus F.: European Migration, Push-pull theories, Proceeding of the World Bank Annual Conference on Development Economics, Munich, 1994 (p.313).

[104] OECD, Labour force statistics 1963-1978 (Paris, 1978), pp. 412-413.

[105] OECD, Labour force statistics 1976-1980 (Paris, 1980), pp. 412

[106] Reuter's News Agency, and Turkish Daily Hurriyet, 2010/10/16.

German public and political opinion suggested that Turks are less integrated than many other groups in Germany.[107] There are also some misperceptions by German public such as Turks resist against being integrated and tend to create a parallel society in Germany. Furthermore, they do not bother to learn German language.

Studies showed that integration of immigrants is easier from the same socio-cultural, political and religious backgrounds. But Muslim immigrants from distinct cultural and religious backgrounds had been problematic[108] Since Muslims did not interact and mix with the mainstream host society (including Turkish immigrants in Germany). This is in spite of the fact that Turkey embraced Western secular political system and west European lifestyle including changes in dress and Latin alphabet instead of Arabic.[109] However, the current ruling religious party government of Turkey changed the constitution by a referendum on 12 September 2010. As Parekh argued interacting and amalgamation with the host society is easier from the same linguistic background such as Britons in Australia and Austrians in Germany. The multicultural integration is not always successful for immigrants from distinct cultural and religious backgrounds. Accusing immigrants by host country's politicians for being uninterested in being integrated; of being unreasonable, lacking an open-mind, common sense and unwilling to learn host country's language is not a solution. The solution lies in dialogue with immigrant representatives from their organisations.[110] Obviously, Turks have a different culture and tradition, which seems an obstacle for Turks' integration within European continent unlike USA.[111] In addition, Turks did not go to Germany to stay forever. Their aim was not to stay in Germany permanently, just to earn and save money rather than staying and living a comfortable life in Germany. They were not interested in participation in social and political activities in Germany. They did not learn German and improve their German skills. Moreover, Germans had no immigration and integration policy because they expected and encouraged Turks return home. Turks postponed returning home every year. Germany's encouraging return policy and restriction of family unification, residential and work permit caused Turks to feel unwanted in Germany and gave them a status of permanent temporariness under the name of foreign residents.[112]

Tourism is also a chain facilitating factor for integration of Turkish immigrants into Germany as well as Turco-German relations. According to Frankfurt Turkish Council, Department for Tourism and Information (1999), 9,732.697 German tourists visited Turkey in 1998 and 2, 338.529 of them were Germans.[113]

---

[107] Berlin Institute for Population and Development, 2009

[108] Tariq Modood, Anna Trandafyllidou and Ricard Zapata-Barrero (eds.): Multiculturalism, Muslims and Citizenship, A European Approach, Published by Routhledge, 2006, Ch.10 'Europe, Liberalism and Muslim question' by Bhikhu Parekh, (p. 180-195)

[109] Ibid., (p. 196)

[110] Ibid., (p. 180)

[111] Amin Maalouf: Çivisi Çıkmış Dünya – Uygarlıklarımız Tükendiğinde, Yapı Kredi Yayınları - YKY Publicatıon İstanbul , 2009 (Turkish version translated by Orçun Türkay) Originally, Le dereglement du monde, Editins Grasset & Fasquella, 2009 (p. 17-18)

[112] Şen, Faruk; Çiğdem Akkaya, Reyhan Güntürk: On the eve of year 2000 Europe and Turkey (*2000 yilinin eşiğinde Avrupa ve Türkiye*), published by Çağ Yayınevi, İstanbul, 1999, (p. 16-20)

[113] T.C. Frankfurt Başkonsolosluğu Turizm ve Enformasyon Dairesi {T.R Frankfurt Turkish Council, Department for Tourism and Information, Frankfurt, 1999

Not only bilateral relations have been affected by Turkish immigrants' integration, but also Turkey's EU membership. According to the Bild's report (October 19 2010), a German public opinion poll on the issue of Turkey's EU membership suggests 73% Germans are against Turkey's EU membership, only 13.5% support its EU membership.[114] If Turks were better integrated into German society, German public opinion would be positive for Turkey's joining to the EU.

As mentioned in introduction of the chapter, the first chapter only deals with Turkish migration to Germany, Germany's immigration policy and theories of migration in general. Then integration theories, changing status of Turkish workers during their presence in Germany within Germany's integration policy, which leads to exclusion/isolation, integration or assimilation, have been examined in the next chapter.

---

[114] Vatan Gazetesi, October 19 2010

Chapter 2

2.1 Chapter introduction

The aim of the second chapter is to explore Germany's integration/assimilation policy and the importance of immigrants' integration for bilateral relations as well as themselves, by examining Turks' integration level into German society. First the key factors affecting integration of Turkish immigrants and bilateral relations positively and negatively had been identified in the light of fifty years' experience such as the interactions and coexistence between the Turkish and German communities. The key factor here for a successful integration of immigrants is for Turks to accept the host country/Germany as a new home and to be accepted by Germans as full members of German society.

As integration is a two way process, this research needs to be investigated and evaluated from both sides' point of view – German preferences and Turkish expectations. As a consequence of historical phenomenon, the majority of Turks experienced a changing status between their rights as ex-guest workers deprived of social, civic and political rights and some of them as integrated/naturalised newly German citizens who have the same rights as native Germans on paper, but in practice they do not receive equal treatment. Germans have benefited from the guest worker system economically, but closed their eyes for emerged integration problems for years by denying that Germany is not an immigration country and they do not have any integration policy.

This chapter has also investigated the changing statuses of Turks from guest-worker to immigrant and Germany's changing attitudes towards the Turkish community by applicable approaches within the framework of Germany' s integration/assimilation, citizenship policy and the EU's integration measures.

In addition, this chapter has discussed the alternative approaches related to the research question on the integration of immigrants which ended up with isolation/ghettoisation, multi-cultural integration and the assimilation. In this research the following question has been addressed and investigated in seven chapters.

'Have Turkish immigrants integrated into Germany (during 1961-2007) and has their integration any impact on bilateral relations, either positively or negatively?'

2.1.1 The concept of integration and its application in the European context

The concept of integration is simply an outcome of mutual interactions or the amalgamation between the host society members and immigrant community members.

John W. Berry argues that integration "requires immigrants to *adopt* the basic values of the receiving society and the receiving society to *adapt* national institutions (e.g., education, health, and justice, labour) to better meet the needs of all groups now living together in the larger plural society".[115]

The concept of integration is not as simple as the saying people use in daily life "When in Rome do as the Romans do"; however, this phrase does not refer to long-term immigrants but to temporary wage-earners.

Although concepts of immigration and integration are interrelated, immigration is used in the course of settlement; integration is applied to long-term residents. As Claudia Roth stated "You cannot call people 'guest' after living forty years in Germany".[116] She urged that immigrants should be granted voting rights at least. So, as a long term residents the Turks in Germany are not guests any more but immigrants and need to be integrated into German society and way of life.

A Danish researcher Peter Nannestad has defined integration as "a process that results in the financial and social equality of ethnic minorities with the majority population".[117] This definition is inspired by British liberal Roy Jenkins as Britain's home secretary in 1966. The liberal view is similar to multiculturalism since both views recognize immigrants' diversity.

Saskia Sassen argues that the integration of immigrants is perceived by the host society members as "what has generally come to be seen as declass, one represented as not belonging to the country of residence, such conditions can indeed produce feelings of being 'invaded' by the other".[118]

Sassen also argues that immigrants are unwilling to cut the ties with their home country and want to remain loyal to their mainland but they want access to the whole rights of the host country as "immigrants are often reluctant to give their rights and within countries of origin (such as returning, owning property, inheriting property, participating in national election), but do want full integration in countries of residence".[119]

The following diagram demonstrates the areas of integration in which the long-term immigrants are expected to be integrated in order to meet their material, socio-cultural and psychological needs as well as their countries' demands.

---

[115] Berry, J. (2004): Fundamental psychological processes in intercultural relations. In D. Landis, J. M. Bennett, & M. J., Bennett (Eds.), *Handbook of intercultural training* (3rd Eds.) (pp. 166-184). Thousand Oaks: Sage.
[116] The Greens Party leader Claudia Roth made a speech in her party's election campaign in Munich on 24 September 2009.
[117] Peter Nannestad, "Integration Is Hard: Danes and the New Ethnic Minorities", in *Uncomfortable Challenges: Current Tendencies in the Danish and European Immigration Debate* (in Danish), ed. Peter Seeberg (Odense: Odense University Press, 2001), p. 13.
[118] Sassen, Saskia: Guests and Aliens, The New Press, New York, 1999, (p. 149)
[119] Ibid., (p. 146)

Diagram 1   TYPES OF INTEGRATION

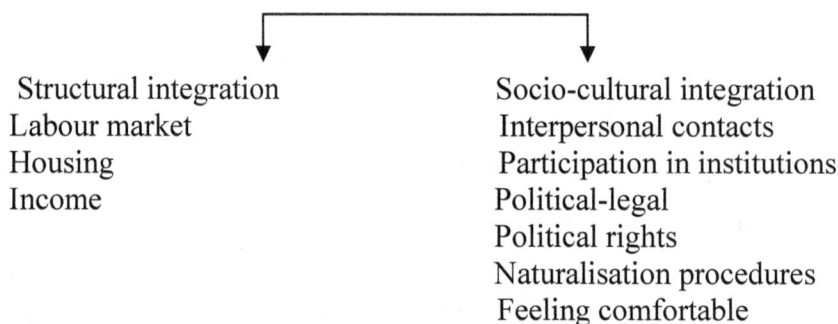

Structural integration	Socio-cultural integration
Labour market	Interpersonal contacts
Housing	Participation in institutions
Income	Political-legal
	Political rights
	Naturalisation procedures
	Feeling comfortable

Source: Author

As the above diagram shows integration has many dimensions; and each needs to be explained separately. Different types of integration are hypothesized on different kinds of rights. For example, economic (labour market, housing and income); social, cultural (interpersonal contracts, participation in society's institutions, political and sportive activities) and political rights which refers to immigrants' background such as educational attainment, language command, age structure, cultural values, tradition and religious affiliation. On the other hand, the attitudes of the host society at both the national and the local level have a mutual effect on the integration process of immigrants positively or negatively.[120]

Milton Gordon argues that once structural integration has occurred such as employment, housing and income, all the other types of integration (including decline of prejudice and discrimination) will naturally follow. [121]

Tariq Modood argues that cultural integration hybridizes host and immigrant culture to produce a multicultural society. Immigrants should adapt to host culture, while maintaining their cultural identity. [122]

As to social integration, a Canadian theorist Jane Jenson developed five social indicators of social cohesion in a society (Jenson, 1998:15).

Table 2: Jenson's Five Dimensions of Social Cohesion

Belonging – Isolation
Inclusion – Exclusion
Participation – Non-involvement
Recognition – Rejection
Legitimacy – Illegitimacy

Source: M. Sharon Jeannotte, 2008 [123]

---

[120] Geddes, Andrew: The Politics of Migration and immigration in Europe, Sage Publication, London, 2003, (p. 5-7).

[121] Milton M. Gordon, 1964. Ethnic Education; Its Purposes and Prospects Assimilation in American Life, Oxford University Press, 1964, p. 27

[122] Modood, Tariq; Anna Trandafyllidou and Ricard Zapata-Barrero (eds.): Multiculturalism, Muslims and Citizenship, A European Approach, Published by Routhledge, 2006, Ch.10 'Europe, Liberalism and Muslim question' by Bhikhu Parekh, (p. 179-203).

[123] M. Sharon Jeannotte: Promoting Social Integration - A Brief Examination of Concepts and Issues, Conference Paper, July 8-10, 2008 Helsinki, Finland (pp. 15)

44

According to Jenson social integration is based on the willingness of immigrants to cooperate with host society members and work together at all levels of society to achieve common goals (Janennotte et.al, 2003:3).

According to Adrian Favell, "Integration is said to hinge on formalising the idea of associative membership within the political space of the nation which, by defining boundaries and the lines of in/out between citizens and foreigners, establishes the shape and unity of a modern nation-state".[124]

Geddes especially emphasises socio-economic integration and suggests that a sharing of the costs of socio-economic integration between the host state and immigrants themselves is necessary.[125] Although the earlier settlement and the length of immigration in the host country is a factor that is most likely to affect the integration process, the most integrative factors for integration of immigrants is participating in sportive, cultural and political activities in the host country.[126] In this way, interaction creates a common interest and association with host's youths.[127] This is one of the key factors, which develops a successful integration.

Integration consists of contradictory terms such as preserving the home culture of the minority in order to facilitate re-migration, but also contained as an expectation that non-German minorities should adapt to the culture of the host country, Germany. Integration experts have argued that the term 'integration' was used to refer to the two-way process of adaptation by both the migrant and the host society in a way that enables the migrants to obtain upwards socio-economic and political status and access to the rights and participation in socio-cultural and sportive activities of host countries.[128]

Comparative research on migration in Europe has been divided into two parts, the first part deals with immigration control, and the second part deals with the integration issue of long-term immigrants into their host societies.

The concept of integration applied to both migrants and national minorities such as ethnic Germans from the former eastern bloc countries in Germany and the Turkish minorities from Greece, Bulgaria and Bosnia (Balkans) in Turkey.[129]

Ursula Mehrländer argued that in the past for many Germans immigration meant that the immigrant was expected to adopt German customs and traditions, however it is now the case that German attitudes are more positive towards immigrants from the EU member states, the US, Japan, Austria and Switzerland who are now considered an enrichment of German society'.[130]

---

[124] Favell, Adrian: Philosophies of integration, Macmillan Press,1998, (p.45)

[125] Geddes, Andrew: The Politics of Migration and immigration in Europe, Sage Publication, London, 2003, (p. 5).

[126] The Times, 20 June, 2006, Germany hosts "World Cup". One of the striking aspects of Germany's football – inspired patriotism has been the number of immigrants openly supporting the national team. Turks talk about the German-players as "Our Boys" .During the games, German fans chanted:"Stand up if you are German", thousands did so.

[127] *The Times,* June 22 2006, Turkish Kebabs became World Cup funs' favourite food in Germany.

[128] Geddes, Andrew: The Politics of Migration and immigration in Europe, Sage Publication, London, 2003, (p. 5).

[129] GeoJournal, Volume 48, nr.2, 1999, Territorial change and national identities in the Eastern and Western Europe, p.67-69 (3)

[130] Spencer, Sarah (Ed.): Immigration as an Economic Asset, Trentham Books, 1994; in Ch.1 Ursula Mehrländer: The Development of Post War Migration and Refugee Policy, (p. 11).

The following figure shows how European countries deal with immigration issues between the EU body and national institutions in the member states by considering national, ideological and regional interest within the institutional frameworks and policy references.[131]

Figure: 3

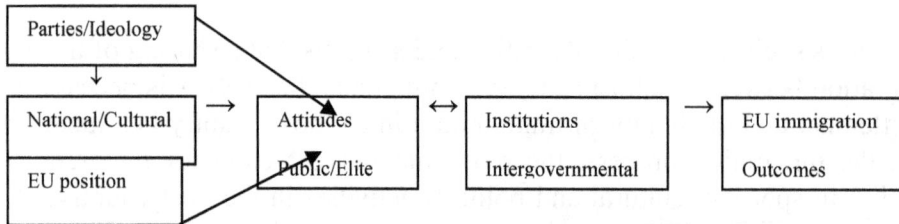

Source: Adapted from Lahav, Gallya (2004): 'Immigration and politics in the New Europe' (p. 3) Figure 1.1 Conceptual map.[132]

Figure 3, indicates the influence of the EU's integration policy on the integration process of immigrants in the member states.

The European Council defines "integration as a two-way process which hinges on the shared responsibilities of the host state and the legally resident third-country nationals."[133]

Figure 4: Factors affecting integration

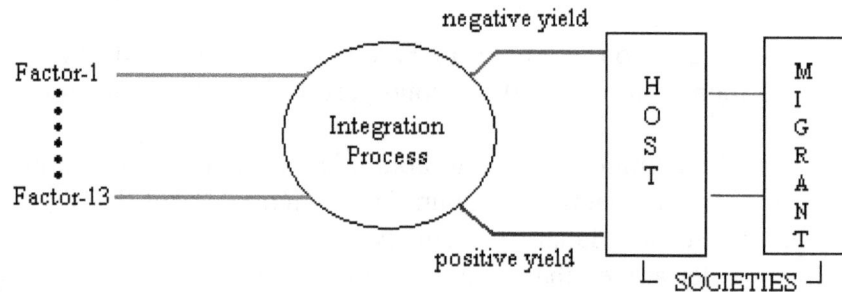

Source: Author

Fig-4 (Chapter 3, p. 128)

The concept of integration has been discussed in chapter two within the framework of EU integration policies. The factors affecting the integration of immigrants have been identified within two opposite groups as facilitating or hindering the process (See also Factors affecting integration in the Methodology Chapter 3, p. 128).

The subsequent Council conclusions on immigrant integration policy identify 11 basic common principles of integration, which are listed by the European Council in The Hague programme (2003). Some of them as follow:

---

[131] Lahav, Gallya: Immigration and Politics in the New Europe, Cambridge University Press, 2004, (p. 3)

[132] Ibid.

[133] Council Directive 2003/86/EC of 22 September 2003 on the right to family reunification, OJ 2003 L 251/12 (transposition deadline 3 October 2005)and Council Directive 2003/109/EC of 25 November 2003 concerning the status of third-country nationals who are long-term residents, OJ 2004 L 16/44(transposition deadline 23 January 2006).

"Integration is a dynamic two way process of mutual accommodation by both the migrants and the residents of Member States. Basic knowledge of the host society's language, history and institutions is indispensable to integration... Interaction between immigrants and Member States citizen is a fundamental mechanism for integration. Shared forums, inter-cultural dialogue, education... equal to national citizens and in a non-discriminatory way." [134]

Further development of The Hague programme is provided for in the Commission Action plan of May, 2005. The non-binding character of the Council conclusions and the three perspectives on the relationship between law and integration has been identified:

"The practice of diverse cultures and religions is guaranteed under the Charter of Fundamental Rights and must be safeguard, unless this practice conflicts with other inviolable European rights or with national law". [135]

In addition, Kees Groenendijk suggests three perspectives for a successful integration in the EU member states:

"A secure legal status will enhance the immigrant's integration in society; a strong residence status and equal treatment are instruments for integration; Naturalisation (or permanent residence status) should be the remuneration for a completed integration; The lack of integration or the assumed unfitness to integrate is grounds for refusal of admission to the country." [136]

Diagram 2

CONSEQUENCES OF INTEGRATION POLICIES IN EUROPE

Isolation	Intégration	Assimilation
Ghettoisation	Multiculturalisme	Acculturation

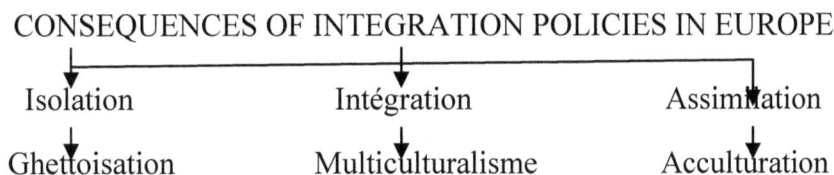

Source: Author

The integration process of immigrants creates three groups in European host countries. These groups are: 1) Isolated; 2) →integrated; 3) →assimilated. These three groups are the basis for a questionnaire designed (in chapter three on methodology) for this research conducted on Turkish immigrants in Germany (analysed in the chapter four and five). These three groups are defined in the methodology chapter as follows:

Members of the first group have isolated themselves from the host country. They are afraid of losing their roots, their social and cultural values, and therefore they are not willing to be integrated into their host country at the expense of losing their cultural identities.

Members of the second group are willing to be integrated, but at the same time they wish to preserve some of their cultural and linguistic values by keeping in touch with their home countries.

---

[134] Council Directive 2003/86/EC of 22 September 2003 on the right to family reunification, OJ 2003 L 251/12 (transposition deadline 3 October 2005)and Council Directive 2003/109/EC of 25 November 2003 concerning the status of third-country nationals who are long-term residents, OJ 2004 L 16/44(transposition deadline 23 January 2006).

[135] Ibid., p. 14

[136] Kees Groenendijk: European Journal of Migration and Law 6: 111-126, 'Legal Concepts of Integration in the EU Migration Law', 2004, p.113.

This is a real and desired "integrative" approach which is regarded as acceptable by both by immigrants and the host country (See Three categories Questionnaire Table Chapter three, p. 131).

Respondents of the third group in contrast to the first and second group become more assimilated into the host society (See Questionnaire Table Column 4 and 5, high level of integration, full assimilation or elimination of ethnic distinctiveness of immigrant group). The third group (mostly the 3rd generation German-born immigrant youths from mixed-marriages, and divorced or broken up families) are more likely to be assimilated into German society easier because they do not know anything about their parents' country of origin, language, and culture and so forth. Because they are highly assimilated they do not feel themselves different from the young native members of the German society. In fact, this highly assimilated group is likely to lose all traces of their ethic distinctiveness and cultural origin in the near future. Because it is inescapable to adopt the new cultural and linguistic identities of the host state, and only a small group of immigrants might preserve some small part of their parents' cultural and linguistic distinctiveness). They turn against their parents' country of origin's national values, they do not or cannot speak their parents' language, criticize their parents' traditions, norms etc. They have been assimilated through the process.

Past experiences from traditional immigration countries such as America, Canada and Australia shows that most of the immigrant youths may be expected at some point in time to stop being minorities and feeling American. Conley, Ellen Alexander calls them hyphenated-immigrants such as German-Americans, Turkish-Americans, but in Germany immigrants are called 'foreigners.' [137] As they move from their native culture, socio-economic and political status and become a part of the existing 'majority' society. This is because, the process of assimilation operates through a common majority culture, through mixed residence, schooling and through intermarriages. Therefore, the third group immigrant youths are likely to lose all evidence of linguistic distinctiveness in three or four generations. As a consequence, some of the immigrants cannot resist against the majority to preserve their distinctiveness forever; eventually, they lose their minority status and become like the majority.

Joe L. Kincheloe and Shirley R. Steinberg describe the term of multiculturalism as "What is Multiculturalism? Multiculturalism means everything and at the same times nothing". Power relations play an important role in helping to shape the way individuals, organizations, groups and institutions react to the reality of multiculturalism. [138]

Diagram 3

TYPES OF MULTICULTURALISM

Conservative Multiculturalism	Liberal Multiculturalism	Pluralist Multiculturalism	Left-essential Multiculturalism	Critical Multiculturalism

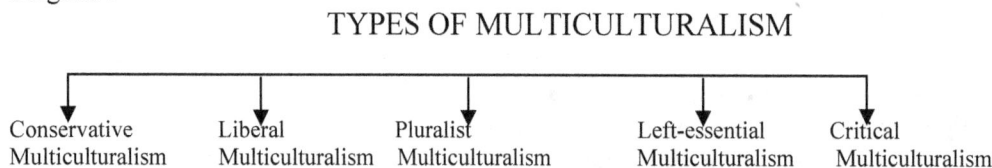

Source: Adapted from Joe L. Kincheloe and Shirley R. Steinberg: Changing Multiculturalism, Open Univ. Press, 1997, (p. 3-23)

---

[137] Conley, Ellen Alexander: The chosen shore, Stories of Immigrants; German-Americans connected by a hyphen or are called 'hyphenated immigrants', University of California Press, 2004; in chapter 14, Turkish-immigrant is called as 'Turkish-American (p.197-207).
[138] Joe L. Kincheloe and Shirley R. Steinberg: Changing Multiculturalism, Open Univ. Press, 1997, (p. 1)

The above diagram shows that there are five types of multicultural approaches and five types of definitions of multiculturalism. Joe L. Kincheloe and Shirley R. Steinberg define each type of multiculturalism as follow:

> "Conservative multiculturalism/monoculturalism: involves the efforts to assimilate everyone who is capable of assimilation to a white, middle class standard, many people have seen this as assimilationism which destroy the cultures of ethnic groups and render them politically powerless, a kind of 'melting pot'. Liberal multiculturalism believes that individuals from diverse race, class and gender group share a natural equality and a common humanity. Pluralist Multiculturalism focuses on difference as opposed to liberalism's focus on sameness. Left-essentialist multiculturalism fails to appreciate the historical situatedness of cultural differences. Critical multiculturalism emerges from the Frankfurt School of Social Research in Germany in the 1020s. Critical theorists want to promote an individual's consciousness of himself or herself as a social being. An individual who has gained such a consciousness understands how and why his or her political opinions, socio-economics, class, role, religious beliefs, gender and racial self-image are shaped by dominant perspectives".[139]

Lise Togeby argues that the idea of multiculturalism is frequently employed as an entire opposite to assimilation and she defines the concept as:

> "Multiculturalism springs from a notion implying that the autonomy of the individual is ... tied to its culturally defined social identity. Thus, a mutual recognition between individuals involves the mutual recognition of the involved cultures. Representatives of a given culture have a collective right to demand that the political community pursues an active policy that secures their cultural prosperity".[140]

Sarah Spencer argues that "Immigration is seen as contributing to the vitality of a multicultural nation while in Europe resistance to multiculturalism remains strong".[141]
Carla Baran, a psychologist from Istanbul who works for the official Bavarian welfare service for Turks, in Munich; her argument contrasts with this view:

> "Some families are growing more liberal, others more traditional. Some youths run away from home, because they can't stand their parents' strictness. These tensions are worse here than back in Turkey, because of the German influence and the fears of Germanising. It is tough situation: but I think integrating is bound to come within another generation or so. The fanatics will lose in the end" she said. [142]

Definition of the term assimilation is regarded as a 'process of social development'; the immigrants adapt themselves to the native society members until the characteristic of the immigrant group has virtually disappeared. The term of assimilation also contradicts with the concept of ethnicity. Since the ethnic group loses its 'ethnic characteristics such as physical, religious and linguistic distinctiveness.[143]

---

[139] Ibid. p. 3-26

[140] Lise Togeby, *From Guest Workers to Ethnic Minorities* [in Danish] (Aarhus: Aarhus University Press, 2003), p. 1

[141] Spencer, Sarah (Ed.): Strangers and Citizens, A positive approach to migrants and refugees, Rivers Oram Press, London, 1994, (p. 11)

[142] Ardagh, John: Germany and Germans, *The United Germany in the Mid-1990s,* Third Ed., Chapter 5 'Turkish Guest Workers' and Other Immigrants: A painful path towards acceptance, Penguin Books, England, 1995, (p. 273-297).

[143] Lermer, Arthur: The Evolution of Canadian Policy towards cultural pluralism. Information and Comment Papers .No. l6 Canadian Jews Congress, 1955, (p. 1)

The 'assimilation' approach is supported by European right-wing political parties and by their supporters. For example, Le Pen's extreme right Front national, placed second in the first round of the French presidential election in 2002.[144]

The question of the integration process of immigrants and governments does not only interest immigrants themselves but also the host society's members. Therefore, such areas of research need to be investigated and evaluated from both sides' perspectives. The key factor for the successful integration of immigrants is that the immigrants accept the host country as their new home, and that the immigrants are to be accepted by host members as members of their society.

Simultaneously, the host society members' concerns that immigrants take jobs away from natives. A survey from the 12 OECD countries in the 2000 suggests that 30.2% of natives in the European immigration countries think that immigrants take jobs away from natives. [145] On the other hand, the Turkish immigrants concerns, such as feeling insecure and not being recognized fully by German authorities as an ethnic minority. They are distinct from Germans in the aspects of culture and traditions, these points should be put into consideration by the German authorities as well as politicians during their integration process. Integration processes need to look at these points and this thesis will focus on the experience of Turkish immigrants in Germany.

Studies in this context, integration means that immigrants adapt to German standards and are accepted into German society, while retaining their own culture and citizenship; but assimilation means a much fuller process of Germanisation which very few Turks wish for. But, the German-born younger generation Turkish youths are not aware of integration which is possible without assimilation. However, German assimilation/integration policy has not become successful socio-culturally and politically, but economically has been relatively successful.[146]

Britain has multi-cultural integration policy, in which minority groups are encouraged to celebrate their distinctiveness, so long as they accept that others can do the same. For British integration policy is better than French and German policy.

Lord Bhikhu Parekh defines the multicultural approach as

> "Multiculturalism thus became part of the nation's received wisdom at the end of the 20th century and the approach had some value. It has done much to teach us about each other's cultures and to have respect for individual differences...Multiculturalism have sometimes been taken to mean that every culture is morally self-contained and cannot be judged and criticized from outside, and that is it self-authenticating and must be respected".[147]

Zig Layton-Henry argues that Britain was already a multicultural society in the 1980s. He also describes the perception of immigrants by people of the host country from a Marxist view as:

---

[144] Geddes, Andrew: The Politics of Migration and immigration in Europe, Sage Publication, London, 2003, (p. 78).

[145] IZA Discussion Paper No.187, August 2000 (12 OECD countries); by Thomas K. Bauer, Magnus Loftstom and Klaus F. Zimmermann, 'Immigration Policy, assimilation of Immigrants and Natives' Sentiments towards Immigrants': Evidences from 12 OECD countries, (p. 21)

[146] Spencer, Sarah (Ed.): Immigration as an Economic Asset, Trentham Books, 1994; in Ch.1 Ursula Mehrländer: The Development of Post War Migration and Refugee Policy, (p. 10-11).

[147] Parekh, Bhikhu: Runnymede Perspectives, Conservatism and Community Cohesion Published by Runnymede in January 2010, (p. 11-14)

"Marx was clearly aware, are often perceived as foreign intruders, illegitimate competitors, for scarce resources such as jobs, accommodation, health, and welfare benefits". [148]

Adrian Favell defines a multicultural society as "Multiculturalism is dependent on being bounded and culturally shared as a specifically national political unity, beyond the multicultural and 'multinational' differences of minority groups and cultures."[149]

Jim Jordan defines it as "The idea of multiculturalism is a product of liberal democracies which ring fence the rights of the individuals within a self-declared secular society". [150]
Integration is a suitable approach when it is desired by both the host society and immigrant society members; as long as Turkish immigrants are willing to be integrated and at the same time maintain their ethnic identities to some degree, and the German society members are willing to accept the Turks as a part of Germany and as new members of the German society. However, integration does not mean immigrants will give up their own culture, language, religion, traditions and rituals in favour of the hosts'. If they abandoned their socio-cultural, political and economical values they would be adopted into the host society totally then the term 'integration' loses its meaning and turns into assimilation. The Turks and the Germans have perceived 'integration' differently. The Germans interpret or perceive 'integration' as assimilation but wish that the Turks integrate into Germany. Patricia Ehrkamp argues that German assimilation policy make Turks feel being unwanted and excluded by German society.[151] The Turks also perceive 'integration' as assimilation and resist against their integration because of their misperception and Turkish politicians' misguiding or misinterpretation of integration and multiculturalism by both the Turkish PM Erdogan and German Chancellor Angela Merkel. So they have different expectations from each other.

The definition of an 'ethnic group' is similar to a minority or immigrant group in the aspects of physical, cultural and religious differences from the majority host society. Simultaneously, the immigrant group feels itself distinct from the majority and the majority society feels that the ethnic minority group is different from themselves.
In Europe there has also been a discourse concerning the notion of "Ethnic Pluralism", is almost the same as interaction between native society members and immigrant community members but under the name of 'interactionism' which means sufficient interaction between two communities by influencing one another.

Another term is isolation or segregation due to lack of integration immigrant group members isolates themselves from the majority members as seen in the French and German case rather than interacting with the host's members.

Don Henrich Tolzmann points out to the importance of German-Americans' multicultural experience in American life since seventeenth century. Former American president John F. Kennedy called America as, "a nation of immigrants". German minorities in America have called themselves 'German-Americans' since their emigration in 1607. The German emigrates constitute USA's largest ethnic group, over 60 million, represent one-fourth of American population, according to 1990 census. The 1990 census also showed that the great majority of

---

[148] Layton-Henry, Zig: The Politics of Immigration, Blackwell, 1992, (p. 5, 14)
[149] Favell, Adrian: Theory and Society, 27: 209-236), Kluwer Academic Publisher, 1998, (p. 215)
[150] Jim Jordan: Migrants in German speaking countries, 2004, published by CILT (p. 100).
[151] Ehrkamp, Patricia, "We Turks are no Germans": assimilation discourses and the dialectical construction of identities in Germany, *Environment and Planning, A* 2006, volume 38, pages 1673-1692

those living in America who was born abroad are citizens of the US now. For instance, Albert Einstein (1879-1955), physicist, recipient of the 1921 Nobel Prize in physics, [152] and founder of the European integration concept as an 'Integration Theory' was Ernst Haas, a German migrant. Henry Kissinger was also technically a German immigrant has become a prominent political figure in US politics.

Obviously, the German-Americans have enriched and contributed to socio-cultural, economic, political and scientific life of America as well as American school system. For example, the state-sponsored universities in the US are based on German model. Celebration of Christmas and the New Year in the US is also a German-Americans' contribution to American culture and tradition which is mainly shaped by German-Americans.[153] The Turks in Germany should have become Turco-Germans as the German emigrants integrated successfully and contributed to American life. The Turks should be integrated into German society in the same way as the Germans succeeded in America. There is no reason for concern why the Turkish immigrants and Turkish politicians to be worried about losing their cultural identity as a result of integration into German society. As the German-Americans have maintained their ethnic characteristic in a distant country like America since 1607, the Turks can also maintain their ethnic trails in Germany which is not far from Turkish mainland, just at the heart of Europe.

As a result, multicultural integration experiences from classical immigration countries suggested that USA, Australia and Canada have been created by immigrants' contributions. Multiculturalism is a good approach if immigrants adapt to majority's socio-cultural values while maintaining their ethnic characteristics. However, it also has some risky aspects, if immigrants' culture and language is dominant, the native or majority culture and language becomes he minority in their own country. The aborigines in Australia and the red-Indians in America became minorities in their own countries.

2.1.2 Germany's integration and citizenship policy from historical perspective

Concept of citizenship is a status and a set of rights that immigration countries include or exclude their immigrants in these rights in accordance with national and the EU's integration policy measures. Roy Gardner defines 'citizenship' as a legal relationship with 'State', or 'nation-state'. Citizenship is not just legal, but also political, economic, and social relationship.[154]

The first German Foreigners Law was passed in 1965; it especially focused on guest workers. In paragraph 2 it stipulates that 'a work permit can be granted if the presence of the foreigners does not damage the interests of the Federal Republic'. Article 73 of the German Constitution gives the government the right to legislate for emigration and immigration, but had nothing to do with integration issues of immigrants with permanent residents in Germany. Politicians were only interested in the issue of whether Germany was an immigration country. Principally, Germany was not a country of immigration and needed no integration policy.

---

[152] Tolzmann, Don Heinrich: The German American Experience, Humanity Books, New York, 2000, p. 225
[153] Ibid., p. 18-19

[154] Gardner, J.P., What Lawyers Mean by Citizenship', Encouraging Citizenship: Report of the Commission on Citizenship, London: HMSO, 1990, p.63-68

Moreover, there has been an attempt to strengthen the recruitment ban in 1974 by not allowing newly arrived wives and families to work. This was abolished in 1979, at a time when the German government tried a different approach.

On 1 December 1978, an Ombudsman for the Advancement of the integration of Foreign Workers and their families was created. Minister President of North-Rhine-Westphalia of SPD-Social Democratic Party, Kühn was the first German politician outlined a report on Germany's status as immigration country. In his report of 1979, Kühn identified 'Germany as a country of immigration' and argued for the necessity of integration measures, rights to naturalisation for second generation foreigners and granting voting rights for long-term residents in local elections.

Immigrants in Denmark, Sweden and the Netherlands have already had voting rights in local elections since 1982, if they had three years residence in those countries. However, Kühn's Report was published at a time of unemployment and anti-foreigner public opinion was rising. The issue of granting voting rights to non-German immigrants had been exploited by the CDU's Chancellor Candidate in the 1980 federal election campaign, for being too 'generous' to foreigners and Kühn's party lost votes in the 1980 election and in subsequent elections. Just one of Kühn's recommendations was adopted. A bill introduced on 2 December 1981 by the re-elected SPD-Free Democrat Party (FDP) coalition granted second generation foreigners the right to naturalisation. It was opposed by the SDU/Christian Social Union (CSU)-controlled Bundesamt and Kühn's attempts to change the law in favour of immigrants became unsuccessful in 1982. The SPD-led government introduced more restrictive measures to reduce the number of immigrants that entered Germany under the 'family reunion' regulations. The same restrictive immigration policy was followed by the new CDU/FDP coalition government rather than emphasising on integration and granting more rights to immigrants. Kühn was replaced by moderate Liselotte Funke (FDP).This was a sign for another change in official policy and an end of Kühn's short-lived integration policy. The new approach was an exclusion of newcomers and repatriation of those long-term residents return to their country of origin by the payment of inducements rather than integrating those immigrants who had definitely settled in Germany. In 1982 the SDP Federal government continued with the same classical 'non-immigration country' policy and that it should not become one. The SDP lost the 1983 election to the CDU, the CDU adopted more restrictive adopted measures for the immigration issues and on 28 November 1983 the government offered financial inducement to promote the foreign workers to return home country. However, only a few immigrants accepted the offer of DM 10.000. This was because the financial inducement was too low, and because of economic and political instability such as military regime in Turkey; these factors made repatriation impossible. This was also unacceptable due to lack of a large amount of German public support. The German political elites and a large part of German public opinion perceived the government's repatriation policy unacceptable by expressing the moral obligation which Germany owed to its guest workers and their families. However, it is interesting that there was no federal legislation to solve the immigration and integration issues and the 1965 Foreigners Law was just replaced with the 1990. In the meantime the problem was left to the Foreigner Offices of the *Länder* (Federal states) to implement administrative regulations as to residence entitlement family reunion etc. Immigration policy of federal states varied widely, with Baden-Württemberg in the south the most restrictive and Bremen in the north the most liberal.

A new bill of the Foreigners Law was proposed by Minister of Interior Zimmermann (CSU) in 1988. It included anti-immigrants ideology and was replaced by the more moderate Schäuble (DCU) in 1989.

Towards the end of the 1980s, 60 per cent of the foreigners in the FRG had been born in the FRG and official thinking favoured the process of gradual adaptation. A new Foreigners Law of 1990 came into force on 1 January 1991. There was no reference to the previous law that 'Germany is not an immigration country', nor was repatriation of the foreigners to return to their home country. In other words, the term country of immigration and integration of immigrants had been virtually accepted.

Christian Joppke suggests that 'these measures indicate the independent workings of moral obligations, not just of legal constraints'. However, the policy still maintained the fundamental distinction between Germans and foreigners, and continued to refer to "the recruitment of guest workers as a unique event in the past which must not be repeated."[155]

From 1974 onwards official policy moved from a 'refugee welcoming' approach to 'control' of the numbers coming in. Thus, visa requirements were introduced for those countries which produced the most refugees, such as Palestine (1974), Afghanistan, Ethiopia, Sri Lanka, and Turkey (in 1980 because of Military Coup in Turkey).

Germany's official immigration policy was based on 'Germany not being an immigration country (kein Einwanderungsland) until Ethnic German inflow in the 1990s. A non-immigration country meant also that Germany had no integration policy until the official declaration of itself as an immigration country.[156] Geddes argues that if Germany was not an immigration country, why it opened its borders to Ethnic Germans from the Eastern bloc countries such as Kazakhstan and Belarus in 1990s. [157] The Ethnic Germans demonstrated their intention of why they immigrated to West Germany with the following phrase: *"Kommt die Deutschmark, bleiben wir; kommt sie nicht, geh'en zu ihr* (If the DM comes we stay, if not, then we leave for it)" (Geddes, 2003:84). [158]

Germany's former citizenship law was historically based on 'blood-tie' and ethnic nation state, which was first introduced in 1913. Collapse of the former Soviet Union and the inflow of the ethnic Germans had played an effective role on the new German law in accordance with the EU integration law. The new citizenship law includes all immigrants including the Turks as long as their applications meet the naturalization criteria. The new German citizenship law gives priority to ethnic Germans and they are considered native Germans even if their descendants spent their entire life out of Germany.[159]

Since reunification German integration policy has changed positively and is becoming a more inclusive and more rights- based policy. German politicians redefined the national political community's boundaries, in response to the immigration of ethnically, culturally and religiously different people. There are two important changes in German immigration policy in this period. The first is that Germany has introduced greater restrictions on immigrants' access to German territory such as border control like all other EU member states. The second change is that simultaneously Germany has introduced a more inclusive policy for immigrants with permanent

---

[155] Christian, Joppke: Immigration and the Nation-state, the United states, Germany, and, the Great Britain, 1999, (p. 84)

[156] Geddes, Andrew: The Politics of Migration and Immigration in Europe, Sage Publication, London, 2003, (p. 99).

[157] Ibid., p. 80.

[158] Ibid., p. 84.

[159] Ibid., p. 84

residence permission. The new policy gave immigrants access to legal rights such as citizenship rights if they are legal residents and have fulfilled the requirements for naturalisation. Before reunification, access to political rights and citizenship was only available to ethnic Germans, where as the new German immigration policy includes non-German origin immigrants such as the Turks. These policy changes affected the number of naturalised Turkish immigrants regarded distinct in the aspect of ethnically, religiously from the majority culture.

By introducing the new German immigration policy a more inclusive and rights-based policy simultaneously affected the integration of Turkish immigrants intensively. This can be explained due to the structural and conceptual changes after Reunification in 1990 in German self-understandings of cultural and political community.

As known, Germans have historically had difficulties accepting other cultures and religions, such as its Turkish immigrants with their Islamic religion and their cultural backgrounds. However, immigrants are regarded as an integral part of the German society.[160]

The Turks have had many statues and titles over forty years. Changing attitude of German public is visible in the terms and statuses they used for Turkish immigrants changed since their migration from 1961 as *(Gastarbeiter)* guest workers to *(Mitbürger)* fellow citizens as permanent residents. They have also called Turkish immigrants as *(Ausländische Arbeitkräfte)*, the foreign work force. With the Turkish family unification in the 1980s these two terms turned into a single term *(Ausländer)* foreigners. When the Turks decided to stay in Germany permanently a new concept emerged *(Inländer ausländischer Herkunft)* which means foreign origin natives or *(Indländer mit nichtdeutschen Pass)* which means foreign origin natives without a German Passport is called natives but not Germans *(Nicht deutsche)*. Non-Germans or *(Zuwanderer)* immigrants have been added to these changing terms, and are being used by the German public daily. Another example is the widely used concept of *(Mitbürger)*: common or fellow citizens with political participation. The voting rights of immigrants emerged as an expression of political rights, which is almost equal with the word citizens who have full rights for political participation. Although practising the rights of political participation does not reflect fully the participation of Turkish immigrants, a positive step has been taken by the German public to accept Turks as members of German society. Besides these positive steps, an increasing number of naturalised Turks in the German public caused a debate about dual-citizenship and added more concepts to migrant literature like *(Deutsche türkischer Herkunft)* Turkish descent Germans and *(eingebürgerte Türken)* newly naturalised Turks. All these changes in German public opinion mean that Germans are tending to accept the Turks as a part of German society.

In the late 1990s, the German public began to accept the reality and Germans eventually realized that the 'guest worker' program was not temporary after all and that the Turks will remain in Germany permanently. German politicians formulated an 'immigration policy' in the 1990s, which meant that immigrants should be integrated into German society through a process of integration or assimilation. Although the German politicians continued to accuse the Turks from time to time of not being keen on integration into the German lifestyle, the public opinion

---

[160] An Article by Zeynep, Gürcanli on German ambassador's report in Ankara, 18th February 2008, Hürriyet Newspaper, [Author's Translation]

polls,[161] and Euro barometers,[162] indicated that there was a positive change of attitude by the Germans.[163]

Experiences from Sweden and the Netherlands show that multicultural integration allows the preservation of home culture and language to some degree, which also means that immigrants still have a chance to return if they wish in the future. Of course, their choice depends on which country has the higher standard of living – Germany or Turkey.[164]

The perception of integration as an approach meant that the Germans and the Turks both have had different expectations from each other. The German perception of the integration of the Turks has meant that Turks will give up their cultural identity entirely in favour of German assimilation. The Turks would become German in their communicative skills, their appearance, their dress, their behaviour, manner and attitudes completely. The Turks' perception of integration was to be regarded as ethnic minorities, different in nationality, background and culture but recognised as legitimate groupings in German society. Especially the third generation Turks believe that the Turkish culture has enriched German culture.[165] Now Germans have accepted the necessity of the integration of Turkish immigrants they should also accept that immigrants have other beliefs and traditions.

On the one hand, the opinion of the German public concerns the fact that Germany is housing 'too many immigrants', and they fear that granting full rights to the long-term foreign residents could damage German social cohesion, cultural heritage and national homogeneity if Germany accepts multicultural integration policy.[166] Therefore, the Germans prefer that immigrants should remain as foreigners and outsiders in Germany rather than integrating and granting them more rights.

---

[161] A Euro barometer survey in1992 indicates that young Germans are more likely to accept the immigrants than older Germans and put an end of exclusion from their rights. 30 percent of young Germans under twenty-five agreed with the statement: I don't like many foreigners in my country, while 51 percent suggest that immigrants should be integrated, 19 percent want all foreigners to leave the country. Among older Germans, forty percent express that they do no t like many foreigners in the country. Thirty one percent of older Germans think foreigners should be assimilated into German society. Twenty nine percent of older people have moderate attitudes to foreigners.

[162] Attitudes toward the presence of people of other nations, 1988-1997).Question: Do you personally find the presence of people of another nationality disturbing in your daily life? Source (n-size): Euro-barometer 30(11,791); 37 (14.82); 39 (15.136); 48 (16.186).

[163] There are also remarkable attitude changes in German individuals toward immigrants. It is interesting that naturalized Turkish immigrant youths represented Germany in the 2005 European song contest in Turkish-German language as bilingual. A third generation Turkish-girl, German citizen represented Germany at World Beauty Contest in 2005.

[164] Geddes, Andrew: The Politics of Migration and Immigration in Europe, Sage Publication, London, 3003, (p. 102-123).

[165] 25 October, 2006-Berlin, German Foreign Minister, Frank Walter Steinmeier, made a speech at the 100th year anniversary of Association of Foreign Journalists, from 60 countries 400 journalists including Turkish Newspaper Hurriyet, joined the celebration. The Minister Stated "Labour immigration caused a lot of social and cultural changes in Germany for the past 40 years; especially Turkish immigrants' impact is great. As a result immigration, *Turkish **Döner Kebab*** became German speciality beside the *Sucuk* 'Sausage" [Author's translation 1, April 2008].

[166] Ibid., p. 102

Bar chart 7a: 'IMMIGRANTS' FROM EUROPEANS' POINT OF VIEW

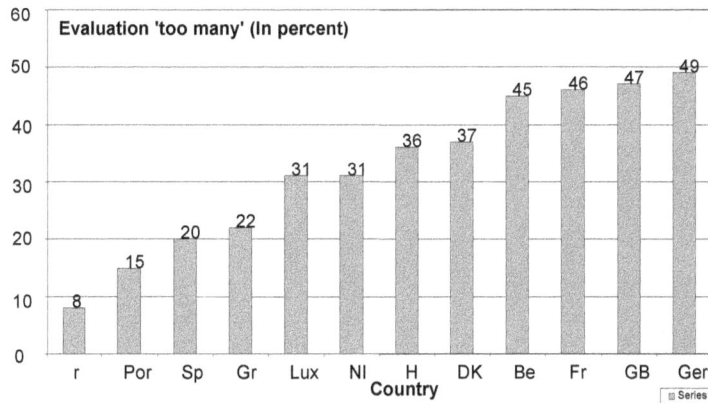

Figure 1: Evaluating the 'others'

Source: Eurobarometer No. 30 (1988)

Above Table shows there has been dissociation from 'others' which was made by respondents who answered that there were 'too many' people of other nationalities in their country in 1988. The percentage of respondents is giving this answer in each of the 12 EU countries. There are wide differences between countries. The range is from 8 percent in Ireland to 49 in Germany.

Below Table 7b shows that Asians, Arabs, and Turks are most negatively evaluated nationalities from another group of nationalities. The lowest values are attained by countries that perceive 'others' to be primarily Western European nationalities. Southern European countries are Ireland, Portugal, Spain and Greece. The suggestion is that primarily foreigners from outside Europe are negatively evaluated.

Table 7b: Ranking of the evaluation of 'others' in the 12 EC countries,[167]

NO.		
1.	Asians	(49%)[168]
2.	Arabs	(48%)
3.	Turks	(47%)
4.	Eastern Europeans	(42%)
5.	Latin American	(41%)
6.	Africans	(36%)
7.	Southern Europeans	(36%)
8.	North Americans	(25%)
9.	Northern and Central Europeans	(24%)

Source: Eurobarometer No. 30 (1988)

A survey by the Allensbach polling institute from 2009 suggested that more than 50 percent of Germans still believe Germany has 'too many' immigrants.[169] However, compared to

---

[167] Weighted by national population.

[168] Number in brackets is percentage of respondents who name the given group as belonging to another nationality and who also believe 'there are too many people of other nationalities living in their country'.

1988 Eurobarometer in the following table a positive attitude change is visible. 47% German perception of immigrants in 1988 fell to 22% in 1991.

Table 8: Attitudes to foreigners in the late 1991 (percentages)

Population from 16 years	West Germany	East Germany
Hostile to foreigners	22	8
Rather hostile	23	16
Rather friendly	43	57
Friendly towards foreigners	8	19
No opinion	2	

Source: POLIS-München/Köln: SINUS-Heidelberg, 1991

On the other hand, Germany has an ageing population and needs young immigrants because of its negative demographic change. [170] The second concern is its demographic decline: It has been estimated that only continued in-migration will stabilize Germany's demographic development and prevent the disproportionate ageing of its population without migration (Dinkel and Lebock, 1994: 36).

According to the below Age-dependency Table and its estimated calculation without migration or lack of its current immigrants' integration Germany's population could decrease between years from 1990 to 2030 from 81.8 million to 50.7 million.

Table 9: Age-dependency ratio for immigrants in Germany, 1990-2030

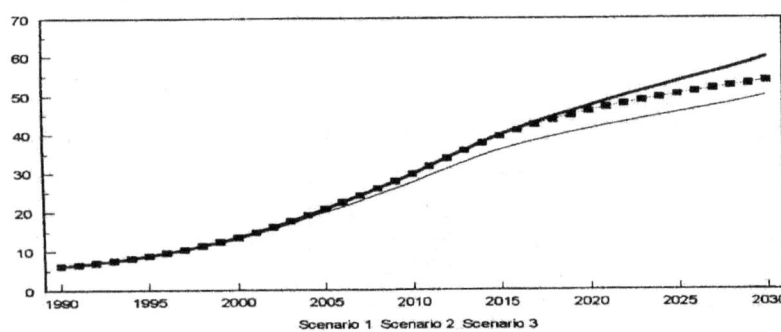

Source: Camphausen, Statistisches Bundesamt, 1990

Table 10 below indicates that the Turks are a young population group, 35.7 being younger than 18 years old. About half of the Turkish population is between 25 and 45 years old and only 5 % is older than 60.

---

[169] http://Spiegel.de/international/Germany/0,1518,561969,00.html, Access on 22 June 2009 (p. 4)
[170] Germany's currently 82 million populations will decrease to 50 million by year 2030 if they do not accept an effective integration policy.

Table 10: Age structure of Turkish population in Germany, 1990

0 - 17 years	597.619	35.7 %
18 – 20 years	127.766	7.6 %
21 – 29 years	332.779	19.9 %
30 – 39 years	192.503	11.5 %
40 - 49 years	249.202	14.9 %
50 – 54 years	100.419	6.0 %
55 – 59 years	49.846	3.0 %
60 – 64 years	17.960	1.1 %
65 and above	7.817	0.5 %

Source: TAM (Türkiye Araştirmalari Merkezi) Turkish Research Center (*Zentrum fur Turkeistudien*), Zur Lebenssituation und spezifischen Problemlage alterer auslandischer Einwohner in der BDR, Kurzfassung, Essen, October 1992.

Table 2.2.1: The age structure of the Turkish population in Germany (2008)

Age ranges	Mainstream German population (%)	Turkish-German population (%)
60 years Plus	25	5
30-39	50	50
Under 30 years	25	45

Source: International Journal of Retail and Distribution Management Vol.36 No.3, 2008 (p.212-223)

Demographic aspects of the Turkish population in Germany, as shown in Table 2.2.1, the age structure of the Turkish population in Germany considerably differs from that of the mainstream German population. The table illustrates the important point that 45 per cent of the Turkish population is younger than 30 (the proportion of the first generation Turks in Germany is about one-fourth) in contrast to the mainstream German population (25 per cent under 30) (Aygün, 2005; Uğurdemir-Brincks, 2002) support the importance of the comparatively young age profile and over 50 per cent of the Turkish population in Germany are between 15- and 55- years old.

One of the most integrative factors for immigrants is participating in sportive, [171] cultural, [172] and political activities in the host country. In this way, interaction creates a common interest and association with the host's youths. This is one of the key factors, which develops a successful integration. [173]

Although integration as an approach has been perceived differently by two community members, a compromising balance of integration is accepted by both sides as very important.

Since a high level of integration means assimilation of immigrants this may create a people without ethnic origin or unaware of their ethnic origins. Not at all integration means

---

[171] The Times, 20 June, 2006, Germany hosts "World Cup". One of the striking aspects of Germany's football – inspired patriotism has been a great number of Turkish immigrants openly supporting the German national team. Turks talk about the German-players as "Our Boys" .During the games, German fans chanted:"Stand up if you are German", thousands did so.
[172] 22 June 2006, Turkish Kebabs became World Cup funs' favourite food in Germany.
[173] Article by Kate Connolly, Guardian, 15 November 2010, Immigration; the rare success story of Mesut Özil

isolation and the formation of ghettos in the suburbs of big German cities as in France (See chapter three, survey questionnaire table, p. 23).

The causes of their migration interact with the factors that shape integration and the factors which are facilitating or hindering the process of integration of Turkish immigrants have been analysed and evaluated statistically in chapters four and five.

2.1.3 Impact of Religious Affiliation on integration of immigrants in Europe

Increase of religiously different communities in West European countries created a new dimension in the area of integration factors of long-term immigrants into their host societies.

Some multicultural theorists such as Bhikhu Parekh argue that radical Islam is a hindrance for Muslim immigrants' integration into West European societies. He claims that Islam needs a reform as Atatürk did in 1923 in Turkey.[174]

Andrew Geddes argues that a moderate attitude to religion makes religiously different immigrants' integration into their host countries easier. In spite of the fact that the Turks are Muslims, the Republic of Turkey constitutionally is a secular state; religious life of Turkish immigrants in Germany had been left to the initiative of private organisations in recent years. Growing numbers of religiously different Turkish communities in Germany needed religious leaders and praying places to practise their Islamic rituals; in response to their demands the Turkish Islamic Union was established as a German branch by Türkiye Diyanet İşleri Başkanliği (Turkish Directorate of Religious Affairs) in 1982. Turks in Germany are practising Islam as it is being practised in Turkey as a secular state.[175] With regards to Turkish immigrants' religious identity, in contrast to France, German Turkish Organizations such as the Turkish Directorate for Religious Affairs and Milli Görüş (the National View) encouraged Turks to become German citizens. In France, loyalty to Islam has been construed as reactionary or as evidence of an unwillingness to integrate.[176]

In some cases the West German educational authorities provide Muslim religious instructions to Guest worker children. German Journalist Günter Wallraff, author of "Ganz Unten" 'Lowest of the low' („Es sind religiöse Gründe." – „Darf ich fragen, welcher Religionsgemeinschaft Sie angehören?"- „Islam"),[177] suggests that a dialogue between religions will help with understanding the distinctiveness between immigrants and natives rather than mutual misunderstanding each other. "Islam should be interpreted again according contemporary European social systems. Muslims do not live Prophet Muhammad's time anymore. If Muhammad lived today, some reforms to Islam would surely be made."[178]

---

[174] Modood, Tariq; Anna Triandafyllidou and Ricard Zapata-Barrero (Eds.): Multiculturalism, Muslims and Citizenship, Routhledge, 2006; in chapter 10 by Parekh, Bhikhu: Europe, liberalism and the 'Muslim question' (p. 180-203).

[175] Geddes, Andrew: The Politics of Migration and Immigration in Europe, Sage Publication, London, 2003, (p. 92).

[176] Ibid.

[177] Wallraff, Günter: 'Lowest of the Low' (Ganz Unten or "Ich Ali"), Verlag Kiepenheuser, Köln, 1985, (p. 127).

[178] An Article by Tuncay Yildirim, Günter Wallraff says, 'If Turks leave Germany, German economy, social and retirement system collapse' Hürriyet, November 11 2006 (p. 6-7)

Hakan Karakuş argues that "Atatürk's social and political ideology which adapted Western European norms to Turkish society is still the best choice for developing politics, education and civic institutions to the level of Western societies and Western European democratic nation states. He also argues that Atatürk's ideological teaching is the best way to help Turkey exploit its strategic location as a bridge between Europe and Asia. In Atatürk's ideology religion, Islam is a private matter".[179]

Although Turkey has been a secular state since 1923, there is a growing tendency towards Islamic religiosity in recent years; the current ruling party is placing more emphasis on religious values. Even German Politician Cem Özdemir, who is Germany's first national party leader of Turkish descent, argues that there is a risk that Turkey could slide into Islamism.[180]

Faruk Şen argues that Turkey is a Muslim country but a secular state and it is not being ruled constitutionally by Islamic Law (Sheriat) like Saudi-Arabia, Iran or Pakistan. Some Turkish parents want religious lessons for their children in German schools. Socio-cultural integration is dependent on German language knowledge and education of immigrants. Therefore German teaching should be taught from the age of 4 in the kindergartens in a natural way. A solid identity will, thus, help to integrate immigrants into the host country. Therefore religious lessons should not only be about Christianity but also cover other religions such as Islam.[181]

Islamic religion's effect on the integration of Turkish immigrants as well as other Muslim groups in major European immigration countries (such as Germany, France and the UK), needs to be investigated from the perspective of religious identity. It is hypothesized that one of the cultural barriers of integration of Muslim immigrants in the EU is the effect of Islamic religion and the lack of its reformation.[182] There are 15 million Muslim immigrants in 25 EU member states (now 27, including Romania and Bulgaria from first January 2007). Of the 4 million living in Germany, 2.7 million of them are Turkish-origin; another 500 of them are from Bosnia and Albania (from former Yugoslavia). The total Muslim population in Germany is 4 million, which consists of 3.9 percent of 82 million. Islam is, thus, the second religion in Germany. In Britain, it is the Hind-Pakistani Muslims. In France, and Holland, the Magrip Muslims from North Africa. Most of the Muslims live in France, 8.1 million in total.[183]

Emine Demirbüken-Wegner, a German of Turkish origin, MP for Berlin State parliament and member of the CDU's National Executive Board since 2004, argues that

> "Religious lessons should be introduced in the German schools. If, immigrants are regarded as an integral part of the German society, religious tolerance is important. Immigrant children should learn their religions and cultural roots. These values will help immigrant youths to form an interfaced, cultural identity". [184]

---

[179] Hakan Karakus: Turkey and the EU, Kemalism's Effects on the Road to the EU, MA Thesis, Naval Postgraduate School, September, 2005 (p. 3-7)

[180] By Michael Giglio, Der Spiegel's article, A Turk at the Top 10/15/2008

[181] Şen, Faruk: Turkish culture and Islam : In Sarah Spencer (ed.): Immigration as an economic asset, The German Experience, IPPR/Trentham Books, London, 1994 (p. 102)

[182] Ibid., p.102

[183] Source: Eurostat , 2006

[184] Article by Janet Schayan: Diversity in focus: living together in Germany , 19 November 2010
http;//www.germantyandafrica.diplo.de/Vertretung/proteria_dz/en/startseite.htlm

Growing anti-immigrant political parties in Europe has seen a threat to immigrants' integration. Since immigrants feel insecure in their host society. In Germany far right NPD (The National Democratic Party of Germany), in France Jean-Marie Le pen's National Front, [185] in Austria FPÖ (Freedom Party), in the Netherlands *Geert Wilders'* PVV (Party for Freedom) became the third biggest political party in Dutch parliament. [186]

The Turks are particularly family-orientated and have tended to come from rural Anatolia; it is inevitable, then, that they have naturally encountered a cultural identity crisis with their Islamic religion in a Christian country but secular and democratic German society. It is interesting that some of the Turks from rural areas in Germany are more religious than their fellow country-men in Turkey. [187]

British and Dutch multicultural societies are more tolerant than German and French societies. A characteristic of immigrants in multicultural societies such as Britain, Holland, Sweden, Denmark and Switzerland are more secular (in this context, secular means moderate attitude to religion) than in France and Germany. However, the Turks in Germany and Austria are more religious and less secular. On the other hand, the Turks in Britain, Holland, Sweden, Denmark and Switzerland are more secular and less religious. [188]

As for the impact of the religious affiliation of immigrants on their integration process, the second and third generation are going through a process of secularization and are distancing themselves from the religious beliefs of their parents. This situation can be explained by their education levels, birth place and host countries integration policy. It is suggested that as immigrants' education level increase their secular and moderate view increase. Contrary to this view, immigrants that have a poor educational background are more religious but less secular. [189] The religious communities in Germany are comprised of Catholics 31.5 %, Protestants 31.1%, Muslims 3.9 % and Jews 0.1 %. The role of the Islamic religion in German society has gained increased importance for Muslim immigrants' as a result of the integration process. There are 4 million Muslims living in Germany, majority of them are Turkish. There are 2, 00 mosques in several German cities. [190] The Basic Law guarantees a variety of religious instruction in several federal states. Since 2006 the German Conference on Islam has created a basis for planned dialog between the German state, Muslim associations, and Muslims who do not belong to any Islamic organization.

The effect of religion can be seen in many different aspects of Turkish immigrants' integration. For example, second and third generation Turkish origin, German-born youths raised and educated in the German education system have arguably a more moderate attitude towards religion. They are more likely to be integrated into the host society and to have found the integration process easier when compared with earlier generations. In a 2000 article, Eren Ünsal,

---

[185] BBC News, 22 April, 2002, when Jean-Marie Le pen succeeded in the French presidential election in 2002 as the third place with 17.02% of votes, the conservative daily Le Figaro's headline was "The earthquake".

[186] Der Spiegel interview with Geert Wilders: 'Merkel is afraid', "She is trying to copy our party's ideology", "My fight is not with Muslims but Islam", He said. 11/09/2010

[187] Şen, Faruk: Turkish culture and Islam : In Sarah Spencer (ed.): Immigration as an economic asset, The German Experience, IPPR/Trentham Books, London, 1994 (p. 102)

[188] Euro-barometer 30, 1988 (15,136)

[189] Facts about *Germany*: Churches and *religious communities*
www.tatsachen-ueber-deutschland.de/.../churches-and-religious-communities.html Accessed on 26 11 2010

[190] Ibid.

an educationalist and spokeswoman of Berlin's Turkish Association commented on barriers to early-years education of Turkish-origin children that parents are "reluctant to put their offspring in a non-Muslim environment in their impressionable early years"[191].

This question attempts to discover the influence of religious belief on the integration process and to investigate whether inflexible religious feelings or politicised religious influences are more likely to be a hindering factor of immigrants' integration into a diverse society.

A view of public opinion (in the EU member states in 1988) on immigrant rights, broken down by religion, is old but is the only available opinion poll on religious attitudes of member states in the EU. Of the five religious categories illustrated as follows: Protestants were the most likely to want to restrict the rights of non-EU immigrants, with nearly one-third (32 percent) expressing this preference. Approximately one-fifth of Catholics, Orthodox, or those with no religious affiliation preferred the restriction of rights for non-EU nationals (17 percent, 20 percent, and 19 percent respectively).The groups that were least likely to wish for such restrictions fell into 'other' category (primarily Jewish, Muslim, Buddhist, and Hindus).[192]

Although the Muslim population in Germany makes up only 3.9 % of the total population, the perception of Islam in Germany is negative. For example, a survey held in 2003 shows that up to 46 % of the respondents think 'Islam is a backward religion'. Another survey was conducted on 2004 shows that more than 60 % of Germans think that 'Islam is oppressing women'. In 2006, only 30 % of Germans have a 'favourable' opinion of Islam.[193]

Differently to France, Turkish Islamic leaders in Germany encourage Turkish immigrants to integrate into German society, gain German citizenship and self-identify as German Muslims.[194]

A survey related to religion suggests that Islam is the third largest religion in Germany, which was carried out by Yasemin Karakuşoğlu, on cultural and religious identity of Turkish immigrants in the German states North Rhine-Westphalia and Hesse in 1995. One third of children under age of six are of immigrant origin. In many German cities, immigrant-descended youths make up 40 per cent of the young German population. [195]

A recent debate on religious lessons was started by Emine Demirbüken-Wegner MP of the CDU from Berlin State council in 2007 on the issue of new religious lessons in German schools. She argues that "Religious lessons should be introduced in the German community. If, immigrants are regarded as an integral part of the German society, religious tolerance is crucial in this context. Immigrant children should learn their religious and cultural roots. These values will help immigrant youths to form an interfaced, cultural identity. A solid identity will, thus, help to integrate immigrants into the host society. Therefore religions lessons should not only be about Christianity but also other religions such as Islam and so on", she concluded.

---

[191] Karacs, I. (2000), Germany's Turkish children sink into the underclass, The Independent on Sunday, 12 November 2000. Accessed via the web 28-June-2009: http://www.independent.co.uk/news/world/europe/germanys-turkish-children-sink-into-the-underclass-622943.html

[192] Eurobarometer, 1988

[193] Die Bundesregierung this article is extracted from (www.euro-islam.info)

[194] Kastoryano, Riva (2003), Research Article: France, Germany and Islam: Negotiating Identities, Immigrants and Minorities, Volume 22, Numbers 2-3/ July 2003, pp.280-297

[195] Horrocks, David, and Eva Kolinsky (Eds.): *Turkish Culture in German Society Today.* Providence, R.I.: Berghahn Books, 1996; in Ch. 5 Yasemin Karakuşoğlu, The role of Islam in the cultural orientations of Turks, (p. 190).

A research by Heinz Streib and Adem Aygün on 'Religious socialization of Turkish immigrants in Germany' which focuses on modernisation and transformation of religion in the migrant situation affect their attitudes to religion and eventually their integration positively in diverse cultural and religious society. Recognising the complex ontological perspective of religious life among persons of Turkish origin, special attention was paid to "issues of multi-religious socialisation which will help to understand and plan religious education in public schools in Germany".[196]

As a result, the religious affiliation is a factor that influences the integration of Muslim immigrants' into West European secular and democratic societies. In the case of Turkish immigrants' integration into German society, although Islamic religion has a negative affecting factor on the Turks' integration into German society, other factors such as Turks' unemployment rates and education level are more affecting factors for their full integration than their religion (See also chapter 4, survey question 4)

2.1.4 Germany's immigration and Integration policy since August 2001

In Germany, until 2001, no immigrant could become a citizen if they were not of German origin, even if they met the conditions (such as being born in the country of parents also born there). British immigrants were able to integrate more successfully due to the British multicultural-integration policy which was more tolerant in contrast to Germany's denial for not being an immigration country until 2001. The proportion of immigrants in Great Britain is lower than that in Germany, and two thirds of them live in the same household as a member of the native population.[197] British immigrants' language skills are also higher than Germans' and since most of the British immigrants are originally from English speaking colonies as in the French case. However, French immigrants have different problems than the Turks in Germany.

In France, for example, governments granted citizenship to its immigrants, but demand that immigrants culturally be assimilated as a price for getting citizenship rights.

The third approach seems to be the approach used in the French case, Isolation (African origin minorities' rebel on October 27, 2005). Isolation and deprivation are the experience of the French immigrants compared with Dutch, Swedish and British policies. Integrating immigrant families from second and third generations was a failure due to poor housing conditions, inadequate school achievements, poorly developed transport facilities, social exclusion and a higher number of young unemployed ethnic minorities whom are unskilled. The unemployment rate is 10 percent, among youths, but is over 20 % among young immigrants it is twice as high. France is home to some 6 million Black Muslim minorities, one-third of the total Black Muslims residing in the European Union, and representing one-tenth of the country's population.[198]

---

[196] Heinz Streib and Adem Aygün: Religious Socialisation and Faith Development of Adolescents in Turkey and Germany: Results from Cross-Cultural Research. Collegial Paper for ISREV XVI (2008) – Ankara, Turkey

[197] Germany has been housing *20 percent* of foreign-born population including ethnic Germans. This is the largest proportion of foreign-born population in other European countries, comparing with France *9 percent*, Britain *7 percent*. However, they accepted themselves as '*immigration countries*' in the early 1990s.

[198] Eurostat: Thomson Data stream, 23 April 2005.

64

Felix Buchel and Joachim R.Frick categorized European welfare states according to their immigration/integration policy and divided the major immigrants receiving countries into four regime types: the first group was identified as "Liberal Welfare regimes", comprising Britain and Ireland; the second group as "Conservative welfare regimes" such as Germany and Austria; the third group was "Social Democratic welfare" states such Denmark and Sweden; finally, the fourth group was "residual welfare regimes" like Italy and Spain.[199] Therefore, Britain, Holland, Sweden and Denmark have a better integration policy than other European countries.

In the German case, the situation is as Stephen Castles has argued that "Germany is becoming a multi-cultural society. But the trend still frightens people in Germany".[200]
The British immigration expert Stephen Castles looks at the issue from a Marxist viewpoint. He suggests that "History shows that labour immigrations always lead to permanent settlement, unless forcibly prevented look at the Asians and West Indians in Britain, or the Polish miners in France".[201]
His quotation suggests that majority of Turkish workers will stay in Germany rather returning to their country of origin.

Obviously, Germany will rely on foreign workers to skills shortages. With declining birth rates and an ageing population, Germany has been forced to reconsider its integration policy. A nation which has traditionally not perceived itself as an immigration country has been forced to accept that immigration may not only be good for the nation, it may even be a necessity for its growth. "An ageing and shrinking population needs goods and services" argued Professor Rainer Muenz of the Immigration Commission, who published recommendations on the future of immigration in Germany. This suggests that Germany should come to terms with its demographic future and recruit immigrants with the correct skills as permanent residents. The commission report recommends using a points system which offers bonuses for their skills, qualifications and their language ability. The chair of the commission, Rita Suessmuth, wants a flexible system arguing that "we know already, starting with the year 2010 we recommend 50,000 we did not count the family. Usually we count at least three persons per average."

Achim Dercks argues that "Immigration is now seen as a answer for the companies need and a new wave of immigration could also change things for Germany's large Turkish community." Forty years since the first guest workers arrived and many of the country's guest worker Turks will still endure a second class status. For the first time four decades is being discussed in a positive light. This will improve the conditions for people who are currently living there because they will have some measures that can give them more equal rights to German nationals. The situation has changed now. Germany has never seen itself as a more multi-cultural society; Germans have begun to discuss the new immigration reforms which could change their society forever.[202]

Reform of Germany's citizenship and nationality law (Harmonization with European standards as of 1 January 2000) The Federal Republic of Germany has had a new citizenship and nationality law since 1 January 2000. Passed by broad majorities in Germany's Bundestag (lower

---

[199] F.Buchel and J.R.Frick: Article, Immigrants' economic performance across Europe, Population Research and Policy Review (2005) 24, (p. 193).
[200] Stephen Castles: Here for Good, *Western Europe's Ethnic Minorities*, Pluto Press, London, 1984, (p. 7)
[201] Ibid. (p. 7)
[202] Germany's immigration revolution-BBC News, July 4 2001

house) and Bundesamt (upper house) in May 1999, this reform of the regulations governing the naturalization of foreign nationals was one of the first domestic measures of major societal importance and European dimension to be launched by the new government under Chancellor Gerhard Schröder.

2.1.5 Germany's Traditional Citizenship and Naturalization Policies

Paul Close argues that Germany has created a class of *'unter-menschen'* immigrant workers are excluded from fights of citizenship because German nationality law was based on *blood tie* rather than residence until 2001 (Close, 1995: 132).

Rogers Brubaker described the German nationality law as 'ethno-cultural' - as if a form of 'institutional racism' - because it excluded the non-Germans and the Turkish guest workers (Brubaker, 1992; 1). In contrast to France, German social and labour market policy disadvantaged the non-Germans and the Turkish guest workers in the socio-economic integration process (Brubaker, 1992: 78). In addition, granting of German citizenship by naturalization to non-Germans and the Turkish guest workers was left to the discretion of Federal States' (*Länder*) authorities to acquire evidence of the immigrants' cultural assimilation. In Bavaria, for instance, immigrants were required to be able to recite the first verse of the Bavarian national anthem (Geddes: 2003; 94). Until 1990 the conditions for naturalisation were still implied according to section 8 of the 1913 Nationality Law. During the 1980s annual naturalisation rates were less than 0.5 per cent for the Turkish guest workers and for other non-German populations. Dual nationality became increasingly common. Of the 630.000 naturalisations between 1975 and 1990, 430.000 required dual nationality for ethnic Germans unable to abandon their previous nationality (Geddes: 2003; 94).

Christian Joppke argues that the 1990 Foreigners Law resulted in a disagreement during the 1980s and 1990s between the French civic nation model and German blood ties models (Joppke, 1999: 200).

The lack of a German integration policy caused the isolation of first generation Turkish immigrants (especially first generation women), [203] in German towns until 1990; these individuals originally come from the rural areas of Turkey. [204] A lack of reform of German naturalisation law resulted in fewer Turkish immigrants gaining German citizenship. For instance, by the year 1980, only 387 Turks gained German citizenship which makes 0.1 % of those who stayed in Germany over ten years (Castles, 1984:84).

It can be argued that, changes in Germany's new citizenship law by Schroder's coalition government in 2000 facilitated the naturalization of immigrants with foreign nationalities. Requirement of continuous residence for German citizenship prior to application shortened from15 years to eight.

---

[203] Changing status of Turkish immigrant women in Germany, Original title of the Article '*Almanya'daki Turk Kadinin degisen Konumu*', (Edit) Centre for Turkish Studies, Essen; published by Cumhuriyet, March 1999, Istanbul (p. 55-63).

[204] In 1980s Berlin, for example, a quart of Turkish immigrants lived in seven of the city's 75 districts. In Cologne, the situation is the same, a heavy concentration of Turks in private housing in the centre (Altstadt Nord) and in a northern industrial suburb (Fuhlingen). This ghetto-style settlement is both a sign and cause of the immigrants' isolation from society at large.

According to the German Ministry of the Interior's figures in 2003, the number of naturalized persons of foreign origin from the period 1997 to 1999 was only 110,990 immigrants naturalized, but from 2000 to 2003 this number almost doubled to 173,100. An increase in the number of naturalizations could be explained with the 2000 changes and the shortened residency requirements. In 1999 the number of naturalisations amounted from 143,270 in 1999 to 187,000 in 2000.[205]

As Germany's naturalisation number varies from one state to the other, implementation of the new citizenship law also changes from one state to state. For Example, In Berlin and Saxony-Anhalt were an increase in the number of immigrant naturalisation respectively 6.9% and 7.8%, but in North-Rhine Westphalia and Bavaria where most of the Turkish population living were a decrease as 17.7% and 14.2% in the number of immigrant naturalisation.

As for the dual nationality issue, the Schröder government's policy was flexible regarding the issue of maintaining former nationality, if an applicant has a good reason for that, such as property inheritance, land and house ownership in the country of origin. However, the government's dual citizenship plan did not succeed because of opposition from the conservative Christian Democrats. According to Population in Focus data in 2001, 48.3% of the naturalised immigrants maintained their former nationality; in 2002, naturalized persons of possessing dual nationality decreased to 41.5%. Since then dual citizenship has remained as a controversial issue in Germany's naturalization process.
Although Germany changed its citizenship (which prior was restrictive and based on blood-tie) law from the ethnic state approach to a mixture of nation state and welfare state citizenship policy, the new citizenship law still remained open to discussion either immigrants should be included or excluded (Geddes, 2003:100-1).

While Germany was engaged with its integration policy debate whether should be a multicultural approach or assimilation policy, other welfare states such as the Netherlands and Sweden were moving from multiculturalism to full integration and a civic nation state integration model rather than implementing multicultural approach (Geddes, 2003:102).

By the year 2000, the number of naturalised Turks was still very low with 220,781, whereas it reaches 838,630 by 2008. Prior to German acceptance of itself as 'an immigration country' caused a delay in Turks' integration and naturalization process in Germany.

2.2.3 Table for number of naturalized Turkish population in Germany from 1995 to 2004

Year	1995	1996	1997	1998	1999	2000	2001	2002	2003	2004
per year	31,578	46,294	42,240	59,664	103,900	82,861	76,573	64,631	56,244	44,465

Source: Adapted from German Official Migration Report, 2005, (p. 175)

The above table shows that 618,849 immigrants of Turkish origin have gained German citizens between years 1995-2004. During the same period 1,278,424 immigrants gained German citizenship by naturalization. This means that 1.5 % of the total German population had been naturalized during the nine years period are foreign origin immigrants.[206]

---

[205] Statistisches Bundesamt (Federal Statistical Office of
Germany)http://www.migrationformation.org/images/0803_germany_fig 1.gif
[206] http://www.bamf.de/SharedDocs/Anlagen/DE/Migration/Publikationen/Migratiosbericht-2005

Table 2.2.4: Turks in Germany with Migration Background, 2007

Detailed migration status	Total	Share of total population (%)
Turkey	2,527,000	16.4

Source: Adapted from Germany's 2007 micro-census, Germany

Above Table 2.2.4 displays that the total number of Turkish people with migration background were 2,527,000 by 2008.

Table 2.2.5: Turks in Germany by Nationality and Gender, 2008

Citizenship	Total	Share of total (percent)	Men	Women	Percent women
Turkey	1,688,370	25.1	889,003	799,367	47.3

Source: Adapted from German Federal Statistical Office and the Central Register of Foreigners, 2006 to 2008

Table 2.2.5 shows that the total numbers of Turkish citizens were 1,688,370 by 2008. These figures mean that the numbers of total naturalized Turks with Turkish origin were 838,630 by 2008.

Table 2.2.6: Number of Turkish Population in Germany remained as Turkish citizens from 1995 to 2007

1995	1996	1997	1998	1999	2000	2001	2002	2003	2004	2005	2006	2007
2.014.3	2.049.06	2.107.42	2.110.2	2.053.56	1.998.53	1.947.93	1.912.16	1.877.66	1.764.31	1.764.04	1.738.83	1.713.551

Source: Population Division of the Department of Economic and Social Affairs of the United Nations Secretariat, Trends in Total Migrant Stock: The 2005 Revision http://esa.un.org/migration, November 2008.

There are different speculations among German public and political elite about the real number of Turkish immigrants living in Germany. Above Table 2.2.6 shows that there are only 1,713,551 Turkish immigrants remained as Turkish citizens in Germany. By 2008 these figures decreased to 1,688,370 and 838,630 gained German citizenship by naturalisation.

2.1.6 Comparison of Germany's treatment of Guest workers and ethnic Germans

First generation Turkish guest workers in Germany have been treated as guests and welcomed by the German public until the economic and oil crisis, and subsequent recruitment stop (*Anwerbesstopp*) in 1973. Since Germany's Foreigners Law (*Ausländergesetz*) from 1965 consisted of restrictive rights to foreigners. At the same time, the law has been encouraging Guest-workers to return home. Therefore, they worked hard with an intention of saving money and returning home to build a better life. Therefore, they are not interested in learning the host country's language properly and participating in the host country's social and political life. Staying in the host country and a half-hearted guest without learning host language with a plan of returning home is a hindering factor to adopting host country's life-style. On host country's side, perception of the 'Guest worker recruitment system' or guest-worker policy was based on temporariness rather than permanent project.

German official integration and citizenship policy was different from state to state, from party to party, in parallel with changes from government to government until the country's official declaration as a 'country of immigration' in 2001 where immigration policy became more unified. The Law was replaced in 1990. In the mean time it was left to the

68

Foreigner Offices of the *Länder* to implement administrative regulations as to residence entitlement, family reunion etc. They varied widely, with Baden-Württemberg in the south the most restrictive and Bremen in the north the most liberal. In addition to socio-economic integration there was also discretion at the Federal State (*Länder*) level to require evidence of cultural assimilation. In Bavaria, for instance, knowledge of the first verse of the Bavarian national anthem was required. This section of the chapter explores the articulation between Germany as a welfare state and the understanding of the German national community as a community of descent based on ethnic ties. Naturalisation was difficult until 1990; implementation of the citizenship law is still at the discretion of (*Länder*) federal state authorities. The role of EU citizenship had very little effect on the German governments' citizenship policy whilst the government preferred to 'repair' of the incomplete membership status of denizen-ship rather than changing it into an appropriate law which is implemented in other European welfare states. Thomas Hammar defines the denizenship in three different ways such as "the alien who is allowed to stay but not granted any of the privileges of a full citizen: (1) *privileged non-citizens*, such as EU migrants or refugees with Convention status, (2) *denizens* and (3) *quasi-citizens*".[207] The term denizen-ship is a kind of semi-citizenship which does not guarantee the access to political rights as a full citizenship grants. Germany's guest worker migrants were '*denizens*'. They possessed legal, social, but not political rights. Exclusive nationality laws meant that this incomplete membership status was likely to persist into later generations with the result that children born in Germany of foreign parents also be 'foreign'. In contrast to France and Britain, in Germany nationality was still considered as a community of descent rather than a territorial community (birth-place). Turkey's former Associate membership of the EEC and its candidate status to the EU following the Helsinki Summit granted Turkey a directly applicable right of residence for their Turkish workers and these workers family members with long-term lawful employment or residence in a Member State.[208] Since Turkish nationals are by far the largest group of third country immigrants in the EU, this case law provided the basis for an EU model of denizenship.[209]

Germany had no appropriate integration policy until its ethnic minorities (ethnic Germans) returned home to Germany in the early 1990s. Germany appears to have two integration policies: when concerned with Ethnic Germans, Germany has an 'inclusion' policy, when the issue is of Turks' integration process; Germany operates an 'assimilation or exclusion' policy (Geddes, 2003: 100-101). In other words, Germany does not want to share the country's resources with its non-German immigrants but seeks to reserve these resources only for the Ethnic Germans.

Although Turkish guest workers guest workers and their descendants lived in Germany more than 40 forty years and contributed to the German economy more than other groups, but they did not received an equal treatment as ethnic Germans (*Aussiedler*) received in the early 1990s. The ethnic Germans were treated equally with West Germans as if they lived their entire

---

[207] Kees Groenendijk: Chapter 10 the legal integration of potential citizens: denizens in the EU in the final years before the implementation of the 2003 directive on long-term resident third country nationals, (p. 3-5).

[208] Seven Council of Europe Member States, Denmark, Greece, Ireland, Norway, Sweden, Turkey and the UK, ratified the Convention on Establishment (long) before they entered the EC or the EEA in order to acquire a higher level of protection for their nationals living and working in the EC and in other states party to the Convention: Article 7 of Directive 68/360/EEC. Denizenship: short history of a concept, (p. 3) and the denizen status in European law (1955-2000), p. 4.

[209] Ibid, (p. 3, 4)

life in West Germany; while the Turks were excluded from the basic rights. For example, upon their arrival the Ethnic Germans were entitled to housing, unemployment and pension benefits, and to access the health system as other Germans. In addition, the ethnic Germans received a language course payment which was called 'a transition payment' (*übergangsgeld*) related to their attendance at a language course. As though ethnic Germans received a positive discriminatory treatment by German political elite, such a mass ethnic German inflow caused a reaction among the West German public. After the German reunification, an opinion poll from the late 1990 showed 76% of respondents preferred an amendment of German foreigners law Article 16. In the same opinion poll, 96% said that they wanted to end economic migration while 73% favoured amending the Basic Law to restrict ethnic German inflow to West Germany (Geddes, 2003: 87).

Although the 1990 Law constituted of some positive changes in the German naturalization law such as a mixture of blood ties and a civic model for a newly reunited Germany. However, the major changes to the naturalisation law came into effect on January 2001. Approximately 200.000 foreigners applied to become Germans. However, only 30.000 achieved this. [210]

The role of EU citizenship had very little effect on the German governments' citizenship policy whilst the German government preferred to repair the incomplete membership status of denizen-ship rather than changing it in an appropriate way. It is the acquisition of German nationality, but does not guarantee effective use of citizenship rights. In this respect, the relationship between Germany as a welfare state and as an ethnic nation state was identified as key to the discussion of the inclusion and exclusion of Germany's immigrant population.

2.1.7 Comparision of integration policies in European welfare societies

Three basic integration policies have been implemented by West European immigration in the 1990s: multicultural integration policies in the UK and Sweden, and the Netherlands which gives immigrants easy access rights to naturalization and Germany has operated the guest worker system which restrict immigrants' access to citizenship and assimilation policy in France which granted citizenship to its immigrants at the expense of cultural assimilation. [211] In the early 1990s Dutch policy makers were discussing how to harmonize the cultural and ethnic differences of immigrants in the concept of multiculturalism.[212] This policy entails that naturalised immigrants will not be treated as a second class citizens. In 2004, Naturalised Turkish immigrants in the Netherlands reached 42 per cent. This was the highest level of naturalisation rate among immigrant groups.[213]

The Netherlands employs a Multiculturalism philosophy in its immigration policy. This policy is aimed at preserving and developing migrant cultures. Dutch authorities endeavour to encourage the establishing of immigrant associations and organizations at the local, regional, and

---

[210] Migration News, March, 2001.

[211] Brubaker, Rogers, 'Immigration, Citizenship, and the Nation-State in France and Germany': Shafir, Gershon ed., *the Citizenship Debates*; Minneapolis; University of Minnesota Press, 1998 (pp.131-167).

[212] Kees Groendendijk, 'The Netherlands' integration policy, 2004, p.113.

[213] Euro-barometer, 2004

national levels. Such associations could follow a policy of immigrants' participation in socio-cultural, political and sportive activities of the country.

Britain has operated a multicultural integration policy for years and, in the last ten years, during the time of Tony Blair's government more than 1 million British immigrants gained British nationality.[214] If the citizenship of the host country through naturalization is regarded as a last step of a successful integration process by integration experts, Britain is the most successful immigration and integration country among other West European countries. There is a phrase in the Danish language which says: 'Politicians talk much but say nothing'. Current German politicians do just this: they talk a lot but they do nothing about their immigrants' integration. German politicians blame Turks for being unwilling to be integrated into German society. In reality, German politicians are unwilling to support Turkish immigrants to integrate into German society, or they use the Turks as scapegoats for the problems in the economy, high unemployment rates and their own failure to win another term in government. In fact, both countries' political leaders are contributing towards the problem: the German chancellor talks about multicultural integration but she does little. The Turkish PM talks against assimilation but he does nothing. Both leaders, however, claim to support Turkish immigrants financially or morally when their respective elections approach.

Between 1990 and 1993, 140.500 people who were already citizens of one Member State acquired the citizenship of another Member State. The number of naturalisations increased suddenly between 1990 and 1993: almost one million people acquired the nationality of the member states by naturalisation. In Germany, most of them were of Turkish and former Yugoslav origin.[215]

Below Table 2.2.7 shows the number of naturalisations in France, Britain, Benelux countries (Belgium, the Netherlands, and Luxembourg), Germany, and Sweden between 1990 and 1993, 890,000 people acquired the nationality of the member states by naturalisation.

Table 2.2.7: Number of immigrants' Naturalisations in the seven EU states between 1990 and 1993

France	223.000
Britain	218.000
Benelux countries	204.000
Germany	129.000
Sweden	116.000

Source: Statistics in focus-Euro-stat, 1995

According to the Euro-state Statistics in Focus in1995, thanks to Dutch and Swedish integration policy, political participation level of naturalised Turkish descent Dutch and Swedish citizens are respectively in Dutch election 62 % and Swedish 64 %, the same level with original citizens.

Table 2.2.8: Acquisition of citizenship (in thousands), EU-27, Germany, the UK and Turkey, 2001-2008

	2001	2002	2003	2004	2005	2006	2007	2008

---

[214] Acquisition of citizenship (in thousands), EU-27, Germany, the UK and Turkey, 2001-2008
Eurostat *Statistics in focus* 45/2010
[215] Statistics in focus, Euro-stat, 1995

EU-27	627.0 s	628.2 s	648.2. s	719.9 s	723.5 s	735.9 s	707.1 s	696.1 s
Germany	180.3	154.5	140.7	127.2	117.2	124.6	113.0	94.5
UK	89.8	120.1	130.5	148.3	161.8	154.0	164.5	129.3
Turkey			24.8	8.2	6.9	5.1	4.4	6.0

Source: Adapted from Eurostat *Statistics in focus* 45/2010

The above table shows that 1,099,000 immigrants in Britain with foreign origins gained British citizenship between years from 2001 to 2008 within the seven years. As to Germany, 1,072,000 immigrant with foreign origin gained German citizenship by naturalization within the same years (2001-2008), 838,630 of them were Turkish immigrants with a Turkish background. Sweden and the Netherlands both have been multi-ethnic societies, but they both no longer pursue multicultural integration policies.

Current Dutch minority policy aims at combating racism and discrimination. In the Netherlands, tolerant multicultural integration and citizenship policy resulted in high naturalization of immigrants in the 1990s. In fact, one person in six in the Netherlands belongs to an ethnic minority group.[216] This is more or less the same proportion as in Sweden, but the declaration of the Netherlands officially as a country of immigration by a Dutch minister was first made in the late 1990s, even later than in the US.

The Swedish Immigration Board was established for the purpose of regulating migration and the integration of immigrants. Swedish authorities guide immigrants as rapidly as possible from denizen-ship to citizenship.[217] Immigrants are entitled to the same social benefits as Swedes, including unemployment benefits. Sweden has pursued an immigration policy rather than a guest worker concept. After one or two years in Sweden migrants can establish permanent resident status with the rights of denizen-ship; after five they can become Swedish citizens. Yasemin Nuhoğlu Soysal argues that Swedish multicultural integration policy considers immigrants as ethnic minorities, and aims at equal treatment between ethnic groups and native Swedes, while immigrants maintaining their ethnic distinctiveness and cultural identities.[218]

The Dutch and the Swedes have moved away from multicultural approaches. This is because certain values of immigrant populations may be in conflict with the fundamental principles of the Dutch and Swedish societies. Therefore, the Netherlands and Sweden was a model for other West European countries with their ethnic minority politics in the 1990s, but now they have changed their policies towards civic nationalism and socio-economic integration similar to the German integration policy.[219]

---

[216] Article by Anita Böcker and Dietrich Thränhardt: Journal of International migration and integration, 'multiple citizenship and Naturalization: An evaluation of German and Dutch Policies. Volume 7, Number 1, 71-74
[217] Brochmann, Grete and Tomas Hammar (Eds.): Mechanisms of Immigration Control: A Comparative Analysis of European Regulation Policies. Berg Publishers, 1999, (p. 200)
[218] Soysal, Yasemin Nuhoğlu: Limits of Citizenship, Migrants and Postnational Membership in Europe, Published by The University Of Chicago Press, 1994, p. 80)
[219] Geddes, Andrew: The Politics of Migration and Immigration in Europe, in Ch. 4 Germany: Normalized immigration Politics, Sage Publication, London, 2003, (p. 101)

2.1.8 Political debate on German integration policies, multiculturalism or assimilation

German public and political opinion currently suggests that Turks are less integrated than many other groups in Germany or not integrated at all. There are also some misperceptions by the German public such as that Turks resist being integrated and tend to create a parallel society in Germany. Furthermore, they do not bother to learn German.[220]

In 1986, the former leader of Religious Virtue Party Necmettin Erbakan accused his German counterpart Helmut Kohl for acting as an enemy of the Turks because of the German Chancellor's repatriation policy towards Turkish guest workers. Necmettin Erbakan became Prime Minister of Turkey in 1998. He repeated his criticism before the federal election of September 1998 by warning naturalized Germans of Turkish descent not to vote Chancellor Kohl, leader of the CDU party. Erbakan's party was closed down by the Turkish Constitutional Court because of its anti-secular activities across Turkey and abroad. However, the Turkish MP's pressure worked against the former Turk Cem Özdemir (a German-born Turk, feels himself German) who was granted German citizenship. Özdemir entered the German upper house (*Das Parliament*) on 5 March 1999. Mr. Özdemir is leader of 'the Greens Party'.[221]
Statements of Prime Ministers and other politicians of the two countries have played an important role on the Turkish immigrants' integration process. During a 2008 visit to Germany Turkish Prime Minister Recep Tayyip Erdoğan implied in his speech that he encouraged Turkish immigrants to resist German assimilation policy by stating "Nobody can expect you to submit to assimilation. Assimilation is a crime against humanity." [222]

The German and the Austrian press criticized Turkish PM Erdoğan's speech in Munich during his visit Germany on February 14, 2008. The German newspaper Westfällische Nachrichten (Münster, February 14 2008) stressed the importance of the role of host country's language for immigrants' integration and criticised the Turkish PM's 'requirement for establishing Turkish schools in Germany'. Immigrants are supposed to be integrated into German society, so integration is an obligation for immigrants. Immigration and assimilation are two different concepts. Integration does not necessitate that Turkish immigrants will put aside their cultural identity entirely. If immigrants wish to become citizens of the host country, they are obliged to know the host's language. Tageszeitung in Berlin supported the above views.

The Turkish PM's speech in Cologne also produced a reaction from the Austrian newspaper 'Die Presse' in Vienna, which argued that the PM's speech will only help to create parallel Turkish speaking sub-societies in Germany and Austria rather than encouraging Turks to be integrated into their host countries by re-defining the integration 'No one wishes in Austria Turks will give up their cultural identities and speaking their language while being integrated into their host societies. [Author's translation]

On the other hand, German chancellor Angela Merkel said during a speech in Potsdam on 16 October 2010 to youth members of her Christian Democratic Union party, "attempts to create a multicultural society utterly failed, and the concept of different cultures can live happily side by side does not work". She also stressed that immigrants need to do more to

---

[220] Berlin Institute for Population and Development, 2008: Untapped potential, The state of integration in Germany
[221] By Michael Giglio, Der Spiegel's article, A Turk at the Top 10/15/2008
[222] Westfällische Nachrichten, Münster, February 14 2008

integrate, including learning to speak German.

Angela Merkel claims that multicultural integration policy totally failed in German society. She does not accuse Turks directly, but implies that the Turks are also responsible for this failure. A Turkish proverb can better explain the meaning of her statement: "mother-in-law talks to the daughter in order that the bride listens too". In fact, multicultural integration policy has never been applied by current the German government. Her claim that the integration policy has failed is incomprehensible given that it is non-existing and unimplemented. During Angela Merkel's period in government, nothing has been done to integrate immigrants into German society. Further, integration was discouraged in 2007 since 60,000 dual nationals (German-Turkish) have had their German citizenship revoked.

In the year subsequent to Germany's official declaration of itself as 'an immigration country', the number of Turkish immigrants who gained German nationality by naturalization was higher than others. According to Populations in Focus data from Statistisches Bundesamt (Federal Statistical Office of Germany) former Turkish citizens were the largest group with 64,631 naturalizing in 2002, this meant 42% of the total were of Turkish origin. Other immigrant groups were Iranians (13,026, or 8.4%), former Yugoslavs (8,375, or 5.4%) and Afghans (4,750, or 3.1%). During the Schroder governments time 618,849 immigrants of Turkish origin have gained German nationality.

2.1.9 Importance of Germany becoming an immigration country and changing multiculturalism

The declaration of Germany as an immigration country meant that Germany is willing to accept long term Turkish Guest workers as legal immigrants with a new integration policy in 2001. Meanwhile, German denial of being an immigration country and lack of integration policy caused a delay in Turkish integration and deprived those immigrants from socio-economic and political rights. [223]

In the late 1990s, Dutch politicians were occupied with changing their multiculturalism policy to full integration, while Germany declared itself as an 'immigration country' on August 3 2001 by Interior Minister Otto Schilly and was seeking an integration model from the Netherlands. However, enacting legislation was overshadowed following the terrorist attack of September 11, 2001, which led to emphasising on security issues.

In the 1980s and 1990s, multiculturalism was a preferred approach in the West European welfare states such as the Netherlands and Sweden. However, the implementation of multicultural approach became more complicated in the Netherlands towards the late 1990s and in the 2000s. Because, multiculturalism claimed simultaneously maintaining the culture of the majority, such as the preservation of Dutch regional cultures as well as the Dutch mother tongue whilst developing immigrants' different cultural, linguistic and religious identities. Therefore, the Dutch politicians decided to change their policy from multiculturalism to civic integration by emphasising to immigrants' socio- economic integration and treating all citizens equal as well as

---

[223] Andrew Geddes and Adrian Favell (eds.): Politics of Belonging: Migrants and Minorities in Contemporary Europe. Ashgate Publication, 1999, p. 181-119

from immigrant background rather than other policy areas in the early 2000s.[224] The same changes occurred in the Swedish multicultural policy which had been regarded as a laboratory of West European democratic welfare societies. Swedish politicians were from multiculturalism because it was difficult to deal with ethnic identities while maintaining Swedish cultural values such as Swedish language at the same time establishing mother tongue classes for immigrant children and developing their languages. It was also difficult to maintain the life and cultural standards of majority with multicultural policy. About 13% of the nine million Swedish residents are immigrants or the children of immigrants. Hammar argued that Sweden should balance its immigration policy as well as the competing goals of maintaining control and protecting human rights.[225]

As a consequence of this section, multiculturalism has had its contradictions while implementing, immigrants could claim that they would the rights to use their mother tongues, but those who do not command the host country's language they could find themselves disadvantaged in the labour market of the host society. Since multiculturalism policy had been delineated and treats equal all society members regardless in the aspect of their socio-economic and political status, gender, language, and ethnic diversity.[226]

2.2.1 Germany has both been an emigration and immigration country

Although officially denied until 2001, Germany has both been an emigration and immigration country throughout its history. For example, in 1992 Germany was the country with the highest immigration and emigration flows in the EU Member States. More than 1.5 million immigrants were counted in the year, more than 720.000 emigrated from Germany and 800.000 immigrated to Germany. Another interesting event is in 15 member states, more than 60% of all emigrants departed from Germany (Eurostat 1995 p.4 Figure 6).

Since Germany opened its doors to East Germans and especially to people of German origin from Eastern Europe and former Soviet Republics in the 1990s. Now Ex-Russians are the biggest single group of immigrants, Turks are the second biggest immigrant group in Germany. In 1989 and 1990 alone, nearly 800,000 Ethnic Germans came to Germany. More than 90 percent of all Ethnic Germans now come from the former Soviet Union, especially from Kazakhstan. This is important insofar as Ethnic Germans from Poland, and even from Romania, find it easier to integrate into German society. Between the years 1988 and 1995 alone, from 2 million total Ethnic German immigrants, 1.1 million entered the labour force.[227]

---

[224] Geddes, Andrew: The Politics of Migration and Immigration in Europe, in Ch. 4 Germany: Normalized immigration Politics, Sage Publication, London, 2003, (p. 120)
[225] Brochmann, Grete and Tomas Hammar (Eds.): Mechanisms of Immigration Control: A Comparative Analysis of European Regulation Policies. Berg Publishers, 1999, (p. 200)
[226] Joe L. Kincheloe and Shirley R. Steinberg: Changing Multiculturalism, Open Univ. Press, 1997, (p. 2)
[227] Zimmermann, Klaus F.: Ethnic German Migration since 1989 - Results and Perspectives IZA DP No. 50 DISCUSSION PAPER SERIES, 1999 (p. 3, 6, 32)

2.2.2 Introduction of a compulsory language courses for immigrants in Germany

On 1st January of 2005, for the first time in German history, a language course was called 'integration course' for immigrants were introduced. This law came into force once immigrants have obtained residency, they are obliged to attend the 'integration courses' which consist of language courses and courses related to the German legal order, culture, history and the way of living in Germany. These courses are aimed to help the immigrants orient the German political and social system. The courses are compulsory, and long term resident immigrants are obliged to attend integration course in which places are available. If immigrants do not attend the courses, their employment benefits will be drawn or reduced over the period during which they do not attend.

The new German Immigration Law 2007 introduced in 2008 has both restrictive and discriminative elements, especially for newcomers from Turkey who arrive in Germany through family reunification. With the Immigration Law of 2005, the German state covers the costs of the integration courses, meaning that integration is defined as a responsibility of the state. However, according to the new Immigration Law of 2007, if an immigrant is married abroad and wishes to bring his/her partner/spouse to Germany, the new immigrant will have to prove his/her proficiency in the German language in order to receive a German visa. The new- comers themselves pay for the German language courses abroad. The requirement of language proficiency as a part of the New German Immigration Law is only being applied to Turkish citizens who wish to enter Germany on ground of family reunification.[228]

2.2.3 A Debate on the German Integration and dual citizenship policy

German Minister for Internal affairs, Wolfgang Schaeuble stressed that "Turks living in Germany cannot become both German and Turkish at the same time". He made a speech at Phoenix TV panel program called 'Nation, Migration, Integration and Foreign Home Germany'. He replied to one of the audience's questions on dual-citizenship, why he is against dual citizenship. "German-born and raised Turkish immigrant youths should decide to which country (Germany and Turkey) he/she belongs and to which country they feel responsibility. One may not feel loyalty to both countries at the same level". In addition, "understanding of living Islam in Europe is different from other Islamic countries. Germany is a tolerant country and people from different religious background chose Germany to live. Muslims in Germany began to discuss their different views comfortably", he said. Then he called for migrant families to talk German language among family members and parents with their children at home.
German MEP Cem Özdemir and Nihat Sorgeç (German Presidential Reward Winner Manager for Kreuzberg Vocational Training Centre in Berlin) also participated in the Panel. At the Panel, Mr Cem said, "Identity of a human cannot be identified with his/ her religion". But reality has not been reflected in German public in this way. For ex., A Greek and a Turkish young have beaten a retired German man at a train station. The media mentioned Turkish boy's name for a

---

[228] Author's Translation from Turkish Daily Hurriyet, 29 June 2009

76

long time, as if he has beaten the man alone and there is only a Turkish problem in the country. Effective legal measures should be taken to encourage more Turkish immigrants to be naturalised in Germany. He desired German born and raised Turkish youths should play for German national team not for Turkish Team and even a Turkish descent German would be a minister in Germany.

Mr. Nihat Sorgeç said "To Turks should be given a good feeling, loyalty that they belong to this country. "Turks are emotional people if you approach them one step, they do not only approach you closer, but also run to you".

Another participant Hayri Hasan said 'There is an American Proverb "if you are Russian, you are Russian forever". "Dual citizenship does not change anything, Turks 'Foreigners' in Germany, 'Germanised Turks' in Turkey". "Germans should give emotional feelings and accept dual citizenship which will be an advantage for both countries. You could not help admiring British Multicultural society, and how Britons can take advantage of this diversity. British Multicultural integration can be a model for Germany".

World Cup 2006 and Euro 2008 reinforced relationship between two countries Turkey and Germany. It naturally affected Turkish immigrants' participation in the host country's sportive activities and eventually their integration of into German way of living. Angela Merkel ruling government's integration and citizenship policies criticized by the Green Party's co-chairman, Claudio Roth. "German born, well-integrated Turkish descent football **stars** Hakan Balta (was born in the county of Charlottenburg of Berlin, grown up there and played for Hertha Berlin) Hamit Altintop, Yildiray Baştürk and Ilhan Mansiz play for Turkish national team because of Germany's wrong integration policy" she cited. "German government's economic and immigration policy is wrong. If you look at economic and demographic structure of the country, this wrong policy can be easily seen. Moreover, Interior Minister Wolfgang Schaeuble's decision to introduce 'Citizenship test' and 'option model' from the 1st September by ignoring the Federal Parliament's approval is a scandal. Restricting citizenship law and forcing these youths to choose one of the nationalities is not favour of Germany. They have once become German citizens on condition of preserving their home country citizenship from birth or later arrangements you cannot force them to choose one of the nationalities, "We kick them out from German citizenship" in this way. Therefore this policy is wrong, you cannot force them lose German citizenship and this implication does not compile with German Constitution when they are already German citizens. They should be given a dual citizenship right to keep both countries citizenship instead of forcing them to prefer one of it. You can give them a felling that they belong to this country as well. In the way we earn these young people. They will be useful for this country than other countries, for they are German born and grown up in this country. Preserving their own identity and culture is natural as well as they has been integrated into German society".[229]

"*Gemeinsamten Feieren* (Celebrating together) …2.5 million Turkish immigrants live in Germany. They do not only tie two countries, but also contribute to enrichment the daily life of Germany. Thousands of Germans settle in various towns of Turkey, they live there happily. It is estimated that 4 million Germans go on holiday to Turkey every year." The French News Agency (AFP) described the celebration of the Semi-final in German towns as follows: "Turkish and German flags exhibited side by side as a symbol of togetherness and brotherhood as they did

---

[229] [Author's Translation] from Turkish Daily Hurriyet, BERLIN, 23 June, 2008

the same in World Cup 2006 in German towns before the Euro 2008 semi-final between two countries with 2.5 million Turkish minorities in Germany as if two German national teams are going to play for Euro 2008 final".[230]

2.2.4 Chapter conclusion

As immigrants' socio-economic position improved and they became more willing to be integrated, their attitudes and behaviour also changed. This can be accounted for the political behaviour of immigrants and cultural differences between immigrants and natives are a matter of staying longer and, more importantly, willingness to take an interest in host countries politics and adopt its traditions. It is quite logical that naturalised Turkish immigrants in Germany participate in political activities as Germans. In Germany non-national residents are not entitled to vote, but naturalised Turks favour with the Social Democratic SPD and Greens (*Grünen*), this is the same in Sweden and Denmark as well. However, increasing number of naturalized Germans of Turkish descent has not been a significant impact on German elections since 2002. Statistical estimates suggest that approximately 500.000 Turks voted in the 2002 national election, helping to re-elect Schröder by a slim margin over CDU-CSU challenger Edmund Stober. Studies indicate that 103,900 Turks became German citizen in 1990. If the Turks continued to gain German citizenship with this pace, 2 million Turks will be on the voting rolls by year 2025. Two million new voters are enough to swing an election.[231]

In Holland, the percentage of Turks voting was almost as high as the percentage of Dutch (1987). In Sweden, the electoral participation of Turkish immigrants was equal to Swedish turn-outs (1985). As a result, this can be explained by the host countries integration policy as identifying factor of immigrants' turn-outs and voting patterns.

As known, the temporary labour recruitment has been turned into permanent settlement and almost in all Western European states the rights for immigrant workers and their access to social, civic and political rights have been extended. But these improvements are not enough to make them feel secure in their new homes. Then these advanced industrial countries of Western Europe, to what extent, are willing to give economic, politic, and civic rights to millions of long-term immigrants and their families.

The big question integration of Turkish immigrants remains unsolved how Germany still tackles with the aspect of accepting Turkish immigrants as a part of its society. In other words, Germany is not perceived to be as tolerable, as its neighbouring countries are, within the other West European societies, e.g., Britain, the Netherlands, Sweden, Denmark and Switzerland.

Germany has 7.2 million immigrants of which over half of these are Turkish immigrants. Although a half of Turkish immigrants feel integrated into German society: (i) some are easily

---

[230] Kai Dickmann-BILD, 25 June 2008

[231] This figures adapted from <u>Official Migration Report, 2005, (p. 175)</u>

accepted, because they are assimilated; (ii) others are only bearable, because they are integrated; (iii) some of them are not accepted yet, because they live in an isolated way.

Turkish immigrants are ordinary, peaceful people, seeking only the opportunity to build decent, secure lives for themselves and their families in Germany. Most of Turkish immigrants admire many aspects of German society. They find German society more democratic, tolerant, and progressive than Turkish society. There is a Turkish proverb which explains the importance of immigrants' integration into their host society. "If you travel to blinds' country, you should cover one of your eyes" to pretend as if you are also a blind. Therefore, Turkish immigrants should be integrated into their host country. Otherwise, those of the immigrants have no chance to benefit from all facilities their host country offers them.

Worldwide famous GEO journal ordered TAM Turkish Research Centre a computer aided telephone questionnaire to find out German and Turkish communities' attitude and feelings towards each other. The question was "What do Germans and Turks think about each other?" The questionnaire was conducted on 600 persons from each country in 1999. Although they see each other in different places they have sympathy towards each other bilaterally. But they think two people are quite different from each other from characteristic aspect. The survey suggested an interesting view that almost all of German respondents think Turkey is economically dependent on Germany. But half of the Turkish respondents disagree with this German view.[232]

---

[232] GeoJournal, Volume 47, nr.3, 1999, A political cultural map of Europe, a survey approach, p.463-475 (13)

Chapter 3

3.1 Chapter introduction

This chapter will explain how the data collection was carried out and the methods that were applied will also look at the way in which the questionnaire was designed and why semi-structured interviews were adopted. And the way sample size was established and how the methods differ from those employed by other studies.

The following figure demonstrates how theories explain the integration of immigrants in relation to the Turkish community in Germany.

Figure 3.1a The Circuit of Scientific Knowledge

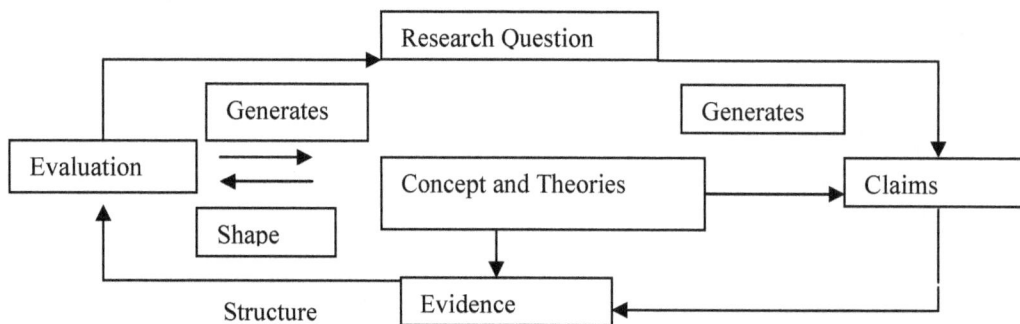

Source: The Circuit of Social Scientific Knowledge, Concepts and theories shape and are shaped by the circuit of knowledge, Peter Redman, Sage Publications, The Open University, London, 2005, (p. 21-23).

Adapted from Sherratt et al., 2000, (p. 18).

Primarily, this chapter deals with research methods, and a skeleton of the survey, which aims to measure the integration level of Turkish immigrants into 16 Federal German States. It will do this by selecting samples from three significant host states housing about 60% of Turkish immigrants, namely the states of Bavaria, Berlin and North Rhine-Westphalia.

The long period of interaction and coexistence between the host and immigrant communities has created opportunities to investigate the level of integration. A bi-lateral agreement facilitating the majority of post-world war II immigration of Turkish guest workers was signed in 1961. Many factors have emerged to facilitate and hinder the integration process of Turkish immigrants into the German way of life. A semi-structured, 5 points-scaled questionnaire with 30 questions (30 testable hypotheses) was used to measure the level of Turkish immigrants' integration into German society. Then a data table, for cross-tabulation with values and percentages was used to show the results of the conducted questionnaire.

Therefore, this chapter explains the methodology, the reasons for choosing the three German states from sixteen, and the integration policy of each federal state and a comparison of the integration achievements with the policy objectives.[233] The Sampling methods chosen are explained, specifically stratified sampling chosen randomly from three major German federal states,[234] since larger samples give more reliable estimates of the population value.[235]

There are two well-known research models in political science, the linear and the wheel model. The linear was chosen for this study. The below figure shows the linear model can easily be amended to include more stages especially if the research involves a sample survey.[236]

Figure 3.1b: The linear research model:

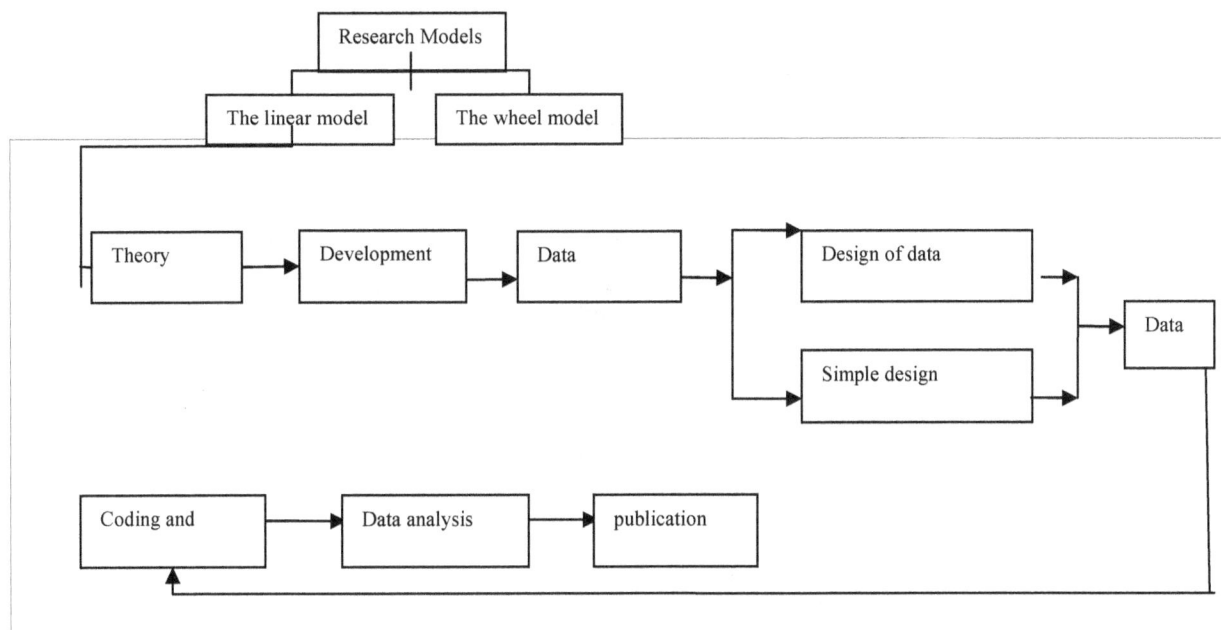

Source: Adapted from Research Methods in Politics, 2004, Figure 2.2 (p. 43).

As seen above figure, the linear model has the great advantages of clarity. It specifies the various steps or stages in the research process in logical and coherent way. However, scientific research rarely involves logical sequences. Research rarely goes according to plan, although this is not an argument against having a plan. David Watson argues that "science seldom involves a straightforward logical sequence. Instead, it involves some guesswork, competition, rivalry and lucky breaks".[237]

---

[233] Janet Buttolph Johnson, Richard A., Joslyn and H. T Reynolds: 'Political Science Research Methods', 5h Edition, 2005 by CQ Press, Washington D.C., (239 – 269).

[234] Simple Statistics: Frances Clegg, Cambridge University Press, Cambridge, 1990 and 2005 (p. 113-120)

[235] Univariate Analysis and Descriptive Statistics by Jonathan Golub, Reading University, Department of Politics, 2005 (p.2)

[236] Burnham, Peter; Gilland, Karin; Wyn Grant and Layton-Henry, Zig: Research Methods in Politics, Palgrave, Macmillan, Basingstoke, 2004 (p.42-50).

[237] Ibid., p. 43

3.1.1 Research Methods

As useable primary data is not available in the study area under research, a sample survey has been undertaken of Turkish immigrants in Germany. This study is supported by available evidence from different scholarly articles, periodicals and other secondary data sources. Since immigrants reside in different states of Germany and the study is necessarily cost effective as well as a fair representation, an interview method of data collection was used for the survey. Also known as opinion polling, it is one of the most familiar political science research methods. Most of the post-1950 political science has focused on public attitude and behaviour, or the study of the political behaviour of individuals and groups. The methods of selection for the sample will be described briefly in subsequent sections of this chapter. The population sample used here should reflect its overall size and major characteristics such as age structure, grade level, ability level, socio-economic status and political participation.

Analytical instruments used in this research method comprise of a survey questionnaire of interviews done to the sample set. To aid the analysis methodically, data was summarized using graphs, figures, and statistical analysis. Qualitative, quantitative and descriptive (inferential) statistics are used to summarize the survey results and analyse the findings in a comparative way, supporting the research outcome. The following data (Table 3.1.2) was taken from secondary sources to explain the growth of Turkish labour migration to former West Germany since 1961.[238]

Although, West German official sources show that the first Turkish guest workers arrived in Germany in 1961, Turkish and British sources show that the arrival of the first Turkish guest workers was in 1956.[239] 150 Turkish people emigrated as an experimental project initiated by West Germany and later in 1961 this was followed by a large scale migration. German officials selected workers according to their age, health, education and employment records. The 1961 Agreement gave the workers entry and work rights in Germany. The recruitment of guest workers was subordinated to the economic interests of the Federal Republic. Article 2(1) of the 1965 Law stated that a residence permit 'may be issued if the presence of the foreigners does not harm the interests of the FRG'. Conditions for these residence permits were all dependent on executive discretion. Residence permits were lined to work permits and both these types of permit were subordinated to West Germany's economic interest.

---

[238] Note: Before Second World War, only Turkish intellectuals, and professionals migrated to Western World. After the War, Turkish migration to Europe was based on economic grounds.
By July 1960, Germany had recruited some 280.000 guest-workers, of whom around *45 per cent* were Italians. In 1960, further recruitment agreements were signed with Spain and Greece and in 1961 with Turkey was signed by Cahit Talas on behalf of Turkish Republic.
[239] Kemal H. Karpat, 'The Ottoman Emigration to America 1860-1914', International Journal of Middle East Studies, 17 (1985), pp. 175-209 and 182, Between 1908 and 1910, for example, 4.261 Turks were admitted as immigrants to the United States, while for the same period, 3,010 Turks, 70 per cent of those admitted, departed. Michael J. Piore, Birds of Passage: Migrant Labour and International Societies (Cambridge: Cambridge University Press, 1979, p.151.

Table: 3.1.1. Number of Turkish Labour migration to Germany between years 1961-1978

Years	Total
1961-67	225,000
1968-73	733,000
1974-78	70,000
Total	1,028,000

Sources Adapted from, 1961-1978 Turkish Labour and Employee Institute (I.I.B.K., 1976, p.6); State Planning Organisation (D.P.T., 1979, p.70)

Table 3.1.1 reveals a rapid growth of the Turkish migrant population in Germany during the bilateral agreement (1961 to 1978) that rises from 225,000 to 1,058,000. During 1968-1973 Germany received the highest number of Turkish labour migrants. However, due to economic recession and oil crisis in 1973, the level of Turkish labour migration has declined drastically. From 1974 to 1978, only 70,000 Turks migrated to Germany to join their families, as a result of Germany stopping further migrant labour recruitment in late 1973.

Table: 3.1.2. The growing number of Turkish labour migrant population in Germany in 1992

Years	Total
1978-1992	1,028,000 - 1.851.000

Source: Calculated from Statistisches Bundesamt (The German Federal Statistics Institute), Wiesbaden, 1992

Table 3.1.2 shows the increase in the Turkish population from 1978 to 1992, which grew from 1,028,000 to 1,851,000. In 1992, the Turks constituted 41% of all non-German population in Germany.

Table: 3.1.3. Turkish-origin population in Germany in 2002 (excluded naturalised)

Host country	Population (in thousands)	Percentage	City	Percentages in main city
Germany	2.014.0	66.4	Berlin	7.0

Source: Adapted from Struder (2003a p.21); Manco (2004, pp.4-5)

Table 3.1.3 indicates the number of Turkish immigrants who stayed in Germany as Turkish citizens in 2002. This accounts for approximately 66% of the total Turkish-origin population in Germany with 7% of them residing in Berlin.

Table: 3.1.4. Turkish population in Germany by status (in thousands) in 2002 plus naturalised

Country	Turkish origin	Turkish nationals	Naturalised number	Percentage
Germany	2.642	1.912	730	28

Source: Adapted from Tumbas (2003, p

Table 3.1.4 presents the total and the status of the immigrants of Turkish origin with only 28% of them naturalised in 2002.[240]

---

[240] Panayiotopoulos, Prodromos Ioannous: Turkish immigrant entrepreneurs in the European Union: International Journal of Entrepreneurial Behaviour & Research Vol. 14 No. 6, 2008, (pp. 399)

3.1.2 Demographic Characteristics of Turkish immigrants in Germany

As argued in chapter one historical development of Turkish migration to Germany since West Germany's guest workers recruitment year 1956-1973 the Turkish population soon overtook all the other guest worker populations. Today over 2.6 million people of Turkish origin live in Germany, including approximately 1 million naturalized Germans of Turkish origin, comprising 36% of the foreign descent population. In spite of the new German legislation of the 1990, the numbers of naturalized immigrants of Turkish descent have not increased. The number of the naturalized Germans of Turkish descent was only 500,000 in 1995.[241] Christian Joppke described the changes in the 1990 German Foreigners Law as a mixture of the French and German immigration law.[242] In order to encourage the Turkish immigrants for German citizenship in 1998 the SPD/Green coalition government relaxed the naturalization rules for dual nationality. Andrew Geddes points out that in 1995 there was some relaxation of nationality laws for the immigrants including the Turks in case of property inheritance in Turkey, former nationals were allowed to regain Turkish nationality if they needed. [243]

The Turks are not the largest ethnic group in Germany anymore. In fact, ex-Russians are the biggest group about 4 million in Germany. The real number of Turkish people with migration background was 2,527,000 by 2008. Then, the total numbers of Turkish citizens were only 1,688,370 by 2008. These figures mean that the numbers of total naturalized Turks with Turkish origin were 838,630 by 2008.[244]

In fact, the total number of naturalized Turks was higher once account is taken of those who were unable to maintain dual citizenship after a change in the law in 2006 by the German coalition government under the Chancellor Angela Merkel's leadership. For example, the total number of Turkish descended Germans was 678,849 in the early 2005.[245] These figures fell to 618,849 in 2006 when 60,000 Turkish Germans lost their German citizenship on the grounds of the change in the citizenship law in 2006. Then, they remained in Germany as Turkish nationals again.[246]

Although the Turkish community is homogenous in Germany there are still some subgroups among them such as four generations and different gender distributions across the age structure. However, the integration problems they face are common in the course of their integration process.

---

[241] These figures adapted from Population Division of the Department of Economic and Social Affairs of the United Nations Secretariat, Trends in Total Migrant Stock: The 2005 Revision http://esa.un.org/migration, November 2008.

[242] Joppke Christian: Immigration and the Nation-state, the United states, Germany, and, the Great Britain, 1999, (p. 200)

[243] Geddes, Andrew: The Politics of Migration and Immigration in Europe, Sage, London, 2003, p. 93-66)

[244] These figures adapted from German Federal Statistical Office and the Central Register of Foreigners, from 2006 to 2008

[245] These figures adapted from Official Migration Report, 2005, (p. 175)

[246] http://esa.un.org/migration, November 2008. Accessed on 12 October 2009

W. Roger Böhning argues that guest workers face mainly four adaptation periods after their arrival in the receiving country.

First male workers emigrate from the urbanized part of the sending country with high skills whose were likely to work in the most marginal of positions until they adapted to the new environment and the labour market of the host country.

In the second stage, the first group return to their home country and they tell their friends and neighbours about their experience abroad. Then the second group with low skills and socio-economic status from villages and agricultural areas of the sending country emigrate to get a job as the earlier group had.

In the third stage, guest workers extend their duration of stay. Meantime other family members join the males. As their expenses increase "they find themselves at the bottom of the socio-economic ladder".[247] Then ghetto style colonies raise, they require mother tongue teachers and imams which bringing more people from their home country.

Final stage, they desire ethnic shops such as helal butchers, home food stores and worship places to feel comfortable in the host country. This means that extra people arrive from the country of origin.[248]

The problems which affect their integration such as economic, social (status and identity) and political (gaining rights, citizenship with access to German social and political institutions) requires harder competition for immigrants in German society compared with the native Germans.[249] For example, poverty (versus feeling comfortable) as an economic problem tends to be defined in comparison with average income in German society. Andrew Geddes argues that job availability of Turkish migrant workers was lower than other migrant workers in 1980s. This was not because they were the least qualified group or poorly equipped for life in Germany, but because, they arrived last and had to accept jobs that were left for them.[250] In 1990, poverty among Germans increased to 11% but had risen to 17% among Turkish immigrants. In 1992, job availability among Germans fell from 9% to 8%, and among Turkish immigrants increased from 15% to 21%.[251] Considering the impact of the economic downturn as a slowing factor on integration of immigrants, the elder generation of Turkish immigrants' already slow process of integration becomes slower.[252] Prodromos Ioannous Panayiotopoulos points out that Turkish Diasporas is becoming an economic power in Europe (2008).[253] In the last decade Turkish immigrants tend to establish self-employment to overcome their economic difficulties which is an effective factor for their integration.[254] The following table shows the increase of Turkish businesses and the types of Turkish businesses only in Berlin.

---

[247]Böhning, W. Roger: The Migration of Workers (*Gastarbeiter in Deutschland*), ILO (1980), p.66-68; and International Labour Review; Year 1991; Volume: 130: Issue: 4; Page 445-59.

[248] Ibid., p. 66-68)

[249] Source: Ralf W. Seifert, 'Am Rande der Gesellschaft? In Informationsdienst zur Auslanderarbeit, No. 3/4,1994,p.19.

[250] Geddes, Andrew: The Politics of Migration and Immigration in Europe, Sage publication, 2003, p.92.

[251] Jeffrey F. Hamburger, 'Migration and Armut', in Informationsdienst Auslanderarbeit, No.3/4, 1994.

[252] Şen, Faruk (July 2003); Historical Situation of Turkish Migrants in Germany (2-3): 28-227,

[253] Panayiotopoulos, Prodromos Ioannous: Turkish Immigrant entrepreneurs in the EU; Journal of Entrepreneurial Research, 2008, Volume 14, Issue 6, pages: 395-413.

[254] Pecoud Antoine (July 2003): "Self-employment and Immigrants' incorporation (2-3): 247-261.

Figure 1: The increase in Turkish businesses in Berlin (1987-2004)

Turkish Businesses in Berlin (Estimated)

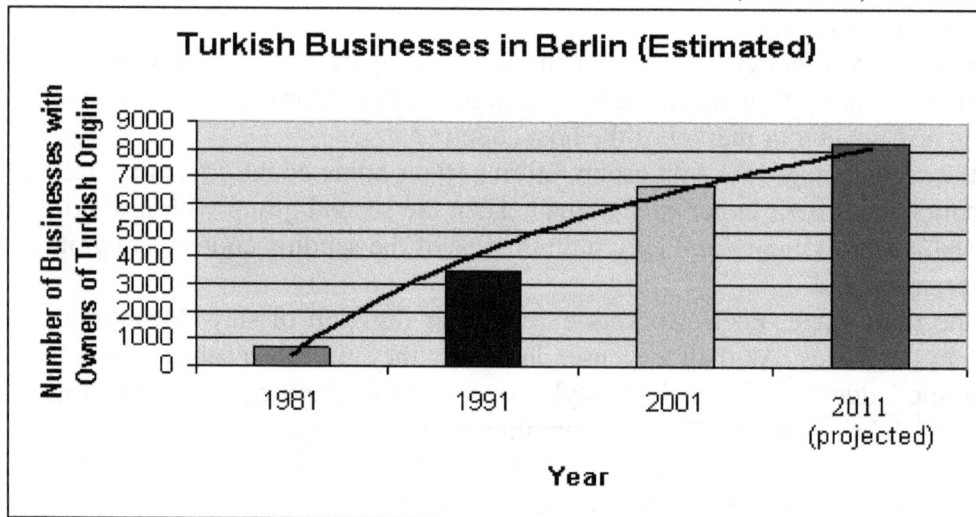

Adapted from Blaschke and Ersöz (1987) and Pütz (2009)

Figure 2: Types of Turkish businesses in Berlin (2002)

2002 Turkish Businesses Industries in Berlin

Adapted from Statistisches Landesamt Berlin, 2002

In summary studies have shown that the economic and social situation of Turkish immigrants is improving continuously. In the 2000s, the situation was better than in comparison to the 1990s and 1980s. Welfare opportunities also had a great impact on integration. The issue will be analysed in the subsequent chapters four and five in detail.

The following histogram 3.1.6 concerns 'Turkish immigrants' demographic change between years 1995-2007. This histogram 3.1.6 histogram is actually based on the data from Population Division of the United Nations Secretariat, November, 2008.

Histogram: 3.1.6. Turkish immigrants' demographic changes between years 1995-2007

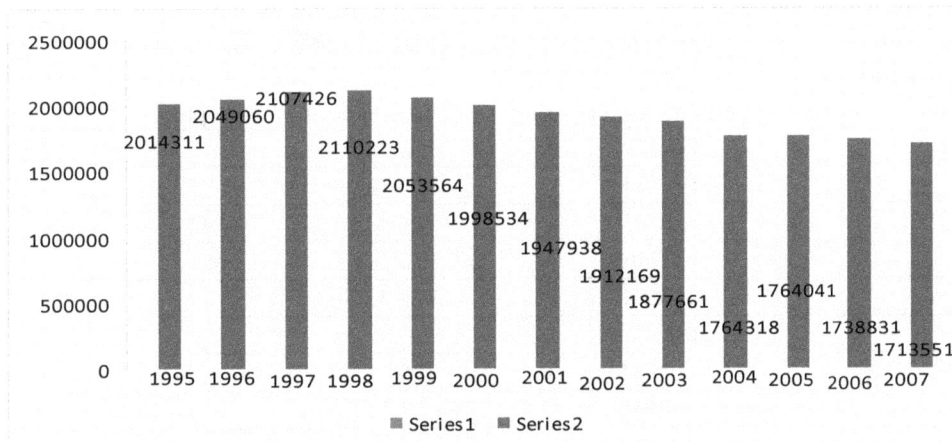

Source Author: Calculated from Population Division of the Department of Economic and Social Affairs of the United Nations Secretariat, Trends in Total Migrant Stock: The 2005 Revision http://esa.un.org/migration, November 2008.

Above histogram 3.1.6 shows only the Turkish-origin population that remained as Turkish citizens. The histogram specifically indicates Turkish immigrants' demographic change between the years 1995 and 2007. While the number of Turkish immigrant population declines steadily, the number of naturalized Turkish-descent Germans increases continuously. These figures will be compared with the findings of the survey research in the conclusion section of chapter six to explore whether they support the main hypothesis or not. Although different sources provide similar figures about the number of Turkish immigrant population in Germany, figure 3.1.6 is simple and displays the relevant figures clearly. The histogram indicates a decline in the number of the Turkish-origin population that remained as Turkish citizens in Germany between the years 1961-2007. Meanwhile, comparing Turkish immigrants' fertility rate which is higher than native Germans, the real number of Turkish descended persons should be higher. Faruk Şen points out that over half (50.5 percent) of Turks are between the ages of 14 and 29, compared with 25 percent for native Germans (Şen, 2002: 30).

The histogram does not only show the demographic characteristic of Turkish immigrants but also their demographic status of how many gained German citizenship and how many remained Turkish citizens. The figures can be helpful to calculate the exact numbers of those of Turkish descent in Germany.

The German Statistics Office suggests that Turkish population's age structure is enormously different from Germans. 25% of German population is older than 60 years. Only 5% of Turkish population is over 60 years old.[255]

One of the Germany's main concerns today is ageing and declining problem of its population. Germany's need of immigrants has also changed, during 1960s-1980s the need was of balance it's in proportionate ageing population. Thus, according to German Statistics Institute estimated figures from 2005, Germany's population without immigration could decrease between the years

---

[255] Statistisches_Bundesamt_2009_loc.3D51-0 Accessed on December 5 2010

2005 and 2030 from 82.1 to 50.7 million. Therefore, Germany needs to integrate immigrants to meet its demographic decline.

The following table demonstrates the age structure of Turkish immigrant population in Germany in 1990.

Figure 3: Turkish population in the FRG according to age structure as of 30 September 1990

0 - 17 years	597.619	35.7 %
18 – 20 years	127.766	7.6 %
21 – 29 years	332.779	19.9 %
30 – 39 years	192.503	11.5 %
40 - 49 years	249.202	14.9 %
50 – 54 years	100.419	6.0 %
55 – 59 years	49.846	3.0 %
60 – 64 years	17.960	1.1 %
65 and above	7.817	0.5 %

Source: Zentrum fur Turkeistudien,Zur Lebenssituation und spezifischen Problemlage alterer auslandischer Einwohner in der BDR, Kurzfassung, Essen, October 1992.

Above table shows Turks are a young population group, 36% is younger than 18 years old. About half of the Turkish population is between 25 and 45 years old and only 5 % is older than 60.

The real number of Turkish immigrants can also be calculated by adding the number of naturalised Turkish descent Germans to the above figure. According to the Berlin Institute for Population and Development 2009, there are only 2.4 million Turkish immigrants including naturalized Germans of Turkish descent living in Germany. So, the factual data on the number of Turkish immigrants and their integration level is not such as the German and Turkish politicians expressed in their statements.

3.1.7 Turkish immigrants remained as Turkish citizens 1961-2000

Year	Population	Year	Population
1961	7,116	1981	1,546,300
1962	15,300	1982	1,580,700
1963	27,100	1983	1,552,300
1964	85,200	1984	1,425,800
1965	132,800	1985	1,400,400
1966	161,000	1986	1,425,721
1967	172,400	1987	1,481,369
1968	205,400	1988	1,523,678
1969	322,400	1989	1,612,632
1970	469,200	1990	1,694,649
1971	652,800	1991	1,779,586
1972	712,300	1992	1,854,945
1973	910,500	1993	1,918,395
1974	910,500	1994	1,965,577
1975	1,077,100	1995	2,014,320
1976	1,079,300	1996	2,049,060
1977	1,118,000	1997	2,107,426
1978	1,165,100	1998	2,110,223
1979	1,268,300	1999	2,053,564
1980	1,462,400	2000	1,998,536

Source: Statistisches_Bundesamt_2009_loc.3D51-0 Dezember 5 2010

Above table shows the total number of the Turkish immigrants remained as Turkish citizens since the years 1961-2000. In 2000 were 1,998,536 Turkish citizens living in Germany. In 2005 the total number of the Turkish immigrants with immigrant background was 2,812,000 which consist of 3.4% of Germany's population. However, the German ambassador of Turkey said that "there are now 3.5 million immigrants of Turkish origin living in Germany". Other informal sources estimate that more than 4 million Turkish immigrants with Turkish background living in Germany.

In 2008, these decreased to 1,688,370 Turkish citizens (889,003 males and 799,367 females) in Germany.

3.1.8 **Naturalisation number of the immigrants of Turkish origin since 1982**

Year	Population	Year	Population
1982	580	1996	46,294
1983	853	1997	42,420
1984	1,053	1998	59,664
1985	1,310	1999	103,900
1986	1,492	2000	82,861
1987	1,184	2001	76,573
1988	1,243	2002	64,631
1989	1,713	2003	56,244
1990	2,034	2004	44,465
1991	3,529	2005	32,661
1992	7,377	2006	33,388
1993	12,915	2007	28,861
1994	19,590	2008	25,230
1995	31,578	2009	

Source: Statistisches_Bundesamt_2009_loc.3D51-0 Dezember 5 2010

In 2005, there were 840,000 naturalized German citizens of Turkish origin. The official number of Turks with Turkish citizenship in Germany is constantly declining, because many Turks became naturalized, and since the year 2000, children born in Germany are entitled to adopt German citizenship. 53% of Turkish immigrants came to Germany through family reunification. Then 17% of Turks who live in Germany were born in the country. 54.2% of Turkish immigrants in Germany are male and 45.8% are female.

3.1.3 Characteristics of German Federal States and reasons for choosing three States from sixteen

Characteristics of the three German Federal States where the survey took place, which were chosen from the total of sixteen are as follows: Germany has a federal system; constituting 16 states (*Länder*), Germany's immigration and integration policy varies from state to state. For instance, Bremen and Hamburg have employed more liberal policies than restrictive Baden-Württemberg State. The three states where the questionnaire survey conducted, the selection of the sample is random. Not only does immigration and integration policy vary but also citizenship policy changes widely with Baden-Württemberg in the south being the most restrictive and

Bremen in the north the most liberal. In Bavaria, for instance, knowledge of the first verse of the Bavarian national anthem was required.

From the aspect of citizenship policy it seems that Hamburg is more hospitable politically and Baden-Württemberg is the least hospitable German state.[256] Political behaviour also changes from state to state. For example, out of the three sampled states SDP (Social Democrats and left parties) has a strong position in Bavaria and Berlin States; alternatively the Christian Democrats are dominant in North Rhine-Westphalia.

It is a characteristic of European political parties that the Social Democrats has moderate and tolerant immigration and integration policy, the left has more liberal approaches such as environmentalism, multiculturalism , the conservatives are restrictive, and the right wings have nationalistic and anti-immigrant views. Some federal state favor dual citizenship, for example, Ralf Stegner, interior minister in the regional state of Schleswig-Holstein suggests that" Those foreigners who are well-integrated, speak the German language and have an income of their own should be offered German citizenship without the precondition of having to relinquish their original nationality first."[257] The current ruling conservative party leader Chancellor Angela Merkel and her party are persistently against granting dual nationality to immigrants in Germany.[258]

Many countries in Europe housing immigrants have developed consultative bodies both at local and national level to deal with immigrants' integration problems and provide them with assistance related to the state's social, health and housing services as well as naturalization procedures. These institutions are shaped in accordance with host country's political and administrative structures. The authority of these institutions differs from one country to another. For example, because of Germany's federative state structure (Länder), these Consultative institutions for immigrants in Germany operate only at the local state level and do not exist at the national level.[259]

The following table shows established immigration offices in Western European countries which deal with immigrant problems. They all have such consultative intuitions both at local and national level. As Table 3.1.9 shows, Germany is the only West European country without a National immigration board and Immigrants' Advisory Council. Germany's immigration and integration policy also differs from other European countries. The federal budget for the integration of immigrants does not include immigrant organizations in Germany. Funding the immigrant organizations is also left to the discretion of local authorities at the municipal level. Local authorities distribute the funds mainly on project basis.[260]

---

[256] Andrew Geddes: The Politics of Migration and Immigration in Europe, SAGA Publications, London 2003, p.81.

[257] Bild am Sonntag : INTEGRATION, German Minister Urges Reversal of Dual Citizenship Policy, 24.04.2007

[258] Ibid.

[259] Soysal, Yasemin Nuhoğlu: Limits of Citizenship in Europe, Migrants and Postnational Membership in Europe, The University of Chicago Press, London, 1994, (p. 82)

[260] Ibid., p.107-108

Table 3.1.9 Consultative institutions for immigrants in major European countries

Country	Central	Local
Sweden	Immigrants' Advisory Council; National Immigration Board (SIV)	Municipal advisory councils
Netherlands	National Advisory Councils for Ethnic Minorities (LAO)	Municipal advisory councils
Switzerland	Federal Commission for Aliens (EKA)	Foreigners commissions
Britain	Commission for Racial Equality (CRE)	Race Equality Councils
France	Social Action Fund (FAS); National Council Immigrant Population	Immigrant Council
Germany	None	Foreigner Advisory Councils

Source: Adapted from Limits of Citizenship in Europe, Migrants and Postnational Membership in Europe, p.82

Due to the lack of poor establishment and many divided groups in Turkish guest worker organizations they have not had any significant impact (with lobbying and socio-cultural activities) on their countrymen's integration problems. Until 1980 Turkish immigrants did not establish any influential organizations to dialogue with German authorities about their problems. Only two of the Turkish immigrant organizations received substantial aid from German local authorities. One 'The Union of Turkish Association in Berlin' was founded in 1990 to create a common action against the new German Foreigners Law; the other 'The Hamburg Union of Migrants from Turkey was founded in 1985. The Union has called for the recognition of 'minority rights for migrants' and dual citizenship, and emphasised the need for 'multicultural policies'. However, due to many divisions among themselves they were not long lived.[261] On the other hand, Italian and Greek were better organized; they have affected their countrymen's integration by lobbying and arranging socio-cultural activities.[262] Some religious organization such as Türkiye Diyanet İşleri Vakfı- TDIB (the Turkish Directorate for Religious Affairs) and Milli Gorus Teskilati-MGT (the National Vision Organization) had also been established. The TDIB was established as a German branch of the TDIB in Turkey, the MGT was supported by former Virtue Party of Necmettin Erbakan, as a mother party of current ruling party AKP in Turkey. In 1990, these two organizations called for recognition of "minority rights for migrants and dual citizenship", and emphasized the need for "multicultural policies" in Germany.[263] Although these two religious organizations have been more influential than others, partly due to Germany's denial that it is 'an immigration country', and partly due to divided views in the organizations, they did not have play any effective role on their countrymen's integration into German society.

Although each German state has its own regional government, immigration policy, integration policy and citizenship test, the national government of the Federal Republic of Germany's policy is decisive and legislative power rests with the national government. For example, the Senate of Hamburg State granted (*Walrecht*) voting rights to its immigrants at local elections in 1989, but the law was cancelled by the German Constitutional Court the following year. The German Constitutional Court is the sovereign authority of the state.[264] However, immigrants including Turks in the Netherlands, Sweden, Denmark, Spain and Portugal have been

---

[261] Ibid., p.109
[262] Ibid., p.109
[263] Ibid., p.109
[264] Andrew Geddes: The Politics of Migration and Immigration in Europe, SAGA Publications, London 2003, p.88.

91

granted voting rights in local elections regardless their nationality on condition of three years residence in the host country since 1983.[265]

As seen in the table 3.2.1 below, the sample is taken from three major federal states which bear they are 'typical' cases almost similar characteristics to the other thirteen. The significance of the three sampled states is that they are home to more than half of the population of Turkish descent.

3.2.1 Number of total immigrants and Turks with percentages in three German Federal

Sampling selected states (Lander)	Number of all immigrants	Number of Turks	Percentages
Bavaria	995,900	224,400	26.0 %
Berlin	382,800	129,800	36.1 %
Nord-Rhine-Westphalia	1,812,300	639,100	37.9 %

Source: Adapted from David Horrocks and Eva Kolinsky 1996: Migrants and Citizens, Berghahn Books, 1996 (p. 71-101).
Adapted from Eva Kolinsky, Turkish Culture in German Society , Chapter 5, Table 5.6 Non-German population in Germany by Country of Origin, 1992 p. 85.
Original source calculated from Federal Statistical Office data and from Statistisches Jahrbuch für die Bundesrepublik Deutschland, 1994

3.1.4 Policy effect of German political parties' on integration of immigrants

As the number of naturalized immigrants increased the political parties of the host countries became interested in the immigrants' integration problems. Those immigrants with voting rights are a factor affecting electoral politics across Europe.[266]

Amongst all German political parties, the Greens as a coalition partner of the German government made valuable contribution to immigrants' integration by supporting the change in the German citizenship law in 2001 which facilitated immigrants' equal access to legal and political rights.[267] The Greens' argument was that immigrants would be integrated within German society. Then they simultaneously should be obedient to the German laws and recognise the basic German values which were defined by the German Constitution. Similarly, the Social Democrats argued that although the German Muslims were entitled to keep their religion, at the same time they had to adapt to the German Democratic secular system, to accept the Constitution, to respect the separation of state and religious affairs, and to avoid establishing parallel societies within the German community

---

[265] Sarah Spencer (Editor): 'Immigration as an Economic Asset', German Experience, A positive Approach to Migrants... (Published by IPPR/Trentham Books) Rivers Oram Press, 1994, p. 104.
[266] Andrew Geddes and Adrian Favell (eds.): Politics of Belonging: Migrants and Minorities in Contemporary Europe. Ashgate Publication, 1999, p.181.
[267] The coalition (2001) agreement between the SPD and Greens acknowledged an irreversible process of immigration and argued that the aim of policy should be the integration of the resident foreign population. The government proposed that children born in Germany would obtain German nationality if one parent had been born in Germany or come to Germany while under the age of 14. The further reinforced civic model, though without automatic acquisition of German nationality because parents had to apply on behalf of their children before they reached the age of 6. The new coalition also proposed the foreign spouses would be able to obtain citizenship independently of their partners, whereas before they lost their residence permit if the marriage broke up.

The Conservatives refused the Greens' model arguing that immigrants would have to abandon their former citizenship, language, ethnic and social values. The Conservatives' argument was in favour of traditional attitudes to protect the homogeneity of the German nation rather than implementing a multicultural approach.

In denying the assimilative model of integration the Conservatives preferred, the Greens argued that immigrants would keep their religious and cultural values while integrating into German society. The Greens persistently favoured a pluralistic model based on a civic and rights-based integration policy.

Another improvement for immigrants in Germany was made by the Social Democrats in the German Parliament (*Bundestag*) in 2004, the Social Democrats justified their support by referring to opinion polls, which suggested that 80 percent of the German population favoured greater security legislation for immigrants; this therefore, represented a fulfilment of the wishes of the German public. [268] As a result, the Citizenship Law of 2005 was an outcome of the Social Democrats and the Greens' Government, as a compromise that the law of blood-tie was no longer the only way; well-integrated immigrants could gain access to German citizenship by birth.

The following table shows the voting distribution of German parliament in accordance with German political parties' representatives in Bundestag since general election on 18 September 2005.

3.2.2 German Parliamentary election results, 18 September 2005

	Party List votes	Vote percentage (change)		Total Seats (change)		Seat percentage
Social Democratic Party (SPD)	3,059,074	37.1%	-5.7%	74	-28	39.6%
Christian Democratic Union (CDU)	3,695,806	44.8%	+7.9%	89	+1	47.6%
Free Democratic Party (FDP)	508,354	6.2%	-3.7%	12	-12	6.4%
Alliance '90/The Greens	509,219	6.2%	-0.9%	12	-5	6.4%

Source: http://www.bundeswahlleiter.de/ Federal Diet, Accessed on 2 December 2010

Below table 3.2.3 demonstrates the distribution of voter turnouts and seats of the German political parties in the parliament in 2009.

3.2.3 Distribution of seats in German Parliament since 2009 election

Political Group	Total	Gain/Loss
Christian Democratic Union (CDU)	194	14
Social Democratic Party (SPD)	146	-76
Free Democratic Party (FDP)	93	32
Left Party (Linkspartei)	76	22
Green Party	68	17
Christian Social Union of Bavaria (CSU)	45	-1

Source: http://www.bundeswahlleiter.de/ Federal Diet (29.09.2009, 15.02.2010)

---

[268] Deutscher Bundestag, Plenar protokol 15/118. 01.07.2004,

Below the table show the number of the Turkish population in the European counties those remained as Turkish nationals in Germany since 2008.[269]

3.2.4 Citizenship of foreigners, as at 31 December 2008 in Germany

Turkey	1,688,370
Italy	523,162
Poland	393,848
Greece	287,187
Croatia	223,056
Russian Federation	188,253
Serbia and Montenegro (former)	177,330
Austria	175,434
Bosnia and Herzegovina	156,804
Serbia	136,152

Source: Federal Statistical Office, Pocketbook: Germany, 2009, p. 33

The following table demonstrates German political parties' impact on immigrants' integration process and citizenship figures.

3.2.5 Acquisition of citizenship (in thousands), EU-27, EFTA and Candidate countries, 2001-2008

	2001	2002	2003	2004	2005	2006	2007	2008
EU-27	627.0 s	628.2 s	648.2. s	719.9 s	723.5 s	735.9 s	707.1 s	696.1 s
Germany	183.3	154.5	140.7	127.2	117.2	124.6	113.0	94.5
UK	89.8	120.1	130.5	148.3	161.8	154.0	164.5	129.3
Turkey			24.8	8.2	6.9	5.1	4.4	6.0

Source: Adapted from Eurostat *Statistics in focus* 45/2010

As the above table shows, whenever, the SPD-Green coalition has come into power at national level, the number of naturalised Turkish-origin people's increases. However, when the CDU-Christian Democrat Party and the Christian Union Party is the ruling coalition, the number of naturalised persons declines.[270]

Political parties integration policy does matter for immigrants' naturalization whereas, statistical data both from Schröder's and Merkel's government's ruling period on naturalization figures of immigrants have shown that in Merkel's 2008 term only about 94,500 foreigners applied to become German citizens; in the Schröder term of 2001 about 183,300 immigrants gained the German nationality. This means that the number of naturalized Germans of immigrant origin fell 60% during the Conservative government's time and it still continues to decline.[271]

---

[269] www.destatis.de Access on December 4 2010

[270] Bild am Sonntag : INTEGRATION, German Minister Urges Reversal of Dual Citizenship Policy, 24.04.2007

[271] Ibid.

The ruling political party always decides the policy which affects integration. As discussed, the SPD-Greens' integration policy is more humanitarian, tolerant and in favour of immigrants. It seems that Turkish immigrants have little chance to participate in German political life unless they have integrated and gained German citizenship. Turkish immigrants favour to join the SPD-Greens. However, the proportion of Turkish members in the total SPD membership lists was not more than 2.5% in 1994.[272]

Integration expert Andrew Geddes argues that if immigrants wish to participate in their host country's politics, they should be integrated and naturalize. A lack of integration of immigrants leads to concerns about political stability, social cohesion and welfare, both at the level of nation and the EU.[273]

Former interior minister Wolfgang Schäuble argues that naturalised Turkish immigrants cannot deal with their dual loyalties. They should decide where they belong – Germany or Turkey.[274]

The SPD and the Greens suggest that when immigrants are as loyal as natives, they should also have the same political rights as natives, those of immigrants with voting rights at least for local elections will be more interested in being integrated in their host society and the political parties than those without such rights. As long as they pay taxes and contribute to the national economy as native Germans, they should also be able to participate in German politics. [275]

Another argument was why, when German citizens have no voting rights in Turkey, the Turks should be given voting rights in Germany. However, naturalized Turkish citizens of German descent obtain voting rights in Turkey. [276] Furthermore, if immigrants are granted voting rights they would be able to establish their own political parties in Germany. They would also be able to undermine German's national interests.

A different argument was by the SPD and the Green Party that they proposed if young Turkish immigrants carry out their compulsory military duty in Germany, they should be granted voting rights and citizenship, since there are not enough young men to recruit into the German army. However, this idea was strongly opposed by the Turkish Defence ministry in 2005.

On the other hand, Christian Democrat and Christian Union parties' policy is known among Turkish immigrants as anti-immigration and intolerant (especially during 1980s leading CDU by Helmut Kohl). Due to the new anti dual citizenship law 60.000 Turkish Germans lost their German citizenship in 2006 under leadership of Angela Merkel government. Andrew Geddes argues that German mainstream the extreme right (like the National Democrats-NDP, the German People's Party-DVU and the Republican Party) and centre-right parties exploit immigration issue (Geddes, 2003:89). For example, Roland Koch, CDU state president of

[272] Sarah Spencer (Editor): 'Immigration as an Economic Asset', German Experience, A positive Approach to Migrants... (Published by IPPR/Trentham Books) Rivers Oram Press, 1994, p. 104.
[273] Geddes, Andrew: (Geddes, 2003:102).
[274] http://www.migratioinformation.org/feature/display.cfm?ID=175 Access on 10.10.2009
[275] In summer 2001 a Commission established by the SPD/Green coalition reviewed German immigration policy. The report of the commission published in summer 2001 began by stating that Germany needs immigrants and that it needed to successfully integrate them.
[276] A German citizen living in Turkey has been elected as mayor for a Turkish town *Didim* at the Aegean cost. This means that there are no legal restrictions for Germans' participation in election and purchasing property such as real estate.

Wiesbaden Hesse, fought on anti-immigrant and anti-dual citizenship platform but he appears to have alienated his voters/supporters in the February 2, 2008 election). CDU-Angela Merkel's right-wing Christian Democrats performed poorly in February 2008 key state election in Hesse, a result that casts doubt on the viability her ruling coalition. The CDU took 36.8%, putting it just one-tenth of a percentage point ahead of the opposition Social Democrats (SPD). In the last state election in 2003, the CDU scored 48.8%, with the SPD a distant second on 29.1%. The result was a blow to the State president of Hesse, Roland Koch, who is known for his anti-immigrant anti-dual citizenship stance (for example, he collected 1 million anti-dual citizenship signatures in 2003 before the election). However, his attempts to win the 2008 election with anti-immigrant propaganda failed. In Lower Saxony, SPD-Social Democrat Party became first party, CDU second, FDP-Free Democrat Party third, the Greens Forth and the Left Party first time entered into the state parliament with 5 percent election-barrage in the election. However, a positive change, on the issue of immigrants' integration and citizenship, is visible even among the CDU leading politicians. Since, they do not insist on their 'nation-state and blood-tie' views on immigrants' citizenship issue as they did before. 'Guest workers' reform' (October 17th, 2007 Berlin) in German society, German Chancellor Angela Merkel said that "Guest workers from southern Europe, who migrated to Germany in 1960s, gave the German society a new face. Speaking at a two-day symposium on 'Integration through education in the 21st century' in Berlin, Merkel said "the Turks now living in Germany for the last four generations contribute a great deal to the country's economy. This flexibility and change on the CDU integration policy is partly due to Turkish decent Germans' joining to the party, partly centre-right parties want naturalised Germans' votes like the SPD and the Greens. The coalition government has also established specific Integration Ministry. [277] German Minister for Integration Affairs Maria Böhmer sacked Professor Faruk Şen, the director of the Centre for Studies of Turkey at the Essen University, because of his statement "Turks became new Jews of Germany" in 2008.

Looking at other Western European countries' migration policies it can be observed that, unlike other post-industrial countries, in the 1980s the German centre-right CDU/CSU coalition governments were less willing to develop long-term integration policies. This omission has significantly influenced present-day integration problems. On the other hand, the United Kingdom, Australia and Canada have encouraged the migration of skilled workers by providing mechanisms for permanent settlement and naturalisation such as points systems. French and German politicians admitted that their governments' assimilation policy failed.[278] The former director of the Turkish Research Centre in Germany claims that speaking the host country's language and gaining its citizenship does not mean immigrants have been integrated into the host society as in the French case. For a successful integration other factors such as employment facilitates, income level and education level all play a key role in the immigrants' integration process.[279] Former French Interior Minister Nicolas Sarkozy, became president of France, is known with his anti-immigrant policy. Mr. Sarkozy's slogan was during the presidential election campaign, "There is no place for an immigrant in France who does not speak French; who does not accept 'Gender Equality'; republic and secularism. One, who beats his wife, has polygamy

---

[277] Andrew Geddes, 2003: The Politics of Migration and Immigration in Europe; Germany's Normalised Immigration Politics, Sage Publication, p.79-101.

[278] Reuter's news agency, 2010/10/16

[279]A speech in Potsdam on 16 October 2010 to youth members of her Christian Democratic Union party

and girls who wear head-scarf or enter in classroom with head-scarf." An Academie Francaise, Helene Carrere d'Encausse, claimed that "Many of these Africans in France are polygamous. In an apartment, there are three or four wives and 25 children."[280]

As a result, German political parties' integration policy played a major role in the integration process of Turkish immigrants into German political life as well as other in other integration areas. Turkish immigrants' participation in German political activities and their interest level in German politics have been measured with two politically relevant questions: survey question 16: are you interested in politics in Germany? And question 17: are you a German citizen? And answers of respondents have been analyzed separately in chapter four and a bivariate analysis has been carried out in chapter five comparatively. When Turks gained German citizenship it means that they have obtained voting rights, are able to stand as an electoral candidate and to be elected as representative both at German local, national at the EU level.

As for the policy effect of German political parties on bilateral relations, it has been compared throughout chapters of the thesis. Both German and Turkish governments and politicians have had a changing influence on Turkish immigrants' problems including their integration process.

3.1.5 Relationship between host state's immigration and integration policy:

Although Germany's acceptance of itself as a country of immigration delayed, Germany has developed a specific integration policy which demonstrates both nationhood membership and incorporation between immigrants and native Germans. This incorporation tries to establish a dialogue between German institutes and immigrants organizations in order to facilitate immigrants' adaptation to German society. German federal sates (Länder) are not a multicultural system, but a kind of multi state system. Integration policy varies from state to state because of German federal state structure. [281] Germany's understanding of integration policy has been defined as follows:

> "Integration implies offering fair and equal opportunities in education and on labour market, and in society at large...Integration also calls for considerable effort from the foreigners themselves to adjust to the living conditions prevailing here...Finally, integration also calls for a gradual reduction of the social and cultural gap separating nationals and non-nationals, together with an increase in mutual tolerance and acceptance."(Commissioner for Foreigners' Affairs of the State of Berlin 1985:9) [282]

German integration policy requires that immigrants would adjust themselves to German living conditions to fill the socio-cultural gap between the German and immigrant communities. German understanding of integration aims to make foreigners a part of German society and the labour market. However, compared to other West European countries' integration policy, German understanding of integration policy remains unclear. [283]

---

[280] Sun Sentinel news, Paris riots, 11/5/2005; Diversity in France,
http://news.bbc.co.uk/1/hi/world/europe/4405790.st
    Accessed on December 5 2010
[281] Soysal, Yasemin Nuhoğlu: Limits of Citizenship in Europe, Migrants and Postnational Membership in Europe, The University of Chicago Press, London,1994, (p. 61-62)
[282] Ibid. 42, (p. 61-62)
[283] Soysal, Yasemin Nuhoğlu: Limits of Citizenship in Europe, Migrants and Postnational Membership in Europe,

Immigrants tend to adapt to a new environment over time. This suggests that length of stay is a factor likely to affect their level of integration. Immigrants are more likely to be integrated in states where they settled earliest and statistical data is available concerning this. The state-size and length of stay of Turkish immigrants in Germany is shown below:

The states in which immigrants are concentrated are more representative than the other states. Various aspects of integration process can be observed in the Table 3.2.6 below page 23. For example, point seven in the table of 'identified factors affecting integration of immigrants', explains 'a small number of immigrant group from distinct culture and tradition' is more likely to be integrated into the host society than a large, concentrated immigrant community.

The level of immigrants' integration is also greatly affected by other factors such as education, gender, interaction with the host society and economic opportunity. Sebastian Gundel argues the length of stay of immigrants helps to assess the success of assimilation and integration of immigrants.[284]

Table 3.2.6 Cumulative number of Turkish immigrants

Sampled States	Number of Turkish immigrants(in '000)	Percentage of total immigrants	
(a) Bavaria	224,4	13 %	13 %
(b) Berlin	224,4+129,8=354,2	8 %	21 %
(c) North Westphalia	354,2 +639,1=993,3	37 %	58 %
Rest of the states	720,2	42 %	42 %
Total	1, 713, 5	100 %	100 %

Source: Calculated from David Horrocks and Eva Kolinsky: Migrants and Citizens, Berghahn Books, 1996 (p. 71-101). Adapted from Eva Kolinsky, Turkish Culture in German Society , Chapter 5, Table 5.6 Non-German population in Germany by Country of Origin, 1996 p. 85.

The regional state's integration policy within the Federal Government's integration framework is a factor which plays an important role in integration and the presence of a large number of Turkish-origin voters is significant to electoral success for the coalitions. Politicians are thus encouraged to further pursue those policies. Turkish origin politician Emine Demirbüken Wagner from the CDU can be taken as an example as a Berlin State Parliament MP. Normally Turkish descent German politicians favour the SPD/Greens. But she prefers the CDU, a centre-right political party, rather than the left. Berlin has the largest population of Turkish origin and arguably due to the state's positive integration policy, Turkish immigrants in Berlin have more integration facilities than in other states. The centre-right regional government of Berlin State has adopted a positive approach to the integration of immigrants. Emine Demirbüken Wagner is the first Turkish descent MP from the CDU.[285]

The University of Chicago Press, London,1994, (p. 62)

[284] International Journal of Social Economics, Vol.36, No 11, 2008, pp 769-782. 'What determines the duration of stay of immigrants in Germany?' By Sebastian Gundel and Heiko Peters or www.emeraldinsight.com/0306-8293.htm

[285] Turkish Daily Hurriyet German Edition, November 14, 2006

3.1.6 Differences among Turkish immigrant communities in the three sample states

The state of Bavaria houses 995,900 immigrants, 224,400 of which are of Turkish origin. 26 % of total foreign-origin persons in Bavaria are Turks. The state capital is Munich and city statistics shows that 43,309 of the immigrant population are of Turkish descent, consisting 23.7 percent of total immigrants.

Bavaria houses the third largest number of Turkish immigrants in Germany, after North Rhine-Westphalia and Berlin. Munich is a gateway for the entrance of Turkish immigrants from other countries to Germany after passing the Austrian border. Turkish-origin travellers who prefer to travel to and from Turkey by motorway stopover in Munich, which is closest German city en route to Turkey compared with Berlin and Cologne. Berlin State is home to the densest population of Turkish immigrants (182,800 of 382,800 total immigrant population of Berlin region, 36.1% of total foreign population).

Figure 4: Berlin-Kreuzberg Turkish Population

Statistical Zone	Name	Total	Age of Registered Residents				Number Turkish Residents	Percentage With Turkish Heritage
			Under 6	6 – 18	18 - 65	65 and Older		
12	Mehringplatz	19,314	1,517	3,095	12,651	2,051	6065	31.4%
13	Moritzplatz	19,189	1,452	2,773	12,199	2,765	5219	27.2%
14	Mariannenplatz	21,473	1,385	2,689	15,601	1,798	7344	34.2%
15	Wiener Straße	26,980	1,644	2,917	20,525	1,894	8445	31.3%
16	Urban	44,422	2,626	4,533	33,623	3,640	10928	24.6%
17	Viktoriapark	15,384	879	1,471	11,705	1,329	2538	16.5%
Kreuzberg total		146,762	9,503	17,478	106,304	13,477	40539	27.6%

Adapted from: Statistisches Landesamt Berlin, 2005

Figure 5: Berlin-Neukölln Turkish Population

Statistical Zone	Name	Total	Age of Registered Residents				Number of Turkish Residents	Percentage With Turkish Heritage
			Under 6	6 – 18	18 - 65	65 and Older		
75	Reuterplatz	33,898	2,002	3,414	25,044	3,438	9288	27.4%
76	Roseggerstraße	28,087	1,856	3,195	19,643	3,393	8875	31.6%
77	Köllnische Heide	15,013	1,071	2,107	9,474	2,361	3588	23.9%
78	Karl-Marx-Straße	38,622	2,796	4,803	27,133	3,890	13981	36.2%
79	Schillerpromenade	32,040	2,259	3,637	22,916	3,228	11246	35.1%
Neukölln (North) Total		147,660	9,984	17,156	104,210	16,310	46,979	31.8%

Adapted from: Statistisches Landesamt Berlin, 2005

Berlin as a Federal State is subdivided into twelve boroughs (*Bezirke*). 40,359 Turkish immigrants live in Kreuzberg. 46,979 live in Neukölln (North); its Turkish population is more than Kreuzberg (Veysel Özcan, Turks in Berlin, 2005 and Statistisches Landsamt Berlin, 2005). The total Turkish immigrant population in Berlin (city) appears to be in decline. In fact, the population are acquiring German citizenship. For example, in December 2006 the total was 147,600, 129,800 in July 2007 and 113,779 in June 2008. Another reason for choosing Berlin for the research sampling is that it is home to many Turkish immigrants and one sixth of the city population is of Turkish origin. One in three school children were born of Turkish immigrants in the late 1990s.[286] Recent figures show that 50% of school children in Berlin are of immigrant origin and 80% of them were born outside Berlin.[287]

North Rhine-Westphalia is the most industrial region of Germany and almost 40 percent of former Turkish guest workers and current immigrants reside in this region. Manco points out that Germany accounts for nearly two thirds of all immigration from Turkey in the EU. Thus, the old industrial state of North Rhineland-Westphalia alone accounts for nearly one quarter of Europe's Turkish population (Manco, 2004: 4). State based statistics indicate that the Turkish-origin population of the region has more than trebled (37.9 % compared with Berlin and Bavaria.[288]

North Rhine-Westphalia is the State of Germany with the largest Turkish-origin population. The purpose of drawing the following table 3.1.8 is to distribute the respondents in accordance with each state's Turkish population density. For example, 120 of 300 total samples were conducted in the North Rhine-Westphalia, because its Turkish-origin population density is higher than others.

3.2.7 Number of Turkish immigrants in the sampling states and their capital cities:

Number of Turks in three states	Capital cities & Nr .of Turks	Percentage state & city based	Percentage	Nr. of respondents
1. Bavaria (224,400 of 995, 900 immigrants)	Munich 43, 309 (07/2007)	26.0 % of	9. 2% of	75 respondents of 300 Turkish immigrants
2. Berlin(182.800 of 382,800 immigrants)	Berlin 147, 600 (12/2006)	36.1 % of	10.3 % of	105 respondents of 300
3.North Rhine-Westphalia 113, 779 (06/2008)	Cologne 120,000 (07/2007)	37.9 % of total	11.4 % of	120 respondents of 300 Turkish immigrants
(639,100 of 1,812,300 immigrants)				Turkish immigrants

Source: David Horrocks and Eva Kolinsky 1996: Migrants and Citizens, Berghahn Books, 1996 (p. 71-101). Calculated from Eva Kolinsky, Turkish Culture in German Society , Chapter 5, Table 5.6 Non-German population in Germany by Country of Origin, 1992 p. 85.

---

[286] Çalar, Ayşe: "Dar Kultur-Konzept als Zwangsjacke in Studien zur Arbeitmigration," Zeitschrift Für Turkeistudien 1991, 1:92-105.or Sozialanthropologische Arbeitspapiere Nr.31, Institute for Ethnology, Free University of Berlin.

[287] Migration Studies are published by the Berlin Senate (Auslanderbeauffrage des Senats von Berlin, Potsdamerstr. 65, 10785 Berlin, Germany; and the Berlin Institute for Comparative Social Research (Potsdamerstr. 91, P.O.1125, 10785 Berlin), 2008.

[288] Statistics fur Bundesamts, 1992, and Dezcember. 2006

3.1.7 Reasons for choosing the three states as sample states:

Bavaria, Berlin and North Rhine-Westphalia house the most Turkish immigrants and their Turkish-origin population density is higher than the other 13 federal states, an obvious reason to select these three states as samples.

Almost 60 percent of the Turkish-origin population live in these three states and form a homogeneous community compared with other immigrant groups. Family members originating from the same village in Turkey may have relatives in Berlin or Bonn.

The sample of the survey consisted of 300 representatives of Turkish origin from a range of status, gender, age and profession groups in the three selected states. The purpose of random sample selection from these states was to investigate the level of integration of Turkish immigrants into Germany society.

Berlin has always been a historical capital of Germany, even after its division post the Second World War. However, after the German reunification the capital of the country Bonn was moved back to Berlin in 1990. Its role is not only as the administrative and strategic capital of the country but also the cultural capital. Berlin has also played a historical role in Turco-German relations since 1600.[289]

3.1.8. Factors affecting the integration of immigrants:

Questions concerning the positive and negative factors which affect the integration of Turkish immigrants into German society are the basis for the survey questionnaire.[290] The table below lists these factors, which will aid the upcoming research in an analytical way. If integration is a process affected by these factors, then each factor that interacts with the integration process may yield a positive or negative effect on the host or migrant society (interaction of factors between host and immigrant societies).

The concept of integration has been discussed in chapter two within the framework of EU integration. The factors affecting the integration of immigrants have been identified within two opposite groups as facilitating or hindering the process.

---

[289] Bosporus Germans, June 6 2008, www.qantara.de
[290] Bryman, Alan: Social Research Methods, Published by Oxford University Press, 2004, 'Introduction to Survey Research' (p. 84-85).

The following table 3.2.8 demonstrates how these factors affect the integration process of immigrants after a certain length of stay in the Turkish case twelve years from 1995 to 2007 is the period used.

Table: 3.2.8. Identified factors affecting integration of immigrants positively or negatively are following:

Factors	*Facilitating factors of integration*	*Hindering factors of integration*
1	Higher education level of immigrants	Host society's restrictive integration policy
2	Skilled migrant workers and employment facilitates in labour market	Unskilled migrants and low job availability
3	Self-employment of immigrants	Unemployment rates among immigrants
4	Income level of immigrants	Poverty level of immigrants
5	Moderate attitudes to tradition and religion	Strong ties with their home country and religiosity
6	Having similar language, tradition, culture and religion	Fear of losing their culture, tradition and language
7	Small number, immigration group	A great deal of immigrants
8	Intermarriage, marrying to a member of host society	Having strong family ties
9	Quickly getting to used to host society's way of living	Identify crises between two culture and societies
10	Hospitalities between host and minorities	Hostile attitudes of host and unwillingness to be integrated
11	Job, education and welfare opportunities	Housing and unemployment problems
12	Participation to social and political activities	Not having common interest with local people
13	Feeling a member of hosts	Feeling deprived in their new country

Note: Above Table is adapted from Gordon's Structural Assimilation, 1964 and developed with purpose of using it to German case. Survey questions are based on affecting factors of integration of immigrants.
Source: Milton M. Gordon, 1964. Ethnic Education; Its Purposes and Prospects Assimilation in American Life, Oxford University Press, 1964, p.27

3.1.9 Questionnaire Design

In designing the questionnaire, factors in table 3.2.8 are categorised into four aspects: economic life, social life, political and personal life to gauge Turkish immigrants' integration level.[291] The questionnaire has two parts. The first part contains questions relating to the subject of the study. The second part deals with Turkish immigrants' demographic characteristics such as gender and age structure, which allow a consideration of generation shift and gender distribution of immigrants' to measure the overall level of integration. 30 specific questions are included. The questionnaire is a semi-constructed interview and easy to follow for both the interviewer and the respondents. The wording of the questions is easy to understand as unclear questions provide

---

[291] Bryman, Alan: Social Research Methods, Published by Oxford University Press, 2004, 'Research design' (p. 56).

inappropriate stimuli and result in unreliable or cause inaccurate responses. Also, the respondent may not be co-operative. The question types are 'closed-ended'.

Each question has only one interpretation and avoids technical terms, is not addressed to specialists and has a precise one word answer like yes or no with five point scale rows. The questions do not require respondents to make calculations. Nor do they contain emotional words therefore avoiding emotionally biased answers.

An awareness of the problems encountered by survey researchers is necessary to draw accurate conclusions. The relationship between natives and immigrants, the willingness to accept the host country as a permanent home and being accepted by the native population as a full member of society may all be decisive factors influencing the problem of integration of Turkish immigrants in Germany.

Before administering the questionnaire, a number of factors which affect the level of integration were identified.[292] Facilitating factors of integration have been explained in the earlier section (and table 3.2.3). After conducting the questionnaire, a data table (3.2.4) was then designed to test the identified hypotheses.

The questionnaire indicators are based on a 5 point scale with mid-point 3-(50 %) representing a *medium level* score in each case; 1-2 *low level* (0-25 by 50 percent) indicating a lack of integration (isolation/ghettoisation or Turkification); and 4-5 indicates '*high level* integration (assimilation or Germanisation). The respondent answers by ticking the appropriate boxes.

Graph 3.2.9 A graphical demonstration of an immigrant's feeling about integration:

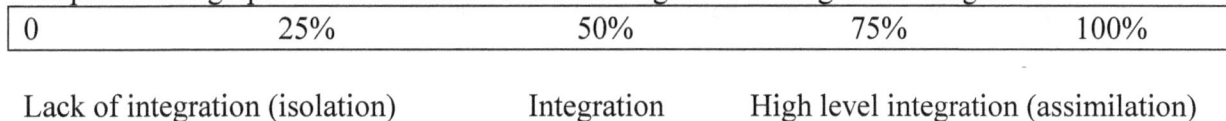

0	25%	50%	75%	100%

Lack of integration (isolation)   Integration   High level integration (assimilation)
Source: Author

A criterion was identified to gauge the level of integration. The criterion is 50%. If they feel 50 percent European or German this has a significant impact on their integration.
The 50 per cent integration (scale) level can be considered as successful integration.

The questionnaire is set out in full below (English version) in Table 3.2.4, which has been drawn to collect data on integration of Turkish immigrants in three sample states in Germany.

---

[292] Bryman, Alan: Social Research Methods, Published by Oxford University Press, 2004; 'The way of administering a research instrument' (p.84).

3.3.1 The Questionnaire Table (English version)

QUESTIONNAIRE SURVEY QUESTIONS ON MEASURING OF INTEGRATION LEVEL OF TURKISH IMMIGRANTS WHO ARE

RANDOMLY SELECTED (Normally invisible)   ISOLATION   INTEGRATION   ASSSIMILATION

[5 point-scale testing]   (1) Lack of integration (2) Isolation (3) integration (4) high level of integ. (5)Assimilation

Question	(1)	(2)	(3)	(4)	(5)
1. How European do you feel?	Not European at all	A little European	European	Quite European	Very European.
2. How German do you feel?	Not German at all	A little German	Ordinary German	Quite German	Very German.
3. Which language do you speak at home?	Only Turkish	Turkish	Both	Mostly German	Only German
4. How religious do you think you are?	Too much	Secular but believes	Normal	not religious	Not at all
5. How are your relations with people at work?	Not good	Not bad	Normal	very good	too good
6. How is local people's attitude to you?	Not good	Not bad	Good	Very good	very hospitable
7. Do you feel equal treated at work?	Feels unfair treated	Sometimes	generally equal	Well treated	More than equal
8. Do you like food here?	Dislikes local food	likes both food	eats only hosts		Totally German
9. Do you like the way of living here?	Very different	different	Yes I like	German better	German is best
10. Do you feel a member of hosts?	Not at all	Not much	Yes I am	I feel	feels too much
11. How strong ties do you have with home?	Too strong	More than German	(50-50)	not much	no ties
12. Is life comfortable here, socially?	Not at all	Hard	Normal	comfortable	More than home
13. Is it hard to find a job, economically?	Too hard	Hard	But possible	Better than Turkey	More opportunities
14. Is it hard to find house here?	Too hard	Hard	But possible	Better than Turkey	More opportunities
15. How are facilities for children education here?	Not good	Not bad	Good	More possibilities	Very good
16. Are you interested in politics, here?	No	Not much	yes	a little	sometimes
17. Are you German citizen?	Yes	Applied for	Accepted	Declined	No

104

18. Do you feel culturally integrated?   No   a little   yes   very well   totally

19. Are you married to a native?   Yes   have been   live together   divorced   No

20. Are you satisfied with your status here?   Disappointed   Not much   Yes   Not bad   Better than I expected

21. Have you been accepted as member of here?   Never   Maybe   Yes   Mostly   Totally

22. Where were you born?   In Germany   In Turkey   In Europe   In America   Other

23. How is your German?   Not at all good   Not good…..   Good   Very good   Fluently…..

24. Where did go to school?   In Germany   In Turkey   Both country   Other European   0ther..

25. What is your last education degree?   Public school….Vocational Technique school….High school…. University…

26. Are you interested in sports here?   Yes, professional   not professional   as hobby   Sometimes   I just watch

27. Where do you want to live in future?   In Germany   In Turkey   Other European   Australia   Other

PART TWO: CATEGORIES OF SAMPLE

28. GENDER: MALE   FEMALE

29.   STATUS: Student   Worker   Unemployed   Businessman/Businesswoman   Academic   Actor

Actress   Retired

30. AGE:15-20   21-30   31-40   41-50   51-60   61-70   71-80   over

(0-25%) Feelings lead to isolation, (50%)   Feelings lead to real integration, (more than 50 %) Feelings lead to assimilation

The questionnaire was produced in three languages: German, Turkish and English due to some Turkish-descended participants from mixed marriages who were unable to speak both languages.

Hypotheses are tested by each question's positive (as a facilitating factor to the integration process) or negative (as a hindering factor to the integration process) effect on integration.

Survey question 18: '*Do you feel culturally integrated*?' is difficult to gain information about immigrants' feelings on integration or question 16 Are you interested in politics, here in

Germany" *Are you politically integrated?*" may also be interpreted as "*Do you vote in elections?*" or '*Do you belong to a political party here?*' The interpretation depends on the host country's political parties' interest in immigration issues and integration on immigrants and also the citizenship of the respondents. Instead of asking '*Do you feel integrated politically?*' Importance of gaining the citizenship of the host country - a lack of citizenship of immigrants means an inability to influence the political system compared with host country citizens. Only citizens can vote in national elections and stand as candidates. The thirty questions are discussed individually in chapter four. Then specific grouped questions for bivariate analysis are treated in a comparative way in the chapter five.

To conclude, the legal status of long-term resident immigrants is important in gaining political rights and subsequently influence in the political life of the host country. Integration and citizenship policy of the host country are interrelated. In other word, immigration policy of a state affects its integration and citizenship policies constantly.

3.2.1 Selection of Sampling Method - Stratified sampling

A survey sample attempts to obtain accurate information about a population by obtaining a representative sample of that population and using the information from the sample to make generalization about the whole population. Surveys provide a quick and affordable means for political scientists on a wide range of immigration issues such as employment facilities, housing conditions and most importantly integration problems of immigrants.

Sampling is a selection of a number of cases for specific study; the sample is used to gain knowledge about a particular population such as immigrants, rather than including the population. Comparative research is based on a sample cases. As Alan Bryman puts it, "given that it is rarely feasible to send questionnaires or to interview whole population (such as all members of a town or the whole population of a country, we have to sample".[293]

Administering survey questionnaire and response rate is an important factor in the success of research. Interviewer effects are perceived to be more or less moderate to the respondent. This may be because of gender, ethnicity, accent, behavior, dress or other attributes. As Shamit Saggar argues conducting survey and analyzing ethnic minority booster sample is not always an easy task. The poor response rate reduces the value of the analysis of the data.[294] For example, this questionnaire survey was conducted in July 2007 in three German states by visiting Turkish societies, workplaces, associations, and clubs. In July young Turkish immigrants were out, some were on summer holiday; some were shy or did not speak English and Turkish speaking. All these factors have a negative effect on achieving a high response rate.[295]

If a research is about proportional representation (PR), making inferences must be an explicit act in order to be reasoned and convincing. Descriptive and causal inferences are used. Descriptive

---

[293] Bryman, Alan: Social Research Methods, Published by Oxford University Press, 2004, 'Research design' (p. 75).

[294] Article by Shamit Saggar and Joanne Drean: *British public attitudes and Ethnic minorities* , July 2001 (pp.24)
Accessed on December 2010 www.cabinetoffice.gov.uk/media/cabinetoffice/strategy/.../british.pdf

[295] Peter Burnham, Karin Gilland, Wyn Grant and Zig Layton-Henry (2004): Research Methods in Politics, Palgrave Macmillan, Basingstoke, 2004 (p. 80-112, 143-4)www.cabinetoffice.gov.uk/media/cabinetoffice/strategy/.../british.pdf

inference is about systematic description of selected cases and what they may look like, or be like. Causal inference is to identify any causal relationship. Although qualitative inference is based on the same principle as quantitative inference, linking what observed in a small sample to much greater population that the sample was drawn from. Some known properties of a normal distribution enable researchers to attach probability statements to the survey question. A probability what the sample shows is also true of the population. When the sample mean is best guess of the true but unknown population mean. If the sample is perfectly representative of the population, the sample mean and the population mean will be the same. If there is sampling error, then the sample mean will deviate from the population mean. In order to find out 'How far away is the sample mean from the population mean?' The chi-square test and the t-test can provide answers to this question.

Stratified sampling is based on sample population's proportionality to the total population. If we want the representatives to reflect the diversity of persons of Turkish origin in Germany, and Turkish immigrant population density varies within a German state, stratified sampling will ensure that estimates can be made with equal accuracy in different parts of the state, and that comparisons of sub-regions can be made with equal statistical power. Randomized stratification can also be used to improve population representativeness in this research.

As immigrants' integration process is influenced by a number of different factors, this suggests using a stratified sampling approach to sampling a population. A stratified sample is a probability sample in which elements sharing one or more characteristics are grouped, and elements are selected from each group in proportion to the group's representation in the total population. Stratified samples take advantage of the principle that the more homogeneous the population; the easier it is to select a representative sample from it. Also, if a population is relatively homogeneous, the size of the sample needed to produce a given degree of accuracy will be smaller than for a heterogeneous population.

As the question of integration is likely to be affected by different socio-economic characteristics such as age, education, sex and income group, this also suggests a stratified sampling approach to find a meaningful understanding of Turkish immigrants' integration into German society. Stratified theory also suggests that each sub-strata needs to have homogeneous characteristics. Even though the Turkish population in Germany is homogeneous; we still need to divide it into independent subpopulations. In this way, no element of the Turkish-origin population such as grouping from economic (employment, income), social (participation of cultural and sportive activities of German society), psychological (feeling member of host, as a home, secure, loyal), political (interests in host politics, political parties and gaining citizenship to obtain voting rights) aspects, and age structure and gender distribution of Turkish immigrants can be excluded. The sample was divided into different homogeneous groups.

In doing so, the age structure of population has been considered as differences in age are likely to affect immigrants' integration. So the questionnaire has been structured an age category in 5 groups ranging from 15-20, 21-30, 31-40, 41-50 and 51-60 over.

There are advantages in stratified sampling over other methods. For example, it focuses on important subpopulations and ignores irrelevant ones, allows use of different sampling techniques for different subpopulations and improves the accuracy of estimation. But it is not useful when there are no homogeneous subgroups.

3.2.2 Sampling procedures/strategies

Different age groups have varying opinions on integration for example, older sections of population who were not born in Germany, can be expected to have a tendency or affiliation with Turkey. On the other hand the younger generation of German born Turkish-descended youths have no current generation connection to Turkey practically. We can argue that they have a natural tendency to be integrated into German society provided that they are given full social and economic support. To consider this issue more respondents are taken from the younger generation.

Because education can be expected to influence the integration process respondents have included professionals, the educated and manual workers. 300 random selects may not include different age groups, professionals, and gender variations and the results of the research would not be so meaningful. That is why 100 respondents have been categorised in different groups or sub-strata. From each category the respondents have been selected randomly.

Although the Turkish-origin population is the most homogeneous community among immigrants and are dispersed evenly throughout Germany, there are still some differences between them in Berlin, Munich and Cologne. For example, in Berlin the largest groups of foreign origin are citizens from Turkey (113,779 in 2004). 6 % of Berlin's population is Muslim (213,000 and 139.000 of them Turkish in 2007).

3.2.3 Question of Sample Size

The sample is used to estimate the characteristics of the target population. Sample size can be smaller for a homogeneous population than for a heterogeneous one and still be as accurate. (If a population is totally homogeneous, a sample of one element will be accurate). Bias will be avoided and thus sampling error minimised. For example, if the population consists of 60% in the male stratum and 40% in the female stratum, then the relative size of the two samples (three males, two females) should reflect this proportion. In the case of this study, the gender distribution of the population of Turkish origin is 57% male and 43% female.

3.2.4 Selection of Sample Size

The selection of individual respondents was made at random, so that every person in the population has a chance of being in the sample. The sample is large enough to avoid the influence of abnormal items. The larger the number of items selected, the more reliable the information provided. The size of the sample depends on the permissible sampling error and the amount of analysis required (it does not depend on the size of the population).

Statistically, there are two sampling techniques: random and non-random. A random sampling method is used to obtain a reliable, fair representation and avoid bias. The Turkish-descended population has similar characteristics in all cases to guarantee each representative has an equal chance of being selected.

The size of the sample is important in avoiding errors (error in this context means differences between expected values and real values).

3.2.5 Weighted mean

The weighted mean is similar to an arithmetic mean (the most common type of average), where some data points contribute more than others. The notion of a weighted mean plays a role in descriptive statistics.

Considered for each state's percentage weighted factor and number of Turkish immigrants in three capital cities with percentages:

3.3.2 Table of weight mean

Sampling selected states/cities	Sampling Number of Turkish immigrants	Percentages
Bavarian State/ Munich	0, 25x300= 75	9.2 %
Berlin city state/Berlin	0,35x300= 105	10.3 %
North Westphalia/Cologne	0, 4 x 300=120	11.4 %

Source: Calculated from table 3.2.7 (.p.25)

The method applied to select the 300 samples, about 100 respondents from each state is weighted percentage/factor or weighted ratio. Obtaining a composite rating or weighted mean of all the factors involves making groups, finding the mean of each group then giving weight to each group and multiplying the mean of these factors by the weighted factor. For example, Munich sample is weighted at 25% of the whole, the Berlin sample at 35% and the Cologne sample at 40%.

3.2.6 The Conduct of the questionnaire

The questionnaire was conducted on a personal basis which guaranteed better results since the questionnaire was carried out in front of the interviewee.[296] In other words imaginary and mass responses were prevented and the results were more reliable. In these way such a method of inquiry saved time, e.g.: time taken by postal deliveries. It was comparatively cheaper since it involved man power rather than finance.

The questionnaire also included 'there-here' comparisons and information about representatives' gender (male-female), age, status (such as student, worker, unemployed, self-employed businessmen/women, service sector, actor/actress; academic or retired, but no name and personally identifiable information is included). In such a way an immigrant could spontaneously compare his/her former life in home country and his/her experience 'here' could be expressed quantitatively.

Descriptive and inferential statistics were used in this survey. (1) Descriptive statistics was employed to summarize/describe the questionnaire results. Then, quantifying was carried out the findings to generalize from a sample group to wider group (the population). (2) Inferential statistics was used as a basis for making estimates/predictions in order to make inferences about finding out what is more likely to happen in relation with integration problems of Turkish immigrants in the future of Germany.

The questionnaire was used as an instrument to measure the impact of dependent variable on the independent variable and simultaneously data related to survey *validity* and *reliability* such as *content, construct, concurrent* and *predictive* validity. For example, content validity was determined by judgement concerning how well the samples represent the correct proportion. Alan Bryman descries 'validity' "a concern with the integrity of the conclusions that are

---

[296] Bryman, Alan: 'Social Research Methods', Oxford University Press, 2004, (p. 85-89).

generated from a piece of research. There are different aspects of validity; particularly, measurement validity. When used its own, validity is usually taken to refer to measurement validity".[297]

3.2.7 Quantifying the indicators of integration

After finishing the data collection from the sample, the following Table 3.2.4, a cross-tab is drawn, which summarizes the whole of the questionnaire results. This will be helpful to comment on the individual items in detail during the rest of the thesis. The cross-tab was helpful to draw pie-charts for the chapter four and bar-chart graphs for the chapter five in order to analyse findings statically.

A cross-tabulation displays the distribution of values as a simple table by listing the categories.

In the Table 3.2.4 the values of the survey results are coded from 1 to 5. The cross-tab reveals also a joint distribution of two or more variables simultaneously. Each cell shows the number of respondents who gave a specific combination of respondents, that is, each cell contains single cross tabulation. Each cell gives the percentage of values that share this combination of traits. In table 3.2.4 the variable has five categories to measure integration from lower level to higher, namely from lack of integration, to integration and high level of integration or assimilation. These categories are all inclusive so the rows sum to 100%. When dealing with a sample, it needs to estimate the proportions in the total population, the obtained figures necessarily needs to convert to *percentages*. This is done in table (3.2.4) that follows, so that readers are in no doubt about the size of the sample.

In addition, using the cross-tabulation can be explained as following because: (i) they are easy to understand. (ii) Cross-tabs can be used with any level of data; nominal, ordinal, interval, or ratio – they treat all date as if it is nominal. (iii) A table can provide greater insight than single statistics. (iv) It solves the problem of empty or sparse cells. (v) They are to conduct.

Moreover, a crosstab shows how many of the respondents who answered one question in a particular way answered another question in a particular way. So for example, it might show how many people who gave as their answer question 9 'the way of life is very different' then gave as the answer to question 13 'it is hard to find a job'. Table 3.2.4 shows that the total number people who answered question 9; in such a way were 23 and the total number who answered 13 as just indicated was 96. A cross-tab would show how many of the 23 also comprised the 96 who found it hard to find a job.

---

[297]Ibid., (p. 545).

Table 3.3.3 Data Table with percentages, standard deviation and means

Question Nr.	1	2	3	4	5	STD	AVG	F	A%	B%	C%	D%	E%	F%
Question 1	53	30	146	21	50	49.91	60		17.7	10.0	48.7	7.0	16.7	16.64
Question 2	26	80	142	30	21	51.72	59.8		8.7	26.7	47.3	10.0	7.0	17.24
Question 3	54	64	158	15	9	59.75	60		18.0	21.3	52.7	5.0	3.0	19.92
Question 4	17	27	192	28	26	75.04	58		5.7	9.0	64.0	9.3	8.7	25.01
Question 5	2	24	171	57	46	65.55	60		0.7	8.0	57.0	19.0	15.3	21.85
Question 6	15	21	170	61	33	63.98	60		5.0	7.0	56.7	20.3	11.0	21.33
Question 7	29	92	139	22	18	53.46	60		9.7	30.7	46.3	7.3	6.0	17.82
Question 8	50	79	161	7	3	64.65	60		16.7	26.3	53.7	2.3	1.0	21.55
Question 9	23	111	128	32	6	55.44	60		7.7	37.0	42.7	10.7	2.0	18.48
Question10	53	56	172	14	5	66.61	60		17.7	18.7	57.3	4.7	1.7	22.20
Question11	101	44	127	21	7	51.86	60		33.7	14.7	42.3	7.0	2.3	17.29
Question12	57	58	141	34	10	49.37	60		19.0	19.3	47.0	11.3	3.3	16.46
Question13	96	86	75	21	22	35.92	60		32.0	28.7	25.0	7.0	7.3	11.97
Question14	27	61	64	54	94	23.97	60		9.0	20.3	21.3	18.0	31.3	7.99
Question15	68	62	105	38	27	30.27	60		22.7	20.7	35.0	12.7	9.0	10.09
Question16	149	66	51	14	20	54.21	60		49.7	22.0	17.0	4.7	6.7	18.07
Question17	98	10	22	10	160	66.87	60		32.7	3.3	7.3	3.3	53.3	22.29
Question18	60	68	115	14	43	37.06	60		20.0	22.7	38.3	4.7	14.3	12.35
Question19	81	20	23	11	165	64.88	60		27.0	6.7	7.7	3.7	55.0	21.63
Question20	50	57	122	36	25	37.86	58		16.7	19.0	40.7	12.0	8.3	12.62
Question21	79	78	123	14	6	49.21	60		26.3	26.0	41.0	4.7	2.0	16.40
Question22	78	191	22	3	6	79.21	60		26.0	63.7	7.3	1.0	2.0	26.40
Question23	7	55	109	32	77	39.46	56		2.3	18.3	36.3	10.7	25.7	13.15
Question24	130	79	6	6	79	53.51	60		43.3	26.3	2.0	2.0	26.3	17.84
Question25	84	106	48	26	36	33.79	60		28.0	35.3	16.0	8.7	12.0	11.26
Question26	35	63	86	37	79	23.45	60		11.7	21.0	28.7	12.3	26.3	7.82
Question27	109	166	13	4	8	73.63	60		36.3	55.3	4.3	1.3	2.7	24.54
Question28	172	128				31.11	150		57.3	42.7	0.0	0.0	0.0	10.37
Question29	45	163	54	16	14	31.11	58.2	9	15.0	54.3	18.0	5.3	4.7	10.37
Question30	36	93	88	42	21	61.23	56		12.0	31.0	29.3	14.0	7.0	20.41

3.2.8 Chapter Conclusion

After completing the conceptual framework, statistical method is established here in chapter three. Then, demographic and quantitative analyses are applied in the following chapters four and five by using graphs and cross-comparison to measure the level of Turkish immigrants have been integrated into German society and the German way of life.[298]

In chapter four a pie-chart type graph was preferable for emphasizing how each category compared in the size with the whole. In order to illustrate category data pie-charts are used throughout the chapter. A circle is divided into slices, with the angle each makes at the centre of the circle being proportional to the percentage in the category concerned measuring the level of

---

[298] Patton, Michael Quinn: Qualitative Research and Evaluation Methods (3rd Ed.) Saga Publication, London, 2002, 'Qualitative Comparative Analysis' (p.477-492)

Turkish immigrants' integration into German society and the way of life. In other words, the intention with using pie-charts is to find a clearer visualisation than other types of chart for comparing each category slice with total.

In chapter five, bar-chart graphs are more preferable to compare the size of one category with that of others. Bar-charts seem clearer to compare one category with another (height of the column or percentages). A series of statistical models are employed in the chapter six.

In chapter seven primary and secondary data are compared to achieve a balanced integration level considered by both sides' point of views (namely Turkish self-perception on their integration and German public opinion on Turkish immigrants' attitudes towards Turkish integration).

As addressed in the research question, integration of Turkish immigrants and bilateral relations between Germany and Turkey are interrelated. Compared to Kohl government, the Schröder government's integration policy had been more positive than Kohl's. The Schröder government policy contributed to both the integration of Turkish immigrants and the bilateral relations, whereas, many Turks became naturalized Germans. Most of the naturalized Germans of Turkish descents have favoured to vote for the SPD and the Greens in German elections.

In the term of the German presidency of the EU, Turkey became a candidate country for the EU at the Cologne summit in 1999, by the aid of positive approach of Schröder government to Turkey's EU membership issue. In contrast to the Schröder government, the Merkel government is against Turkey's full membership of the EU and has employed a restrictive integration policy, especially with anti-dual citizenship policy. Merkel's policy has not been regarded as favourable by those Turkish immigrants who wish to maintain their Turkish nationality at the same time. They have been disappointed by Merkel government's anti-dual citizenship policy.

From historical perspective, Germans have contributed more than Turks to the bilateral relations. The Turco-German relations date to back to the 16th century. An Ottoman style mosque and Berlin's Turkish cemetery from 1863 shows that the bilateral relation is deep rooted in the common war time history between the Ottoman Empire and Germany. The Ottoman history shows that the Ottoman Empire was also a multinational, multi-religious and multicultural state which housed many ethnic nations over 8 centuries such as Greeks, Hungarians, Serbians, Romanians, Bulgarians and Caucasians included from the African states to Indian Oceans. The earliest record of Turks residing in Germany was in the early 1800s, but they were a small proportion of the German and other European countries' population. Ottoman Turks have long visited and perhaps some hundreds of them settled in the Holy Roman Empire as invading Ottoman troops advanced towards Vienna in the 1600s. Any troops who remained were eventually assimilated into the majority Christian European populations of the host countries.[299]

Towards the end of the Ottoman period, many German soldiers, industrialists and craftsmen who settled in the Ottoman capital Istanbul in 1889 were guests of Sultan Abdülhamid II. If someone wonders now why Germans called the Turkish labour migrants in the 1960s 'Guest workers', this is because the Germans were called 'guests' in Turkey. German General Colmar Freiherr von der Goltz, also known as Goltz Pasha, was the chief advisor of the Ottoman army; and General Otto Liman von Sanders who served as advisor and military commander of

---

[299] Article by Christina Schlötzer, June 6 2008, www.commongroundnews.org.de

the Ottoman Empire during the World War I. The Krupp family from Essen manufactured ammunition and armament in Istanbul. The German Foundation at the Sultanahmet square; Haydarpasa Train Station was constructed by German engineers in Istanbul. Sirkeci Train Station was also designed by the German architect August Jachmund in 1890. Berlin-Istanbul-Baghdad Railway was planned by Otto von Bismarck to connect Berlin to Baghdad through the Ottoman capital. The railway was built from 1903 to 1940. This project aimed to enhance the economic, political and strategic ties between Germany and the Ottoman Empire. Theodor Heuss a Bosporus German designed the German Cultural Centre in Istanbul and later he became the first president of West Germany from 1949 to 1959. The Ethnic Germans settled on the Bosporus, called 'Bosporus Germans'; Bosporus Germans held German nationality, spoke German and established German secondary and high schools. The Deutsche Schule is one of the oldest high schools of Turkey from 1884. When Turkish PM Erdoğan suggested Turkish schools in Germany in his visit in February 2008 in Munich, his speech was criticized by his German and Austrian counterparts. [300]

In the aspect of cultural relations between the two countries, there have also been many constructive developments. German professors helped to establishment of the Istanbul University in 1933, Atatürk encouraged the Germans to live in Istanbul who fled from the Nazis. Another ethnic German Ernst Reuther was also refugee from Nazis, lived in Ankara from1935 to 1946 and founded Daimler-Benz CEO, later he became major of West Berlin. His son Edzard Reuther grew up in Ankara designed a German-Turkish university (DTU) on the Bosporus in Istanbul. Edzard Reuther delivered a speech at the foundation ceremony of the DTU, "This is a glorious day for Turkish-German relations", he said in 2008. His dream came true last month. On 32 October 2010, the German-Turkish University (DTU) was opened by presidents of the two countries' in Istanbul. The DTU aims at contributing to bilateral relations as an educational asset. [301]

In the aspect of economic relations, until recent years Germany was the most exporting country of the world. Although Germany lost its title as 'the world's most exporting country' against Chine, it is still the largest trade partner of Turkey. [302]

---

[300] Ibid

[301] http.cbc.ca/world/story/2010/10/19turkey-germany-president.html Accessed on 20 October 2010

[302] Article by Sevil Küçükkoşum; Hürriyet Daily News, June 20 2010

Chapter 4

4.1 Chapter introduction

This chapter analyses Turkish immigrants' integration level within the thirty survey questions as a univariate or single variable by addressing the research question. The main question of this thesis is: 'Have Turkish immigrants integrated into Germany between years 1961-2007 and has their integration any impact on bilateral relations, either positively or negatively?' is intended to understand integration level of persons of Turkish origin into German society, their way of life and impact of their integration on bilateral relations. This study has undertaken a qualitative analysis of data taken from surveys of the Turkish-origin population conducted by the author in 3 cities in Germany and aims to investigate a range of issues. The research question has been critically analyzed and contains thirty questions and a literature review of existing scholarship which helps to test the main argument and discover new findings. Each is addressed individually to identify the most important facilitating and hindering factors of immigrants' integration.

This chapter focuses on single variable effects on integration of Turkish immigrants living in Germany and chapter six employs a bivariate analysis to explore connection between the survey questions, variables which have a joint effect.[303] The thirty questions were asked of respondents to investigate the level of Turkish immigrants' integration in Germany.[304] They relate to the economic life of immigrants, their social life, their personal life and their attitudes towards the German state and people. Some of the questions are closely related and interact with each other. For example, education and integration are most likely to be positively associated. The nature of these joint variables is dealt with in chapter five and six. The major purpose of this empirical analysis is to search for relationships among variables and test the main hypothesis as political phenomenon.

4.1.1 Question 1: How European do you feel?

The intent of the first question is to understand Turkish immigrants' feelings about their integration into European life. This is critical in supporting the main research question and a factual debate about European identity provides some structure to the many inter-connected

---

[303] Janet Buttolph Johnson, Richard A., Joslyn and H. T Reynolds: 'Political Science Research Methods', 5ʰ Edition, 2005 by CQ Press, Washington D.C., (339-402).

[304] Note: The term "migrants" to mean the total of emigrants and immigrants is often used interchangeably with immigrants, foreigners, foreign-born, ethnic minorities, and non-nationals. Immigrant is a legal term, while foreign-born is not. Layton-Henry argues that migrants to whom integration programs apply are not always migrants, but "ethnic minorities" a term generally used to refer to established communities founded by post war immigrants (Layton-Henry 1990: 6). They may be the children or even the grandchildren of migrants, commonly referred to as "second generation" or "third generation" immigrants. Germany's migrants are (i) labour migrants-Guest workers; (ii) ethnic migrants-Germans; (iii) illegal migrants: as tourists, asylum seekers, refugees or entering Germany through different ways.

issues. The hypothesis formulated is that if respondents 'feel' European, they are more likely to be substantially integrated into European host societies. To be fully aware of the complex nature of this question, readers need to understand concepts of 'Europeanness', what and who is a European and whether the concept of 'European identity' is sufficiently developed to have meaning in the everyday life.

The question of 'feeling European' is a multifaceted and sometimes emotional matter for many people who consider themselves for or against European commonality. It is possible for a respondent with European cultural and racial origins to express views entirely compatible with codified European values while denying and objecting to the idea that these values are representative of 'Europe'.

Post World War II, the concept of a common 'European identity' has been closely linked to pan-European institutions and since 1992 the European Union (EU). From its origins as a Western European customs union, the EU has grown through numerous treaties to represent common economic, political and social interests. The promotion of a common identity based on common values is intended to help further these interests. Common 'European values' in this context can be best described as a perspective on EU issues as influenced by political considerations rather than purely ethnocultural values derived from individual countries or peoples. Examples of this 'perspective' include positions on economic co-operation, fundamental human rights and infrastructure development. According to a Eurobarometer survey in 1996, about 51% of residents of the European Union felt 'European'.[305]

These questions will help to determine respondents' feelings of European identity, a factor which contributes to the integration of Turkish immigrants into post industrial German society. Secondly the question of the benefits to Turkish immigrants in being integrated into German society from aspects such as economic, social, cultural and political life will be explored and also the challenges and benefits to society as a whole for immigrants' integration.

The integration of immigrants interests both the European Union and Germany. Andrew Geddes notes that to exercise the legal, social and political rights of EU citizenship usually first requires being a citizen of a member state.[306] Thus, obtaining German citizenship might result from an administrative motivation rather than a question of identity in the case of Turkish immigrants in Germany. A very narrow interpretation is that Turks gain German citizenship only to have access to rights and benefits rather than feeling German and loyalty to the German State.[307]

This question will also help to find out where respondents feel they 'belong' when they live in Germany (geographically, at the heart of European continent). Do they feel a sense of belonging to somewhere else (for example, Anatolia - the Asian part of Turkey) or do they feel that they belong to both places at the same time? Because of Turkey's unique geographic position they might consider themselves belonging to both the European and Asian continents. They may feel European to a significant level but with some feeling of connection to Turkey and not necessarily hindered in their integration into German society. Ideologically, Europe and

---

[305] Eurobarometer, 1996
[306] Andrew Geddes / Adrian Favell (ed.): 'Politics of Belonging: Migrants and Minorities in Contemporary Europe'. Ashgate Publication, 1999, p.181.
[307] Ibid., p. 181

"European" has not only a meaning for Turkish immigrants in Germany, but also for Turks in Turkey since the Turkish Republic was founded by Kemal Atatürk in 1923. Atatürk's main goal was to achieve a European social environment, a European style democratic state and a similar level of economic development and welfare for Turkey. Since the foundation of the republic in 1923, Turkey has tirelessly tried to be accepted, culturally, politically and economically by the West in order to achieve the status of a modern European state. Turkey continued to follow western oriented policies based on democracy and the Market Economy. Within Turkey, the lobby of western Europeans and the Turkish German-educated elite is strong and would like Turkey to be westernised and secular. The Turkish army's role is also important as a guardian of Atatürk's ideas, and principles and secularism of the state which is guaranteed by the constitution.[308] Therefore, the integration of Turkish immigrants into German society is also a benefit for Turkey itself as the sending country.

Answers to these questions are related to the personal feelings of respondents. Therefore this survey starts with a direct question, to research how people feel about the continent of Europe. It is sometimes called Euro-Asia. From the 1490s onwards it is defined as the mainland of Europe. This question investigates Turkish immigrants' feelings as European while living in any European country, in Germany or somewhere else in Europe, on a 5 point scale. In this way, the questionnaire can be applied to Turkish immigrants in other European countries. Germany accommodates 2.4 of the 5.2 million population of Turkish origin in Europe and can be seen as representative of all European countries with regards to Turkish integration. Furthermore, Turkish immigrants who have any other EU state's nationality can live and work in Germany. [309]

Graph 1: Turkish immigrants' feeling as European

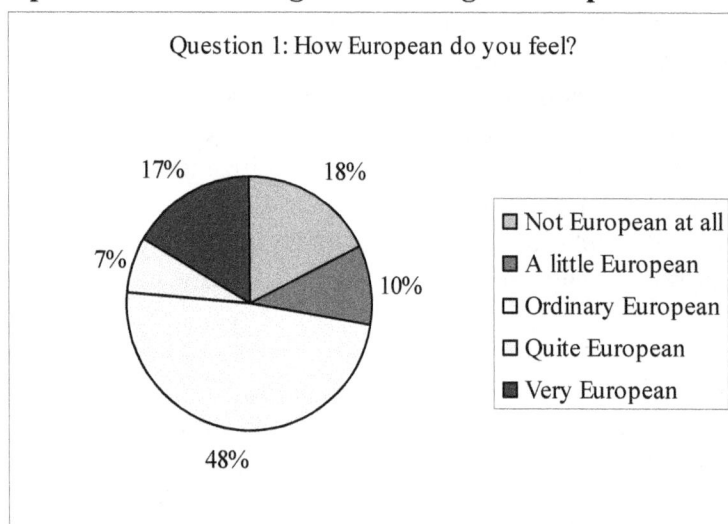

Question 1: How European do you feel?

17%   18%   7%   10%   48%

- Not European at all
- A little European
- Ordinary European
- Quite European
- Very European

Source: Author

---

[308] Facts about *Germany*: Churches and *religious communities*
www.tatsachen-ueber-deutschland.de/.../churches-and-religious-communities.html Accessed on 26 11 2010

[309] Source: Euro-stat July 1998; August and December, 2006

In the answer to the first question; 53 respondents or 18% responded that they feel 'not European at all'. This suggests these respondents suffer from a lack of integration; and are likely to belong to the first generation of Turkish guest workers (the older age group). 30 respondents or 10% replied "a little European", that they do not feel integrated into German society. Most of the respondents (146), 48% responded that they feel like 'Ordinary' Europeans and almost integrated into German society and the German way of life. 21 responded that they feel 'quite European', constituting 7% of Turkish immigrants that feel well integrated into German society. 50 respondents or 17% replied they feel 'Very European' meaning they are most likely to be very well integrated/assimilated into German society. In other words, these findings suggest quite a high level of integration at least on the single measure of feeling European. 49% consider themselves 'normally' European and a further 17% + 7% = 24% feel both very European and well integrated. The indicator of 'Very European' can be interpreted as a high level integration/assimilation which means that 17% of Turkish immigrants consider themselves as being assimilated into German society.

The second and third generation of Turkish descent are German-born, raised and educated in Germany. Of course, the lifestyle and personal values of these generations in Germany differ from Turks in Turkey. People's descent or origin is not important if they feel a member of the host society where they live in. Paula Casal explains that people's descent is not important but their feelings as follows:
"It doesn't matter where you've come from; it is where you are going that counts"
As a conclusion of the debate on the first question, considering 50 percent as statistically significant in integration (the majority), 72 percent (48% Ordinary + 7% Quite + 17% Very) shows an overwhelming majority of respondents feeling European or integrated into European society and the way of life.

4.1.2 Question 2: How German do you feel?

The purpose of the question is to explore the extent to which respondents feel German and to what degree they feel loyal to the German state and its institutions. For instance, if they feel German they are most likely to become integrated or are already integrated in German society. The first survey question 'How European do you feel?' could be asked of any EU or non-EU national including German citizens. 'How German do you feel? is aimed more specifically at German residents. 'Feeling European', while encompassing common values does not include national identity or sentiment and does not mean immigrants desire or are necessarily integrated into contemporary German society. Therefore, the second question was formulated.

Graph 2: Turkish immigrants' feelings of German identity

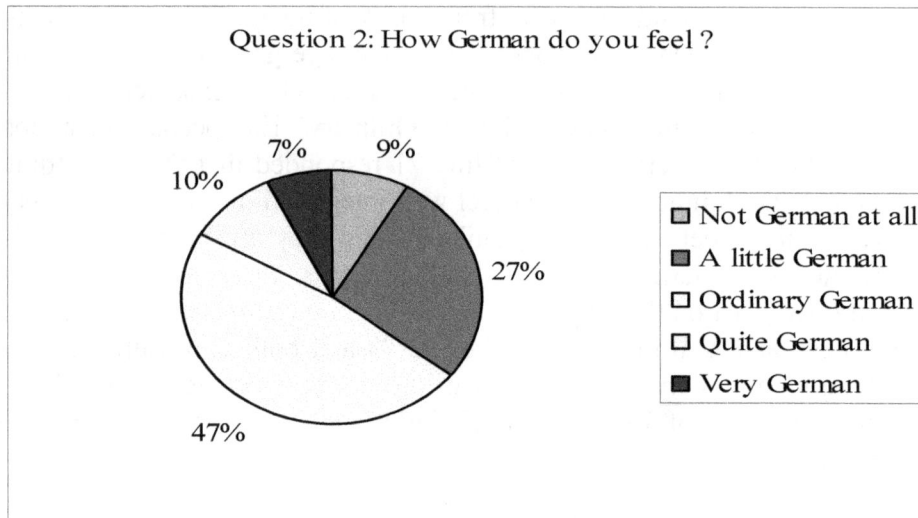

Question 2: How German do you feel ?

7%   9%

10%

27%

☐ Not German at all
■ A little German
☐ Ordinary German
☐ Quite German
■ Very German

47%

Source: Author

Graph 2 shows 9% of respondents feeling 'not German at all', 27% feeling 'A little German'. 47% of respondents feel 'Ordinary German'. Thirty respondents or 10% replied that they feel 'Quite German' and 21 respondents or 7% responded 'Very German'. Overall, 47%10%+7%=64% of respondents fell into the upper 3 categories, feeling German to a significant extent.

Adrian Favell argues that when immigrants are integrated into a national political and social culture, they are tolerated and welcomed more by the native society and politicians.[310] Asking the question in this way, gives information about socio-cultural and political feelings of "belonging" of immigrants in German society, their new identity (feeling degree of German ranging from 'A little' to 'fully German') as well as their loyalty level, whether to Germany or Turkey. Bruce Thornton argues that Turks are assimilated into German society but have little loyalty to Germany and benefit from the prosperity of German welfare.[311]

The result that more than a quarter of respondents or 27% feel 'A little German' may be explained by their age structure (comparing these two scores with age related question of the survey question 29 results which shows that this group's ages are 41-50 (18%) and over 50 (5%). Possible reasons for first and second generation Turkish immigrants' feeling 'not German at all' or 'a little German' could be barriers such as deprivation and homesickness after living in Germany for decades. Their social, cultural and educational background is certainly different from the younger generation's which creates a barrier to accepting German culture as well as a notable "generation gap". Due to their advancing age, lower level of education and lack of German language knowledge this group of Turkish immigrants are less willing and less likely to be integrated into German society than the German born generations of Turkish-origin youths. Significantly, their initial objective was not to stay in Germany permanently but to earn money

[310] Andrew Geddes and Adrian Favell: Politics of Belonging, Migrants and Minorities in Contemporary Europe. Ashgate Publication, 1999, p.220.
[311] Thornton, Bruce: Decline and Fall; Europe's slow motion suicide, Encounter Books, New York, 2007 (p. 48, 107,116)

and return home to build a better life. Economic circumstances changed however and some of them prolonged their stay in Germany until reaching retirement age.

A significant 64% of respondents feel 'Ordinary German', 'Quite German' and 'Very German'. This figure can be explained through integration factors such as school attendance and German language level. According to the survey question 24, 43.3% of them attended to German schools; and question 23 conducted as (How is your German?) in the mid-point 36.3% answered that their German is 'good'. It is likely that German is their first language or they are bilingual. If German-born Turkish youths feel integrated into German society and culture, this is a good sign but there is still a great challenge for them in the areas of educational achievement, career opportunity and making the most of employment facilities that Germany offers.[312]

For a comparison with the general population, results from a questionnaire on German National Identity by Hillary Burbank in 2003 suggest that feelings have changed across generations and vary between the states of the former GDR (East Germany) and West Germany[313].

Figure 4.1: Pride in German National Identity

COHORT	Pride in German Identity	Happiness in German Identity	Shame in German Identity	Desire for non-German Identity
Born before 1946	4.10 (1.24)	4.05 (1.22)	2.26 (1.60)	1.71 (1.27)
Born after 1976	3.05 (1.25)	3.18 (1.15)	2.39 (1.35)	2.47 (1.30)

Source: Burbank, H. (Table 2, 2003)

The above table shows the mean results from the 5 point scale of the 2003 questionnaire which was conducted with a representative sample of 2 age cohorts of the German population. A higher numerical result indicates a stronger positive response to the question asked. The younger cohort of respondents (born after 1976) show notably less pride and happiness in German identity and notably more shame and desire for a non-German identity than the older cohort. Further results show younger Germans holding more positive attitudes about immigrants' culture and acceptance of them. They are also less likely to describe themselves as patriotic. By contrast, the older generation expressed more pride and happiness to be German. People who self-identified as patriotic Germans were most likely to show signs of ethnocentrism rather than patriotism.

Looking at the two response groups of '9% do not feel German at all'; and '27% feel only a little German', it means 36% of respondents still feel themselves more Turkish than German. This group suffers from lack of integration into German society and is likely to live in an isolated (or a kind of Turkish) way in German society. A similar situation of disintegration is seen in the French case, which caused to rebellion of immigrants in 2005. The reasons behind the French immigration rebel turned up to be as isolation, lack of integration into French labour market and high unemployment rates among French immigrants. As a consequence, it is French

---

[312] Söhn, Janina and Özcan, Veysel: The Education Attainment of Turkish Migrants in Germany, Turkish Studies, March 2006, 7(1); 101-124.

[313] Burbank, Hillary (2003) German National Identity: Patriotism and Stigma, in the *Stanford Undergraduate Research Journal*, Volume 2 – Spring 2003. Via web 21-06-2009: http://surj.stanford.edu/2003/pdfs/GermanIdentity.pdf

governments' ignorance and wrong integration policy.[314] As to, the percentages of scale four (10%) and five (7%), total 17% feel 'quite German' and 'very German' are most likely to be from the third generation German born Turkish descent youths) feel Germany as a true home for themselves. It means that 17% is deeply assimilated into German society and the way of life. However, these percentages are far from 50% significant percentage and German public expectation.

In conclusion, question two is also age influenced which shows us that there is a generation gap between the first generation Turkish guest workers and the third generation German born and German educated Turkish descent immigrant youths. Thus, their feelings changes in accordance with their age structure (Further investigation of Turkish immigrants' age structure and its impact on their integration into Germany is in question 29).

4.1.3 Question 3: Which language do you speak at home?

The purpose of asking which language persons of Turkish origin speak at home is to explore their use of language in daily life. Putting the question in this way is intended to investigate issues of language use in the public and private sphere. Firstly, there have been allegations in German media and newspapers that Turks do not speak German at all at home and tend to establish a (*Parallelgesellschaft*) Turkish speaking parallel societies in Germany; and "the Turks are moving away from integrating into German society to create a parallel society. Even the younger generation of Turkish descent speak Turkish in the street".[315]

An increasing use of German can be regarded as an indicator of improving integration. In a 2005 article, Sefer Çinar, the Turkish Union of Berlin spokesman commented:

> "Until the 1990s, nobody demanded that the Turks speak German, because they were just expected to do the dirty jobs, and everyone thought they would go back to Turkey and not stay here," he said. "So people didn't bother learning the language or putting down roots. They didn't integrate, they didn't adapt."[316]

If respondents speak German at home they are able to speak German everywhere. A common assumption to be tested is that immigrants might speak Turkish at home and at least get by in German outside the home. This question also aims to investigate respondents' general proficiency in German and importantly for the purpose of this thesis the impact of use of the

---

314 Newsweek, April 10 2006, By Oliver Roy, Seen on the Streets: The French protests are about much more than jobs, Elites don't get it.

[315] The NewYork Times. "German society fears is the entrenchment of a Turkish-speaking parallel society"; Nicholas Kulish's Article based on Victor Homola's contribution from Berlin, Published 11 November 2007

An article by Baron Bodissey, Published on 5 January, 2009 in Cologne Vingst (Leftist newspaper) on a research of Jürgen Friederichs from University of Cologne. "Germany's Parallel Society Is Intact".

An article by Aaron Erlich 'Germany's Second Doubts About Its Turkish Immigrants', Published in History News Network, George Mason University, July 11, 2005.

[316] Collier, R. (2005), Germany copes with integrating Turkish minority Immigration reform on agenda after decades of separate, unequal treatment. *San Francisco Chronicle* 13-11-2005. Accessed via web 28-06-2009: http://www.runder-tisch-usa.de/berlin-ankara/site/reports/pdfs/Germany_copes_with.pdf

German language on the integration process. A discussion about Turkish immigrants' German language level and the role of German language on Turkish immigrants' integration in Germany will be continued in question twenty-three 'How good is your German?"

The significance of learning and using the host language can be considered as one of the key influences of German society on Turkish immigrants whether first-generation or of subsequent generations, because a language can only be adapted marginally by its users and has multifaceted effects on the integration of immigrants. From a social aspect the German language is relevant from their first contact with host society members. More interaction means speaking more German and less Turkish in daily life.

Early use of German is important for child development. In a 2000 article, the headmaster of a Berlin primary school noted that "many children are struggling at school because they learn no German at home".[317] From a political aspect, the capability of speaking German well would help them access the political mechanisms of the country and subsequently German nationality through integration. All mainstream German political parties show an interest in Turkish immigrants' integration. They use Turkish-language posters during election campaigns and welcome Germans of Turkish descent to become member of their parties to target naturalised Turkish Germans' votes. In summer 2001 a Commission established by the SPD/Green coalition reviewed German immigration policy and attempted to speed immigrants' integration into German society. The report of the commission published in summer 2001 began by stating that Germany needs immigrants and that it needed to integrate them successfully. The commission looked across the border to Dutch policy to argue that all foreigners should learn the German language and raised the possibility of 'integration contracts' offering a quicker path to unlimited residence and work permits for foreigners who passed a language test. The Commission also proposed that more German language courses be offered to resident foreigners, with funding doubled to teach 220,000 persons a year. Furthermore, EU measures for successful integration underline 'the importance of knowledge of the host society's language, history and institutions is indispensable to integration; enabling immigrants to acquire this basic knowledge is essential to successful integration within the framework of EU integration policy'.[318]

From an economic aspect, immigrants' linguistic abilities are a major factor in their capability to earn a livelihood. Concerning French immigrants' protests in the suburbs of Paris in 2005 Faruk Şen argues that 'Most of the French immigrants are French citizens and they speak French fluently, but speaking host country's language and gaining its passport is not sufficient for integration'.[319]

Including a linguistic question aids the investigation of the role of the German language in integration. Proficiency in the host country's language is a key facilitating factors which enables immigrants' access to social and legal institutions of the host country as well as to enable

---

[317] Karacs, I.: Germany's Turkish children sink into the underclass, *The Independent on Sunday*, 12 November 2000. Accessed via the web 28-June-2009: http://www.independent.co.uk/news/world/europe/germanys-turkish-children-sink-into-the-underclass-622943.html

[318] EU Commission's Action plan of May 2005 (Conclusion 10 on immigrant integration policy Annex, Point 2)

[319] Şen, Faruk: TAM – Türkiye Araştırmaları Vakfı - Stiftung Zentrum für Türkeistudien – Turkey Research Centre Association, University of Essen, 2005

their integration into host country socially, politically and culturally. Conceptually, if a Turkish immigrant has good proficiency in the German language, this is most likely to contribute towards their integration into German society.

Graph 3: Which language do you speak at home?

Question 3: Which language do you speak at home?

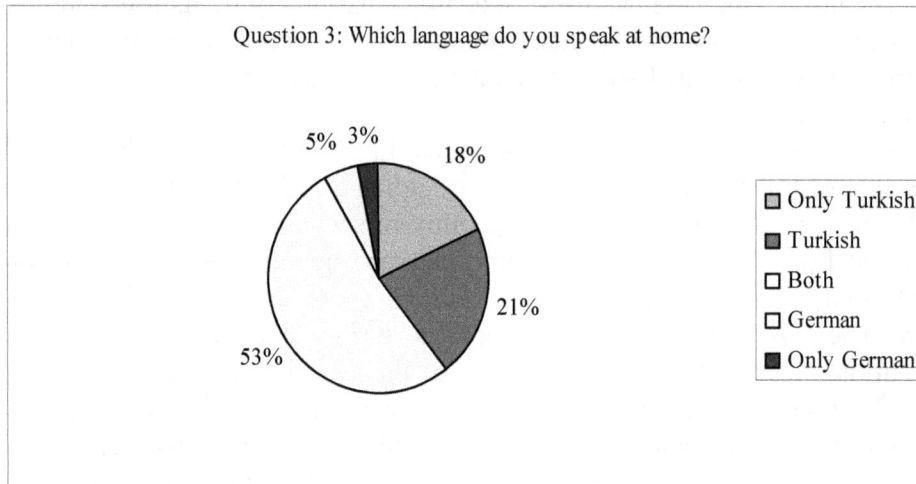

Graph 3 shows that 54 respondents or 18% of them speak 'only Turkish' at home (their mother-tongue). 64 respondents or 21% speak 'mostly Turkish' at home. 158 people or 53% of respondents say that they speak both languages (German and Turkish). 15 people or 5% speak mostly German. 9 people or 3% speak German at home all the time.

As a conclusion, the majority (53%+5%+3% = 61%) speak both languages (Turkish and German) and this percentage has a significant impact on integration of Turkish immigrants and for keeping a balance between two cultures and languages. They are likely to be integrated into German society and at the same time maintain some degree of connection to their home culture and social values. Use of German at home means they are bilingual to an extent. Linguist Vivian Cook argues that bilingualism increases communication skills and language awareness. She also argues that the first language or mother tongue has an important effect on learning a second language.[320] Due to the high birth rate of Turkish immigrants in Germany, the Turkish language community of pupils is the second largest in German schools after German speakers. By the way of comparison in the United Kingdom; the Turkish language is the seventh most commonly used language. In general, Turkish speakers constitute Europe's third largest minority language community. A significant limiting factor is that the maintenance of a true dual linguistic identity requires formal language tuition in both languages.[321]

---

[320] Cook, Vivian; Basetti, B.: Bilingual Cognition and Language Teaching, EUROSLA Basel, 2002 (pp. 13-37).

[321] Faist, Thomas & Özveren, Eyüp: 'Turkish Migrant Broadcasting in Berlin'; Turkish-German Transnational Social Spaces, Ashgate, 2004, p. 194, 201-202).

4.1.4 Question 4: How religious do you think you are?

The aim of asking respondents this question is to investigate the effect of Turkish immigrants' religious feelings and from religious aspect on their integration into German society. This is an important consideration because religious distinctiveness is a notable factor in the lives of Turkish immigrants and the assumption, that a moderate attitude to religion is a positive affecting factor which makes integration easier, can be tested. The religious communities in Germany are comprised of Catholics 31.5 %, Protestants 31.1%, Muslims 3.9 % and Jews 0.1 %.[322] The effect of religion can be seen in many different aspects of Turkish immigrants' integration. For example, second and third generation Turkish origin, German-born youths raised and educated in the German education system have arguably a more moderate attitude towards religion. They are more likely to be integrated into the host society and to have found the integration process easier when compared with earlier generations. In a 2000 article, Eren Ünsal, an educationalist and spokeswoman of Berlin's Turkish Association commented on barriers to early-years education of Turkish-origin children that parents are "reluctant to put their offspring in a non-Muslim environment in their impressionable early years"[323].

This question attempts to discover the influence of religious belief on the integration process and to investigate whether inflexible religious feelings or politicised religious influences are more likely to be a hindering factor of immigrants' integration into a diverse society.

A view of public opinion (in the EU member states in 1988) on immigrant rights, broken down by religion, is old but is the only available opinion poll on religious attitudes of member states in the EU. Of the five religious categories illustrated as follows: Protestants were the most likely to want to restrict the rights of non-EU immigrants, with nearly one-third (32%) expressing this preference. Approximately one-fifth of Catholics, Orthodox, or those with no religious affiliation preferred the restriction of rights for non-EU nationals (17%, 20%, and 19% respectively).The groups that were least likely to wish for such restrictions fell into 'other' category (primarily Jewish, Muslim, Buddhist, and Hindus).[324]

Although the Muslim population in Germany makes up only 3.9% of the total population, the perception of Islam in Germany is negative. For example, a survey held in 2003 shows that up to 46% of the respondents think 'Islam is a backward religion. Another survey was conducted on 2004 shows that more than 60% of Germans think that Islam is oppressing women'. In 2006, only 30% of Germans have a 'favourable' opinion of Islam.[325]

The complexity of the question of religious attitudes affecting the integration of persons of Turkish origin is increased by the effects of Atatürk's secular ideology. The Turkish Republic

---

[322] Euro-barometer 30, 1988 (15,136) reveals Public opinion on the rights of non-EU immigrants by religion (Catholic; Orthodox Protestant, Other, None. Other includes primarily Jewish, Muslim, Buddhist and Hindu). Question: Talking about these people living in(name of country) who are neither (nationality) nor citizens of the European Community, do you think we should extend their rights, restrict their rights or leave things as they are? (restrict, keep the same, extend)

[323] Karacs, I. (2000), Germany's Turkish children sink into the underclass, The Independent on Sunday, 12 November 2000. Accessed via the web 28-June-2009: http://www.independent.co.uk/news/world/europe/germanys-turkish-children-sink-into-the-underclass-622943.html

[324] Eurobarometer, 1988

[325] Sources: www.euro-islam.info Die Bundesregierung this article is extracted from (www.euro-islam.info)

was founded by Kemal Atatürk in 1923 after the collapse of the Ottoman Empire. Hakan Karakuş argues that "Atatürk's secular state was based on Western norms to create a new western style society and secular nation-state. The Turkish military, as designated by the constitution is the 'protector' of Ataturk's ideology and has authority to intervene in the political system under certain condition."[326]

Since foundation of the Turkish Republic by Kemal Ataturk in 1923, the Turkish Army functioned as a valve of democracy in Turkey beside its main defence duty against threats from inside and outside. A strong army is always good for maintain of democracy in Turkey, since political parties from time to time fail to protect democratic system in Turkey. From democratic perspective, the Turkish army resembles a trade union in the Scandinavian welfare states (Denmark, Sweden and Norway). Scandinavian welfare states are considered a democracy laboratory of Europe due to their strong trade unions.

Mehmet Okyayüz, a migration expert and professor of political science at Middle East Technical University in Ankara, the Turkish capital, said many Turks in Germany are "caught in a time wrap," clinging to traditions that in many parts of Turkey no longer exist. "The majority of Turks in Germany are more traditional than many Turks here."[327] He lived for 33 years in Germany and returned to his native country in 1994. He cited the case of a friend who has long lived in Germany, "a normal Turk, not an intellectual," and who has visited his country of origin many times in recent years. "I invited him to speak to my classes, and he was astonished by what he saw there among the students; young men with long hair and earrings, women in the same kind of dress you probably see in San Francisco." [328]

With question four the aim was to link an investigation into respondents' level of belief with the main research question; to what extent they have been integrated into German society and whether Islam is a hindering factor for their integration into German society! Udo Steinbach argues that Turkey's secular system and moderate Islamic dimension have not constituted a problem during the cold war period for the integration of Turkish immigrants across Europe. Although Turks arguably do not share the same religious culture as Western Europeans, Turkish immigrant workers in Europe are not considered hindered in their integration into their host European countries including Germany. [329] So there must be additional factors outside the religious sphere at work such as cultural, economic, political or linguistic barriers.

For some sections of the Turkish-origin community, especially those who immigrated from communities with a strict traditional manner there is a difficulty in framing their religious views without the accompanying traditional modes of behaviour (such as strict separation of males and females in public places). The difficulty of separating religious views from the culture

---

[326] Karakuş, Hakan: Turkey and the EU, Kemalism's Effects on the Road to the EU, MA Thesis, Naval Postgraduate School, September, 2005 (p. 3-7)

[327] Collier, R., San Francisco Chronicle. (2005) Germany copes with integrating Turkish minority Immigration reform on agenda after decades of separate, unequal treatment. *San Francisco Chronicle*, 13 November 2005

[328] Ibid.

[329] Udo Steinbach, 'Turkey-EEC relations: The Cultural Dimension: In Erol Manisali ed., Turkey's Place in Europe Economic, Political and Cultural Dimension (Istanbul: Logos, 1988), p.13.
Bernard Lewis, 'The Return of Islam; Community, 1 (1974) pp.40 and 76 'Turkey and the West, Changing Political and Cultural Identities' Ed., Metin Heper, Ayşe Öncü and Heinz Kramer; published in 1993 by I. B. Tauris & Co Ltd., London.

of religious practice is especially difficult in societies with liberal cultural values such as Germany.[330]

Differently to France, Turkish Islamic leaders in Germany encourage Turkish immigrants to integrate into German society, gain German citizenship and self-identify as German Muslims. Moreover, Osman Yumakoğullari, as the president of the National View Organisation in Germany, declared at a congress of his organisation in June 1995. "The expectation that Turkish Islam in Europe will increasingly focus on Integration of Turkish immigrants into Western European society, therefore, seems not at all far-fetched". [331] A survey related to religion suggests that Islam is the third largest religion in Germany, which was carried out by Yasemin Karakuşoğlu, on cultural and religious identity of Turkish immigrants in the German states North Rhine-Westphalia and Hesse in 1995. One third of children under age of six are of immigrant origin. In many German cities, immigrant-descended youths make up 40% of the young German population.[332]

Emine Demirbüken-Wegner argues that "religious lessons in German schools should not only be about Christianity but also other religions such as Islam."[333]

Graph 4: Measuring of Turkish immigrants' attitude towards religion

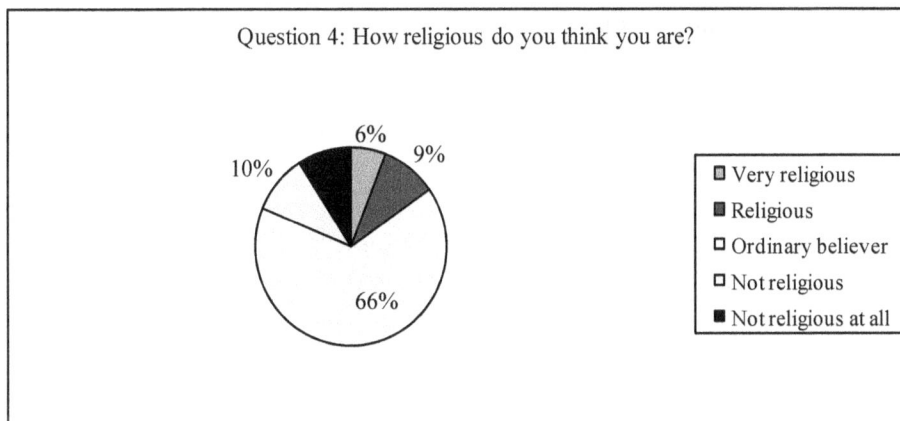

Question 4: How religious do you think you are?

- Very religious
- Religious
- Ordinary believer
- Not religious
- Not religious at all

Source: Author

Graph 4 shows that 17 respondents or 6% feel very religious but they do not feel themselves extremist or fundamentalist. 27 respondents or 9% feel religious but also consider themselves 'ordinary believers' in German society. Such small percentages 6% and 9% should not create for them a barrier on their integration. 192 respondents or 66 percent answered that

[330] Çınar, Alev (2005): Modernity, Islam, and Secularism in Turkey, University of Minnesota Press, 2005, p.240 ISBN:0-8166-4411-X

[331] Kastoryano, Riva (2003), Research Article: France, Germany and Islam: Negotiating Identities, Immigrants and Minorities, Volume 22, Numbers 2-3/ July 2003, pp.280-297

[332] Yasemin Karakuşoğlu: "Turkische Muslime in Nord Rhein Westfalen", research paper for Turkish Studies Centre, Universiy of Essen, , 1995

[333] Article by Janet Schayan: Diversity in focus: living together in Germany , 19 November 2010 http;//www.germantyandafrica.diplo.de/Vertretung/proteria_dz/en/startseite.htlm

they are ordinary believers. 28 respondents or 9.3 percent immigrants believe but they feel more secular than other immigrants. 26 respondents or 9 percent expressed that they do not felt at all religious.

As a conclusion, the outcome of survey question four implies that having a different belief from the host majority is not a hindering factor as economic or unemployment. 66% of respondents classify themselves as 'ordinary believers'. Therefore religion is not a huge barrier to their integration. If we include in this point respondents who are 'not religious' and 'not religious at all' add other percentages upon this i.e. 66 % + 10 % + 9 % = 85 %? If just ordinary levels of beliefs are not barriers to integration, then, a fortiori, absence of religious belief is also not a barrier. 192 respondents answered [the mid-point 3] into consideration which the percentage is higher than 50% and has significant impact on their integration. It means that Turkish immigrants' moderate attitude to religion and specifically Islam is not a hindering factor for their integration into German society and way of life.

4.1.5 Question 5: How are your relations with people at work?

This question concerns the quality and development of immigrants' workplace relations with native Germans, which is a significant factor in their overall social integration. The survey findings are discussed and related to issues of social and cultural interaction in the workplace.

The first (guest-worker) generation of Turkish immigrants has a well documented profile. They were mostly men and approximately one-third was qualified or specialised workers. They worked overwhelmingly in factory environments, in the manufacturing, heavy industry and materials processing sectors.[334]

In a BBC interview in 2004, a manager who came to Germany from Turkey in 1969 commented on the working environment at the time which is a good first-person account of the starting point from which the extent of integration can be measured; "When we first came here we were treated like children who don't know anything, I was a real professional, but the German workers wouldn't let us touch the machines. These machines were like toys for us in Turkey, we were used to them."[335]

Research from 1969, concerning workplace satisfaction or grievance concurs with the personal statement above, that the guest worker generation were competent and found suitable for the jobs they were assigned to[336]. Nevertheless, they faced identifiable social obstacles to workplace integration, which relate directly to the main research question of this thesis and are still in the process of being overcome. Most significantly, the effect of how the socio-economic status, meaning of job, salary level, housing and lifestyle of the guest workers was perceived by Germans was not fully understood or compensated for by the authorities. For example, the poor living conditions of guest workers and their initial lack of understanding of German social life caused a perception that the Turkish immigrants lived to substantially lower standards than

---

[334] Minority Rights Group International, *World Directory of Minorities and Indigenous Peoples – Germany: Turks, 2008,* accessed via web 30-06-2009: http://www.unhcr.org/refworld/docid/49749d1a41.html
[335] Furlong, R. 2004, German Turks question EU fate, *BBC News Online,* 10 Dec 2004 - Accessed via web 30-06-2009: http://news.bbc.co.uk/1/hi/world/europe/4086507.stm
[336] Abadan Unat, N. (1969) Turkish Workers in West Germany: A Case Study, *109th Wilton Park Conference – Immigrant and Migrant Labour – The resulting tensions in affluent countries,* Feb 2-15 1969, Steyning Sussex

126

Germans, creating a considerable barrier to social acceptance.[337] This issue is investigated further in questions 6, 9, 10, 12, 14, 18, 20 and 21.

Significantly, as discussed in Chapter one, guest workers were seen as temporary workers who would return home after a few of years. This status was used by the West German government to counter anti-immigration and protectionist arguments so it can be argued that native German workers did not see the purpose of expending time and effort to get to know them personally. Further information from the 1969 research reveals that 77% of guest workers had never visited a native German family.[338] The language barrier was also significant as German language teaching provision was inadequate in the 1960s, also due in part to the guest workers' perceived temporary stay. Issues relating to language are discussed further in survey questions 3 and 23. Economic factors also played a role. In the 1960s there was general agreement that Germany's labour shortage should be reduced with immigrant workers. The main reasons for this were generational workforce losses due to the aftermath of World War II and political restrictions on surplus East German labour moving West during the "cold war" years. Nevertheless there was a feeling that Turkish immigrant, seen as "cheap" labour would suppress wages among working-class Germans.[339] Related to this, their objectives, to earn as much money as possible in the shortest possible time often through large amounts of overtime clashed with the established balance of productivity of the native German workforce. Later, rising unemployment caused by the 1973 oil crisis among other factors, caused tensions between native workers and guest workers who were seen as taking jobs that would otherwise go to Germans. These factors led to bad feelings and mistrust in the workplace which further hindered the integration process.

A comprehensive study of Turks' social contact with Germans was conducted in 1985 among 43,343 Germans and 9,676 Turkish members of the workforce at Ruhrkohle AG in the Ruhr industrial region. The study showed that most Turks were interested in developing social contacts with Germans both at work and more generally but were still hindered by the previously mentioned obstacles. In 1971, 25% of the guest worker accommodation in North Rhine-Westphalia was found to be barrack rooms.[340]

---

[337] H., Korte, V., Eichener, G., Koch and K., Schmidt (1986): Die situation der auslandischen Arbeitnehmer und ihrer Familiengehoringen in der Bundesrepublik, Reprasentativuntersuchung 1985,ed.Bunderminister fur Arbeit und Socialordnung, Bonn, 1986. Forschungsbericht im Auftrag des Bundesministers fur Arbeit und Socialordnung, Bonn, 1986, p.345.

[338] Abadan Unat, N. (1969) Turkish Workers in West Germany: A Case Study, *109th Wilton Park Conference – Immigrant and Migrant Labour – The resulting tensions in affluent countries*, Feb 2-15 1969, Steyning Sussex

[339] Günter Wallraff: 'Lowest of the Low' (*Ganz Unten* or "*Ich Ali*"), Verlag Kiwepenheur, Kö ln, 1985, (p. 127).

[340] H.Korte,, V. Eichener., Koch and K.Schmidt (1985): Die Wohnsituation der auslandischeen Mitarbeiter der Ruhrkohle AG.Forschungsbeicht, Bochum-Essen, 1985-Schrift-enreihe Landes-und statentwicklungsforschung des Landes Northrhein-Westfalia.

Graph 5: Measuring of Turkish immigrants' feeling towards German colleagues

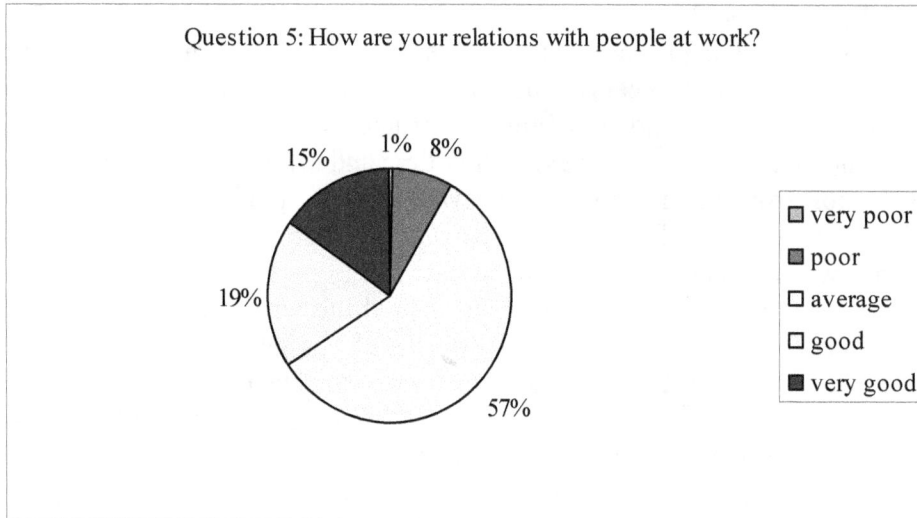

Question 5: How are your relations with people at work?

15% 1% 8%

19%

57%

- very poor
- poor
- average
- good
- very good

Source: Author

Graph five shows that only 2 respondents or 0.1% have 'very poor' relationships with native German workers; 24 respondents or 8% of immigrants answered 'poor'. 171 or 57% answered that they have 'average' relationships at work. 57 respondents or 19% stated that they have a 'good' relationship. 46 respondents or 15% find their relationships 'very good', or excellent at work. A significant point from graph five are the figures for 'good relations' 57% + 'very good relations' 19% + 15% 'too good relations' = 91% of respondents in total feeling at least satisfied with their working relationships. This is an indicator of a successful level of integration of Turkish immigrants. This figure also indicates they are less likely to be unemployed when they are socially integrated. It is easier for socially integrated immigrants to find a job in a technologically developed post-industrial country like Germany where team working and good communications are essential.

Legal and social changes since the 1990s have resulted in considerable improvements in workplace relations and are relevant to understanding the extent to which overall integration has improved. Most significantly, the interaction between native Germans and persons of Turkish origin in the workplace helped to reduce the initial misconceptions and mistrust between the two groups. To put it simply, they got to know each other. A study on German and Turkish Managers in Joint Ventures in 2004 investigated how colleagues contend with the interaction process. The conclusion was that a clear focus on the business objectives and good communication without assumptions of common "social and mental representations" helped to overcome subjective opinions when Germans and Turks are interacting as colleagues.[341] The study indicates however, that its respondents were highly motivated to optimise their interactions in the interests of their business. Such positive action to further integration may not be possible if the parties are unwilling. Further conclusions are that cultural and religious differences do not affect interaction but relative socio-economic status is an important factor. Improvements in socio-economic status

---

[341] Pécoud, Antoine (July 2003). "Self-Employment and Immigrants' Incorporation: The Case of Turks in Germany". *Immigrants and Minorities* 22 (2-3): 247–261. doi:10.1080/0261928042000244853.

are highly relevant to the extent to which the latest generations of Turkish origin are perceived in Germany.

Compared with the guest worker era, there are now many examples of successful and high achieving persons of Turkish origin in business, politics and sport. They are able to act as role models and provide practical advice through mentoring and civic activities. In 1997, Turkish employers created 47,000 jobs in Germany. In 2004, Germany's approximately 65,000 Turkish origin entrepreneurs had sales of €29.5 billion. Increased numbers of Turkish origin managers and supervisors provide role models in the workplace and help to dismiss negative stereotypes that Turkish origin workers are only manual labourers.[342]

From a political perspective, the mainstream political parties now give the issue of integrating immigrants much more priority and their more positive national policies affect public and private sector employment practices directly. The most significant change is to the German nationality law which now facilitates the naturalisation of persons of foreign origin. It is now more accepted (compared with the 1960s) that immigrants intending to stay in Germany should become citizens who have certainly changed the earlier view that persons of Turkish origin were only temporary residents. An increasing proportion of persons of Turkish origin were born, educated and trained in Germany. (The significance of this is explored further in question 22, "where were you born?") In relation to workplace issues all of the identified obstacles to integration have less impact on someone who has spent their entire life in Germany. Improvements in the representation of Turkish origin workers have caused a significant impact on their perception and treatment in the workplace. This is partly due to the increased numbers naturalised as German citizens but mostly due to awareness of and participation in the process of gaining workplace rights. There are numerous trade union and works council representatives of Turkish origin and trade union representation has increased protection against discrimination and harassment. EU-driven anti-discrimination and human rights legislation has also had a positive effect.

In the social aspect, the living conditions of persons of Turkish origin have improved considerably as people moved out of employer-provided accommodation and into privately rented and purchased property. The younger generation are surrounded by German culture.

Certainly, limiting factors are still evident. The overall economic situation and the year-on-year decrease in demand for unskilled labour is reflected in the lack of training and apprenticeship opportunities for those with a low level general education. Unqualified workers may find themselves unable to progress in any prospective career or gain skills and this problem appears to affect immigrant workers disproportionally. Developments in Europe, notably German re-unification and EU enlargement have allowed large numbers of ethnic German workers to enter the former West German labour market, reducing opportunities for other groups including workers of Turkish origin.

It can be concluded that some of the factors that limited the integration of workers from the "guest worker" generation have been overcome through increased interaction and the improved legal and regulatory environment. The Turkish origin workforce is no longer seen as

---

[342] Ibid.

"temporary" and a much higher proportion are able to communicate effectively in German. Increased political representation through trade unions and political parties resulted in significant gains. Social barriers to integration in the workplace remain, however and the key issue of relative socio-economic status, as reflected in the limited opportunities and negative perceptions of Turkish origin workers is a significant barrier to the process of integration.

4.1.6 Question 6: How is the indigenous people's attitude towards you?

This question is designed to examine local Germans' attitudes towards Turkish immigrants in German society. Integration is a two-way process associated with the interaction between Germans and immigrant community members and an important factor for Turkish immigrants is being accepted by host society members and feelings about treatment they receive from native Germans, both as neighbours and workmates in German society.

At a local level the perception of the status and lifestyle of persons of Turkish origin as neighbours and community members is the most significant affecting factor of native Germans' attitudes towards them. The different regions of Germany have diverse standards in terms of community behaviour (compare inner-city Hamburg with rural areas for example) and the ability and willingness of persons of Turkish origin to "fit in" with the local community is essential.

A survey in 1992 indicates that young Germans are more likely to accept immigrants than older Germans and measures put an end to their exclusion from their rights. 30% of young Germans under twenty-five agreed with the statement: "I don't like many foreigners in my country", while 51% suggest that immigrants should be integrated, 19% want all foreigners to leave the country. Among older Germans, 40% express that they do not like many foreigners in the country. 31% of older Germans think foreigners should be assimilated into German society. 29% of older people have moderate attitudes to foreigners.[343]

As Turkish immigrants' integration process has become one of the key issues in German politics, an increasing number of Germans migrate to Turkey on a permanent basis every year. Those Germans who settled earliest in the 1920s are called Bosphorus Germans, whose roots go back to the time of the Ottoman Empire and Kaiser Wilhelm II. The second wave of Germans migrated to Turkey from 1933 onwards when the National Socialists came to power in Germany. They were granted Turkish citizenship and maintained dual nationality. Cem Şentürk describes Germans in Turkey as

> "The descendants of trades' people, military personal, and academics of German origin that came to Turkey during the Ottoman Empire since 1847. The German migration continued also during World War II, thousands of Jews refugees and political activists fled from Germany to Turkey". [344]

A large number of Germans go on holiday to Turkey and they discover Turkish society first hand. They interact in the Turkish language and many buy a summer house or flat on the

---

[343] The Conference on Security and Co-operation in Europe (CSCE) become the Organization for Security and Co-operation in Europe (OSCE) in December 1994.
[344] Article by Cem Şentürk: 'The Germans in Turkey' TAM (Turkish Research Centre-Essen University) Publication, Monday 15 October 2007, 14 percent Germans are interested in purchasing real estate in Turkey.

Mediterranean coast (especially in towns of Alanya, Manavgat, and Side), where there are more than 60,000 German residents, and the Aegean coastal towns of Fethiye, Bodrum, Çeşme, Didim, and Marmaris. [345] A good level of relationship between the two countries reflected by the sending and receiving of people makes the integration of immigrants easier. Such social contacts and interaction contributes to increase mutual understanding between the two societies which is vitally important to integration. According to TAM, "As of April 2005, of the 49,567 immovable properties owned by foreigners, 41,413 belonged to German nationals". [346] The number of German migrants in Turkey, estimated at 60,000 is not as large as the number of Turkish immigrants in Germany. [347]

Graph 6: Measuring the perception of Germans' attitude towards Turkish immigrants of German attitudes

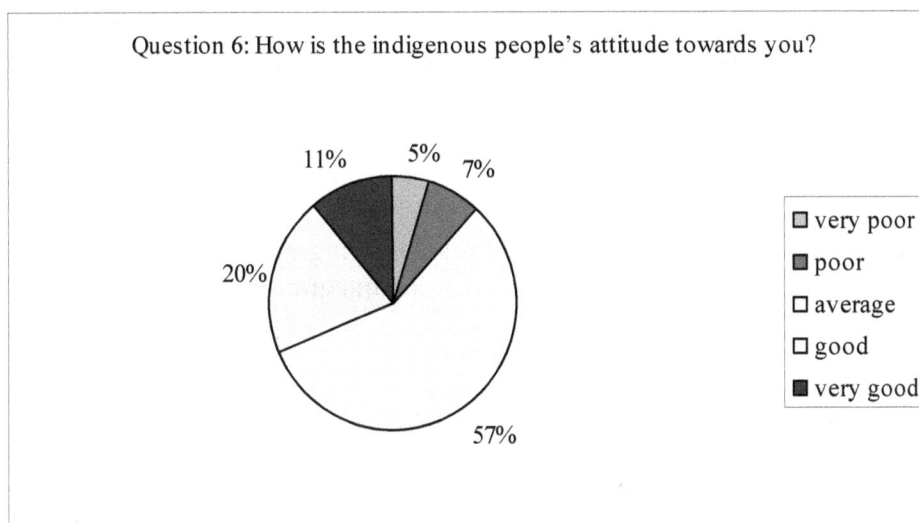

Question 6: How is the indigenous people's attitude towards you?

- very poor
- poor
- average
- good
- very good

Source: Author

Graph six shows that 15 respondents or 5% think that native Germans have negative attitudes towards them; 21 respondents or 7% felt the hosts are 'not bad'; 170 respondents or 56% like to associate with local people and felt content, 61 respondents or 20% find local people 'very good'; 33 people or 11% think their hosts are 'very hospitable'.

Negative sentiments of the native population make immigrants feel less loyal to their host state, eventually less willing to be integrated into a seemingly inhospitable host society. As argued earlier in chapter three, the integration policies of the 16 German federal states are

---

[345] The Turkish Ministry of Housing and Public Works Report, Ankara; 16 June 2008. *Turkish parliament allows property sales to foreigners.*

[346] Turkish Research Centre-Essen University, Publication October 2007, 26th Issue

[347] Faist, Thomas & Özveren, Eyüp: 'German Migrants in Turkey' Turkish-German Transnational Social Spaces, Ashgate, 2004 (p. 91-110)

different and policies change from state to state. Statistically it seems that Hamburg is more hospitable and Baden-Württemberg is the least hospitable German state.[348]

Baden–Württemberg State conducted a citizenship-test in 2006 on its immigrants which is called by German media as 'conscience-test' consisting of 30 questions. "The first question was, what will be your answer 'if your son tells you that he is a gay, and he will get married to a homosexual?' The second question was about the 11th September attack in the US. Are those who carried out the attack, in your opinion, terrorists or freedom-fighters?" One of the Turkish candidate for German citizenship reacted angrily to these kind of the questions by saying: "If you ask this question to Pope, he will never become a German citizen." One of the Greens Party MP Aynur Söylemez said that "One of 16 Federal States in Germany choosing a wrong way for citizenship-test. This State doesn't respect human rights. "[349]

In 1989, Hamburg State was the first one which gave voting rights to its immigrants in local elections, but this state parliament decision was cancelled by German Constitutional Court subsequent year with the initiation of opposition political party. [350]

4.1.7 Question 7: Do you feel equally treated?

This question is intended to find out whether Turkish immigrants receive fair treatment from host society members. The EU integration principles for integration of immigrants in the member states as follows:

> "The dominant conception of integration in EU law and policy is that a secure residence status and equality of treatment with nationals clearly assist integration and thus contribute to the greater social cohesion, security and stability in the country."[351]

Due to restrictive employment conditions and residence status in the member states, integration principles are not always applicable to immigrants in full and they are not always treated on equal terms with host society nationals.[352] According to the German Constitution, all citizens including Turkish immigrants have equal rights and receive equal treatment. In practice across Germany, access to legal rights, positive integration policies towards immigrants and the actual treatment of Turkish immigrants changes from state to state. Each of Germany's 16 federal states has its own parliament and executive.

---

[348] IRR news-Independent race and refugee news network, by Liz Fekete, March 22 2006 Baden-Wurttemberg: discriminatory citizenship test introduced.

[349] Hürriyet Turkish Daily, 1 June 2006

[350] Green, Simon: 'The Legal Status of Turks in Germany' *Immigrants and Minorities*, July 2003, 22 (2-3): 228–246. doi:10.1080/0261928042000244844

[351] Eiko R Thielemann, 2004 European Journal of Migration and Law, Volume 6, No 1, pp. 43-61.

[352] Ryszard Cholewinski, 2005, Migrants as Minorities: Integration and Inclusion in the Enlarged EU, JCMS Volume 43, Nr 4, pp. 695-716

Graph 7: Perceived equality of treatment with Germans

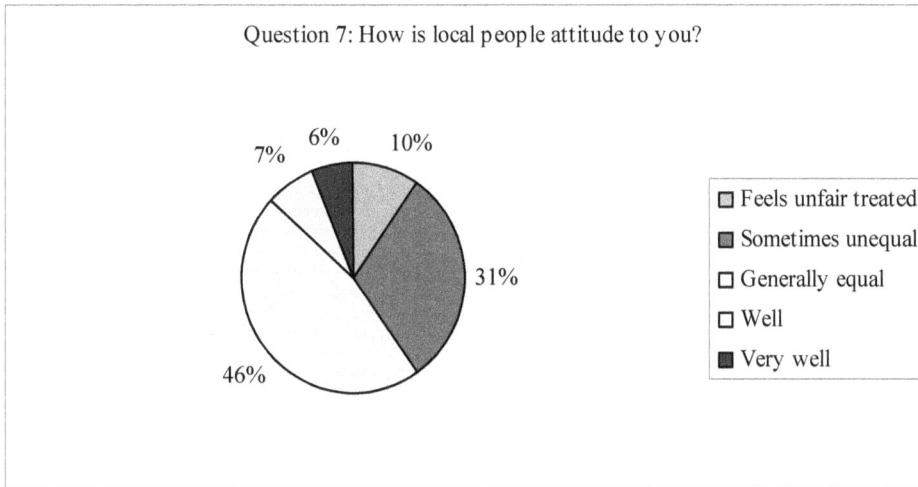

Question 7: How is local people attitude to you?

- Feels unfair treated
- Sometimes unequal
- Generally equal
- Well
- Very well

6% 7% 10% 31% 46%

Source: Author

Graph seven shows 29 respondents or 9.7% replied that they felt 'unfairly treated' or Germans discriminate against them; 92 respondents or 30.7% think that they 'sometimes have been treated unfairly'. 139 respondents or 46.3% felt they have been 'generally equal treated'. 22 respondents or 7.3% felt 'well treated' by hosts. 18 respondents or 6% think that they have been treated 'more than equal' or positively discriminated.

Previous studies suggest that negative public attitudes make immigrants feel insecure and less willing to be integrated into their host society. Especially in a period of economic recession they feel less welcome in their host country. A report (2007) by the centre for Turkish minorities at the University of Essen in Germany has shown that Turkish immigrants in Europe face discrimination in jobs, education, and housing, and this gives rise to feelings of hopelessness and exclusion. The report suggests that Turks face discrimination with issue like employment, education and housing. Unemployment plays a role in discrimination, even more so than religious differences, as it leads jobless German youths to depression and desperate action against immigrants. These unemployed youths look for a scapegoat for economic downturn and crises. In Germany in 1991, especially after the unification, a number of opinion surveys showed a clear decrease in anti-foreigner attitudes.[353] However, arson (the crime of intentionally setting property on fire) on the houses of Turkish families in Mölln (November 1992) and Solingen (May 1993) are examples of right-wing crimes and violence against immigrants. From 1994 there was a decline in these crime rates. More recently is an arson attack 9 Turkish immigrants (5 of them children) lost their lives in Ludwigshafen. Police suspect that a racist person or group set fire to the building where mostly Turkish immigrants lived (10 February 2008). A number of right-wing extremist organisations (such as Neo-Nazis and skinheads) were banned and tough sentences were imposed on criminals. According to the German Ministry of the Interior's Report (2008), there have been 35,150 criminal cases of actions against immigrants from 1991 to 2008 on an average 3,156 annually. This includes recent fire-raids, the use of explosive, violent attacks on immigrants' properties, and in these 13 cases, acts led to death (17 of 20 were Turkish

---

[353] Esser, H.: Generation und Identität, ausländischer Kinder und JugendlicheEdited by H. Esser and J. Friedrichs. Opladen, Westdeutscher Verlag, 2003, (p. 2, 35, 127–146)

133

immigrants who lost their lives). This kind of violent behaviour which happened in Ludwigshafen on 10 February 2008 by criminals provoked the German public to react and caused to participating in one of the largest demonstrations of the post war period in Germany in Dresden, 18 February 2008.[354]

Comparing the general situation of Turkish immigrants in Germany with the French case and other European welfare states such as the Netherlands, Sweden, Denmark, and the UK, Turkish immigrants in Germany have probably less economic and social problems than North African immigrants in France.[355] Although Turkish immigrants in Germany have fewer legal rights than immigrants in Britain, France and in other European countries, they do not feel treated totally unequally and the kind of large-scale social unrest as happened in France in 2005 is unlikely. French authorities granted citizenship to its immigrants in return for cultural assimilation and French integration policies resulted in isolation and assimilation of its immigrants. The French case has little to offer other countries in terms of integration policy.

The Dutch, Swedish and British integration policies seem better than German policy and immigrants in those countries have better access to the legal system and have more rights. More important, Turkish immigrants in those countries feel better treated than those in Germany. Even if there is little evidence for discrimination cases against Turkish immigrants in some German states, Turkish immigrants sometimes face unequal treatments when they seek housing and work[356]. Apparently, some European welfare states such as Sweden and the Netherlands are more sensitive to the issue that their naturalized immigrants should not be treated as second class citizens in their new home country.

4.1.8 Question 8: Do you like the food here?

This question is intended to investigate which country's food persons of Turkish origin in Germany mostly consume either German or Turkish, since maintaining home cuisine and traditions affects their cultural integration into their host society. In previous studies related to cultural integration, Turkish immigrants were found to add diverse cultural values to their host society while they adapted to the host culture and one important aspect of this is food.

Eryilmaz points out that "For the first generation Turkish guest workers food was also a problem until the German supermarkets took note of the demand and ordered Mediterranean fruits and vegetables and until the first Turkish groceries opened in the 1970s. Pork was avoided for religious reasons, veal was expensive and lamb was not available. As a result of being uninformed and with a desire to save money they had an unbalanced diet." [357]

Nermin Abadan-Unat argues that the first generation guest workers experienced some alimentation or diet problems in the 1960s due to lacking knowledge of the German language.

---

[354] Author's Translation from Turkish Daily Hürriyet German Edition, February 18 2008. (Dresden Demonstration took place on February 18 2008).

[355] Vatan Gazetesi, November 5 2005: African immigrants set fire on cars in Paris. The rebel was like revolution in France which lasted 8 days, 1260 cars were burn down by immigrants. Reasons for this rebel seem poverty, unemployment and bad living and housing conditions.

[356] An Article by Kate Connolly in Daily Telegraph, 31st December 2005 on the State of Baden Württemberg citizenship test (kate.connolly@telegraph.co.uk)

[357] Eryilmaz, Aytaç & Jamin, Mathilde (Eds.): *Fremde Heimat. Die Geschichte der Einwanderung aus Turkie*, Essen, Klartext, 1998 (p. 4, 93, 123)

They turned to the traditional Turkish way of feeding themselves. A health survey carried out in Cologne 1964 shows that only 14% of the Turkish workers were benefitting from the heavily subsidized, cheap, warm lunch served in almost all German enterprises, most of the first generation workers were cooking for themselves in traditional Turkish way.[358] Generally their diet consisted of eggs, noodles, Turkish macaroni (pasta), and lots of bread, cheese and yoghurt. This unbalanced diet for heavy manual labour came about through looking the knowledge how to cook a variety of dishes and resulted in a heavy carbohydrate, protein poor nutrition (which lowers the morale and represents a pacifying psychological factor). The nutrition problem still remains a major source of grievances among immigrants.[359]

A survey in 2007 conducted on 1500 people in Germany shows that Döner Kebab has become the top fast food, more popular than hamburgers, and people in Germany eat or consume more döner than anything else. Pizza is the second most consumed food, which is followed by cheeseburgers, sausage sandwiches, hamburgers and French fries. 4% of 1500 respondents prefer 'take-away'; 8% consume 3-5 times weekly; 35% of them consume 'take-away' once or twice weekly.[360] Fast food aside, Turkish fine cuisine is regarded as one of one the three most famous cooking arts, it is said that three major kinds of cuisine exist in the world; Turkish, Chinese, and French. Examples include Meze appetizers, Dolma (stuffed fruit and vegetables) and a wide range of speciality fish and meat dishes. Baklava and Lokum (Turkish delight) are sweet desserts that are world renowned. "Turkish Cuisine fully justifying its reputation is always a pleasant surprise for the visitor".[361]

Graph 8: Measuring the food preferences of Turkish immigrants

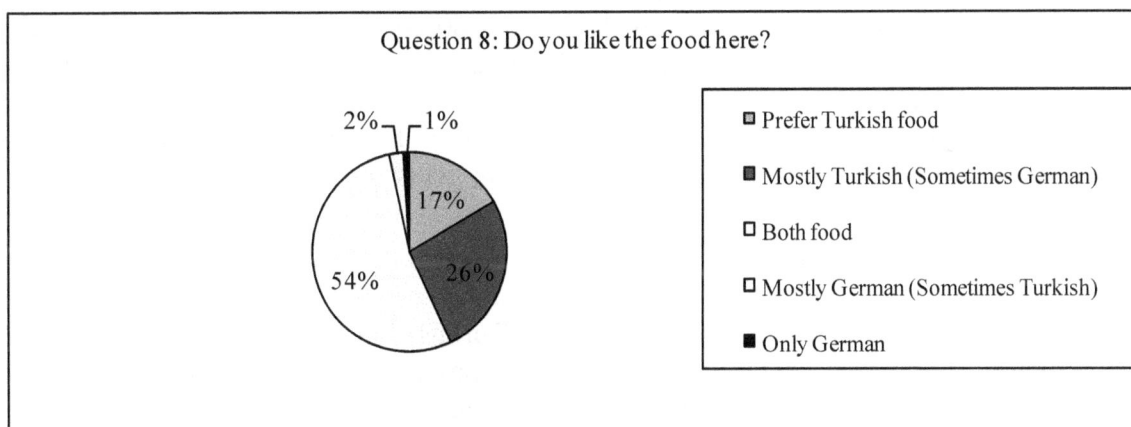

Question 8: Do you like the food here?

2% 1% 17% 54% 26%

- Prefer Turkish food
- Mostly Turkish (Sometimes German)
- Both food
- Mostly German (Sometimes Turkish)
- Only German

Source: Author

---

[358] Abadan-Unat Nermin (1969) :*Turkish Workers In West Germany: A case Study,* Faculty of Political Science, University of Ankara, Ankara, (p. 1-36)

[359] Ibid., (p. 37)

[359] Hürriyet 28 June 2008 [Translation]

[360]All About Turkey – Turkish Cuisine. Accessed via web 12/07/2009: http://www.allaboutturkey.com/mutfak.htm

Graph eight revealed that 50 respondents or 17% preferred Turkish food but they do not dislike German food. 79 people or 26% of immigrants prefer Turkish food, but they 'sometimes' eat German food too. 161 respondents or 54% 'like both countries' food. 7 respondents or 2% consume only German food. 3 people or 1.0% preferred 'only German' food. The answers suggest that most Turkish immigrants consume both countries foods, which indicates a significant integration of eating habits. First and second generation Turkish migrant workers have not only been economic contributors to Germany but also added their fast food culture to German life such as Döner and sausage (Sucuk).

Unat argues that 86% of the first generation Turkish guest workers were particularly male, experienced dietary problems. They usually consumed noodles, macaroni and lots of bread. This unbalanced nutrition affected their working life and daily behaviours.[362] It means that unbalanced nutrition affects immigrants' adaptation to the labour market and the socio-cultural life of the host country.

Panikos Panayi, multicultural history professor and food specialist argues that without studying immigration it is impossible to understand food's effect on integration. "What people eat is a really important symbol of the integration process…dishes don't have nationality"[363] He argues also that "British eating habits have been reshaped by immigration."[364] Multicultural cuisine of immigrants enriched British cuisine by adding to its diverse food traditions. As in Britain, Turkish immigrants enriched German cuisine and their food traditions.

On 25 October, 2006 Berlin, German Foreign Minister, Frank Walter Steinmeier admitted that Turkish guest workers enriched German food culture with a speech at the 100th year anniversary of Association of Foreign Journalists, from 60 countries 400 journalists including Turkish Newspaper Hürriyet, joined the celebration. The Minister stated that "Labour immigration caused a lot of social and cultural changes in Germany for the past 40 years; especially Turkish immigrants' impact is great. As a result of Turkish labour migration, Turkish *Döner Kebab* became German speciality beside the *Sucuk* 'Sausage.'"[365]

4.1.9 Question 9: Do you like the way of life in Germany?

This question is intended to discover whether Turkish immigrants are happy to live in Germany or not. If they feel happy with their lifestyle possibilities they are more likely to be integrated into German society and way of life. Similar interests (for example social and sportive contacts) between the host and immigrant communities make the integration of immigrants easier because the interaction influences the host community's attitude in a positive way and creates interest in immigrants and their background.

German society is complex and there are significant regional differences in culture and outlook. Therefore new immigrants might struggle with the nuances of life in Germany until they

---

[362] Ibid. 50 (p. 37)

[363] Panayi, Panikos: The Guardian, April 15 2008: Article interviewed by Harriet Swain, 'Bites of life'.

[364] Panayi, Panikos; Spicing up Britain, 'The Multicultural History of British Food', The University of Chicago press, 2008, (p. 220-8)

[365] HÜRRIYET Turkish daily, April 1 2008 [Author's translation].

are more integrated. As explained earlier each region of Germany has its own spoken accent, dialect, speciality foods and cultural outlook. For example, it is not surprising if a Turkish immigrant resident in Munich speaks German with a Bavarian accent.[366] Therefore, this question is intended to explore how persons of Turkish origin feel about their particular local environment.

Turkish-origin author Dilek Güngör expresses sentiments about her southern German upbringing, "As a child I wanted to be Catholic. I wanted to be like all my classmates. I always felt like my family did things the wrong way. I was very sensitive to all the small differences. For example, the others had a cold meal in the evening while my family cooked; they washed with flannels before going to bed while we took a bath." [367] This describes a first-hand experience of cultural difference and the struggle that children of Turkish immigrants go through in discovering the different way of life of the host community. Those who are happy with the way of life are more likely to have reconciled these differences with their own culture and lifestyle and therefore feel more integrated.

Opinion polls indicate that changing attitudes over time and increasing diversity are resulting in increased acceptance of immigrants as a part of German society and the integration of immigrants is a desired outcome by both sides. There are remarkable attitude changes in German individuals toward immigrants. It is interesting that naturalized Turkish immigrant youths represented Germany in the 2005 European song contest in Turkish-German language as bilingual. The German ambassador, Eckhart Kuntz in Ankara officially declared that the Turkish community in Germany is a component of German society on behalf of the German government in Berlin.[368] One example is that of a third generation Turkish-origin woman, and German citizen, Asli Bayram who represented Germany at the Miss Universe beauty contest in 2005.

Faruk Şen points out that the Turkish-descended generation should keep their ties with Turkish culture while adapting to German culture and the way of life.[369] Şen cited that "Turks in Germany have become German-Turks. Their language draws on both cultures, although they are treated as foreigners in both Turkey and Germany. Among the younger generations, some writers, journalists and academics have begun to communicate (in German) between the two cultures and contribute to a new cross-cultural identity. They find their own voice, their own advocates, and their own understanding of what it means and what it should mean to be of Turkish origin in German society".[370]

---

[366] A research Article by Jenny B. White, from the *Middle East Studies Association Bulletin*, (1995): Turks in Germany: Overview of the Literature, University of Nebraska-Omaha, July 1995 (p.1-4) (with changes in orthography to HTML standards. Ed note: Turkish orthography may be modified by Web-browsers); Middle East Studies Association of North America.

[367] "German author grew up battling Turkish cliches", Reuters May 3, 2007. Accessed via the web June 10, 2009 http://uk.reuters.com/article/sippsNews/idUKZWE35199820070503

[368] An Article by Zeynep Gürcanli on German ambassador's report in Ankara, 18th February 2008, Hürriyet Newspaper, [Author's Translation]

[369] Şen Faruk: 'Identity Crises and Integration Constraints of Turkish Migrants in the Federal Republic of Germany'; German Socio-economic Panel Study, ILO, Geneva, 1989 (p.2). In Sarah Spencer (Ed.),"A Positive Approach to Migrants" Rivers Oram Press 1994, Chapter 5, (p. 93-103) ,See also Zentrum für Türkeistudien, Essen, 1993

[370] Ibid.

Graph 9: Turkish immigrants' attitude towards the German way of life

Question 9: Do you like the way of living here?

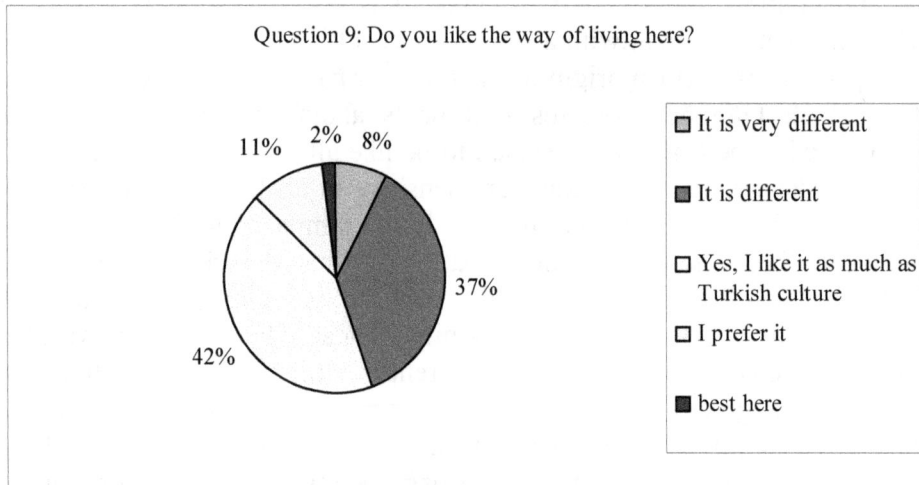

☑	It is very different
◼	It is different
☐	Yes, I like it as much as Turkish culture
☐	I prefer it
◼	best here

Source: Author

Graph nine shows that 23 respondents or 8% think that life is 'very different' in Germany. 111 people or 37% find life somewhat 'different' in Germany but they still prefer to live there. 128 respondents or 42% (almost half of the immigrant population) feel adapted to life in Germany. 32 respondents or 11% of immigrants felt that 'life is better in Germany'. 6 people or 2% enjoy living here in the German way to the extent that they want no further ties with their parents' birth country.

Although there are some allegations in the German media that Turks deliberately exclude themselves from German society and are unwilling to be integrated, there is no evidence to support such a hypothesis. Rather, social exclusion appears to be a much more complex process linked to hindering factors of integration such as unemployment, low social status, low self esteem, lack of family support and lack of confidence in dealing with the local language and culture.

4.1.10: Question 10: Do you feel a member of the host country?

The purpose of this question is to examine Turkish immigrants' feelings about whether they feel accepted or excluded by native Germans and how this affects their willingness to integrate into German society. Sociologists use the term 'integration' to mean the two-way process of adaptation by both migrants and the host society that enables migrants to prosper and move towards attaining equality of access, participation and outcomes.[371] If they feel a part of German society it means that they are more likely to feel loyalty to the German state and its institutions and be integrated into German society.

---

[371] Geddes, Andrew: The Politics of Migration and Immigration in Europe, Sage Publication, London, (p. 5, 79, 101).

Graph 10: Measuring the acceptance of Turkish immigrants by Germans

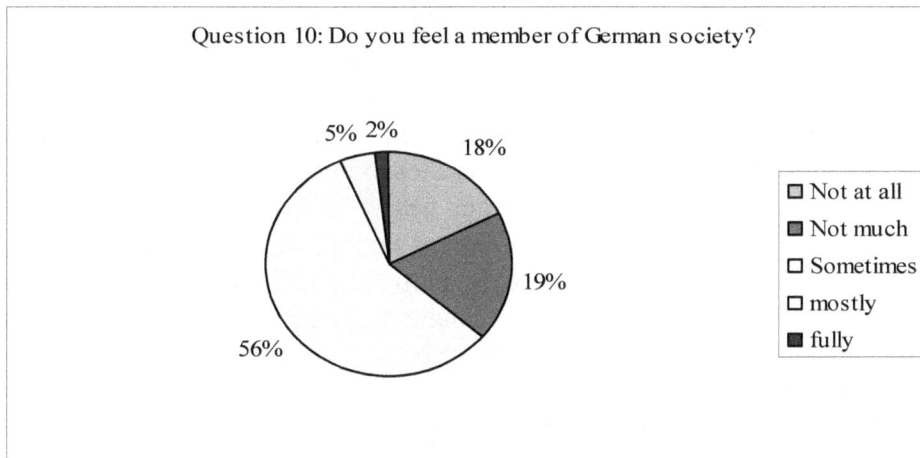

Question 10: Do you feel a member of German society?

Legend:
- Not at all
- Not much
- Sometimes
- mostly
- fully

(5% 2% 18% 19% 56%)

Source: Author

Graph ten indicates 53 respondents or 18% felt 'not at all' a member of the host society, 56 respondents or 19% of immigrant population felt 'not much' a member of the host society, 172 respondents or 56% felt as an ordinary member of host society which means that they are more likely to be integrated and feel a part of German life. 14 people, 5% felt happy at being a member of German society. 5 respondents, 2% felt very happy with their perceived level of acceptance in German society. For immigrants to be accepted as members of the host society, the acceptance should be from both sides' point of view. Feeling accepted or integrated one-sidedly has no meaning unless it is accompanied by the views of host society members.

From the hosts' point of view, previous studies show that some young Germans with a low level of education are less likely to accept immigrants as members of the host society and immigrants perceived competition with them for jobs and housing.[372] Philip N. Jones argues that ethnic German immigrants and former Guest workers face similar difficulties in the field of housing, social and economic integration and degree of acceptance by native Germans.[373] Times of economic recession and high unemployment rates which affects both host members and immigrants may cause reactions or increasing pessimistic opinions towards the presence of immigrants. Another survey from 1992 on how Turks feel they are perceived by Germans indicates that young Germans are more likely to accept immigrants than older Germans. 30% of young Germans under twenty-five agreed with the statement: "I don't like many foreigners in my country", while 51% believed that immigrants should be integrated, and 19% want all foreigners to leave the country. Among older Germans, 40% indicated that they do not like many foreigners in the country. 31% of older Germans think foreigners should be assimilated into German society, and 39% have moderate attitudes to immigrants.[374]

In conclusion, 56% feel as an ordinary member of host society which means that they are more likely to be integrated when they feel a part of German life.

---

[372] Ibid., (p. 101, 120)
[373] Philip, N. Jones, 'Destination Germany'; Population Migration and the Changing World Order (Ed. By W.T.S. Gould and A.M. Findlay), Published by John Wiley and Sons, 1994, West Sussex, (p. 40)
[374] Eurobarometer, 1988

4.1.11. Question 11: How strong are your ties with Turkey?

The aim of asking this question is to investigate Turkish immigrants' connections with their or their parents' home country. Although this question is entirely valid for first generation Turkish guest workers, this study is also interested in the German-born second and third generation of Turkish origin and their loyalty to Germany as their birth-place and residence. The issue of feeling connected to one or both societies directly relates to integration or lack thereof.

The guest worker generation has arguably stronger ties with Turkey than the younger generations because they migrated to work with the intention of saving money and later returning to live in Turkey. Early on they were less interested in participating in German social and political life by, for example learning the host country's language. Living as a temporary guest without learning the host language and with a plan of returning home is obviously a hindering factor to forming new ties with the host country's society. On the German side, the perception of the 'Guest worker recruitment system' or guest-worker policy was as a temporary rather than a permanent project.

Maintaining the ties with country of origin is an emotional factor, which affect immigrants' integration motivationally. Michael Richter describes Turkish guest workers' situation in his book, 'They came and Stayed' (*gekommen und geblieben*), on issue of how difficult to maintain ties with Turkey, Nermin Özdil (2004), one of the Turkish immigrant women who migrated to Germany in 1973 and stayed in Hamburg over 30 years, admits that how and why their ties so weakened with their country of origin.

> "Turkey is not a home for us anymore. Hamburg is my home.
> Turkey is for us a country of memories and holidays."[375]

In the same book on migration issues, Richter identified the themes which cause Turkish immigrants to maintain ties with Turkey;

> "the risk of breaking away from the safety net of the family, the uncertainty that awaits migrants in a foreign country, the increasingly weak ties to the homeland without an adequate substitute in Germany and even the need to redefine one's own identity."[376]

Researchers point out that access to communication technologies and level of ties with their home country affect immigrants' integration. For example, locally produced Turkish language radio and television programmes such as Berlin's *Radio MultiKulti* existed from the 1970s onwards, earlier called 'guest-worker programmes'.[377] This reflects the local dimension of migrant life and ties people closer to the new country of residence while creating a bridge back home and encouraging identification with their country of origin through the use of references to their native language and culture. Turks in Berlin think of themselves primarily as Turkish Berliner, and secondly as Turkish Europeans. The term European has become an important

---

[375] Richter, Michael: They came and stayed, *'Gekommen und Geblieben': Deutsch-Türkishe Lebensgeschicten*, German-Turkish life stories, published by the Körper Foundation, Hamburg 2004, pp 225.
[376] Ibid., p. 225
[377] Kosnick, Kira: Migrant Media: Turkish Broadcasting and Multicultural Politics in Berlin. University Press of New England, 2000, pp.319

concept particularly in Turkish Academic circles in Western Europe which suggests a secular and westernised community that is not intent on maintaining ties with Turkey.[378] On the other hand, Eyüp Özveren argues that Turkish satellite television programmes tend to convey a rather negative image and are seen as a hindering factor to migrants' integration, as those programmes from Turkey have little to say on life in Germany and the integration process.[379] Gaby Strassburger argues that ties to the home country are assumed to be less important to the children of immigrants since the younger generations have spent their entire lives in Germany and only visited Turkey as tourists. Their ties with their descendants' family members, kin and friends might easily narrow down to only a few contacts through the generations. Social contacts of the second and third generation are likely to be located mainly in Germany except for marriages with partners from Turkey.[380]

Turkish immigrants' experience across Europe demonstrates, especially in Germany, when it comes to exercising rights some citizens are treated better than others. This can be interpreted as native Germans receive better treatment than naturalized Germans.[381] On the other hand, first generation guest-workers and their German-born children who returned Turkey experiences re-integration problems. Their German-born children were frustrated because of social and cultural alienation. They are given a new name (*Alamanyali*) 'Turks from Germany' or (*Alamanci*) 'Germanised Turks'. Their children are victims of 'culture differences'. For many of them it is first contact with Turkey and face problems with Turkish language, education system, socialisation, and making new friendships in a new environment.[382] Şen argues that Turks are showing an increasing interest in participating in the mainstream political parties. However they need to feel secure in German society and to have rights which incorporate them economically, socially, and politically as productive members of society. On the other hand, Germans needs to recognise and accept the contribution which Turkish immigrants make, at least they should feel grateful.[383]

During the 1960s and 1970s through its guest worker recruitment system large-scale of migration of Turkish citizens to West Germany contributed to the "economic miracle" or *Wirtschaftswunder* in Europe. At the same time, Germany's, German Foreigners Law (*Ausländergesetz*),[384] generally encouraged guest-workers to return after Germany's recruitment freeze (*Anwerbesstopp*) in 1973 until the first German Immigration Act came into power in 1990.

---

[378] Kira, Kosnick: Building bridges: Media for migrants and the public-service mission in Germany European Journal of Cultural Studies 2000, 3: 319-342

[379] Faist, Thomas & Özveren, Eyup: Transnational Social Spaces, Published by Ashgate, 2004, (p.211)

[380] Ibid.

[381] Layton-Henry, Zig: The Politics of Immigration, Blackwell, 1992, (p. 5-6)

[382] Norman Fumus, Ilhan Başgöz, and Nermin Abadan Unat 'Turkish immigrants in Europe, Identity Crisis of Turkish Migrants', An interdisciplinary Study, Indiana University Turkish Studies, 1985, (p.3-22)

[383] Şen, Faruk (July 2003): The Historical Situation of Turkish Migrants in Germany, *Immigrants and Minorities* 22 (2-3): 208–227.

[384] *Note: The recruitment of guest workers was subjugated to the economic interests of the Federal Republic. Article 2(1) of the 1965 Law stated that a residence permit 'may be issued if the presence of the foreigners does not harm the interests of the FRG'. Conditions for these residence permits were all dependent on executive discretion. Residence permits were lined to work permits and both these types of permit were subordinated to West Germany's economic interests.

This new German policy aimed to integrate immigrants including Turks into German society. Before this law, Germany did not encourage permanent settlement and integration facilities for immigrants. The unclear circumstances caused guest workers and their families to maintain stronger ties with Turkey. For the younger generation, being born in Germany, having a German education and speaking German better than Turkish means that they have weaker ties (and in some cases, maybe no ties at all) with Turkey and are more integrated than the older generation.

Graph 11: Measuring Turkish immigrants' level of ties with Turkey

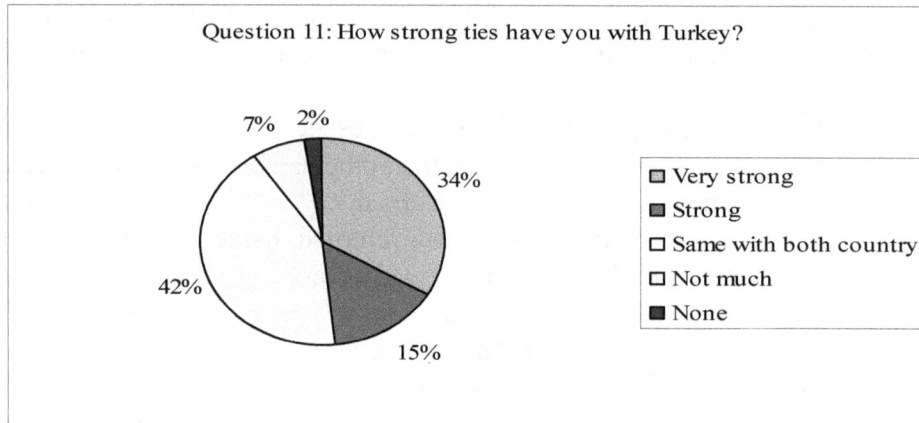

Question 11: How strong ties have you with Turkey?

2%
7%
34%
42%
15%

- Very strong
- Strong
- Same with both country
- Not much
- None

Source: Author

To this question, 101 respondents or 34% expressed that they have stronger ties with Turkey, 44 people 15% have more ties with Turkey than Germany. One can predict that these groups felt relatively isolated and found it harder to be integrated into German society. 127 immigrants 42% (nearly half) of the immigrants have normal ties (50-50) with both countries and felt content with having ties with both countries. 21 participants 7% felt 'not much' ties with their home country, which means that they are on the way to be assimilated into Germany. The last group 2% has 'no tie' with Turkey any more, meaning that they are completely assimilated and have lost their roots.

Having closer ties with their homeland is a slowing factor for the integration of first and second generation Turkish immigrants. The first generation especially had more nationalistic feelings and closer homeland ties compared with later generations.

It follows that the German-born generations may have weaker ties with Turkey, they are almost integrated into German society and way of life which can be considered their native society. They are certainly dependent on their parents and family members for the maintenance of those ties and issues of language and acceptance are significant factors. They therefore risk feeling torn between two cultures as their daily life is German in nature to a significant extent.

Though some businessmen of Turkish origin in Germany such as Vural Öğer and Kenan Polat, are quite capable of maintaining strong ties with Turkey and integrating successfully into German society. They are, in fact, a bridge between two countries and contribute to bilateral relations considerably.

4.1.12. Question 12: Is life comfortable in Germany?

This question investigates their satisfaction level from different aspect of their life in Germany from the first generation guest worker to fourth generation Germans with Turkish origin.

The first survey concerning the housing conditions of the first generation guest workers in 1963 revealed interesting findings as 65% evaluated their lodging as comfortable, sunny, clean; whereas 20% qualified them as cold, neglected, dark and run down. The same survey concerning work place satisfaction from 1964 showed that 69% did not find any difficulty and adjusting themselves to their job, 40% were able to master their duty. 93% conformed they were able to adapt themselves to the working speed. Furthermore, 78% of Turks are able to collaborate with their colleagues, 46% prefer to work with German peer-groups. 63% preferred Turkish colleagues to the Germans. It also should be cited that in 1963, 81% of the workers evaluated their direct superior (Meister) as just, protective, minded, and morally high standing person. [385]

The purpose of asking question twelve is to examine whether Turkish immigrants find life comfortable (in other words, do they feel at home) or not in Germany and as a result gauging their well-being and level of happiness, since "comfort" helps immigrants to feel willing to be integrated into German society. Including this question helps to understand perceptions about their standard of life in Germany. If they feel at home they are more likely to feel integrated. If not, it could mean that they suffer from a lack of integration into German life. Responses to this question also provide information about their feelings towards Germany and German living conditions after staying a decade in the country. It also gives information about their level of loyalty, for example, which country they feel more loyal to, Germany or Turkey. Since their psychological feeling is an important factor which affects many aspects of their integration such as loyalty, political interests, cultural interests, satisfaction status and sports interests.

Integration experts argued that the term 'integration' was used to mean the two-way process of adaptation by both migrant and host society that enables the migrant to prosper and move towards attaining quality of access, participation and outcomes. [386]

A survey conducted by The Bertelsmann Foundation showed that half of immigrants to Germany feel like outsiders in German society. However, 69% of those interviewed feel comfortable in their adopted country. While 58% of survey respondents felt like an integral part of German society. Dr. Jörg Dräger, a board member of the Bertelsmann Foundation, has also stressed the term integration as a two-way process and cited.

---

[385] Abadan-Unat, Nermin: *A case Study,* Turkish Workers in West Germany – immigrant and Migrant Labour – The resulting tensions in affluent countries 109th Wilton Park Conference, Steyning Sussex. Faculty of Political Science University of Ankara, Ankara, 1969, (p. 34)

[386] Spencer, Sarah : 'Immigration as an Economic Asset'; German Experience, A positive Approach to Migrants, River Oram Press, 1994, (p.11-13)

> "That most immigrants are happy with their lives here is a positive signal for Germany as a place to immigrate to. However, integration isn't a one-sided process. If more Turkish and Russian immigrants are to make themselves at home in Germany, they need more recognition and chances to redesign the future." [387]

The same survey reveals that 79% said they were happy with their jobs and 77% were content with their current living conditions. 42% of immigrants said their children have fewer educational opportunities than their native German classmates.

On the issue of immigrant children's education facilities, "Without fair opportunities at education, neither integration nor participation can succeed"

Pie-chart graph 12: Life comfort of Turkish immigrants in Germany

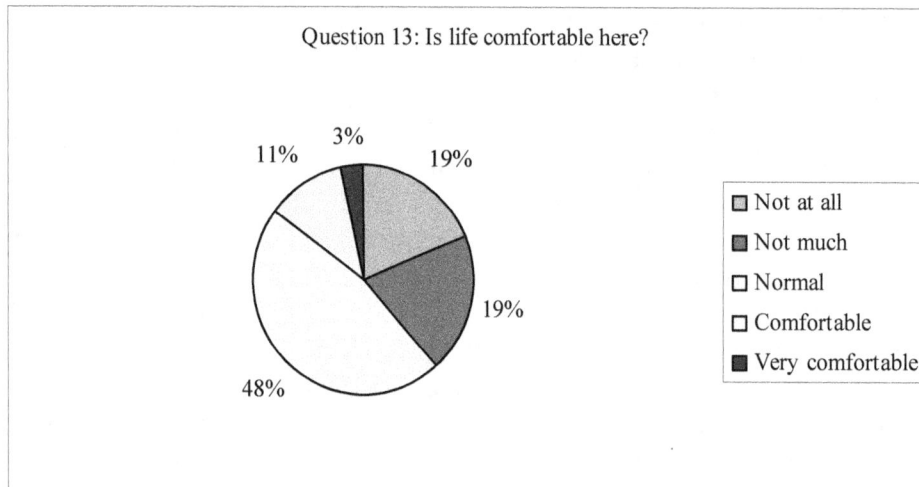

Question 13: Is life comfortable here?

3%
11%
19%
19%
48%

- Not at all
- Not much
- Normal
- Comfortable
- Very comfortable

Source: Author

Graph twelve shows that 57 respondents or 19% of immigrants answered 'Not comfortable at all'. It is interesting that even though they do not feel comfortable they are not deprived. Apparently they live in a isolated way, arguably in a "Turkish" way in German society, probably belonging to an older generation who long for the lifestyle they left behind in Turkey; 58 respondents or 19% of immigrants find life 'hard' in German society. 141 people or 48% find life 'normal' in Germany. 34 respondents or 11% feel happier for being in Germany. 10 respondents or 3% think life is very comfortable in Germany and they are very happy that they settled in Germany. These findings can be interpreted that, summing 48% (that feel life comfortable) + 11% (feel more comfortable) + 3% (very comfortable) equals = 62% that feel life is significantly comfortable in German society.

[387]Study finds half of German immigrants feel like outsiders - The Local. Published: 15 June 09 17:30 CET
On line: http://www.thelocal.de/society/2009/06/15-19945.html   (15 June 2009)
144

4.1.13. Question 13: Is it hard to find a job here?

The purpose of this question is to explore the economic effect on Turkish immigrants' integration and employment facilities when integration in employment, identified as access to job is a desired outcome.

The problem with the EU integration principles is its very difficult to speak in terms of employment as 'a key part of the integration process'[388] if immigrants do not have access to employment on equal terms with nationals. EU Member States feel more comfortable referring to immigrants and using the language of integration rather than minority protection[389].

Hof argues that employment of immigrants has made a positive impact on the German Economy from 1983 to 1992.[390] Anticipated developments mean that Germany will be even more dependent on immigrants in the future. Klaus F. Zimmermann argues that immigrants' contribution will continue to be a positive economic factor for German labour market as in the past.[391]

Turkish immigrants *former guest-workers* and their dependents have not only influenced since 1960s, the composition of the labour force, but they have also had an impact on the economy and heavy industry in Germany. As they had strengthened their decision to consider Germany a home and to stay after uniting their families, investing more of their income in Germany in their living standards for buying a house for their family and investing more money for a better education of their children in German schools instead of sending money home and investing in the country of origin.[392] Originally, Turks are mostly labour migrants with a largely agricultural background. They are primarily recruited for unskilled or semi-skilled work in German industries like metallurgy, mining and textiles, and although some of the Turks were skilled labourers, they have had to accept dangerous and tiring jobs, since their contracts may have tied them to specific jobs in industries. Günter Wallraff documented Turkish guest workers' working conditions in the 1980s in his book "Lowest of the Low" (*Ganz Unten* or "*Ich Ali*") by posing as a Turkish guest worker, and document the mistreatment he received in that role at the hands of employers, landlords and the German government.[393]

In 1996, unemployment rates among Turkish immigrants were higher than in other immigrant groups and amongst Germans. Other immigrant group experience 19% unemployment, the Turks experience 22.5% and among Germans only 10% are unemployed. On the other hand, many Turkish immigrants are establishing businesses in Germany. There were 150,000 foreign-owned

---

[388] Conclusions on immigrant integration policy, Conclusion 11; Council Directive 2003/86/EC of 22 September 2003 on the right to family reunification, OJ 2003 L 251/12 (transposition deadline 3 October 2005) and Council Directive 2003/109/EC of 25 November 2003 concerning the status of third-country nationals who are long-term residents, OJ 2004 L 16/44(transposition deadline 23 January 2006).

[389] Kees Groenendijk: European Journal of Migration and Law 6: 111-126, 'Legal Concepts of Integration in the EU Migration Law' and The Netherlands' integration policy, 2004, p.113.

[390]Hof, B.: Arbeitskraftebedarft der Wirtschaft. Arbeitsmarktchancen fur Zuwandrer, in: Friedrich-Ebert-Stiftung (Hrsg.), Zuwanderungspolitik der Zukunft ,Reihe Gesprachskreis Arbeit und Soziales, Nr. 3, Bon, l992, (s.7-22)

[391] Zimmermann, Klaus F.: European Pull-Push Migration, University of Munich, l994, (p.313).

392 Pries, Ludger: Labor migration, social incorporation and transmigration in the New Europe; The case of Germany in a comparative perspective Transfer: European Review of Labor and Research Autumn 2003 9: 432-451,

[393] Wallraff, Günter: 'Lowest of the Low' (*Ganz Unten* or "*Ich Ali*"), Verlag Kipenheuser, Köln, 1985, (p. 122-6).

businesses by 1992, including 33,000 owned by Turks .The Turkish-owned businesses generated 700,000 jobs in l99l and recorded sales of DM 25 billion (about US $ 17 billion) and invested DM 6 million in Germany.[394] Since better life standards with higher income means a better integration facilities for them.

Pie-chart graph 13: Measuring employment facilities of Turkish immigrants' in Germany

Question 13: Is it hard to find a job?

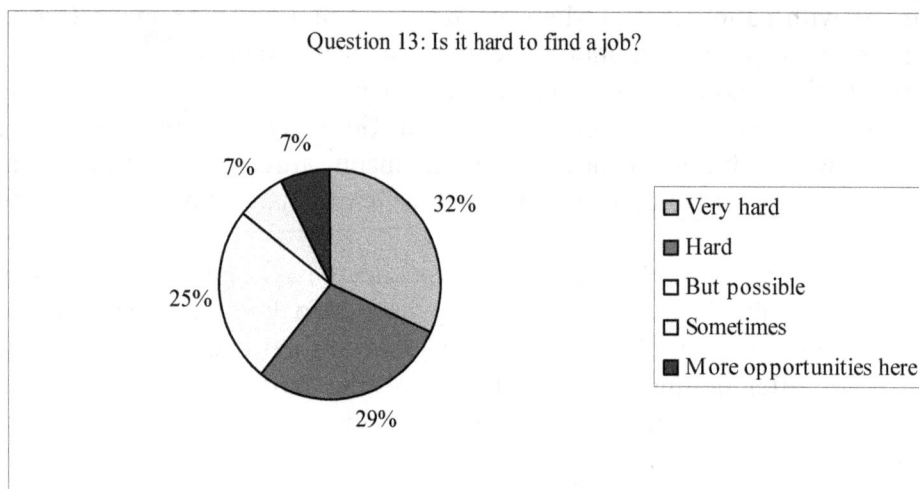

- Very hard
- Hard
- But possible
- Sometimes
- More opportunities here

32%
29%
25%
7%
7%

Source: Author

Graph 13 shows that 96 respondents or 32% of Turkish immigrant respondents think that to find a job in Germany is 'very hard', in other words nearly impossible to find a well-paid job. 86 respondents or 29% think that to find work is 'hard'. 75 respondents 25% of Turkish people in Germany say it is hard to find a proper job 'but it is still possible' to find a job that might be low-paid. 21 respondents 7% think to find a job is 'sometimes' difficult. 22 respondents 7% think that there are 'more job opportunities' in Germany than Turkey. As a conclusion, most of respondents 32% think finding a good job is hard in Germany; and it gets even harder in times of economic downturns, with low income compared with their German peers.

4.1.14 Question 14: Is it hard to find housing here?

Integration in housing is defined as access to safe, affordable accommodation and "safe" meaning not only within the property but also in the surrounding neighbourhood. Housing conditions are an important influence on immigrants' sense of belonging, for their health, and access to jobs and services.

Housing conditions of immigrants and their integration are interrelated. Immigrants living in residentially dispersed and diverse areas are more likely to be integrated into German society than immigrants residing in concentrated Turkish neighbourhoods or in the districts mixed with few native Germans. The ghettoisation and isolation of immigrants which is a barrier to their association with native Germans can be prevented and unintentional ghettos can be dispersed into districts of cities where fewer immigrants are residing to achieve this outcome.

---

[394] Hof, B.: *Job opportunities for immigrants*, in: Friedrich-Ebert-Stiftung (Ed.), immigration policy in the future, discussion series, Labour and Social Affairs, No. 3, Bonn, 1992, (p. 7-22)

First study concerning the housing conditions of 1963 suggested that 65 % of the first generation Turkish guest workers evaluated their housing conditions as comfortable, sunny, clean where as 20% considered them as cold, neglected, dark and run down.[395]

Aytaç Eryilmaz describes the first ten years' accommodation conditions of Turkish guest workers in Germany such as

> "Their accommodations were the hostels arranged by the employers. Germany already had a housing shortage. Apartment buildings; dormitories, barracks, old buildings, attics, basement flats or storerooms were turned into lodgings. The hostels needed to have 6 m2 of space per person, arranged for about four workers."[396]

Research from the German centre for Studies on Turkey (*Zentrum für Türkeistudien*) has established that 15% of the discriminatory cases were reported in housing market.[397] For first generation Turkish guest workers in the 1970s West German employers were obliged to provide dormitories to specified standards to house single or unaccompanied men. A survey in 1971, ten years after the first workers from Turkey arrived, gave the following results:

> "10% of the worker hostels in North Rheine Westphalia were uninhabitable, 25% consisted of barracks, 46% did not provide the needed space per person, 52% of the hostels were erected on factory grounds and 16% of them were fenced in with barbed wire. 40% of the hostels in Hamburg were substandard. On an average 20 persons shared one shower and 10 persons one toilette." [398]

Data from 1980s on housing conditions of Turkish immigrants of German sources show that only 10% still lived in the hostels whereas 80 percent lived in apartment building. Prior to the German reunification in Berlin, a quarter of Turkish immigrants lived in seven of the city's 75 districts. In Cologne, the situation was similar, with a heavy concentration of Turks in private housing in the centre (Altstadt Nord) and in a northern industrial suburb (Fuhlingen). This ghetto-style settlement is both a sign and cause of immigrants' isolation from society at large.[399] However, in the 1990s the number of housing loan accounts among the Turks rapidly increased, Turkish immigrants started to their houses and move into their own houses or flats. As mentioned in the introduction, poor housing condition is a hindering factor of integration of immigrants. Such an isolation of some Turkish immigrants was not only because the Turks were unwilling to live next with German neighbours or wish to live a Turkish neighbourhood, but Germans were unwilling to live within the mixed districts.[400]

---

[395] Abadan-Unat, Nermin: *A case Study*, Turkish Workers in West Germany – Immigrant and Migrant Labour – The resulting tensions in affluent countries 109th Wilton Park Conference, Steyning Sussex. Faculty of Political Science University of Ankara, Ankara, 1969, (p. 30)

[396] Ibid., (p. 34)

[397] Şen, Faruk: 'The Historical Situation of Turkish Migrants in Germany', *Immigrants and Minorities* 22 (2-3), July 2003, pp. 208–227. doi:10.1080/0261928042000244835

[398] Eryilmaz, A.: *40 years in Germany - At Home Abroad*: DOMIT –Documentation Centre and Museum of the Migration from Turkey, Cologne, 2002, (p.3-5) [Translation from Turkish: Bengü Kocatürk – Schuster]

[399] Ibid., (p. 2-5)

[400] Ibid., p. 5-9

The following Table 4.1 shows the ranking German preference as neighbours in their distinct.

Table 4.1.1 Desirability of Various Groups as Neighbours by Germans, 2000

Group	Valid Percent Saying "rather not"
East/West Germans	9.1
Jews	18.9
Vietnamese	28.5
Turks	33.9
Africans	34.2
Poles	37.1
Arabs	45.5
Gypsies	63.9

Adapted from Fetzer, (2000), Pedagogies of Teaching 'Race' and Ethnicity in Higher Education: British and European Experiences, Sociology, Anthropology, Politics (C-SAP) University of Birmingham, 2006, p. 216

Above Table 4.1.1 shows that almost 19% Germans are unwilling to live with Jewish neighbours. 45.5%, a large number of Germans do not wish to live next to people from Arabic countries. 9.1% Germans do not want to live them next to their own countrymen as neighbours. It means that former East and West Germans do not want to live as neighbours with each other.[401]

In 1989, Germans lived in accommodation with on average, 2 rooms per person. Considering this level as a norm or regularity, a definition for proper housing would mean that per person has one room at least to live in a flat or house. In 1984, this applied to 40% of Germans but 81% of Turks; by 1989, poor housing among Germans had declined to 34% but remained at 80% for Turks. In the early 1980s, 41% of non-Germans lived in areas where more than 12% of the inhabitants was foreigners. By the mid-1980s, their share risen to 45% for non-Germans generally and 49% for Turks. In the 1980s, low income is not the sole reason of poor housing. There is little evidence for claims, repeatedly made in the literature, that the housing conditions of Turks are determined by their unwillingness to pay more rent, by their primary concern was to save as much as possible rather than invest in better housing in Germany.[402]

On the contrary, evidences from 1990s points to Turks are more willing to invest and improve their poor housing condition in German society. A study of the housing conditions of Turks in Germany was conducted in the late 1980s among 43,343 Germans and 9,676 Turkish members of the workforce at Ruhrkohle AG in the Ruhr industrial region. The average income of Turkish workers at Ruhrkohle, many of whom worked at the coal-face-lay 9% above that Germans, and 59% were even willing to pay higher rents in order to improve the quality of their housing. One in three Turks (30%), but only one in six Germans (16% lived in flats without a bathroom. Ninety-three percent of Turks compared to 48% of Germans wished to have a larger home. In addition to the discrepancies in housing quality, various studies have revealed that

---

[401] Jacobs, Susie: Pedagogies of Teaching 'Race' and Ethnicity in Higher Education: British and European Experiences, Sociology, Anthropology, Politics (C-SAP) University of Birmingham, 2006; In Chapter 9, Robert Grimm: Outlooks on Teaching 'Race', Ethnicity and Migration in Selected German Universities, pp. 210-230

[402] Kolinsky, Eva: 'Multiculturalism in Making. Non Germans and civil society in the new Länder', in Flockton, G. and Kolinsky, E. (ed.) *Recasting East Germany,* London: Frank Cass, 1999, pp. 22-39)

Turks have to pay 20% more rent than Germans for property of the same standards.[403] The study of housing conditions among the Ruhrkohle workforce also showed that most Turks were interested in developing social contacts with Germans. 13% preferred to live in a segregated neighbourhood, 53% in a mixed neighbourhood, while **33%** even expressed a preference for neighbours who were solely German. The 1985 survey showed that a mere 9% of Turks, given the choice, would have preferred a predominately Turkish neighbourhood. Despite these findings, the allegation has persisted among Germans that Turks unwilling to integrate sufficiently into German society and the German way of life. [404]

Although most of the Turks have been evenly distributed across Germany in the 2000s some of the Turks still tend to be concentrated in certain parts such as in Kreuzberg of Berlin, Cologne, Frankfurt, and Duisburg. A quarter of Turks live in smaller towns in southern parts of Germany like Hessen, Wurttemberg and Bavaria. These concentrations in certain city quarters, often labelled 'little Turkey' or 'little Istanbul' have led to label as a form of ghettoisation. [405]

In the 1990s, more Turks started buying houses although predominantly in those parts of town where they already live. The disappearance of Turkish 'ghettos' will largely depend on social mobility of German–born generations of the Turks. Data from Turkish sources show that numbers of house-owners of Turkish immigrants are increasing. Turkish Housing Minister Faruk Nafiz Özak cited that Turkish immigrants own 220,000 properties in Germany; however, the number of properties sold to foreigners mainly Germans was only 65,000 in Turkey.[406]

Pie-chart graph 14: Measuring the housing conditions of Turkish immigrants in Germany

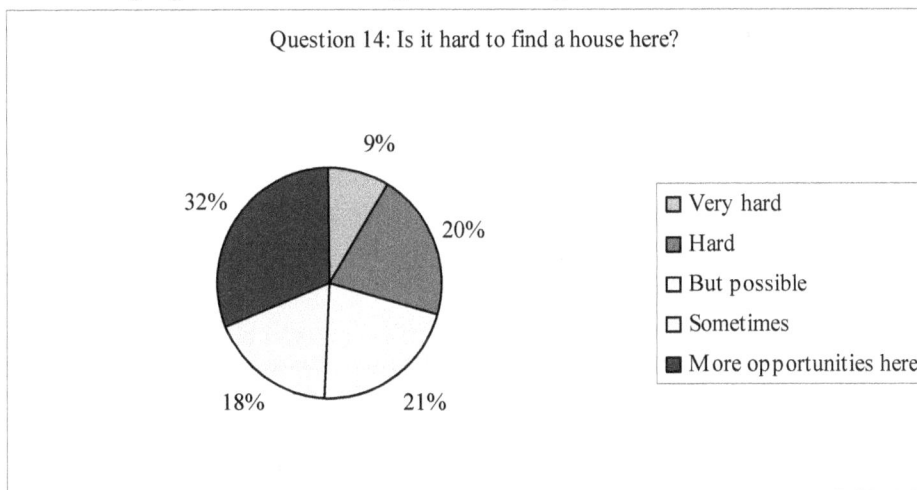

Source: Author

---

[403] Eryilmaz, Aytaç: *40 years in Germany - At Home Abroad*: DOMIT –Documentation Centre and Museum of the Migration from Turkey, Cologne, 2002, (p.4-5) [Translation from Turkish: Bengü Kocatürk – Schuster]

[404] Ibid.

[405] H.Korte, V.Eichener, G.Koch, and K.Schmidt (1985): Die Wohnsituation der auslandischeen Mitarbeiter der Ruhrkohle AG.Forschungsbeicht, Bochum-Essen, 1985-Schrift-enreihe Landes-und statentwicknungsforschung des Landes Northrhein-Westfalia. Forschungsbericht im Auftrag des Bundesministers fur Arbeit und Socialordnung, Bonn, 1986, p.345

[406] Turkish Ministry of Housing and Public Works' Report, Ankara, Turkey, 16 June 2008.

Table 14 reveals that 27 respondents, 9% of Turkish descent said that it is 'very hard' to find a proper house. 61 respondents, 20% said it is 'hard' but possible to find house. If one compares with the situation a decade ago. 64 respondents, 21% think that finding a house is easier than prior to German reunification, especially in Berlin where there are more available houses for rent or to buy. 54 respondents, 18% said that facilities are even 'better than Turkey'. 94 respondents, 32% stated that 'more opportunities' appeared after reunification.

Previous data on the housing conditions (of Turkish immigrants in Germany from 1985-1994), shows that poor housing resulted in slower integration of Turkish immigrants into German society. Those studies also suggest that Turkish immigrants experience greater instability in poorer housing conditions and have a greater reliance on the rental sectors than the native population. Turkish immigrants represent the largest group of foreign residents, 26% of whom live in social housing, followed by 25% of people from the former Yugoslavia, 12% of Italians and 11% of Greeks.[407] Although 32% of Turkish immigrants state that their housing conditions have improved since German unification. 2/3 of Turkish immigrants still feel that they need some more improvement is due in their housing conditions to further their integration from housing aspect.

4.1.15. Question 15: How are the facilities for your children's education?

The purpose of this question is to investigate the feelings towards the education facilities provided in Germany for the children of Turkish immigrants which is the most significant factor in their integration into the German school system and social life and gives access to other facilities such as social, legal, political and sportive activities.

If adequate facilities are not provided for immigrant children they are not to be able to be educated and the extent of their integration into German society will be constrained. The availability of language tuition and language support services is a key factor affecting integration of immigrants in a host country. Integration of Turkish immigrant children into the German education system is not only necessary for their school integration and educational achievement but also necessary for their integration performance from all aspects of German life such as economic, social, politics and sportive participation of activities in German society in the future.

Below the table gives data from 1974-5 which is representative of the educational status of the Turkish immigrant guest worker generation. The data shows 65.1% of the survey sample as having a primary school education only. It can be concluded that the low socio-economic status of guest worker parents has been perpetuated through the discrimination of their children.[408]

---

[407]Sarah Spencer (Ed.): Immigration as an Economic Asset, Trentham Books, 1994; in Ch.1 Ursula Mehrländer: The Development of Post War Migration and Refugee Policy, (p. 11).
[408]William Hale: Turkish immigrants in Western Europe -The Turkic Peoples of the World-Edited by Margaret Brainbridge, Published by Kegan Paul, 1993, (p.383)

4.1.2 Educational attainment of emigrant workers and total population of Turkey, 1974-5

Turkish School system prior to 2000	Workers abroad, 1974	Turkish population, 1975
Literate but not completed Primary	17.8	30.1
Primary school (ages 7-12)	**65.1**	54.9
Middle school (ages 12-15)	9.4	4.9
High School ages (16-18)	1.9	4.8
Above (ages 18-24)	4.0	5.0
Unknown	1.8	0.3

Source: Devlet Istatislik Enstitusu-DIE (State Statistics Institute of Turkey), 1979, p.23

Above table shows that Turks immigrated to Germany as guest workers', their literacy rates was even lower than they stayed in Turkey during 1970s.

A survey conducted in 1998 show that only 8% of the German youngster, 33% of all foreign youth and 40% of the youth of Turkish do not even start vocational training. In 1999 the number of Turkish origin pupils in Germany was 503.000. About 91.000 of them attended trade schools. 194, 000 of them attended kindergarten and primary schools, while 22, 400 pupils attended grammar schools. Furthermore, 19,000 studied in the same year at a university.[409]

German educationalists and politicians argue that contemporary integration of immigrants can be achieved only through education. Kenan Kolat President for Turco-German Society in Frankfurt argues that, "Turkish Parents should participate to Education system in Germany",[410] and Prof. Ingrid Ditrich argued that "German education system is discriminatory".[411] Journalist Yalçin Doğan points out how education is important for immigrants' integration from all aspects of host society '*Fighting on identity issue of Turks*'. "Immigrants are unwilling to be integrated because hosts want to abolish their identity through assimilation under the name of integration". German chancellor Angela Merkel underlines the importance of education for immigrants' integration, "Integration of immigrants will be successful but only by education". Now many German companies grant scholarships to immigrants' children for their training and education which aim at helping their integration.[412]

At Germany's third integration summit in Berlin November 6 2008, German politicians Angela Merkel, Anne Maria Böhmer and Olaf Schölz emphasized that "Education and language skills are key to integration".[413]

There are very real and quantifiable challenges facing Turkish-origin youth, their parents and educational policy makers in finding a solution to the under-performance in the education system. Comparative research from Konsortium Bildungsberichterstattung 2006 by Crul and Schneider reveals that only 14% of Turkish immigrants aged 25-35 at the time of writing finished a preparatory track that would provide direct access to university. 2006 Research shows an 18% secondary school dropout rate among German Turkish-origin youth aged 25-35 at the

---

[409] Eryilmaz, A.: '*40 years in Germany - At Home Abroad*' DOMIT –Documentation Centre and Museum of the Migration from Turkey, Cologne, 2002, (p. 6) [Translation from Turkish: Bengü Kocatürk – Schuster]
[410] Kenan Kolat, President for Turco-German Society, Frankfurt, 28.8.2006
[411] An article by Yalcin Doğan: '*Fighting on identity issue of Turks*'18 October, 2007 [Author's translation from Turkish Daily Hürriyet, 18 October, 2007].
[412] Ibid.
[413] DW-World: Berlin Promises Better Education Chances for Immigrants (07.11.2008) DW-WORLD.DE
   An article by Maurice Crul and Jens Schneider, 2009, (p.9)

time of writing. However the overall educational situation of the second generation is significantly better when compared with the first generation. The total percentage of the first-generation individuals between 20 and 26 years of age not working and not studying is 18.6%, whereas this is the case only for 8.5% of the second generation.[414]

In Germany, a survey of 2000 shows Turkish-origin girls have overtaken boys, the percentage of Turkish-origin women with a diploma from the more prestigious levels of schooling (Abitur or Fachhochschulreife) is rising. About 1 in 5 Turkish women aged 18-30 at the time of the research had a diploma on this level, a clear improvement compared with the micro-census data of 1995. German micro-census data 2002 shows that Turkish-origin girls in German preparatory tracks for higher education more than doubled compared with a 1988 survey, which means that females first closed the gap with the males and have overtaken males even with better school results.[415]

Graph 15: Measuring education facilities of Turkish-descent children in German schools

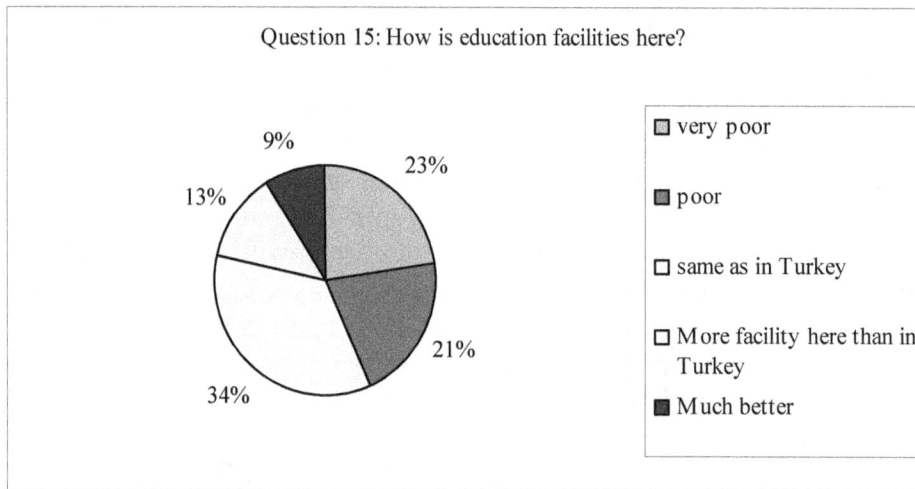

Question 15: How is education facilities here?

- very poor
- poor
- same as in Turkey
- More facility here than in Turkey
- Much better

23% 21% 34% 13% 9%

Source: Author

Above graph shows that 68 respondents, 23% find the education opportunities 'Not good' for their children. 62 respondents, 21% find education and training opportunities 'not bad'. 105 respondents, 35% find the German education opportunities 'good' for their children. 36 respondents, 13% think that there 'more education opportunities' in Germany. 27 respondents, 9% find education facilities 'very good' in Germany.

Previous studies show that several factors contribute or hinder the integration process of immigrants. One important facilitating factor is the level of skills and education of immigrants entering into the host society. German Chancellor Angela Merkel said that "Guest workers from southern Europe, who migrated to Germany in 1960s, gave the German society a new face.

---

[414] Konsortium Bildungsberichterstattung, 2006.
[415] German Microcensus data from 1995 to 2002

152

Speaking at a two-day symposium in Berlin, Merkel said "the Turks now living in Germany for the last four generations contribute a great deal to the country's economy."[416]

German born children of Turkish descent who have been brought up in a bicultural environment with schooling in standard German classes with mastery of the German language are likely to complete their studies and to be integrated into their country of birth and education successfully. When they are exposed to the German language; to the German society; and to the German way of living from an early age this is more attainable. However, for the majority of the two-thirds of non native-German children born in Germany, educational opportunities differ sharply from those of their native-German peers with a heavy concentration at lower education levels.

The German-born children of Turkish guest workers up brought in a bicultural environment, schooled in standard German classes and with mastery of the German language are more likely to complete their studies successfully. The essential factors are exposure to the German language; to German society; and to the German way of living.

The German Federal Minister of Education left the issue of educational and school integration of immigrant children to the discretion of the eleven states of former West Germany. The school integration was first discussed in the late 1970s how much cultural and linguistic preservation would be implemented.[417]

To achieve a viable integrated educational program for immigrant children, Berlin schools actively pursue and enhance contact and interaction among Turkish-descent and native German children. Further, schools support programs which allow children to reconcile the cultures of home and school. Most specifically, the schools should facilitate language transition programs rather than simply assuming that being in Germany is sufficient to learn German.

Comparing two German states' in Berlin and Bavaria education policies towards the integration of Turkish-descended children in the early 1980, the Bavarian approach in Munich looks bilingual containing flexible elements that have isolated and segregated Turkish-descended children under the name of bilingualism. As a number of critics about linguistic debates have noted that the Bavarian approach resulted in failure for second generation Turkish-descended children in both languages. Turkish parents were undecided whether to stay in Germany permanently in the mid of 1980s. Before 1980 German Federal States considered bilingual instruction to be the best solution for education of the children of immigrants with the expectation that the parents would return home one day and those children could continue their education in the home country and without a need to master the German language. In the case of those parents who decided to stay in Germany earlier, their children mastered the German language and have been integrated into the German school system.

---

[416] German Chancellor Angela Merkel delivered a speech at the symposium of 'Integration through education in the 21st century' in Berlin, 17 October 2007

[417] Eryilmaz, A.: '40 years in Germany - At Home Abroad' DOMIT –Documentation Centre and Museum of the Migration from Turkey, Cologne, 2002, (p. 6) [Translation from Turkish: Bengü Kocatürk – Schuster]

The 'integrationist' Berlin education approach for immigrant children is more realistic and humane than the bilingual Bavarian approach. It acknowledges the fact that those Turkish immigrants and their German born children are staying in Germany and need to be integrated into German society. The integrationist approach of Berlin is built on the diversity and heterogeneity of cultures and experiences of those children since Germany recognised and legitimated itself as a culturally pluralistic society, considering the cultural and linguistic background of these immigrant children. A third characteristic of Berlin schools which are based on bicultural and bilingual educational approach is the background of the immigrant children is not ignored and so that parents need not worry that in schools their children will lose their ethnic and religious values and cultural heritage.

The Berlin program is grounded in the view that an educational environment for guest worker children must encourage bilingualism. Immigrant children have the option of integrating into the society and maintaining closer homeland ties. One sixth of Berlin city schools and one of every three school children in Berlin-state is from immigrant background.

Table 4.1.3: German, non-German and Turkish Pupils in German Schools, 1994 (in %)

Type of School	German and Non German Pupils	Non-German Pupils	Pupils from recruitment countries	Turkish Pupils
Junior	37	37	36	37
Main	17	26	29	29
Middle	11	9	10	8
High	20	10	8	6
Special	4	6	6	7
Auxiliary*	10	11	11	13
Overall Number of pupils	9,133,000	800,241	600,000	360,912

Auxiliary*: A special school for slow learners. Figures in Table are rounded up and may not total 100.
Source: Adapted from Bundesanstalt für Arbeits and Socialstatistik-Hauptergebnisse 1993, Nuremberg, 1993

Youth of Turkish origin, including those born in Germany and holding German school qualifications, are deemed to be foreign applicants if they are not naturalised and must compete for places reserved for foreign students in the University System. For instance in 1990-1991, only 0.8% of student in at German universities were of Turkish origin with German educational qualifications. In 1994, 25% of young non-Germans but only 6% of young Germans failed to gain a school leavers' certificate. Also in 1994, 5% of German applicants but only 1.5% of non German applicants (1, 829 individuals) were accepted for public sector employment. This data shows bare educational inequality: only 28% of native German but 44% of Turkish-origin pupils leave school with the lowest educational qualification, the high school graduation: 28% young Germans but only 6% young Turks pass their Abitur (University Entry Examination),[418] and gain the right to study at German universities.[419]

---

[418] **German school system**: Preschool classes (*Vorklassen*), Schulkindergarten (*preparatory classes*), and Primary school (*Grundschulen*), Secondary school (*Hauptsschulen*), Multi aimed schools (*Schularten mit*

Table 4.1.4: Number of immigrant children attending school in Germany 1997-1998.

Type of schools	others	%	Turks	%	Total foreigners
Vorklassen	3.404	0.3	3.267	0.3	6.671
Schulkindergarten	4.653	0.4	5.219	0.4	9.872
Grundschulen	218.693	17.7	181.730	14.7	400.473
Hauptsschulen	130.521	10.5	100.497	8.1`	231.018
Schularten mit mehreren Bildungsgangen	3.278	0.3	1.366	0.1	4.644
Realschulen	48.084	3.9	30.352	2.5	78.436
Gymnasium	65.604	5.3	22.222	1.8	87.826
Gesamtschulen/Freie Waldorfschulen	33.557	2.7	31.255	2.5	64.812
Abenschulen und Kollegs	5.335	0.4	3.089	0.2	8.424
Sonderschulen	34.004	2.8	24.577	2.8	58.581
Berufschulen	190.951	15.4	97.190	7.0	288.141
Total	738.084		500.764		1.238.848

Source: Ministry of Federal Education and Science "*Grund und Strukturen*" 1998-1999

The problem with competition for university places isn't only due to the students' qualifications, but the national origin of the parents which determines their children's access route to university. Given that a university education is a requirement for all professions, even the best educated Turkish-origin youth in Germany continue to be penalised (in 2009) because of their parents' background.

In the 1990s, low-status jobs were increasingly taken up by ethnic-German immigrants from former Warsaw Pact countries. Those German born and educated children of Turkish guest workers who were successful were free to move from blue-collar to white-collar careers and from low-paid employment to the professions.[420]

Among German states Berlin has the best municipal record of trying to help the youths of Turkish origin for their educational integration; this was due to Richard von Weizsäcker, later to be President of Germany. He was former CDU governing mayor in 1981 increased funds and staff for Berlin's new State (*Land*) welfare centre for immigrants. Richard von Weizsäcker (Mayor of West Berlin 1981-1984; President of Germany 1984-1994) has been an advocate of democratic principles, tolerance, and social responsibility. The city itself with 165,000 persons of Turkish origin has the biggest Turkish population outside Turkey with many writers, lawyers, and exhibitions by Turkish artists, while the number of Turkish university students is far higher than elsewhere.[421]

---

mehreren Bildungsgangen), Preparatory for vocational schools (*Realschulen*), High schools (*Gymnasium*), mixed school (*Gesamtschulen/Freie Waldorfschulen*), Evening schools and colleges (*Abenschulen und Kollegs*), Special classes (*Sonderschulen*), Vocational Technique schools (*Berufschulen*), Universities (Universität).

[419] Spencer, Sarah (Ed.): Immigration as an Economic Asset, Trentham Books, 1994; in Chapter 5, Faruk Şen,'Pre-school Education and School Problems and Transition from School to Employment, (p. 100- 101)

[420] Kolinsky, Eva: 'Multiculturalism in Making. Non Germans and civil society in the new Länder', in Flockton, G. and Kolinsky, E. (ed.) *Recasting East Germany*, London: Frank Cass, 1999, pp. 22-39)

[421] Ibid.

Table 4.1.5: Distribution of Turkish students in German universities between 1980 -1998

Years	Total Turkish Students	Other non-German students	Turkish students %
1980	6.542	57.713	11.3
1985	9.215	74.574	12.4
1990	12.962	99.760	13.0
1992	15.859	123.052	12.9
1994	19.317	141.460	13.7
1995	20.631	146.471	14.1
1996	21.858	151.870	14.4
1997	23.031	158.435	14.5
1998	24.050	162.510	15.2

Source: Statistisches Bundesamt, Wiesbaden, 1998

Table 4.1.6: Turkish Students in German Universities in 1996/7

Departments	Students grown up in Germany	Total Turkish Students %
Language and History	1,692	53.0
Sports	75	64.1
Law, Economy Social Science	5,831	95.2
Mathematics Nature Science	1,704	66.8
Medical	1,246	84.7
Veterinary	3	13.6
Forestry/Agriculture	39	35.5
Engineering	4,651	78.0
Art Academies	181	63.7
Total	15,442	70.6

Source: Statistisches Bundesamt, 1998.

There are 113 universities, 157 vocational high schools and 45 Art academies in Germany. The number of Turkish-descent students in German universities increased 259% between 1980 and 1997 whereas the number of German students increased only 163%. In 1980 there were 6,542 students, in 1997-8 this number increased to 23,031 or 15.2% of the total. 70.6% (37.4% of those are female students) of these numbers completed their gymnasium (high school) in Germany.[422]

In furthering the integration of Turkish immigrants and their children, the role of emigrant and immigrant countries' attitudes are also important. Here, to clarify this matter, the education policies of Germany and Turkey did not help the educational integration of Turkish-origin children. On the contrary, it hindered it. The Turkish government sent mother tongue teachers to meet the perceived educational need, but some of those teachers did not speak German.

Successful educational projects have emphasised common values, building solidarity through shared activities, for example theatre performances and bringing parents together for

---

[422] Jacobs, Susie: Pedagogies of Teaching 'Race' and Ethnicity in Higher Education: British and European Experiences, Sociology, Anthropology, Politics (C-SAP) University of Birmingham, 2006; In Chapter 9, Robert Grimm: Outlooks on Teaching 'Race', Ethnicity and Migration in Selected German Universities, pp. 210-230

contact and discussions regarding the education of their children.[423] Considering the importance of parental involvement however, we can see that only 10% of Turkish immigrants were technically educated. For successful school integration, parents should participate in school activities in a cooperative way and help with their children's homework. Such a low proportion of adults with a post-secondary educational background may indicate that the children would need significant additional support particularly with language learning.

4.1.16. Question 16: Are you interested in politics here?

The purpose of this question is to investigate Turkish immigrants' interest in German politics and political activities. The political integration of persons of Turkish descent can be determined by the extent of their participation and representation at local, national and European parliament levels. Affecting factors include the attitudes and policies of German political parties towards Turkish immigrants' integration, their interest in naturalised German Turks' votes and the number of naturalised Turkish immigrants gaining voting rights with citizenship.

Immigration experts assert that if immigrants wish to be integrated and naturalize they should participate in their host country's politics. They also claim that "illegal migrants have already been portrayed as a challenge to security, identity, welfare and the principles of Western European democracies and controlling unwanted migration is also important for EU states." [424] A lack of integration of immigrants causes concerns about political stability, social cohesion and welfare, both at the level of the nation state and the EU.

The growing numbers of naturalised Turkish immigrants have affected electoral voting patterns in Germany. The existence of Turkish-descent political representatives in mainstream parties is an important criterion for their feeling of integration. Their participation in German politics is directly related to citizenship policy as only German citizens may vote in general elections. Each state has its own citizenship test and in this may create an undue barrier to participation in the electoral process. One of the female political representatives of Turkish origin Lale Akgün, a Social Democrat in the Bundestag, describes the difficulties of the German political system as a "glass ceiling" once in office. This may go some way to explain the fact that just five of the Bundestag's 613 members claim Turkish heritage and the number of Turks holding elected office throughout all levels of government including local, state and national typically hovers around 80.

German political parties' integration policies play an important role in this issue, for example; if the country's ruling and opposing parties agree on a common and favourable integration policy for immigrants, this will facilitate the integration process of the immigrants.

If the host country's ruling party is in favour of integration of immigrants and the opposition is not in favour, this situation will bring uncertainties to the integration process as there is no commitment to continue if the party in power changes.

---

[423] European Commission Video "Integration of immigrants: a challenge for Europe", 09/12/2005, European Commission - Audiovisual Service REF : I-049849, playback at 6 minutes, accessed via the internet
http://ec.europa.eu./avservices/video/video_prod_en.cfm?type=detail&prodid=408 (link checked 20/05/2009)
[424] Thielemann, Eiko, A.: 'European Journal of migration and Law-JCMS', 43 (1): 695-716, Volume 6, No 1, 2005, pp.43-61

Graph 16: Measuring the political awareness of Turkish immigrants in Germany

Question 16: Are you interested in politics here?

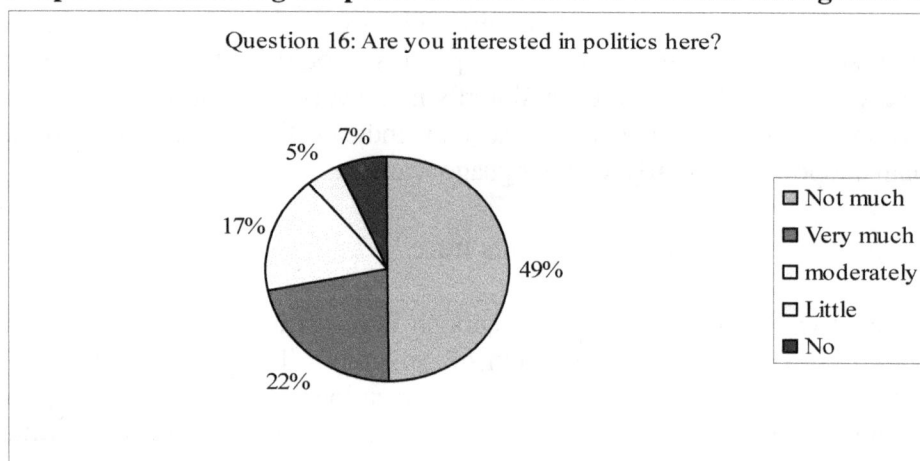

☐	Not much
■	Very much
☐	moderately
☐	Little
■	No

Source: Author

Graph 16 shows that 149 respondents, 49% answered this question as 'Not much'. This does not mean that they are not interested at all in German politics. Rather, they find politics meaningless without having German citizenship. In other words, they feel excluded from political rights such as voting rights, participating in German political activities and joining to German political parties as a member without being fully integrated into the German socio-political life and obtained German nationality. 66 respondents, 22% said 'very much' that they are generally interested in politics in Germany. 51 participants or 17% said 'moderately' meaning that they take notice of political issues that affect their lives; 14 respondents, 5% said that they are interested in political issues but do not necessarily have a preference of political party. However, their attitudes might change 'sometimes'. 20 respondents, 7% said 'No' they do not engage with politics in Germany.

Some Turkish immigrants show a willingness to get involved in Germany's politics and adopt its traditions. It is logical that naturalised Turkish immigrants in Germany should participate in political life as Germans. Politically integrated immigrants bring a new generation of representatives to their host country's legislature. Turkish immigrant women in particular are doing better than men in the field of university education, business and in political participation. A number of Turkish immigrants are involved in parliamentary and local government. For instance, Cem Özdemir, the first naturalized Turkish immigrant-German elected MP in the Bundestag, is co-leader of the political party "Alliance '90/The Greens" and Turkish descent MEP Vural Öger is representing Germany in European Parliament. In Germany, non-citizens are not entitled to vote in general elections, but naturalised Turks tend to favour the Social Democratic SPD and The Greens (*Die Grünen*). An opinion poll in late 1998 suggested that dual citizenship was not desirable by German conservatives (CDU-Christian Democratic Union) and if integration of resident immigrants is achieved successfully, those immigrants would constitute a fifth of the German population by the year 2020, forming a significant voting block. It is obvious that immigrant electoral behaviour and voting patterns are connected with the process and policies of integration. Immigration has been affecting electoral politics across Western democracies (including Germany) as growing numbers naturalise, obtain voting rights and express their political opinions at the ballot box. One example is the 2000 citizenship law reducing barriers to citizenship for persons of foreign parentage born in Germany. Cem Özdemir lobbied successfully in favour of this change. Thomas Scharf points out that the German Greens Party is encouraging local people including Turkish immigrants to participate in political activities in Germany. "Cem Özdemir, the Green Party politician, born in 1965 in Bad Urach in south western Germany, is both a bridge-builder and a self-starter. He was the first member of the German parliament, the Bundestag, of Turkish descent. On talk shows, he liked to refer to himself as the "Anatolian from Swabia," a region in the south western German state of Baden-Württemberg" [425]

The low number of Turkish-origin representatives in Germany can be explained by the fact that the first generation of Turkish guest workers migrated mostly from a rural environment. Industrial societies such as Germany and other Western European countries have ways of living and institutions that differ greatly from those in Turkey and the process of political acclimatisation took time. The longer immigrants stayed in Germany and as their socio-economic position improved, they became more integrated and their political attitudes and behaviour also changed. Importantly, immigrants show an increased willingness over time to take an interest in host countries politics and adopt its political traditions.

4.1.17. Question 17: Are you a German citizen?

The purpose this question is to investigate the relationship between the integration of immigrants and German citizenship and integration policy.
As discussed earlier in the chapter three, the Federal Republic of Germany has 16 constituent states; each with its own immigration, integration and style of citizenship test. [426] At the beginning of the Turkish labour migration, many immigrants did not consider the citizenship requirements and bureaucratic process in force in the state they were migrating to. This is possibly due to a lack of information or a lack of sophistication in the guest workers' planning due to the original short-term intention of their stay. In fact, during Germany's foreign labour recruitment years (1960-1973) the intention of most was to return home after saving money. Germany did not consider itself an immigration country until year 2000. After Germany's official declaration of itself as an immigration country, the citizenship law was changed in favour of immigrants with long-term residency and their children. Prior to this, German citizenship depended on blood ties (since 1913).

A new citizenship law of Germany was passed by broad majorities in Germany's Bundestag (lower house) and Bundesrat (upper house) in May 1999. This nationality reform of the naturalization of foreign nationals was one of the first domestic measures of major societal importance under Chancellor Gerhard Schröder. The new citizenship law came in force from January 1 2000.

The new law substantially changes the principle of descent (*jus sanguinis*) which has long been the country's traditional basis for granting citizenship. Now, it will also be possible to

---

[425] Thomas Scharf (1994): 'The Rise Of the New Local Politics' (The Greens in Germany's Local Politics), The German Greens-Challenging the Consensus, German Studies Series (Ed. Eva Kolinsky, Keele University); Berg Publisher,1994
[426] Each federal state of Germany has its own citizenship criteria/test to grant citizenship to its immigrants. For example, Baden-Württemberg had a notorious test

acquire German citizenship as the result of being born in Germany (*jus solis*) as is the case in most other European countries. Further, the reform also takes into account the fact that more than seven million foreigners live in Germany on a long-term basis. One third of them have lived here for more than 30 years; half of them have lived in Germany for at least 20 years. The lives of most of the foreign nationals living in Germany center on Germany. The new citizenship and nationality law offers them a shorter mandatory waiting period for naturalization, which is reduced from 15 years to eight. It is an offer to facilitate their integration into the civic community, an offer that is not based on blood tie anymore. A large portion of Germany's population now has the opportunity to participate in and help shape social and political issues with all inherent rights and obligations. This reform is aimed at closing the gap that has existed to date between social reality and citizenship status. This gap exists because, in practical terms, most of these people have become Germans. In legal terms however, they continue to be foreigners. This offer to facilitate the integration of foreign nationals living in Germany however also involves obligations. These obligations include in particular that the respective individual learns German and professes loyalty to the Basic Law, Germany's constitution.

The individual state's current integration policy is therefore an important facilitating or hindering factor.[427] The increasing numbers of Turkish-descent Germans is a good indicator of the progress of integration of Turkish immigrants. Individuals applying for citizenship are most likely to be integrated or substantially integrated into German social, cultural and political life.

Graph 17: Measuring the number of Turkish descent German citizens

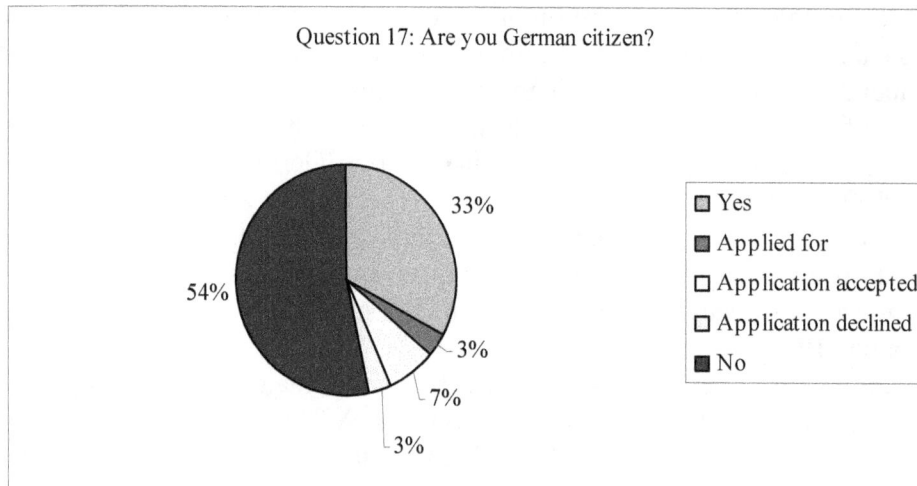

Question 17: Are you German citizen?

- Yes
- Applied for
- Application accepted
- Application declined
- No

Source: Author

Of the 300 respondents, 98 or 33% said "yes"; they became German citizens. 10 of the respondents, 3% indicated that they applied for German citizenship, but their application is in

---

[427] Bös, Matthias: The Legal Construction of Membership: Nationality Law in Germany Retrieved 2007-02-09. German Minister Urges Reversal of Dual Citizenship Policy, DW-World

progress. 22 respondents or 7% said that their application for German citizenship has been accepted by German Federal authorities but is still in process. 3% or 10 respondents said that their application for German citizenship has been 'declined'. Exactly 160 participants or 53% of the 300 said 'No' they had not applied and are living in Germany as Turkish citizens.

The positive side of the results, 33 % +7 % = 40 % citizenship gained or accepted is a good indicator but shows a significant lack of political integration. There is a definite gap between the number of persons of Turkish origin living in Germany and their level of political representation and a shortfall in the number of potential voters and political candidates caused by persons not holding German citizenship partly explains this. Turkish immigrants who gained German citizenship are able to play a fuller part in national life, revealing the self-perceived advantages and disadvantages of gaining German citizenship as a complex issue.

In Germany, the 1913 Nationality Law defined the German nation as comprised of a community based on 'descent'. This law was one of the hindering factors for non-Germans and as well as Turkish immigrants becoming German citizens until the end of 1990s.[428] Another hindering factor comes from the Turkish side. Turkish loyalty to the homeland is stronger than other immigrant communities in Germany, especially for first generation guest workers for whom national pride is an important consideration.

Veysel Özcan points out that the changes to German law help boost naturalization numbers. For example, former Turkish citizens made up the largest group with 64,631 naturalizing in 2002, accounting for 42 percent of the total.[429]

The low rate of naturalization can be explained as many first generation Turks do not want to give up their nationality and de-emphasise their Turkish origin as a defensive social posture adopted by the community in the face of perceived hostility. Another important factor is a sense of insecurity, which the guest-worker system was designed to produce, and which reinforces any unwillingness to give up Turkish nationality for German nationality. Many see dual nationality as preferable and some form of insurance. A *dual nationality* policy which would have addressed these concerns was rejected by both the political centre-left and centre-right except from the Greens Party in Germany. Former Co-chairman of the Green Party Claudia Roth advocates dual citizenship for second and third generation German born Turkish descent immigrants after the Euro 2008 semi-final between Turkish and German National Football Teams when many German-born Turkish descent footballers played for Turkey. Although dual citizenship is restricted under German law, it can be held in limited circumstances: (i) where a child born to German parents acquires another citizenship at birth (e.g. based on place of birth, or descent from one parent); (ii) where a German citizen acquires a foreign nationality with the permission of the German government; (iii) where a naturalized German citizen, or a child born to non-German parents in Germany, obtains permission to keep their foreign nationality. A senior Social Democratic member Ralf Stegner, who is the interior minister in the regional state of Schleswig-Holstein, has asked the German chancellor to change dual-nationality law to allow

---

[428] Geddes, Andrew: The Politics of Migration and immigration in Europe, Sage Publication, London, 2003, (p. 95).

[429] Source: Federal Statistical Office of Germany (*Statistisches Bundesamt*), 2002

dual-nationality to all citizens of Germany. He feels that Germany should allow multi-nationality to integrate many of the Gastarbeiter who live in Germany.

Turkish immigrants remaining as Turkish citizens in Germany permanently have lawful residence. Some subsequently acquired German citizenship, but the process is difficult for immigrants and even their German-born children. The decision to grant citizenship to immigrants and conditions for naturalisation is left to the discretion of 16 different states' authorities in Germany.

In the case of naturalisation (gaining German citizenship) of Turkish immigrants, German naturalisation policy and the mostly first generation Turkish loyalty to their homeland contradict German citizenship requirements. However, Germany is home for the German-born second and third Turkish-descent generations who tend to be well integrated into German society and plan to stay there in future (discussed further in survey question 27). It is important to consider and evaluate the extent to which cultural differences are accepted. In the three major European immigration countries, the preconditions are almost the same, such as a minimum cultural adaptation required for naturalization including a basic knowledge of the host country's national language.

In most western European countries, the route to citizenship for immigrants has been defined using criteria like acceptable integration, length of residency, financial security, lack of criminality, linguistic proficiency, etc. The challenges posed by immigrants, including Turks, with distinct cultures and religions have raised the issue as to what extent they must adapt to the culture of the host country as a precondition for gaining citizenship and formal social and political rights. Integration for Turkish immigrants is defined as an adaptation to Germany's mainstream culture and an acceptance from German society of Turkish cultural and religious differences and diversity. Turks in Germany have become *German-Turks* in the same way that German emigrants in the United States call themselves '*German-Americans.*[430]

Don Henrich Tolzmann argues that the German-Americans have contributed to agriculture, industry, religion, education, music, art, architecture; politics, military service, and literature in the USA. They constitute USA's largest ethnic group, over 60 million, represent one-fourth of American population, according to 1990 census. Most of the German emigrates from German-speaking `states Switzerland, Austria and the Austro-Hungarian Empire, and Russia (from the Black Sea and the Volga) settled in the Western plain states, especially in Dakota, Nebraska, Kansas, and Colorado. They founded settlements in America with German names such as Kassel, New Danzig, and Leipzig.[431]

A German TV panel program called 'Nation, Migration, Integration and Foreign Home Germany' on German Integration and dual citizenship policy, the German Minister for Internal affairs, Wolfgang Schaeuble argues that "Turks living in Germany cannot become both German and Turkish at the same time. German-born and raised Turkish immigrant youths should decide to which country (Germany or Turkey) they belong and to which country they feel responsibility.

---

[430] Kaya, A.: 'Citizenship and the hyphenated Germans' *German Turks*, in F. Kerman and A. Içduygu (eds.) Citizenship and Identity in a Globalizing World: European Questions and Turkish Experiences, Routhledge, London, 2005
[431] Don Henrich Tolzmann: 'The German-American experience', published by Prometheus, 2000, New York, (p.18-19).

One may not feel loyalty to both countries at the same level."[432] Then he called for immigrant families to talk German among family members and parents with their children at home.

German MEP Cem Özdemir and Nihat Sorgeç Manager for Kreuzberg Vocational Training Centre in Berlin also participated in the Panel. Mr Cem said, "Effective legal measures should be taken to encourage more Turkish immigrants to be naturalised in Germany. German-born and raised Turkish youths should play for German national team not for Turkish Team."[433]
Mr. Nihat Sorgeç said: "Turks should be given a feeling, a loyalty that they belong to this country. Turks are emotional people if you approach them one step, they do not only approach you closer, but also run to you."[434]
Another participant in the Panel Hayri Hasan said 'There is an American proverb,

> "If you are Russian, you are Russian forever. Dual citizenship does not change anything; Turks are 'Foreigners' in Germany, 'Germanised Turks' in Turkey. Germans should give in to emotional feelings and accept dual citizenship which will be an advantage for both countries. You could not help admiring British Multicultural society, and how Britons can take advantage of this diversity. British Multicultural integration policy can be a model for Germany".[435]

As a result, some German politicians, scholars, Turkish origin businessmen, artists and actors favour dual citizenship for immigrants, the conservatives and some of the right (wing) parties oppose it.

4.1.18. Question 18: Do you feel a part of German culture?

The purpose of this question is to find out to what extent Turkish immigrants feel culturally integrated into German cultural and social life, considering the fundamental differences between Turkish and German culture and general difficulties integrating into an unfamiliar culture. Having a distinct culture makes integration harder as Turkish immigrants have to make more effort to understand the differing expectations, structure and common values among other factors. The research question requires their integration to be investigated from all aspects and cultural integration is highly significant. Therefore this question was directed to representatives of Turkish immigrant community/population in Germany.

Previous studies reveal that Turks show an increasing interest in participating in mainstream cultural trends and they have added new values to German literature. Turkish immigrants' literature and authors bring the heritage of their forefathers into present-day Germany. Improvement of social and cultural contacts between Germans and Turks in Germany can create communication and bridge gaps.

The younger generation of Turkish origin and Germany's Turkish origin business people are optimistic on integration of Turkish immigrants into German society. For example, Vural Öger believes that their success in business will help to integration of Turkish immigrants and Turkey's political efforts to become part of Europe. Öger says, "The majority of Turkish

---

[432] German TV Panel Program, 'Nation, Migration, Integration and Foreign Home Germany' [Author's Translation] May 7 2008 http://haberyorumlari.hurriyet.com.tr/
[433] Ibid. [Author's Translation]
[434] Ibid. [Author's Translation]
[435] Ibid. [Author's Translation]

immigrants call Germany home". He has also entered into German politics to change the image of Turks in Germany and Europe. He was elected to the European Parliament for a second term this year as a Social Democrat. [436] A young Turkish immigrant from Berlin, Abdullah Güneş, identifies himself as a Berlin Turk, not as a Turk from Turkey. 'Living in Berlin' refers to the city rather than to Germany as a whole. Turkish immigrants living in Berlin feel themselves as a part of life in Berlin. "Some of the troubles in Turkey do not interest me much. I watch sports from Turkey; it is a bit important to me, but what is going on in Berlin, in Germany, is more important. Germany is our second mother country. Our children will say, Germany is our first mother country. But they will say so as Turks!"[437]

This is an attempt by a new generation to try to make their voices heard and to advance their own understanding of what it means and what is should mean to be of Turkish origin in German society. The literature itself (in the German language) creates contacts and provides explanations through characters and stories and establishes a new mode of communication that can bridge social gaps between Germans and persons of Turkish origin.[438] Turkish immigrants wish to be integrated culturally and the positive view of integration among young persons of Turkish origin in German society means that they will contribute to form a new cultural identity as German-Turks. This bicultural and bilingual double identity is a theme of this research.

Turkish descent authors in German language and literature can create communication and bridge gaps. Migrants' literature itself creates contacts through its characters and stories, bridges gaps, and establishes communication.

This is an indicator of the level of integrated Turkish immigrants and increasing education level of second and third generation Turkish immigrants and raising the number of naturalised immigrant's added new values to German everyday life. These values aroused curiosity and interest of Germans in migrant culture and literature. Migrant authors reflected their cultural values in German society by writing books in German. A few of them can be mentioned here. For example Feridun Zaimoğlu, who regards himself as a 'Schleswig-Holsteiner' and writes his books in German including *Kanak Spraak*, *Abschaum*, and *Koppstoff*. Renan Demirkan's *Schwarzer Tee mit drei Stuck Zucker* (1990), and Emine Sevgi Özdamar's short stories (*Mutter Zunge*) 'Mother-Tongue' and (*Grossvater Zunge*) 'Grandfather-Tongue'(1990).These two are related by female Turkish immigrants to Germany and the experience of immigrant women in German society.

Themes of his books are related to racial treatment of immigrants and calling for immigrants to maintain their identities and rights. The second generation author, Selim Ozdogan with his book '*Ein gutes Leben ist die beste Rache*', 'a good life is the best revenge'. Nine of the 15 'Adalbert von Chamisso' Literature Prizes have been given to Turkish descent immigrant writers. Including Aras Ören, Güney Dal, Yüksel Pazarkaya, Zafer Şenocak, Zehra Çırak, Alev

---

[436] An article published in The New York Times' European Edition by Carter Dougherty, 'Turks in Germany are in bullish mood'; November 15 2005 (p.1- 4).

[437] Faist, Thomas & Özveren, Eyüp: Turkish-German Transnational Social Spaces, Ashgate Publication, 2004 (p. 194-202).

[438] Horrocks, David and Kolinsky, Eva (eds.): Turkish Culture in German Society Today. Providence, R.I.: Berghahn Books, 1996.

Tekinay, Ismet Elçi, Emine Sevgi Özdamar and Selim Özdoğan. Turkish immigrants born and raised in Germany have become successfully integrated into German society and better accepted than less integrated immigrants. Turkish descent movie stars (actors and actresses) do not act on the stage as stereotype guest worker role such as self-employed (*Dönerci*) Kebabman or Turkish girls escape from their fathers' strictness and oppression.

In the field of TV programming German-born and raised girl ARD TV's sport speaker Yasemin Kalkan can be a good model for successfully integrated immigrants. Another second generation Turkish immigrant Fatih Akin, whose film (*Kurz and Schmerzlos*) 'Short and Painless' narrating three German youths from Hamburg, won a prize in Salonika and Locarno. Kutlu Ataman's (*Lolia und Billidi Kid*)' is another example which won a best prize at the Berlin Film Festival. The theme of the film is a story of a Turkish travesty, narrated from a different point of view, a different diversity, if you compare it with Turkish movie set (*Yeşilçam*) Turkish Hollywood. In the field of cultural activities, like theatre and cabaret which deal with migration have taken place in German cultural life since 1980s. Bilingual presentations of *Tiyatrom* 'My theatre' in Berlin or (*Kamerad*) 'Comrade' theatre in Cologne are good examples of cultural activities. Among the first Turkish cabarets and playwrights, there are Şinasi Dikmen and Muhsin Omurca. These two actors first acted at the theatre with (*Knobibonbon*) together and then played 'Coup in Bonn' and 'Circumciser of Ulm'. Both plays are dealt with the integration and perception of Germans from the point of Turkish views and perception of Turks from the point of German views. In the framework of this (*Gastarbeiterlos*) 'Guest unemployed' with Sedat Pamuk's (*Putzfrauenkabarett*) 'Cabarets of Cleaner Women' or (*Bodenkosmetikerinnen*) 'Floor make-uppers'.[439]

This question simultaneously explores Turkish immigrants' adaptation into German culture, at the same time maintaining their country of origin's culture. It provides information that allows German readers for a better understanding of cultural and literary works expressions by Turkish German authors, and artists since they are written in German language. At the same time this question investigates the impact of Germans' living in Turkey on Turkish immigrants' integration into German society as well as minimizing and understanding of cultural differences between two communities in German society. Eva Kolinsky argues that

"Over the years, some Turks have responded to the unspoken rules of exclusion and exchanged their Turkish for German citizenship in order to become doctors, politicians, or journalists. Turkish immigrants wish to be regarded as ethnic minorities, different in nationality, background and culture but recognised as a legitimate grouping in German society. That would be ethnic minorities in Germany have developed lifestyles, identities, cultural diversity and a voice or voices of their own, has yet to be acknowledged fully in the German society and the country which has become their home."[440]

---

[439] 'Entrance of (*Gastarbeiterliteratur*) Turkish guest worker-literature into German Culture and literature world' is summarized and translated from Turkish Daily Hürriyet, German Edition/Culture and Magazine section, August 2006 [Author's Translation]

[440] Horrocks, David and Kolinsky, Eva (Eds.): 'Turkish Culture in German society today', Non-German Minorities in Contemporary German Society, Published by Berghahn Books, 1996, (p. 79-84).

Graph 18: Measuring cultural integration of Turkish immigrants in Germany

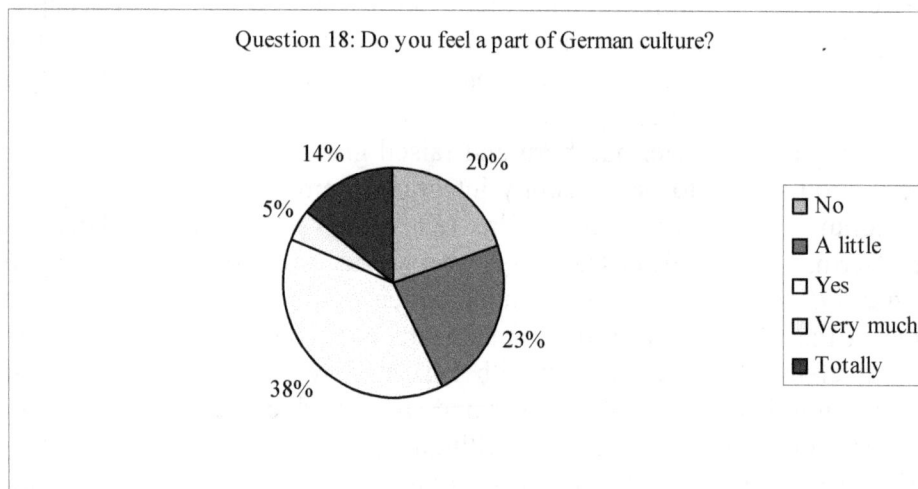

Question 18: Do you feel a part of German culture?

14% 20%
5%
23%
38%

- No
- A little
- Yes
- Very much
- Totally

Source: Author

Graph 18 shows that 60 respondents, 20% said 'no', they do not feel culturally integrated; 23% of the 68 respondents said that they are culturally integrated 'a little'; 115 respondents or 38 percent said 'yes', answering positively and acknowledging they felt integrated from cultural aspect; 5% of the 14 respondents said 'very well'; 14% or 43 respondents said that they felt 'totally' integrated meaning that they feel assimilated into German culture.

Researchers emphasize democratic, economic and administrative problems in host countries, the manner in which immigrants adapt themselves to their native born hosts until eventually immigrant groups' distinctiveness's vanished, with no history and no literature and immigrant origin has become almost irrelevant. Arthur Lermer claims that "assimilation' is anti-democratic; while allegedly solving problems arising from differences, it actually undermines some of the basic tenets of Democracy" [441]

Turks in Germany wish for better security, increased acceptance by the German people and the possibility to keep a connection to their culture of origin to some extent. Turkish migrant workers and their families have made significant progress in building new lives in Germany; they have bought houses, established businesses. It would be very difficult for well-established immigrants to return home, therefore co-existence is important. [442]

If the host society knows nothing about immigrants' original positions (class, race, sex, natural talents, religious beliefs, individual goals, and cultural values), how can they accept immigrants as members of their society? A Turkish proverb says "Man is enemy of his unknown". As Michael Richter points out a lack of dialogue between two communities in his book 'They came and stayed'. Some Turks in Germany feel rejected and excluded, even if they

---

[441] The Evolution of Canadian Policy towards cultural pluralism, Information and Comment Papers.No.16, Canadian Jews Congress, 1955
[442] Guardian 1 September 1993, 'Old Germans need young migrants' pay'.

are third generation in Germany. Often there is a lack of will on both sides to enter into an open dialogue and insufficient knowledge about each other's culture.[443]

German politicians emphasise 'diversity' as a more politically acceptable approach. A balance of integration for Turkish immigrants is importance; a high level of integration means assimilation of immigrants which may create a people without ethnic origin or unaware of their ethnic origins.[444]

As discussed earlier, Turkish immigrants are not only from diverse culture, but also majority of them from rural Anatolian regions of Turkey (Turkey has seven different geographic and cultural regions). Therefore, cultural integration of Turkish immigrants caused a long heated debate in German political circles recently. In 2009, a survey conducted by The Bertelsmann Foundation showed that half of German immigrants feel like outsiders in German society. While 58% of survey respondents felt as a part of German society.[445]

4.1.19. Question 19: Are you married to a German?

The purpose of this question is to investigate intermarriage between persons of Turkish origin and Germans and the impact on integration. Intermarriage is a significant influencing factor for the integration of Turkish immigrants in German society. In mixed marriage households one adult is native-born and the other is foreign-born. Persons of Turkish origin living in mixed marriage households are more likely to be integrated into German society compared with those in non-mixed marriages. They are also likely to have a higher level of interaction with host society members, for example with friends and relatives of the German partner.

Journalist Hans Kirchmann argues that intermarriage is not only an important influencing factor of Turkish immigrants' integration into German society and its life standards, but also determinative factor for immigrants' stay in Germany. A German married is establishing a kind of binding ties to Germany. One of the first Turkish immigrants, Onur Dülgers, came to Germany when he was 22, married a German, owns a house in the Cologne suburb of Chorweiler. His pretty garden has fig and olive trees reminding him of his homeland. First, he wanted to return instantly, but he stayed, bought a used car, drove around and met his wife Monika. Then he stayed." Onur cited proudly "We helped build this economy. When we visit Turkey now we stay in hotels, and we feel like tourists."[446]

The method of asking this kind of sensitive question concerning respondents' personal life calls for caution but gives useful information on their integration. For example, asking 'Are you married?' means nothing for their integration level in German society, but marrying a native German means the respondent is more likely to be integrated or is already more integrated than a respondent married to a non-German.

---

[443] Richter, Michael, 'They came and stayed',' *Deutsch-Türkishe Lebensgeschicten '*, German-Turkish life stories, published by the Körper Foundation, Hamburg, 2004, (p. 225)

[444] Euro-barometer: 30 (11,791); 37 (14.82); 39 (15.136); 48 (16.186). Attitudes toward the presence of people of other nations, 1988, Question: Do you personally find the presence of people of another nationality disturbing in your daily life?

[445] Study finds half of German immigrants feel like outsiders - The Local. Published: 15 June 09 17:30 CET
On line: http://www.thelocal.de/society/2009/06/15-19945.html

[446] Article by Hans Kirchmann: German-Turkish Fundation (*Deutsch-Türkische Stiftung – DTS*) 2003

Graph 19: Intermarriage rates of Turkish immigrants in Germany

Question 19: Are you married to a German?

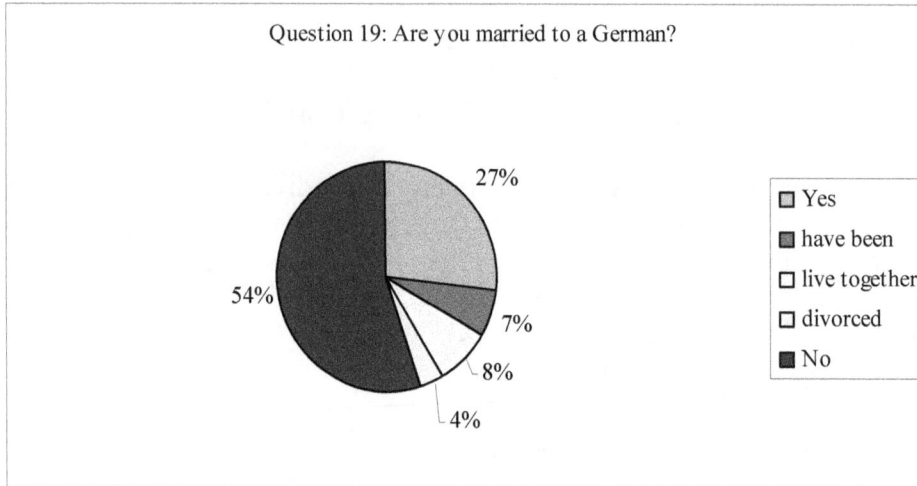

- □ Yes
- ■ have been
- □ live together
- □ divorced
- ■ No

Source: Author

Graph 19 shows that 27% or 81 respondents said 'Yes'. 7% or 20 respondents said they 'have been' married but now live separately; 8% or 23 respondents 'live together' or are cohabiting; 4% or 11 respondents said they are 'divorced' and finally 55% of the 165 respondents said 'No', they are no married to a German citizen.

The growing openness in the domain of marriage is a remarkable indicator of progressive integration. A slow integration process is characterised by low intermarriage rates among first generation Turks, limited upward social mobility and the perseverance of trans-national ties. Many tended to choose a spouse from their country of origin. Partly for linguistic, cultural and religious differences or possibly an intention to return to Turkey they tended to be opposed to intermarriage. In contrast, the increased rate of intermarriage between persons of Turkish origin and Germans, which was happening at the rate of about 1,000 per year at the end of the 1970s, is a hopeful sign. The 1996 data on civil weddings of Turkish nationals given in the table below shows the intermarriage rate with Germans to have risen to more than 4,600 by that year. In 1980 only about 28 % of unmarried Turks could imagine marrying a German. Within two decades this had doubled with men being slightly more positive than women about intermarriages. At the same time, negative opinions about intermarriage decreased from 45 % to 28 % indicating increasing integration.[447]

---

[447] Turkish Labour Institution (*Turkiye Is ve Isci Bulma Kurumu*), 1980 Data (*Verileri*)

Civil weddings of Turkish nationals residing in Germany 1996

	Absolute Numbers	Percentage
German-Turkish marriages at German registry offices	**4,657**	**16.1**
Marriages between Turkish nationals and third-country nationals at German registry offices	747	2.6
Turkish-Turkish marriages at German registry offices	917	3.2
Turkish-Turkish marriages at Turkish consulates in Germany	4,920	17.0
Visas issued by German consulates in Turkey to residents of Turkey for joining their non-German spouse in Germany	17,662	61.1
Total	**28,903**	**100.0**

Sources: Federal Statistical Office, Turkish Consulate General, Foreign Office
Transnational Social Spaces, Faist & Özveren, Ashgate 2004

There is an assumption that Turks for cultural and religious reasons are different to Germans. When people are from a different cultural and religious background, they tend to instinctively oppose intermarriage. However, there has been a steady increase in Turkish-German marriages, amounting to several thousand each year; whereas in 1996 they amounted to 6,000 marriages, numbers reached to 9,000 by 2001.[448] Although there is a belief among Germans that Turkish immigrants have a preference for marrying within their own ethnic group, the percentage of persons of Turkish origin who choose a German partner has been rising since the 1990s.[449] This increase may have been because of the growing numbers of naturalised Turks.

According the German Federal Statistics Institute (Statistisches Bundesamt), a research on intermarriage suggests that German women preferred Turkish men over other immigrant groups as a marriage partner in 2007. The result of the research indicates that 3,900 German women married Turkish men. 1,700 German women married Italian men and 1,200 German women married Americans.[450]

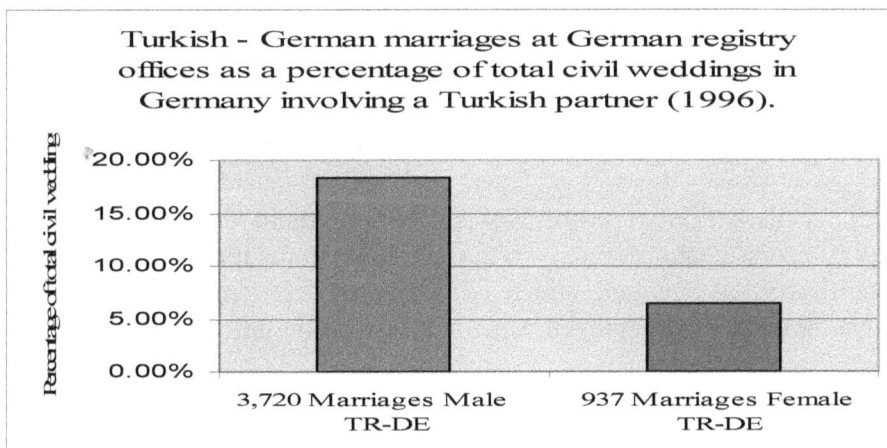

Sources: Federal Statistical Office, Turkish Consulate General, Foreign Office, Transnational Social Spaces, Faist & Özveren, Ashgate 2004

---

[448] These figures were announced by the Director of the TAM (Turkish Research Centre, Faruk Şen, and quoted in the online edition of Turkish Daily News, accessed on August 08, 2002 and these figures do not include Turkish-German marriages made outside Germany.

[449] A recent data (from German Federal Statistics Institute records, 20 November 2008) on marriages between the Germans and Turks show that most of the German women marriage preference was to Turkish men in 2007.

[450] Turkish Daily 'Hürriyet', November 20 2008

The survey results indicate that an immigrant married to native or who is cohabiting with a native is integrated more and found the process easier than one married to a non-native and almost all immigrants who married a native gained German citizenship. This means that literature review or previous surveys supports these results.

As a conclusion of the survey question, previous studies show that the numbers of Turkish-German marriages have been increasing about 1000 every year until 1980s. In 1996 it has risen to 4,600 that year and reached 28,903 the end of the year.[451] In 2001 amounted to 6.000 each year, in the end of the year totalled 9, 000.[452]

The 2007 survey indicates only 81 respondents or 27% have been married to Germans or Turkish origins. A clear majority 165 respondents or 54% is not married to German or naturalised Germans with immigrant background. 4% divorced, 7% live together not married. Although 45% of Turkish immigrants have affected by intermarriage but this percentage is still under the significant level to be considered as having impact on their integration.

4.1.20. Question 20: Are you satisfied with your status here in Germany?

This question aims to measure Turkish immigrants' feelings about their social status in Germany which is strongly related to their integration into German society. One of the reasons for the migration of Turkish guest workers to Germany in the 1960s was to improve their socio-economic status. Therefore this question is directed to respondents from four generations of persons of Turkish origin to research the status they achieved in Germany.

Since the 1960s, the raising of the social status of persons of Turkish origin (former guest-workers, their dependents/children and more recent immigrants) is linked to many factors. They have not only influenced the composition of the labour force, but they have also had an impact on the socio-economic, political, cultural and educational life in Germany. They strengthened their decision to consider Germany a home by uniting their families, investing more of their income within Germany and buying property all of which contributed to increased socio-economic status. [453]

Research into the labour market outcomes of Turkish immigrants in Germany using data from 2002 has shown that the second generation have improved their status mainly due to higher educational achievement and improved language ability.[454] If they feel satisfied with their status it is also more likely that they have already achieved some degree of integration into the German way of life.

---

[451] Faist, Thomas & Özveren, Eyüp: Turkish-German Transnational Social Spaces, Ashgate Publication, 2004 (p. 194-202).

[452] Şen, Faruk, TAM (Türkiye Araştımalar Merkezi) or *Turkish Research Centre's* report, University of Essen, 2001

[453] Turkish guest workers sent money to their relatives in Turkey by 1990.Because they could not decide to stay permanently or return home until 1990s.

[454] Euwals R., Dagevos J. Gijsberts M., Roodenburg H. (2007) *The Labour Market Position of Turkish Immigrants in Germany and Netherlands: Reason for Migration, Naturalisation and Language Proficiency.* IZA DP No. 2683 Forschungsinstitut zur Zukunft der Arbeit – Institute for the Study of Labour. March 2007.

Philip N. Jones argues that even before the new German citizenship law, Federal German policy was to achieve a full and rapid integration of both ethnic German immigrants from former Warsaw Pact countries and former Guest workers into German society. He points out that there is a parallel tendency between ethnic German immigrants and Turkish guest workers in term of socio-economic status. Both communities faced similar difficulties in the field of housing, social and economic integration.[455]

Graph 20: Measuring the satisfaction of Turkish immigrants in Germany

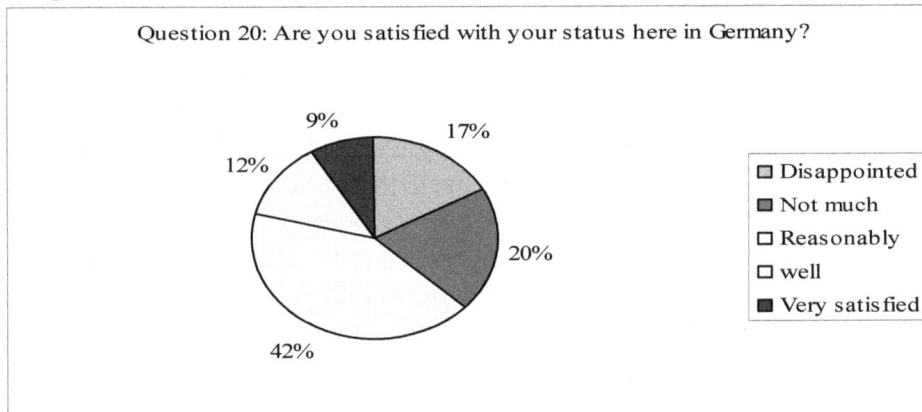

Question 20: Are you satisfied with your status here in Germany?

9%   17%
12%
20%
42%

- ☐ Disappointed
- ■ Not much
- ☐ Reasonably
- ☐ well
- ■ Very satisfied

Source: Author

Graph 20 shows that 17% or 50 respondents answered 'disappointed'; 19%, 57 respondents said that their satisfaction level is 'not much'. 42% t or 122 respondents said 'yes'; 12%., 36 respondents said 'not bad'; 9%, 25 respondents said 'better than I expected'.

Summing up the three nominally satisfied categories ('yes'- 42%, 'not bad'- 12% and 'very'- 9%) = 63% feel at least satisfied with their current status in Germany. This result shows that a majority of persons of Turkish origin achieved or exceeded their expected social status (in aspects such as economic, political and cultural life).

The first generation of Turkish guest-workers mostly came from a rural environment with a poor educational background (see question 25 in this chapter for more information), seeking opportunities to build decent and secure lives for themselves and their families.[456] Most Turkish immigrants admire many aspects of German society. They find German society more democratic, tolerant, and progressive than Turkish society. For example, persons of Turkish origin from Mannheim feel that they achieved an excellent level of economic and social status in German society. On the 400th anniversary of Establishment of Mannheim city, which was celebrated on 14th November 2006, the head of the Turkish Business Association, Mustafa Baklavacı, said that "We came here with wooden luggage and we are today businessmen of Mannheim", ('*Wir sind stolz darauf Mannheimer zu sein', 'Wir sind dabei...*") We are proud of being Mannheimers, we are part of it all...".Then he added that "Turks in Europe will form the future of Europe". In this context, in order to integration of Turkish immigrants a German-Turkish Academicians' Platform was established in the body of the Cologne University in 2006. Another Turkish

---

[455] Philip, N. Jones, 'Destination Germany'; Population Migration and the Changing World Order (Ed. By W.T.S. Gould and A.M. Findlay), Published by John Wiley and Sons, 1994, West Sussex, (p. 41)
[456] Author's Translation from Turkish Daily Hürriyet German Edition, 14 November 2006

171

businessman from Berlin, Kemal Şahin, head of the Turkish-German Chamber of Industry and Commerce, said that second and third generations in Berlin are two-cultural and bilingual'.[457]

4.1.21. Question 21: Have you been accepted as a member of society?

The purpose of this question is to gauge immigrants' feelings on the extent to which they feel accepted in German society and way of life. Acceptance as a minority implies that the cultural diversity of immigrants is perceived as a social reality and acknowledged as an enrichment of German society. Therefore, there is a delicate balance between whether Turkish immigrants wish to be regarded as distinctly Turkish, different in background and culture but recognised as a legitimate grouping in German society. Individuals would like to be acknowledged fully in German society in terms of their lifestyle and identity. For acceptance to displace exclusion, it has to be recognised that identity itself is not solely linked to national specificity, but can embrace cultural diversity, too.

The EU Commission describes integration of immigrants (similar to the OSCE definition) as a two way process which involves mutual respect and understanding. The EU Commission's integration principles also impose further requirements on immigrants: the EU basic values are also to be respected;[458] basic knowledge of the host society's language, history and institutions is viewed as 'indispensable' to integration;[459] and practices of diverse cultures and religions must be safeguarded, as long as maintaining these do not conflict with European human rights or national law, which includes the prevention of 'individual migrants from exercising other fundamental rights or from participating in the host society'.[460]

However, some German states appear reluctant to apply the EU commission's Conclusions. The EU integration policy actually focuses on the adaptation, and integration of immigrants into the host society rather than recognizing and celebrating cultural diversity.

One of the facilitating factors of integration is gaining the acceptance of the general public in the host society. Encouraging a wide distribution of immigrants into a host country's regions will prevent the formation of ghettos and facilitate the acceptance of immigrants by the local population. Philip N. Jones points out that a clustering tendency is not seen only in Turkish guest workers' residential areas, but also in immigrant ethnic German communities. This clustering tendency is regarded as a factor which hinders integration and causing isolation. As a result, it contributes to a low level of social acceptance by native Germans.[461]

Vural Öger, Turkish descent businessman and a second term elected MEP, points out that to be accepted easily by German natives as member immigrants have to do economically well

---

[457] An article by Carter Dougherty, The New York Times, 'Turks in Germany are in bullish mood' November 15, 2005

[458] The EU Conclusion on immigrant integration policy, Conclusion 10.These values include 'respect for the principles for the provisions of the Charter of Fundamental Rights of the Union ,which enshrine the concepts of dignity, freedom, equality and non-discrimination, solidarity, citizen's rights and justice'. Conclusions on immigrant integration policy Annex, Point 2, 2003.

[459] The EU Conclusion on immigrant integration policy Conclusion 12, 2003

[460] The EU Conclusion on immigrant integration policy, Conclusion 16 and Annex, Point 8, 2003

[461] Philip, N. Jones, 'Destination Germany'; Population Migration and the Changing World Order (Ed. By W.T.S. Gould and A.M. Findlay), Published by John Wiley and Sons, 1994, West Sussex, (p. 43)

and integrated into mainstream of German society. "Turkish entrepreneurs are integrated here better than almost any immigrant group. Someone who runs a business is someone whom German society always welcomes."[462] Germans are selective if an immigrant is good enough and integrated fully into German society they accept skilled immigrants easily. Another good example for being accepted by Germans is a Turkish descent girl; Gülcan Karahanci became first German-Turk Speaker of German Music Channel VIVA since January 2003. She left behind her 500 rivals at the selection.[463]

Graph 21: Measuring of acceptability level of Turkish immigrants by Germans

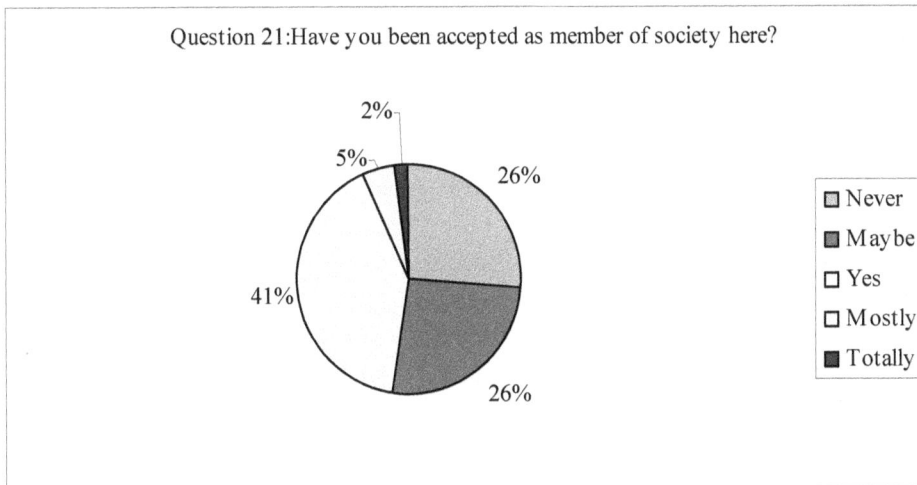

Question 21:Have you been accepted as member of society here?

2%
5%
26%
41%
26%

- Never
- Maybe
- Yes
- Mostly
- Totally

Source: Author

Graph 21 shows 26% of the 79 respondents said 'Never' meaning they have negative feelings about being accepted by Germans. 26% or 78 respondents said 'maybe' means that they have doubts about being accepted and think inclusion or accepting immigrants as full members of German society takes time. 41% or 123 respondents felt that they have been accepted as a member of German society. 5% or 14 respondents felt that they are 'mostly' accepted as member by host society's members. Only six respondents, 2% felt that they have been 'totally' accepted.

Summing the results of those feeling nominally accepted as a member of the host society: 41 % feel accepted + 5 % feel mostly accepted + 2 % feel totally accepted = 48 %. Although this percentage is less than a majority of those surveyed, a significant proportion feel accepted and integrated.[464]

In Germany, an important economic argument since the 1950s has been to gain acceptance for guest workers and immigrants as net contributors to the welfare state.[465] Germany

---

[462] *The New York Times* – European Edition: An article by Carter Dougherty 'Turks in Germany are in bullish mood' Published: November 15 2005
[463] Politic, Culture, Economy and Science Forum Deutschland, No. 2/2003 April/May. www.magazine-deutschlad.de

[465] Ulrich, Ralf: German Socio-economic Panel Study; 'A Positive Approach to Migrants', Sarah Spencer (Ed.), Rivers Oram Press, 1994, Chapter 4, p. 65.

would have struggled to sustain its place as one of Europe's economic giants without additional manpower through migration.[466] Large-scale migration of Turkish citizens to West Germany developed during the 'economic miracle' (*Wirtschaftswunder*) of the 1960s and 1970s. Then as now, Germans have been especially proud of their economic achievements. Economic success, rising living standards and improved social opportunities were of paramount importance for the acceptance of post-World War II political democracy by the German population, for the social and political integration of its immigrants, and for the development of the contemporary welfare state.

In spite of their valuable contributions they have not been accepted as a member of majority of German society. For example, Ursula Mehrländer cites "in 1989 immigrant workers contributed 12.8 billion DM to the state pensions fund, 7.8 % of the total payments (164 DM); but only 3.43 billion DM (1.9 %) of the total pension volume was paid out to immigrant workers in 1992. A study (1993) suggests that each German worker would have to spend about 40 % of their income on pension contributions without the presence of a mainly young migrant population".[467] In the same way, Ralf Ulrich (1994) points out his SOEP macro-data analysis showing that immigrants contribute more to the public purse than they receive from it.[468]

For persons of Turkish origin to feel secure in German society it is essential for them to have rights which incorporate them economically, socially, and politically as productive members of society. However, the other side of the process is that the indigenous population needs to recognise and accept the contribution which immigrants made for Germany over years.

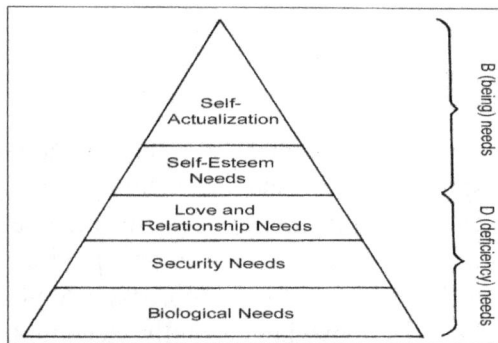

Source: Maslow's Pyramid, Hierarchy of Needs, 2001-4

As Abraham Maslow argued in his ranking of needs five-stage model, Germans should be grateful or become satisfied for Turkish immigrants' contributions, especially from the first

---

Horrocks, David, Kolinsky, Eva (Ed.): 'Turkish Culture in German society today, Published by Berghahn Books, 1996 (p. 79-85). [Prof. Eva Kolinsky, director of the Centre for the Study of German Culture and Society at Keele University."Non-German Minorities in Contemporary German Society" 1995]

[466] Mehrländer, Ursula: A Positive Approach to Migrants", Sarah Spencer (ed.), Rivers Oram Press 1994.Chapter 4, (p. 65)

[467] Guardian 1 September 1993, 'Old Germans need young migrants' pay'.

[468] Ralf Ulrich: German Socio-economic Panel Study," A Positive Approach to Migrants", Sarah Spencer, (ed.), Rivers Oram Press 1994.Chapter 4, (p. 65)

generation guest workers. Then some of the Turkish immigrants from time to time feel insecure in Germany.[469] Maslow's pyramid continues, as one's needs in life to become satisfied, the next stage becomes more convincing. First are natural or survival needs like eating and sleeping, on the basic stage. All humans must have those things, if nothing else. Subsequently are security or safety requirements: having a place to stay, knowing where your next food is coming from, and avoiding threat. Then the next stage becomes love or belongingness, the need to associate with other people.[470]

4.1.22. Question 22: Where were you born?

This question explores an interesting characteristic of Turkish labour migration to Germany or factor related to their background which affects their integration process in Germany is their regional belongingness or birth place in Turkey. Since, there are huge cultural, educational and traditional differences among migrant people from large cities and rural areas in Turkey.

A survey from 1963 two years after the bilateral recruitment agreement in 1961 show that although 41% indicated Istanbul as their last resident (which means that 33% migrated to Istanbul earlier as internal migrants from other regions of Turkey such as East Anatolia and South Eastern Anatolia), only 18 % were born there and they were highly skilled workers. Theodor Marquard, Director of the German Liaison Office Istanbul in 1966, his citation was quoted as "Most of them will begin a new life in Germany; they will strike roots and visit their home countries only as guests."[471]

This inclination did not change notably; in 1966 again Istanbul and European part of Turkey turned out 41.5%, Central Anatolia only 18 % of all Turkish labour force going to Germany.[472] Eryilmaz, Aytaç points out that between 1961 and 1973, Turkey sent the highest proportion of skilled workers to Germany as 30% of all recruits were skilled. Moreover, 20% of the recruits were women.[473]

The latest data from Berlin-Institute for population and development (*für Bevolkerung und Entwicklung*), showed that half of the total 3 million Turkish descents (*Türkischstammigen*) population were German-born, and are under 15 years old age group.[474]

The purpose of asking this question is to investigate the relevance of place of birth for Turkish immigrants' integration and the importance of being born in Germany in relation to integration issues, for example a German-born person of Turkish descent will learn everything about German society and culture through immersion but significantly less about their parents'

---

[469] Five Turkish children were burnt to death in 1993, when skinheads set fire on the Turkish house in Solingen and in Ludwigshafen 9 people were burnt to death in February 4 2008

[470] Alan Chapman: Maslow's Hierarchy of Needs www.businessballs.com or www.Questia.com/Abraham_Maslow

[471] Abadan-Unat Nermin :(1969) *Turkish Workers In West Germany: A case Study,* p. 27 Faculty of Political Science University of Ankara, Ankara; A Conference Paper from Sussex 1969
[472] Ibid., p.28-30
[473] Eryilmaz, Aytaç "40 years in Germany – At home abroad" DOMIT – Documentation Centre and Museum of the Migration from Turkey, Cologne [Translation from Turkish: Bengü Kocatürk-Schuster]
[474] Berlin-Institute for Population and development (*für Bevolkerung und Entwicklung*), Edition 63, 26 January 2009

(Turkish) society. Comparing German-born and Turkish-born persons, those born in Germany will always have been exposed to German as the language of public interaction. In addition, according to the new German citizenship law (owing to a very positive change in 1999) many Turkish-descent German-born youths are now German citizens and can benefit from a new legal structure which is now closer to other Western European countries.

Graph 22: Measuring of German-born Turkish immigrants' effect on integration

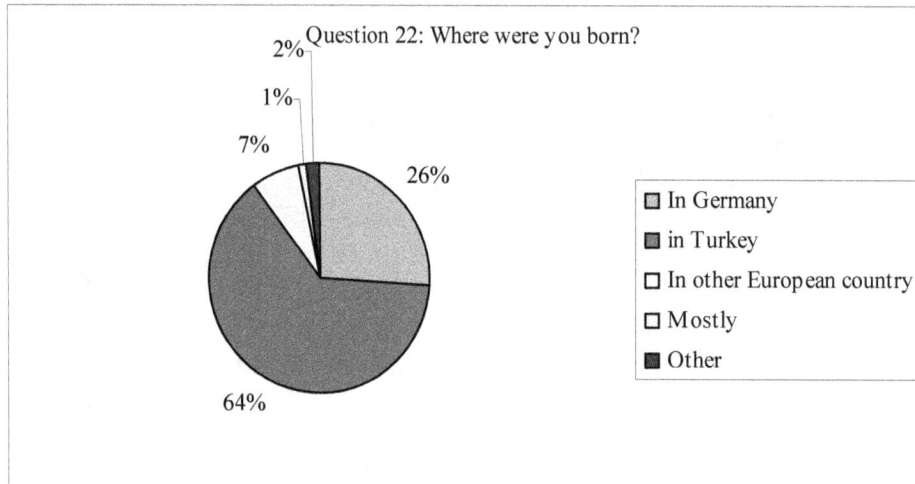

Source: Author

Graph 22 shows that 78 respondents or 26% replied that they were born 'in Germany'; 64% or 191 participants answered that they were born in 'in Turkey'; 7% or 22 respondents said that they were born 'in Europe' meaning other European countries. One percent or three respondents said 'in America'; and two percent of the six respondents answered as 'other' countries.

Analysing the non-German born Turkish immigrants, 36% were born out of Turkey with a western background, language and education meaning they are more likely to be integrated into German life than those who are Turkish-born and subsequently migrated to Germany.

As discussed in the first chapter of this thesis concerning the background of the Turkish migration to Germany, the situation of first generation Turkish 'Guest workers' 1956-1973 changed following the oil crisis in 1973. As a result of the deteriorating economic situation there was a parallel change in attitude towards the guest workers. Whereas they were seen as necessary temporary workers up to that point, after 1973 they have been called 'foreigners' and the issue has been referred to as the *Ausländer problem*, or the foreigners problem ever since.

The second generation migrated to Germany through family unification as family members of the guest workers between 1973-1983; the third generation Turks were born in Germany. The second generation was already in transition from temporary guest worker status to permanent immigrant status when the first German Immigration Act came in power in 1990. New German policies aimed to integrate immigrants including Turks into German society.[475]

---

[475] Brubaker, Rogers: *Citizenship and Nationhood in France and Germany*, Cambridge: Harvard University Press, 1992, p. 177-180

One interpretation is that before the 1990 Law, Germany did not offer an encouraging settlement and integration framework for its immigrants. The unclear circumstances caused the guest worker generation to maintain stronger ties with Turkey.

As seen in Britain and France, the end of labour migration did not mean the end of immigration. In the late 1970s Germany had to face the issues of family reunions, integration of foreign-born children into the education system, and the demands for voting rights and citizenship by immigrant workers and their relatives. Foreign-born children who joined their immigrant parents at a later stage of the family life cycle and second generation immigrants, that is, children born to foreigners in the country of immigration, children are not foreign-born but remain foreign citizens.[476] Thus the challenge of integration has become even more acute in the 1990s than in previous decades. The perception that the national debate over immigration was divisive was prevalent in Germany (90%) and France (70%), but 13% in the UK, where immigrant figures are lowers, MEPs reported.[477] In other surveys conducted from 1988 to 1997, fewer than 15 percent of Europeans ever said that the presence of people of other nations was disturbing on a personal basis.[478]

4.1.23. Question 23: How good is your German?

This question is intended to examine proficiency in the German language among persons of Turkish origin. Competency in the language of the host country is a key facilitating factor for integration which enables immigrants' interactions with the native population as well as access to and participation in the social and legal institutions of the host country.

Generally, first and second generation Turkish immigrants found their integration into German society limited by their poor knowledge of the German language. On the other hand, they had stronger ties with Turkey than the younger generation have now. Since, they came to Germany with the intention of returning home after a number of years, it can be argued that they were not motivated to learn German beyond that which was essential. It is doubtful that manual work in factories in the 1960s and 1970s resulted in exposure to the German language beyond a very basic level. Participation in the Germany's social and political life was probably not an immediate priority. [479]These circumstances amount to significant hindering factors in adopting the German language and lifestyle which became apparent in circumstances where effective communication is necessary for example when seeking medical attention. As early as 1967, researchers noted that Turkish guest workers and their families faced problems communicating directly with health service providers in Germany with possible negative outcomes.[480]

---

[476] King, P., Schultze, G., Wessel, R, 1986: The situation of foreign workers and their families in the Federal Republic of Germany; Representative survey, 1985, Bonn.

[477] Source: Euro-stat population statistics for 1985 and 1990, data published by the Council of Europe (1993).

[478] Source: Euro-stat population statistics for 10 MEPs report that immigrant rights should be extended, by country and party group, 1992 survey of members of European Parliament(Interview No 51, Brussels, April 14, 1992;2 ,p.167)

[479] Hamburger, F., (1990): On the way to hike society – migration process and political realities in the Federal Republic of Germany, in: Learning German, Issue 1, p. 3-29.

[480] David, Pachaly and Vetter : Perinatal outcome in Berlin Germany among immigrants from Turkey, Published 8 June 2006 Springer-Verlag

From the native-German point of view, the perception of the 'Guest worker recruitment system' and associated policies was definitely based on temporariness rather than encouraging permanent immigration. The unclear circumstances were a further disincentive for the promotion of language learning among the guest worker community. Thirty years on, the younger generation face intense competition with their German peers in order to enter the highly advanced labour market and upgrade their work skills. It is essential that they are able to communicate in German at a native level. Otherwise, they will not only be disadvantaged in employment opportunities, but will also be limited in a similar way to the first generation from being integrated into German social and political life.

Graph 23: Measuring German language proficiency of Turkish immigrants

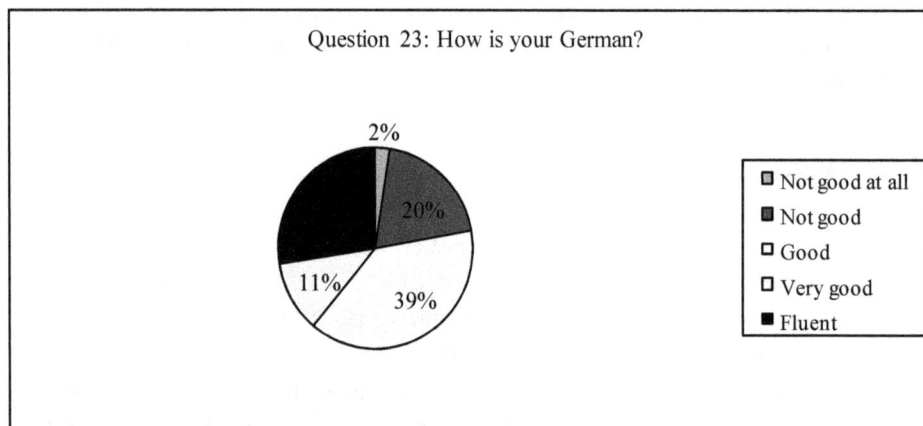

Question 23: How is your German?

- Not good at all
- Not good
- Good
- Very good
- Fluent

Source: Author

Graph 23 shows that 7 respondents or 3% said that their German was 'not good at all'; 55 respondents or 20% said that their German was 'not good'; 109 respondents or 38% said that their German is 'good'. 32 respondents or 11% said that their German is 'very good'. 77 respondents or 28% responded that they are able to communicate 'Fluently' in German.

These figures show nominal German language capability among 36 % 'good' + 11 % 'very good' + 26 % 'fluent' = 73% of respondents, a promising positive indicator for their integration into life in Germany.

The social, political and cultural integration of all persons of Turkish origin is highly dependent on knowledge of the German language. German-Turkish bilingual scholars advise German should be taught from the age of 4 in kindergartens in a natural way. Faruk Şen argues that 'Speaking host country's language and gaining its passport is not enough for integration', regarding French immigrants' protests in the suburbs of Paris in 2005. "Most of the French immigrants are French citizens and they speak French fluently, but speaking host country's language and gaining its passport is not sufficient for a successful integration".[481] These events are the consequence of French immigration policies of previous French governments. Even with the current high unemployment rates in German society, many persons of Turkish origin are

---

[481] Vatan Gazetesi, November 5 2005

working in jobs with a career path and establishing their own businesses. In Germany immigrants of Turkish origin have strong family ties and economic and moral support from family members.

There are also possible negative outcomes. Carla Baran, a psychologist from Istanbul who works for the official Bavarian welfare service for Turks in Munich, she said:

"Some families are growing more liberal, others more traditional. Some youths run away from home, because they can't stand their parents' strictness. These tensions are worse here than back in Turkey, because of the German influence and the fears of Germanising. It is tough situation: but I think integrating is bound to come within another generation or so. The fanatics will lose in the end."[482]

There was also a critic debate on integration of Turks in Austria last month. During an interview on the integration of the Turkish in Austria, a Turkish-origin Austrian politician, Alev Korun (a Vienna Green Party MP), expressed the importance of the German language for Turkish immigrants' employment, training and future career. She commented,

"The key factor for integration of Turkish immigrants is basic education, especially, learning the host country's language. Unskilled immigrants need vocational training. In order to support social integration should be identified key points such as work-places and schools. The most important problem here is unemployment. There are 300,000 Turkish immigrants in Austria, 100,000 of them are Austrian citizens. In general, unemployment rate is 7%, but among Turks, it is 17%".[483]

Another politician of Turkish descent in Austria, Nurten Yilmaz, Vienna Democrat Party MP, said,

"We belong to here, Austria; we are a part of this society. We have to integrate into this system. First of all, we should send our children to kindergarten. You can't live in this society without *German* language. Market places, supermarkets are full of the Turks. At least the third generation children should be integrated. If they attend to vocational training, they will not be unemployed and will be easily integrated".[484]

On 1 January 2005, for the first time, an integration course for immigrants was introduced in Germany. Once immigrants have obtained residency, they are obliged to attend the course which consists of language lessons and studies relating to the German legal system, culture, history and the way of life. These courses are aimed at helping immigrants navigate German society. The courses are compulsory and long term resident immigrants are obliged to attend. If they do not, their employment benefits can be withdrawn or reduced over the period during which they should attend.

The new German immigration law introduced in 2008 has both restrictive and discriminative elements, especially for newcomers from Turkey who arrive in Germany through family reunification. Under the immigration law of 2005, the German state covered the costs of the integration courses, meaning that integration was defined as a responsibility of the state. However, according to the new law of 2007, if an immigrant is married abroad and wishes to

---

[482] Ardagh, John: Germany and the Germans, in chapter 5: Turkish 'guest workers' and other immigrants: a painful path towards acceptance, Penguin, 1995 (New Edition: The United Germany in the mid-1995), p. 273

[483] Austrian Independent, November 11 2010

[484] Ibid.

bring their partner to Germany, the partner will have to prove their proficiency in German in order to receive a visa. The newcomers themselves pay for the German language courses abroad. The requirement of language proficiency as a part of the new German immigration law is only being applied to Turkish citizens who wish to enter Germany for family reunification.

4.1.24. Question 24: Where did you go to school?

This question investigates which country's school system persons of Turkish origin attended. If their education was entirely in Germany, they are more likely to feel (or have felt) integrated into the German education system and social life than those who attended to school in Turkey or elsewhere. Apart from the language barrier, difficulties in the educational integration of children of Turkish origin arise partly from differences between the German and Turkish school systems and training of teachers.

The educational integration of the children of immigrants is the first step to economic, political and cultural integration, representing a key facilitating factor. Similarly to the integration process of adults, education and learning are two-way processes, involving mutual respect and understanding.

Graph 24: Investigation of the school system attended by persons of Turkish origin.

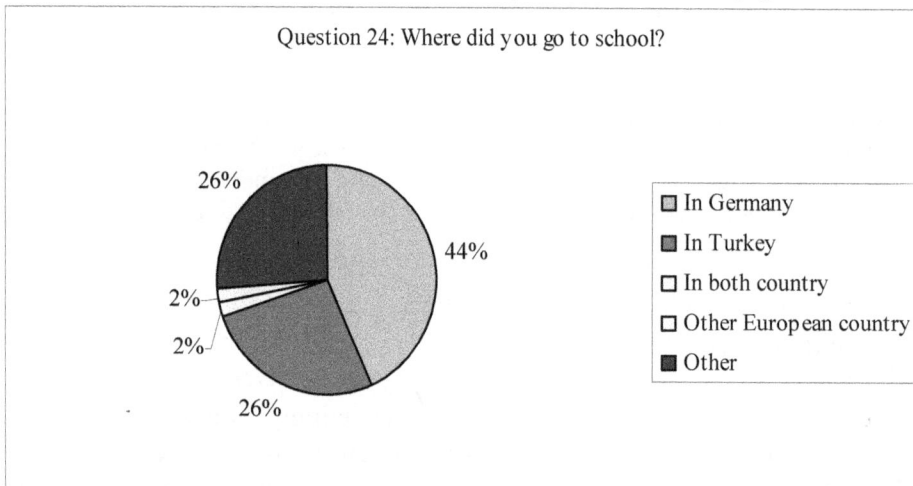

Source: Author

Graph 24 shows that 130 respondents or 44% replied 'in Germany'; 79 respondents or 26% replied 'in Turkey'; 6 respondents or 2% replied in 'both countries'; 6 respondents, 2%.0 percent said in 'other European' countries; 79 respondents or 26% said 'other' non-EU countries. Nearly double the number of respondents attended school in Germany 44% than attended school in Turkey 26 percent.

This is related to next question 25 concerning the level of education achieved, which provides relevant findings such as that most persons of Turkish origin (35 percent) attended the 'Vocational School education' in Germany. 26% of Turkish immigrants have a secondary school education and only 12% received a university degree in Germany.

In conclusion of this section, empirical studies and this survey suggest that Turkish immigrants who are more educated are also more integrated in Germany. In education, qualifications and fluency in the host language are key goals of the integration process, aiming for parity in outcomes at each stage of education, including pre-school take-up. Each year the Turkish Ministry of Education sends about 200 Turkish teachers to support Turkish children linguistically in big German cities where many Turkish immigrants live in order to meet their mother-tongue educational needs.[485]

4.1.25. Question 25: What is your education level?

This question investigates the education level of persons of Turkish origin and the effect on their integration in Germany as it is a significant affecting factor. There is considerable evidence that furthering integration into German society is largely a function of the level of skills and education of incoming immigrants.[486] The availability of language tuition and language support services is a critical factor in the case of highly educated immigrants who wish to continue their professional careers and maximise the contributions they yield to their host country.

For example, in 1991, only 0.8% of students in at German universities were Turkish-origin with German educational qualifications. In 1994, one in four secondary school pupils of non-German origin failed to gain a school leavers' certificate but only six percent of those of German origin. Also in 1994, 5% of German-origin applicants but only 1.5% of non-German origin applicants or 1,829 individuals were accepted for public sector employment. Anyone with limited educational achievements is highly disadvantaged in the current German labour market.

Yasemin Karakusoglu argues that "a poor educational background and weak language skills have particularly bad prospects in the Germans school system. For forty years The Turks were not offered enough in term of education."[487] Therefore, language and education equips immigrants to build capacity not only to get a better-paid job but also to adapt better to their host society. For Turkish immigrants in Germany technical education is more demanding and it helps youth of Turkish origin find career based employment rather than manual labour. It also enables immigrant to create a comfortable life and achieve upward social status. Being educated themselves help immigrants to educate their children in Germany. Since they are working and paying taxes to the host country, the public finances also benefit. German industry also benefits from the immigrants' skilled labour.

Considering the educational achievement of Turkish immigrants' integration into German school system, society, we can see that only 10% of Turkish immigrants were technically educated.

---

[485] Source: Turkish Ministry of Education, January 20, 2008. This year 515 teachers will be sent; 400 German-speaking, 100 French-speaking and 10 English-speaking and finally 2 music teachers.
[486] Regarding 'Guest workers' reform' October 17 2007 in Berlin, German Chancellor Angela Merkel said that "Guest workers from southern Europe, who migrated to Germany in 1960s, gave the German society a new face. Speaking at a two-day symposium on 'Integration through education in the 21st century' in Berlin, Merkel said "the Turks now living in Germany for the last four generations contribute a great deal to the country's economy".
[487] http://Spiegel.de/international/Germany/0/0.1518.561969,00 html Access 22 06 2009

Pie-chart graph 25: Measuring Turkish immigrants' education level in Germany

Question 25: What is your education level?

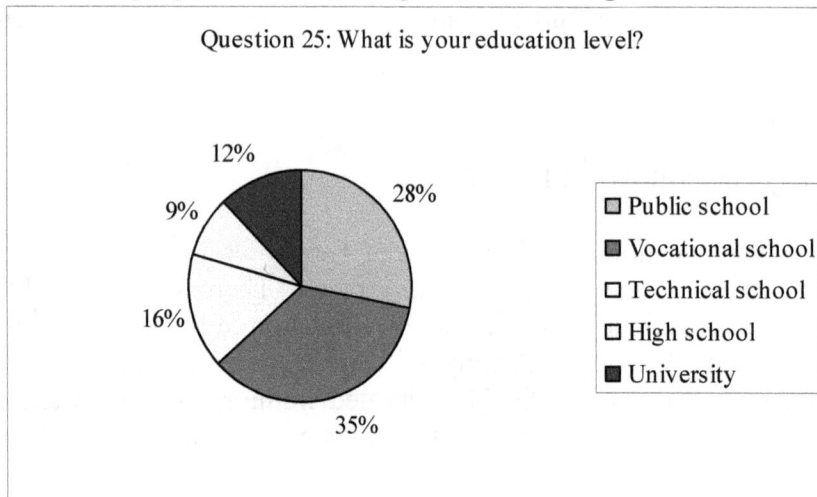

Source: Author

Graph 25 shows that 84 respondents or 28% replied 'Public school' (8-9 years); 108 respondents or 35% 'Vocational school' or (secondary); 48 respondents or 16% 'Technical school' (and high school); 26 respondents or 9% responded 'High school'; 36 respondents or 12 said that they have a 'University' Degree.

The education level of the second and third generation of Turkish origin is higher than the first generation and they found integration easier.[488] There are 113 universities, 157 vocational technical schools and 45 art academies in Germany. The numbers of Turkish students in German universities increased 259 percent between 1980 and 1998. The number of German students increased only 163% during those years.

This survey result and previous studies show that education level of the younger generation is higher than the older. However, they still face difficulties in school integration due to their parents' limited and different educational background as well as their different upbringing. For example, German educationalist Ingrid Ditrich pointed out that the Turkish parents should participate in education system in Germany, cooperate with teachers and help their children with homework at home.[489]

Their parents' educational background and system of schooling plays a part for their integration into German society. First of all, their Turkish parents' needs to be oriented and informed or educated about school system and how German parents participate, for example by helping with their children's homework. Fewer Turkish parents do this in Germany.

Statistisches Bundesamt, Educational attainment of Turkish guest workers' children in Germany between 1974 -5 and 1998 Turkish students in German universities between 1980 and 1998.
[489] An article published in The New York Times' European Edition by Carter Dougherty, 'Turks in Germany are in bullish mood'; November 15 2005 (p.1- 4).

4.1.26. Question 26: Are you interested in sports here?

Finding common interests with host country members is one of the most motivating factors of immigrants' integration and participating in sports, cultural[490], and political activities in the host country is a natural way of achieving this. In this way, the interaction creates a common interest and contact especially between youth of the immigrant and native-German communities leading to opportunities for integration in the country.

The Times reported the World Cup in 2006 as following way.

"Germany hosts 'World Cup'. One of the striking aspects of Germany's football –inspired patriotism has been the number of immigrants openly supporting German national football team. Turks talk about the German-players as 'Our Boys'. During the games, German fans chanted: 'Stand up if you are German', thousands did so." [491]

Mahmut Özgener, head of Turkish Football Association, argues that increasing number of Turkish origin players is an important factor which creates social interaction with majority youths and contributes to integration of Turkish immigrants into German sport life. He points out interesting figures such as "There are 6 million licensed professional football players in Germany, only 225, 000 in Turkey. The number of Turkish origin licensed professional players reached 250, 000 in Germany which is even higher than those of Turkey." [492]

Graph 26: Measuring interest in sport of Turkish immigrants in Germany

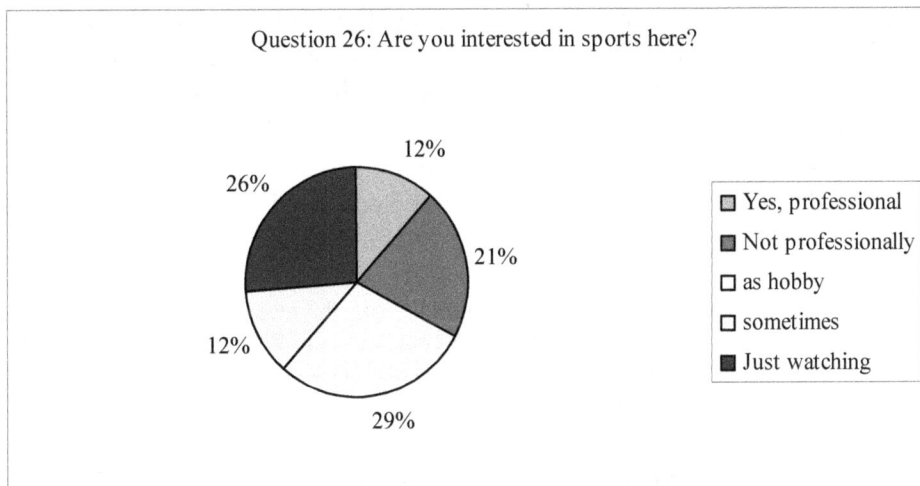

Source: Author

Graph 26 shows that 36 respondents or 12% replied 'yes, professionally'; 63 respondents or 21% said 'not professionally'; 86 respondents or 29% said 'as hobby'; 37 respondents or 12 said that they 'sometimes' play; 79 respondents or 26% said they 'just watch' sports programmes

---

[490] June, 22, 2006, Turkish Kebabs became World Cup funs' favourite food in Germany.
[491] Times, 20 June, 2006
[492] Author's Translation from Turkish Daily Hürriyet, 22.6.2006
    Accessed on January 17 2009 Turkish Daily Hürriyet Website www.hurriyet.com.tr

such as football, basketball, volleyball matches and so on. The result of survey question 26 indicates that 12% of respondents are professional sportsmen and women including footballers, basketball players, wrestlers, and boxers both at the German national and local level. This number is significantly increasing annually.[493]

Angela Merkel ruling government's integration and citizenship policies was criticized by the Green Party's former co-chairman, Claudio Roth. She argued that "German born, well-integrated Turkish descent football stars like Hakan Balta and Ilhan Mansiz are playing for Turkish national team because they are not allowed to have dual citizenship." Roth continued to criticize the government's new citizenship law with following statement,

> "They have once become German citizens on condition of preserving their home country citizenship from birth or later arrangements you cannot force them to choose one of the nationalities. We kick them out from German citizenship in this way. We cannot force them lose German citizenship and this implication does not compile with German Constitution when they are already German citizens. They should be given a dual citizenship right to keep both countries citizenship instead of forcing them to prefer one of it. You can give them a felling that they belong to this country as well. In this way we earn these young people. They will be useful for this country than other countries, for they are German born and grown up in this country. Preserving their own identity and culture is natural as well as they has been integrated into German society".[494]

Both World Cup 2006 and Euro 2008 reinforced the relationship between Turkey and Germany. The Turkish immigrants' participation in the host country's sportive activities and eventually facilitate their integration of into the German way of living. Turkish newspaper *Hurriyet* put a German heading *Gemeinsamten Feieren* means 'Celebrating together' on the day of European Championship Semi-final between two countries' national teams. The newspaper's comment was as following: "Turkish-origin players do not only tie two countries, but also enrich the daily life of Germany. 4 million Germans go on holiday to Turkey every year. Thousands of Germans settle in various holiday towns of Turkey, they live there happily."

French News Agency (AFP) described the celebration of the Semi-final in German towns as follows:

> "Turkish and German flags were exhibited side by side as a symbol of togetherness and brotherhood as they did the same in World Cup 2006. On the eve of the Euro 2008 semi-final the flags are exhibited together again in many German towns. Germany has about 3 million citizens of Turkish origin. The atmosphere here is as if two Turkish national teams are going to play together for Euro 2008 final."[495]

Participation in socio-cultural and sportive activities in the host country creates interaction avenues and common interests between immigrant and native youths. These, in turn, facilitate integration. In recent years many Turkish-origin footballers, basketball players and boxers who have grown up in Germany play for German national teams. Among many others, we can name

---

[493] Ibid.

[494] Hurriyet, BERLIN, 25 June, 2008, [Author's Translation]

[495] Kai Dickmann-BILD, 25 June 2008 [Author's Translation]

Mesut Özil, Mehmet Scholl, Patrick Malik, and Yildiray Baştürk, Altintop brothers Hamit and Mesut and Mithat Demirel.

4.1.27. Question 27: Where do you want to live in future?

The aim of asking this question is to investigate whether persons of Turkish origin intend to live in Germany permanently, plan to migrate to another country or will return to Turkey.

Karin Hunn describes the history of Turkish guest workers how their temporary stay turned into permanent residing as follow. *"Nächstes Jahr kehren wir zurück..."* 'Next year we will go back...', why they postponed their return every year for some or another reason from 1961 bilateral agreement until unification. Hunn demonstrates that treaties regulating economic relations between two countries were consistently connected to political relations. The West German government also agreed to pay monthly child benefit or support even for children of Turkish migrant workers who lived in Turkey. The convention to privilege labour migration with European Union member states (Europäergrundsatz) was suspended with regard to Turkey. However, Turkey held a distinct status as a member of NATO and aspiring/associate member of the EU. Turkey was also favourably regarded for having been an ally in the two world wars. In fact, Hunn points out that in the early phase Turkey was considered to be part of Europe. Hunn demonstrates that initially, Turkish labour migrants were allowed to stay in West Germany for only two years. This plan was also supported by the Turkish government, which hoped that labour migrants would return to Turkey to apply the knowledge they had acquired during their stay in Germany and develop the Turkish economy. This was Turkey's expectation from its Guest workers, which wanted unskilled workers to return as skilled workers; instead, it lost many skilled workers. Hunns's study counters widely held beliefs about the social regional origins of Turkish migrant workers in Germany. With regard the first generation of workers, for example, *only 18 percent* hailed from villages with less than two thousand inhabitants; whereas *41 percent* came from Istanbul. Indeed, many Turkish workers were accustomed to far more developed sanitary facilities than those that awaited them in Germany and were shocked when confronted with the substandard sanitary situation and heating equipment in areas of Berlin. The percentage of skilled workers was higher among immigrants from Turkey than, for example, those who came from Italy, Spain or Greece. Over time, circumstances changed Turkish-Germans continued to lack basic civil and political rights.[496]

For example, a survey published with an article in Der Spiegel, suggests that 38% of young academics of Turkish origin are not happy in Germany and do not believe that Germany has a good integration policy. It means that they have future plans to immigrate to an English-speaking country like Canada, Australia or the USA.[497]

In the 1980s, German governments were encouraging 'guest-workers' to return home.[498] However, the British sociologist and immigration expert Stephen Castles, affirmed that guest-

---

[496] Hunn, Karin, "Nächstes Jahr kehren wir zurück..." 'Next year We will Go Back...'*The history of Turkish Guest Workers in Germany*; Gottingen; Wallstein, 2005, pp. 598
[497] Der Spiegel, dated on 19.5.2008,
[498] Castles, Stephen: Here for Good, 'Western Europe's Ethnic Minorities', Pluto Press, London, 1984.

workers including Turks will stay in Germany permanently, from a Marxist viewpoint in his interesting book.[499]

Another expert on integration, Eva Kolinsky, pointed out that "guest-workers (*Gastabeiter*) from Turkey were the least willing to leave and the most likely to settle and reunite with their families".[500] A willingness to stay in Germany means that they are at least comfortable living in Germany and are more likely to be integrated into German society. Those who are not satisfied with German society and do not feel comfortable in Germany are more likely to migrate to another country. If immigrants are settled and well established in their lives, they are more likely to be integrated in into German society.

Graph 27: Exploring Turkish immigrants' decision for living in Germany

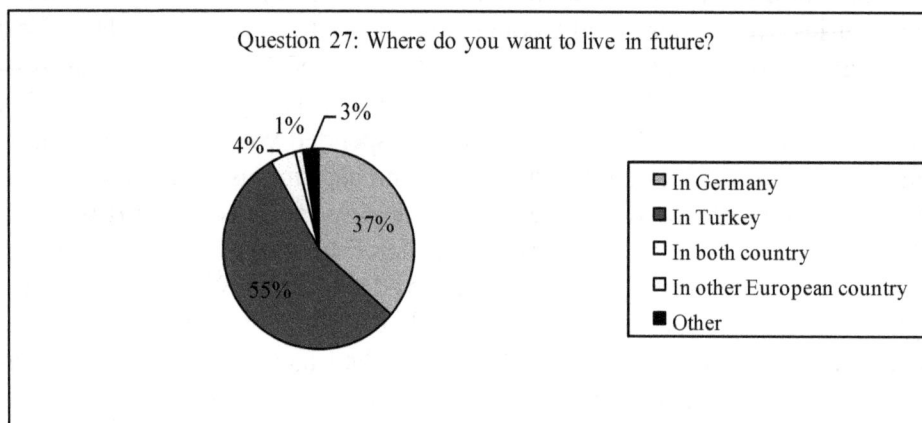

Question 27: Where do you want to live in future?

- In Germany
- In Turkey
- In both country
- In other European country
- Other

37%
55%
4%
1%
3%

Graph 27 shows that 36% answered 'in Germany'; 56% said 'in Turkey'; 4% said 'Other European' in both countries; or 1% said that they want to live in 'Australia'; 3% answered 'other' countries, possibly indicating an as yet unplanned desire to leave Germany.

An earlier survey on immigrants' future plan reveals meaningful finding which is related to survey question 27 'Where do you want to live in the future?' as follows:

Table 4.1.8: Preference for staying in Germany or returning home, 1993 (% by ethnic origin)

Preference	Turks	Yugoslavs	Italians
Return planned	31	18	25
Wish to return, w/out date or time	12	13	20
Undecided	14	29	20
Decision to stay in Germany for good	43	40	35

Source: Adapted from Turkish Culture in German society, 1996, published by Berghahn Books (p.119)
Original Source: Ausländer in Deutschland, no.4, 1993, p.4. Report findings from Emnid survey of 1993.

---

[499] Castles, Stephen and Miller, J. Mark: 'The Age of Migration'; International Population Movements in the Modern World, Second Ed. Published by Macmillan, London, 2003 (p. 5, 13, and 48).
[500] Horrocks, David, Kolinsky, Eva (Ed.): 'Turkish Culture in German society today, Published by Berghahn Books, 1996 (p. 83)

Young German-raised and educated academics of Turkish descent are tending to leave Germany for other countries.[501] The reasons for this are that they are not happy in Germany and feel Germans are not grateful for the contributions they have made to Germany. Therefore, many academics do not plan to live in Germany in the future. Apparently, not only academics but also other Turkish immigrants who do not feel comfortable with life in Germany plan to leave because they are not satisfied with their status and do not believe that Germany has a proper integration policy for immigrants. For these reasons they are more likely to emigrate especially to English speaking countries such as Australia, Canada or America. Those remaining tend to be considerably more positive about life in Germany, feel that life is comfortable there and are most likely to be integrated into German society and the way of life.[502]

The first and third responses shown in graph 27, respectively 36% answered 'want to live in Germany and 4% answered 'want to live in both Germany and Turkey', giving a total of 40 % of respondents wanting to live in Germany. Comparing this 40 % survey result with the previous research from 1993 where 43 % of Turkish immigrants expressed a wish to live in Germany shows long-term consistency in the proportion of those of Turkish origin wishing to live in Germany.

4.1.28. Question 28: Gender distribution of Turkish immigrants

The purpose of this question is to investigate the demographic characteristics and gender distribution of the Turkish-origin population in Germany. The structure of the population plays an important role in their integration into German society.

Previous data from the German Ministry of Employment shows that the total Turkish immigrant population in Germany are 2,110,223 excluding naturalised Turkish descent Germans; 965,116 of whose are female; while 1,145,057 are male. Another important point the data suggests that the largest subgroup consists of ages between 15 and 29 are 316,073 females and 365,643 males, total 681,716.[503] These figures indicate that the age structure of Turkish immigrant population is younger than native German population as well as than other immigrant groups. Furthermore, a ÇYDD - Association for Supporting Contemporary Life data shows that proportion of working Turkish immigrant women is higher than men. For example, in 2000, 400,174 men and 170,474 women are in paid employment.[504] Earlier in 1960 by recruitment year, the number of migrant female worker was just 173, however by 1974, the number had increased to 159,984 (SPO, 1994, p.106).[505] Hanife Aliefendioğlu describes the first generation Turkish women's living conditions in Germany as follows. "Immigration does not always result in immigrant women's interaction with Western culture and their emancipation. Some first

---

[501] Wasted Opportunities-Why Turkish academics are leaving Germany. Highly educated academics with Turkish roots are in a minority in Germany. They could make valuable contributions to German society, but increasingly, they are leaving the country (Der Spiegel-19.05.2008).

[503] These figures adapted from Turkish Culture in German society, 1996, published by Berghahn Books p.119; Turkish minority in German society-Elçin Kürşat- Ahlers. Original source: Ausländer in Deutschland, no.4, 1993, p.4. Reporting findings from Emnid survey of 1993.

[504] ÇYDD-Cagdas Yasami Destekleme Dernegi (Association for Supporting Contemporary Life), 2000 p. 9 - 12; Konur II Sok. 51/6 Kizilay/Ankara-Turkey

[505] Faist, Thomas & Özveren, Eyup: Transnational Social Spaces, Published by Ashgate, 2004, (p p. 59-60)`

generation migrant women who went to Germany along with their husbands had no opportunity to work outside the home. This was due to the patriarchal nature of traditional Turkish society, especially in rural areas. This ideology tends to project women first and foremost as housewives and mothers. In fact, these ideologies are reflected in all societies, whether the women are migrants or not. Employers, on the other hand, tend to view migrant women as a source of cheap labour due to their status as 'dependants'.[506] Ayşe Kadioğlu points out those migrant women not only face discrimination within the family and the labour market of the host societies, but also as members of marginal ethnic or racial groups.[507]

Earlier studies on gender distribution suggest that the percentage of Turkish immigrant women increased greatly in the late 1970s because of the family unification process.[508] A survey of female immigrant workers in North Rhine-Westphalia has shown that the employment rate of Turkish women (30%) has more or less reached the level of German women. It is also important to emphasise that 44% of the immigrant residents are women.[509]

Social scientist Nermin Abadan Unat claims that the self-perception of Turkish women concerned changed considerably and their confidence was raised. Unat admits that Turkish women did not voluntarily decide to migrate to Germany. Some women are from rural regions of Turkey, "brought up traditionally, totally unprepared intellectually" and "without any knowledge of life in German city, highly disciplined working conditions or production standards and a new surroundings". Everything was different for them. They had to adapt themselves to German discipline, timing, punctuality, trade union activities and entitlements.[510] Necla Kelek, a sociologist from Hamburg, describes Turkish women's situation from rural areas in her book "import brides" and "40 Quadratmeter Deutschland" (40 Square Metres of Germany) in 1985. The bride was locked up by her husband and was not allowed to leave the small apartment by herself. She also argues that some Turkish women agree to arrange marriages in the hope of an interesting life and more opportunities for personal development in Germany.

Canan Topçu is an editor of the German daily '*Frankfurter Rundschau*'. She focuses on gender roles among the Turkish migrant community. She writes that

> "Turkish women in Germany show a great interest in education and want to advance professionally. Germans tend to consider Turkish women as victims of a patriarchal society shaped by religious beliefs.

---

[506] Köksal, Sema Erder (1993), Uluslararasi Göc Sürecinde Kadinin Gündeme Gelişi ve 'Ghetto'da Kadin'; Kadin araştirmalari Dergisi, KAUM Yay, Istanbul, Vol. 1, pp.110, 113-125.

[507] Kadioğlu, Ayşe: Migration experiences of Turkish Women; Notes from a Research Diary', In International Migration, Vol. 35 (4), (1997, p. 538) pp. 537-56.

[508] Schultze, Günter: Social situation of foreign girls and women in North Rheine-Westphalia, Düsseldorf. Schultze, Günter: Soziale Situationen ausländischer Mädchen und Frauen in Nordrhein-Westfalen, 1987,Düsseldorf. Schultze, G., 1991: Berufliche Integration türkischer Arbeitnehmer. Vergleich der ersten und zweiten Generation, Bonn. Statistisches Jahrbuch der Bundesrepublik Deutschland, 1991, Wiesbaden.

[509] Schultze,G.,l987:Soziale Situationen ausländischer Mädchen und Frauen in Nordrhein-Westfalen, Düsseldorf.   Lessons from Germany and Job Security in America: By Katharina G. Abraham and Susan N. Houseman; 'Labor Market Performance in Germany and the US, Univ. of Maryland, 1987 (p. 47-50), and General Anzeiger, 23.3.1992

[510] Abadan-Unat Nermin (2002) Unending Migration: from Guest-worker to Transnational Citizen (*Bitmeyen Goc: Konuk iscilikten Ulus-otesi Yurttasliga*), Istanbul Bilgi University Press on Migration Studies.

Turkish women are oppressed, forced into marriages and beaten by men. The media nurture such clichéd prejudices; even though a single woman from Turkey covers her hair".[511]

She also argues that "Germany meant liberation for Turkish women from restrictive relationships; a chance to escape from dysfunctional or forced marriages to uneducated Turkish men who saw women as second-rate beings obliged to obey."[512] A survey shows that female Turkish students at German universities increased almost *tenfold* from 1980 to 1996, whereas the number of male students only increased *2.5 times*. For example, in 2002/3 academic year there were 2400 Turkish citizens (excluding German naturalised) studying at German universities, 9300 of them were female. As a result, female Turkish immigrants are more likely to be integrated into German society and subsequently to gain German citizenship.[513]

In Germany, the BiB survey of 2000 shows Turkish origin immigrant girls have overtaken the boys, the percentage of Turkish women with diploma from more prestigious levels of schooling (*Abitur* or *Fachhochschulreife*) is rising. About 1 in 5 Turkish women living in Germany aged 18-30 now have a diploma on this level, a clear improvement compared with the micro-census data of 1995-2002 survey shows that Turkish girls in German preparatory tracks for higher education more than doubled compared with 1988 survey, which means that females first closed the gap with the males and overtaken the males even with better school results.[514]

Graph 28: Investigating the gender distribution of Turkish-origin people in Germany

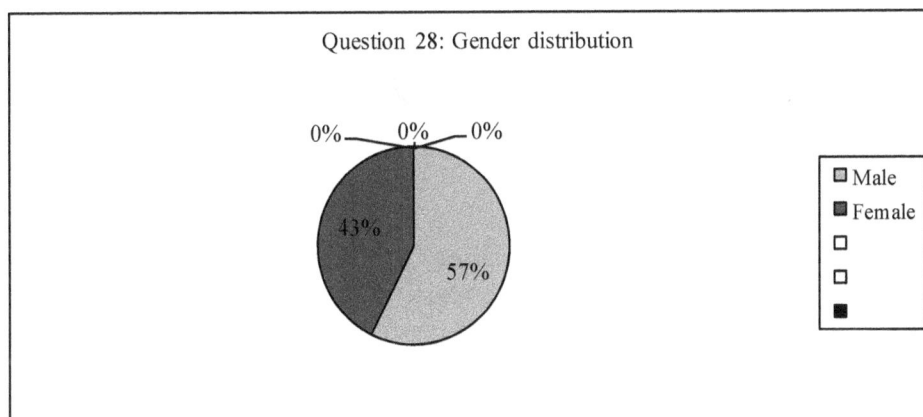

Question 28: Gender distribution

0% — 0% — 0%

43%

57%

Male
Female

Source: Author

Graph 28 shows that 172 respondents or 57% were male participants; 128 respondents or 43% were Female participants.

The Multiple Worlds of Turkish Women: www Magazine for development and Cooperation. Published first March 2005 and last 16.05.2005

[511] The Multiple Worlds of Turkish Women: www Magazine for development and Cooperation. Published first March 2005 and last 16.05.2005

[512] Ibid.

[513] Ibid.

[514] An article by Maurice Crul and Jens Schneider, 2009,(p.9)

Http://webmail.fmg.uva.nl/exchweb/bin/redir.asp?URL-http://www.terecord.org/Home.asp ID Number: 15333, Date Accessed: 9/12/2008

Although, among Turkish immigrants the number of males outnumber females and Turkish women migrated to Germany in significant numbers almost 10 years later than men; previous studies suggest that Turkish women are doing considerably better in the process of integration in all areas. For instance, in the aspect of school integration Turkish girls are doing better than boys; there are more Turkish descent female political representatives in Germany both at Länder and national parliamentary level, even in business women do better than men. Educational data from 1997 shows girls are doing slightly better than boys in following table. Furthermore, the number of Turkish students who attend to university is also rising. Further evidence shows gender differences are conspicuous and women and girls are doing considerably better.

Table 4.1.9: Gender distribution of Turkish students in German universities 1980-97

Years	Total	Number of male students	%	Number of female students	%
1980	6.542	5.731	87.6	811	12.4
1985	9.215	7.512	81.5	1.703	18.5
1990	12.962	9.350	72.1	3.612	27.9
1992[515]	15.859	10.955	69.1	4.904	30.9
1993	17.912	12.105	67.6	5.807	32.4
1994	19.317	12.811	66.3	6.506	33.7
1995	20.631	13.498	65.4	7.133	34.6
1996	21.856	14.125	64.6	7.731	35.4
1997	23.031	14.734	64.0	8.297	36.0

Source: Statistische Bundesamt, Wiesbaden, 1998

In 1980, the proportion of Turkish female students was 12.4%; in 1997 this increased to 36%. The current gender distribution of the Turkish immigrant population in Germany is 57% percent male and 43% female. Data from 1997 indicates that Turkish immigrant students' first preference is law, economy and social sciences 42.2%, language and history follows this. Their third preference is engineering departments. Another interesting point Turkish female students' number is doubled. For example, Turkish female students consist of 9.7% of medical students, and male are only 4.9% of those in German universities.

Emine Altiok points out her experience in Germany as following:

"Turkish women have become emancipated in Germany; they earn their own living and won't accept the usual role of a Turkish wife. But, we have new problem of identity: Are we Turkish or Germans? We cherish our own culture and religion, but we see positive things in European society especially for women. Many women who go back to Turkey just can't cope any more with the restrictions, at least not in provinces – it is easier in Istanbul or Ankara. We, who plan to stay in Germany, intend to work out a middle way between Turkish female subservience and German excess of liberty."[516]

---

[515] East Germany is included to these data after 1992.

[516] Ardagh, John: *Germany and the Germans;* Third Edition Published by Penguin, 1995, p. 273-297
Note: Emine Altiok had studied at Berlin University and was now with the state broadcasting (Rundfunk), making radio programmes for local Turks:

4.1.29. Question 29: Professional status of Turkish origin workers

This question is related to Turkish origin workers' job distribution and employment status which is an affecting factor of their integration. The aim of asking this question is to measure their integration level according to strata from different professional groups in German society.

Table 4.2.1: The employment of Non-Germans and Turks by Economic Sector, 1993 (in %)

Economic Sector	Non- Germans	Turks
Agriculture/ Fisheries	1.0	0.8
Mining/ Energy	1.2	2.8
Manufacturing	42.2	**53.4**
Construction	19.0	7.6
Trade/Commerce	10.4	8.9
Transport/Communication	4.8	4.5
Banking /Insurance	1.1	0.4
Public Services	2.5	1.9
Private Services	25.7	18.9
Charities	1.5	1.0
Total (N)	2,150,114	619,053

Source: Bundesanstalt für Arbeit and Sozialstatistik, 31 December 1993.

Table 4.2.1 shows Turkish-origin workers in 1993 concentrated in certain manual occupations such as plastic production 16% of the workforce, foundry work 24%, hygiene services 20%, fish processing 34% and leather processing 28% and only 1.9% working in the public services. Turkish and other foreign workers are particularly strongly represented in these occupations. The economic restructuring which has transformed labour-market opportunities and occupational status in post-reunification Germany benefited Turks and other non-Germans less than Germans.[517]

By 1993, employment in manufacturing had decline to 42 percent for non-German workers generally; among Turks it still constituted over 53%. Conversely, service sector employment had increased from 7% in the 1980s to almost 19% in 1993. In 1993, 35,000 Turks ran their own businesses and had created 13, 000 jobs between them. Overall, just over 200,000 immigrants were self-employed. The emergence of an entrepreneurial middle class, including a small Turkish sector, had begun, although most of these businesses were on small scale and

---

[517] Bundesanstalt fur Arbeits and Sozialstatistik-Hauptergebnisse 1993,Nuremberg,1993 shows that in 1993,38 percent of Germans worked in manufacturing,22 percent in service sector, while white-collar employment had displaced manufacturing as the largest employment sector among Germans but not among immigrants.

frequently employed family members. In many cases, unemployment had led to people setting up in business in accept to reduce economic insecurity. Some Turkish businessmen, however, also stressed that their key motivation had been to achieve independence 73%, higher income 60%, higher status 62% and more security for their families. Today, the motivations of persons of Turkish origin in pursuing self-employment can be explained as follows. The Turkish community in Europe as well as Germany is made up of a significant younger population when compared to the average of the EU population, motivated to work in order to become established. Self-employment is an option for many unemployed first-generation former guest workers but it also increasingly an option for second generation youth, often assisted by parents who had in mind securing the future livelihoods of their children. The overall proportion of Turks who are self-employed in the EU lies at 4.8%, which is significantly below the EU average of 12.3%. Nearly 70% of all Turkish-origin business owners in the EU are in Germany, of which four fifths is in only three sectors: (1) retail; (2) restaurants and takeaways; and (3) the service sector. Over one third 39.7% of the Turkish immigrant businessmen have lived in Germany for 11-30 years.[518] In one study of Turkish self-employed businessmen in Germany found that only 15% were German citizens in 2003 and that 41%, whilst born in Germany, had Turkish nationality.

Remzi Kaplan, a businessman who is the founder and the present chairman of the Berlin Chamber of Commerce (IHK), states that they serve as a bridge between the two communities of the business world. According to data gathered by the society in 2008, the annual revenues of these businesses amounted to a total of 3.5 billion Euro and they provide employment for over 29,000 people. The Berlin Brandenburg Society of Turkish-German Businessmen today has 380 members and it is the voice of approximately 9000 Turkish owned business establishments in and around Berlin. The number of German members constitutes about 10% of the whole. In 2006, the number of Turkish owned businesses in Berlin, small and large, was around 6800.[519]

On the other hand, a survey related to German family firms, conducted by Deutsche Bank on 400 medium-scale family companies revealed that one in three has no heir to take over the management after the owner's retirement or death. 62% of those have already declared the future management of the company. The rest of companies are seeking a solution for the problem. Especially, 10% of those have serious concerns about the problem due to Germany's population decline. Sven Jezoreck, president of Deutsche Bank for Münster and Ruhr Branch stated the survey results.[520]

Table 4.2.2: Unemployment among immigrants from former recruitment countries, 1980-1994 (in%)

Years & 1994 Unemployment	Labour Force Overall	All Non Germans	Turks	Former Yugoslavs	Italians	Greeks	Spaniards	Portuguese
1980	3.5	4.8	6.3	2.8	5.5	4.1	3.2	2.1
1985	8.7	13.1	14.8	9.0	14.7	11.4	8.7	7.6
1990	6.6	10.0	10.0	9.0	10.6	11.4	6.8	5.5

---

[518] TAM-Türkiye Araştirmalari Merkezi or TRC-Turkish Research Centre, Essen, 2003

[519] The Voice of the Turkish Business world in Berlin Friday, 29 August 2008

[520] An Article by Ziver Ermiş on Germany's demographic decline causes heritage concerns for German companies (Cologne) February 2nd 2009. The survey results are published in West deutsche Allgemeine Zeitung.

1994	8.8		15.8	**18.9**	9.8		17.0	16.2	11.2	11.2
Total	391, 6		141, 851	45,141	38,339		22, 643	21.123	6, 837	6, 036

Source: Compiled from statistics published by the Bundesanstalt für Arbeit for the relevant years. Unemployment: (30 August 1994)

Table 4.8 shows that in 1994, the unemployment rate among Turks was twice the national average and had trebled since 1980.

Graph 29: Professional Status of Turkish immigrants

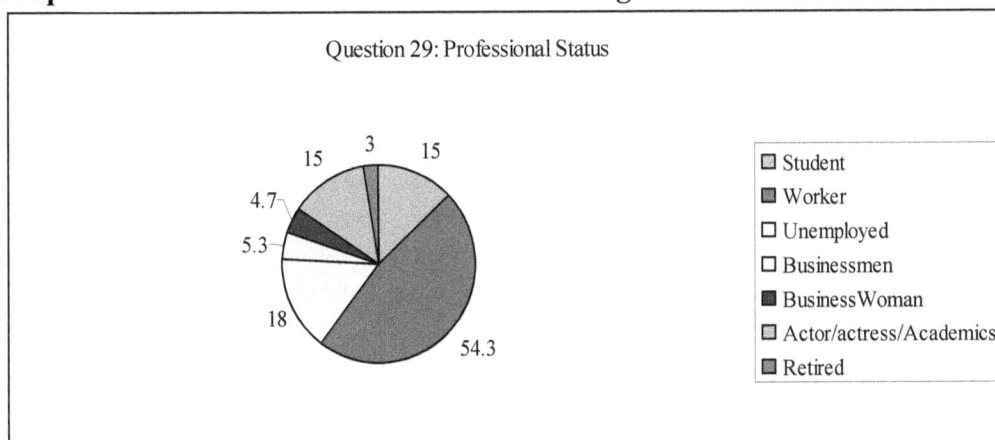

Source: Author

Graph 29 shows that 45 respondents or 15% said that they are 'students'; 163 respondents or 54.3% said that they are 'workers'; Six point scale bar chart shows that 54 respondents or 18 percent replied that they are 'unemployed'; 16 respondents or 5.3% responded 'businessmen' (self-employed); 14 respondents or 4.7% said 'businesswomen' (self-employed); 9 respondents or 3% responded 'retired'.

The unemployment level of persons of Turkish immigrants was 18.9% in 1994; in 1996, unemployment rates among Turkish immigrants were higher than other immigrant groups and amongst Germans. Other immigrant groups experienced 19% unemployment, Turks experienced 22.5% and among Germans only 10% are unemployed. [521] The survey results show that in Germany, according to the 2002 census, 11% of Turks were unemployed compared to a national average of 4% Unemployment rates of both men and women are higher than for the general population, especially among those between the ages of 16 and 24. Although the 2007-survey result shows little decline, unemployment rates among Turkish immigrants are still high with 18%, which is one of the negative affecting factors of immigrants' integration into the host society. In other words, unemployment and economic downturns are a slowing factor of integration which plays a role in negative attitude of Germans towards Turkish immigrants, even more so than religious differences, as it leads jobless Germans to scapegoat immigrants; however, there is no evidence to support such an allegation.

---

[521] Şen, Faruk: "The Historical Situation of Turkish Migrants in Germany". *Immigrants and Minorities*, July 2003, **22** (2-3): 208–227, doi:10.1080/0261928042000244835.

The author of 'Lowest of the Low' (*Ganz Unten* or "*Ich Ali*"), (1985), Günter Wallraff, claims that 'if Turks leave Germany, Germany economically collapses' (2006). He also pointed out that Turkish guest workers in 1980s have accepted dangerous and tiring jobs, which are dirty and potentially damaging to health, in shift or piece work and often in plants with a fluctuating workforce and little job security; since their contracts may have tied them to specific jobs in industries or to avoid becoming unemployed (1985).[522] On the other hand, many Turkish immigrants are establishing self-businesses in Germany. There were 150,000 foreign-owned businesses by 1992, including 33,000 owned by Turks .The Turkish-owned businesses generated 700,000 jobs in 1991 and recorded sales of DM 25 billion (about US $ 17 billion) and invested DM 6 million in Germany.[523]

4.1.30. Question 30: Exploring the age structure of Turkish origin population

Question 30 is intended to find out about the age structure of the Turkish origin population in Germany. This is a relevant factor as the younger German-born generations tend to be more integrated than older Turkish immigrant population. Due to negative demographic changes Germany still needs immigrants but specific age groups namely young immigrants at the peak age for work. The demand is arguably less than the post-war years but there is still need for them.

Pie-chart graph 30: Evaluating the age structure of Turkish immigrants in Germany

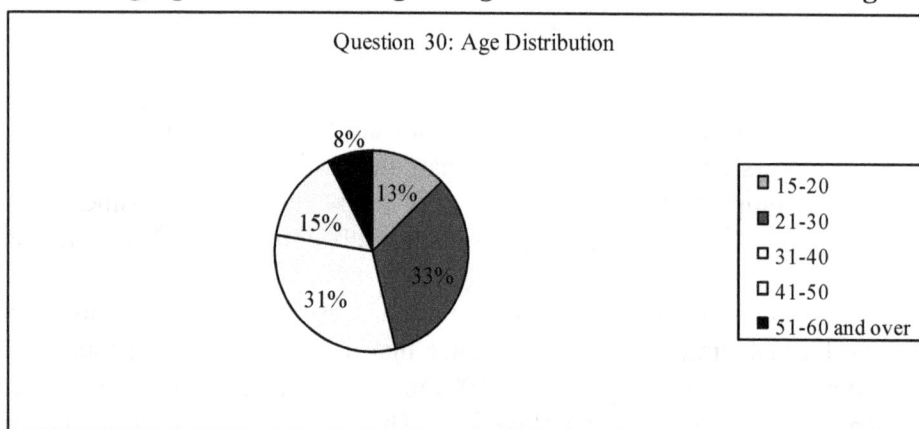

Source: Author

Graph 30 shows that 36 respondents or 13 percent are between '15-20'years old (no data under 15); 93 respondents or 31 percent are between '21-30'; 88 respondents constituting 33 percent are between '31-40' years old; 42 respondents or 15 percent are between '41-50'; 21 respondents or 8 percent between '51-60' and over. Persons under 15 years and over 60 years old haven't been included in the survey results, only from the first group (15-20 years old) and to last group (51- 60 years old) have been interviewed.

---

[522] Wallraff, Günter: 'Lowest of the Low' (*Ganz Unten* or "*Ich Ali*"), Verlag Kipenheuser, Köln, 1986, (p. 122-6). Günter Wallraff: http://writing.learnhub.com/lesson/5849-gnter-wallraff-undercover-journalist#ixzz0HUti6GD7&A
[523] Journal 'This Week in Germany', 18 September, 1992:4.

The survey result indicates that Turkish immigrants have constituted a younger population in Germany. One important finding the survey results suggest that only continued inward migration can stabilize Germany's demographic trend and prevent the disproportionate ageing of its population. One in three children, under the age of six, is of immigrant origin. In big German cities, those youths consists of 40% German population.

German Statistics Institute's figures also concur, according to their figures and calculations Germany's population without migration could decrease between the years 2005 and 2050 from 82.1 to 50.7 million. Another important finding (the survey results indicate) is 'young (Turkish) immigrants pay old Germans receive'. The study also shows that each German worker would have to spend about 40% of their income on pension contributions without the presence of a mainly young migrant population[524]. Most of the first generation Turkish guest workers returned home before their retirement age because of German assimilation policy, pressure and racism. There are over 8 million retired people in Turkey, in fact one in four of them returned from Germany and retired on a Turkish national pension instead of receiving funds from Germany.

Table 4.2.3: Turkish population in the FRG according to age structure as of 30 September 1990

0 - 17 years	597.619	35.7 %
18 – 20 years	127.766	7.6 %
21 – 29 years	332.779	19.9 %
30 – 39 years	192.503	11.5 %
40 - 49 years	249.202	14.9 %
50 – 54 years	100.419	6.0 %
55 – 59 years	49.846	3.0 %
60 – 64 years	17.960	1.1 %
65 and above	7.817	0.5 %

Source: Zentrum fur Turkeistudien,Zur Lebenssituation und spezifischen Problemlage alterer auslandischer Einwohner in der BDR, Kurzfassung,Essen, October 1992.

The Turks in Germany are a comparatively young population group, 35.7 being younger than 18 years old. About half of the Turkish population is between 25 and 45 years old and *two thirds* of immigrants belong to the *20-49 age group*. Only 5 % is older than 60.

The latest data from Berlin Institute for population and development show that 29% of total population of Turkish immigrants are younger than 15 years. This proportion with native German is only 12%, which means that Turkish descents are the youngest ethnic group in Germany.[525]

---

[524] Guardian 1 September 1993, 'Old Germans need young migrants' pay'.
[525] Unused Potential or *Ungenutzte potenziale-Berlin-Institut für Bevolkerung und Entwicklung*, Edition 63, 26 January 2009 or http://www.berlin-institut.org/newsletter/ newsletter_archive.html

The age dependency ratio of the immigrant population in Germany has escalated since 1990 and is predicted to continue to do so until 2030 (Sarah Spencer Ed., 'Immigration as an Economic Asset', A positive Approach to Migrants... Rivers Oram Press, 1994, p. 84.). This means that Germany will still need immigrants in the future as labour force and to stabilise its declining population. Spencer has three scenarios:

Scenario 1 implies continued net migration of 200,000 immigrants annually. Here the age-dependency ratio of immigrants would grow to 50% in the year 2030.

Scenario 2 assumes a linear decrease in net immigration to zero by the 2000. Then the ageing of the foreign population would develop even faster and reach an age-dependency ratio of 60% in 2030.

Scenario 3 shows us the impact of a stop in fertility decline. In this case the age – independency ratio would increase only 53.8% in 2030.

Conclusion

This chapter is concerned with a univariate analysis of survey responses to gain an understanding of the main research question of this study, namely the level of Turkish immigrants' integration into German society and its impact on Turco-German relations. The key factors that have been taken into account for this purpose are the respondents' attitude towards Germany and Europe as a whole, birthplace, citizenship, education level, employment status, German language ability, level of interaction with native Germans at work and in civic life (political, social and sportive activities), tendency to permanent residence, political awareness and relative social status (compared with Germans). Environmental factors identified include the EU and German political parties' integration policies, equal opportunities legislation, German reunification in 1990 and Turkey's the EU membership. From the analysis and review of previous studies, the hypothesis to be examined is that progress towards the integration of persons of Turkish origin is highly dependent on a number of factors, which affect individuals and groups in different ways depending on their characteristics and that the success (or lack) of integration in the long term is dependent on how the factors are addressed by German society as a whole.

For a visual representation, the following table shows the percentage of respondents that chose the positively "satisfied" response categories for questions that encompass the most important affecting factors of integration. The respondents of Survey 2007 expressed their self-perception of their integration level and their life in Germany.

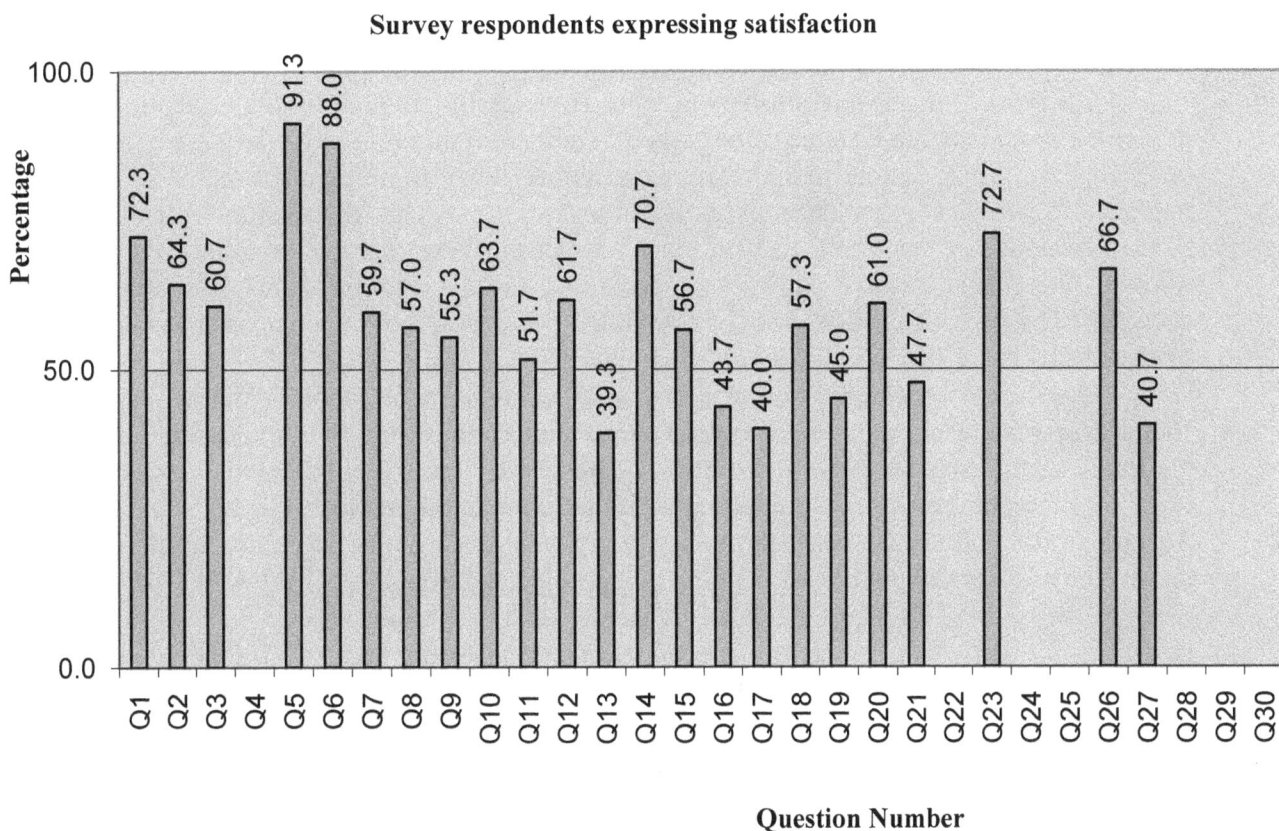

Survey respondents expressing satisfaction

Percentage / Question Number

Q1: 72.3
Q2: 64.3
Q3: 60.7
Q5: 91.3
Q6: 88.0
Q7: 59.7
Q8: 57.0
Q9: 55.3
Q10: 63.7
Q11: 51.7
Q12: 61.7
Q13: 39.3
Q14: 70.7
Q15: 56.7
Q16: 43.7
Q17: 40.0
Q18: 57.3
Q19: 45.0
Q20: 61.0
Q21: 47.7
Q23: 72.7
Q26: 66.7
Q27: 40.7

Source: Author

Survey summary

The study found 49% of respondents to question one self-identified as "ordinary" Europeans with almost equal numbers expressing a greater and lesser feeling. Because of the cultural, political and geographical dimensions, "Feeling European" is a complex question for Turkish-origin people. For example, an individual born in European Turkey is European in a geographic sense regardless of their feelings. The most significant affecting factor is political awareness (from both German and Turkish media and politicians) which increases the likelihood of an individual forming an opinion.

Question 2, "How German do you feel" finds 48% of respondents expressing German identity in an ordinary sense. More respondents, 36% express a lesser sense of identity than for "Feeling European" 28%. In part, this can be explained by the birthplace and citizenship of respondents as the "guest worker" generation emigrated from Turkey and are less likely to feel German. However, the finding that 64% of responses are in the top three categories is a strong indicator of integration.

Responses to question 3 about language use show that a considerable minority (39%) speak mostly or only Turkish at home. Speaking German at home accustoms the speaker and their household to social and interpersonal language use which is of benefit in other situations and is a good indicator of integration. The question of language use is complex and the key

197

factors in this study are Birthplace, German language ability, tendency to permanent residence and overall level of interaction in German. An individual born, educated and interacting in public in German is more likely to use the language at home.

Question 5, about relationships at work is primarily affected by the Education level and perceived socio-economic status of persons of Turkish origin (skilled workers are more likely to be accepted). Other factors include language ability, level of interaction, equal opportunities, tendency to permanent residence and political awareness (which includes union representation). 57% of respondents feel that their workplace relationships are "normal" and only 9% worse than normal. Other studies have shown that perceived socio-economic status is a key factor for acceptance by native Germans. 91% of respondents feel their workplace relationships are normal or better which is a strong indicator of integration.

Question 6 concerning how respondents feel about local people's attitude towards them found a similar response to the previous work-related question, 34% indicating a better than "normal" relationship (31% for question 5). The key affecting factors are also similar, with the level of interaction being most significant. Social interaction between Germans and persons of Turkish origin can be increased through participation in activities of common interest such as sports, the arts, recreational clubs, cultural and political activities.

Question 7, "Do you feel equally treated?" sounds similar to question 6 but the response pattern is not, indicating a different interpretation and affecting factors. 41% of respondents feel sometimes or often unfairly treated. Previous studies have shown these feelings most often arise over access to education, employment and housing. The most significant facilitating factors in this type of situation are good German language ability and high perceived socio-economic status while environmental factors such as political integration policy and equal opportunities also have an effect.

In response to question 8, "Do you like the food here?" 54% expressed liking both German and Turkish food. Only 1% said that they like only German food implying a strong link to Turkish cuisine in both the German-born and Turkish-born generations. The most significant factor for adopting German food is the level of interaction with native Germans who have reciprocated by developing a taste for Döner Kebab.

Question 9 investigates whether persons of Turkish origin are satisfied with the lifestyle they achieved in Germany. Culture and lifestyle vary noticeably between the individual states (Länder) because they have distinctive characteristics and limited political autonomy. Survey responses therefore reflect local conditions. The pattern is different to previous questions as 37% of respondents chose the second of five responses "Its different" and 42% chose the third, "Yes I like it", a noticeable division of opinion. The key factors of an individual's satisfaction are their employment status, German language ability, relative social status and level of interaction. Environmental factors such as the integration policies of local political parties and equal opportunities are also important.

Question 10, "Do you feel a member of the host country" is concerned with whether respondents feel accepted or excluded in society by native Germans. The 56% response of "Yes, I do" is a strong indicator of integration. 7% feel strongly accepted while 37% feel excluded to some extent – a considerable minority. The key influencing factors are birthplace, citizenship, German language ability, level of interaction and relative social status. The integration policy of the Federal government is also a key factor of how persons of Turkish origin are perceived by native Germans and can positively influence anti-immigrant feelings.

Question 11 examines the connections respondents have with Turkey. The Turkish-born guest-worker generation originally intended to return and maintained contact through family links and Turkish-language literature and media. The second generation, both the German-born and the Turkish-born who immigrated to be with their parents have maintained links to some extent. 49% of respondents said that they have strong links with Turkey and 42% said they had equal links with both countries. The key influencing factors are birthplace, level of interaction and tendency to permanent residence.

In response to question 12, "Is life comfortable in Germany", 48% of respondents found life comfortable to a normal level, implying that their living conditions are reasonable. Previous studies show that the guest worker generation struggled in the 1960s with long working hours, poor accommodation and inadequate access to Turkish foods which made their lives uncomfortable. 38% of respondents expressed dissatisfaction with the level of comfort in their lives suggesting that there is still progress to be made for a substantial minority. The key influencing factors are employment status, German language ability, level of interaction and relative socio-economic status.

Question 13, concerning the difficulty of finding a job in Germany finds 61% responding "Hard" or "Very hard". A 2007 study found 18% unemployment among persons of Turkish origin. Two-thirds of the guest worker generation were unskilled workers who migrated to meet the demand for manual labour in the 1960s. Environmental factors such as the reunification of Germany and later EU expansion increased the supply of labour and EU freedom of movement has resulted in labour subcontracting, where whole teams move internationally to carry out work at lower rates of pay than locals. Additionally, Germany has experienced a reduction in manufacturing and growth in professional employment which does not favour the unskilled. The most significant affecting factors are citizenship (non-citizens are excluded from certain occupations), education level, German language ability, tendency to permanent residence and relative socio-economic status.

Question 14, "Is it hard to find a house here" examines housing conditions for persons of Turkish origin. Better housing means higher socio-economic status to the casual observer, an important factor in acceptance by native Germans. The first generation of guest workers were mostly single men and the barrack room accommodation provided reflected their perceived short-term stay. When bringing families to Germany, they faced discrimination and limited availability of rented housing. Previous studies have found evidence of ghettoisation or concentration in certain districts of cities, a hindering factor to integration. German reunification in 1990 eased the rented housing shortage and home ownership is a growing trend as increasing numbers acquire the means to buy. 29% of survey respondents replied that it is "Hard" or "Very hard" to find adequate accommodation, 39% replied "But possible" or "Sometimes" and 32% replied "More opportunities here" showing a relatively even split in the range of experiences. The key influencing factors are employment status, German language ability (in order to persuade landlords) and relative social status (again, to persuade landlords of suitability).

Question 15 examines opinions about education facilities provided for the children of Turkish immigrants. Historic education policies did not help the integration of Turkish-origin students into the German school system as they were expected to return to Turkey with their parents in the future. Education policy and outcomes vary substantially between states. Studies have found them underperforming substantially, 40% do not start any kind of vocational training. An adequate education is essential for success in Germany due to the economic shift towards professional services and high-value manufacturing. School life also provides opportunities for interaction with native Germans. Those who have not naturalised as German citizens are treated as foreign students not as home students when applying for university, a substantial hindrance. 34% of survey responses deemed the facilities "Good", 21% "Not bad" and 22% better than good giving a total of 77% at least satisfied. Key facilitating factors include Education level, German language ability and employment status as educated parents are more likely to raise their children to value education and help them make the most of the system.

Question 16, "Are you interested in politics here?" found 49% responding "Not much", meaning they find politics irrelevant. 39% responded "Yes" and "A little". The first generation of Turkish immigrants were unable to vote or become candidates in national elections therefore trade unions were their earliest form of representation. Growing numbers of naturalised Turks gained voting rights with citizenship but only 5 of the 613 members of the national Parliament (Bundestag) claim Turkish heritage and the number of Turkish-origin politicians in all levels of government is about 80. Significant affecting factors of involvement with politics are citizenship, education level, German language ability and level of interaction.

Question 17 to Turkish-origin respondents, "Are you a German Citizen", found 33% replied "Yes" and 54% replied "No", evidence of a substantial number living in Germany as Turkish citizens. German nationality law is a significant hindering factor as there is no automatic right to citizenship by place of birth. Children born to foreign parents must naturalise when they are 18 years old. In the past dual citizenship was permitted for the children of German citizens born in other countries but more difficult for those intending to naturalise in Germany and retain their citizenship of birth. Loyalty to Turkey is a further reason why immigrants may not wish to naturalise. The most significant factors are birthplace, employment status, German language ability, level of interaction and tendency to permanent residence. Individuals applying for citizenship are most likely to be substantially integrated into German cultural, political and social life.

In response to question 18, "Do you feel part of German culture?", 61% replied "Yes" or "A little" and 19% "Very much" or "Totally", a strong indication of identity and participation. Turkish immigrants had to adapt to the different expectations, structure and common values in Germany. The German-born generations have been exposed to German society from childhood and do not have to adapt. Their difficulty is in reconciling the values of society around them with possibly different values held by their parents and the Turkish-born generation. The key affecting factors are birthplace, citizenship, education level, German language ability, level of interaction and relative socio-economic status.

Question 19 concerning intermarriage found 27% of respondents answering "Yes" to the question "Are you married to a German?". Together with the 7% answering "have been", this is good evidence of interpersonal integration. Previous studies show negative attitudes towards intermarriage decreasing from 45% to 28% from 1980-2000. 1996 data shows a substantial disparity in the number of marriages involving a Turkish man and German woman (18% of all marriages involving a Turkish partner) and a German man and Turkish woman (6% of the same group), possibly due to differing cultural values. The most important affecting factors are employment status, German language ability and level of interaction.

Question 20 asks respondents if they are satisfied with their socio-economic status in Germany, one of the most important affecting factors of integration. 42% replied "Yes" showing that a substantial group are satisfied with their status. 37% replied "Disappointed" or "Not much" indicating that there is still progress to be made. Persons of Turkish origin have raised their status by educational achievement, gaining promotion at work, buying property, improving their language ability and starting businesses. The most important affecting factors are citizenship, education level, employment status, German language ability, level of interaction and tendency to permanent residence.

41% of respondents to question 21, "Have you been accepted as a member of society here?" replied "Yes" while 52% replied "Never" and "Maybe" indicating they have doubts about whether they are accepted by native Germans. A significant issue concerns whether persons of Turkish origin can be accepted as part of German society while retaining their cultural diversity. The 2% of respondents who replied that they had been "Totally" accepted is an indication that it is possible. Previous studies show that key factors such as education level, employment status, German language ability and relative socio-economic status affect whether immigrants are viewed positively.

Question 22, "Where were you born" is intended to investigate the place of birth of respondents. 64% replied "in Turkey" and 26%, "in Germany" while 7% were born in other EU countries. Being born in Germany is a significant factor in the integration of persons of Turkish origin as they will have been exposed to German culture, language and society from birth. Data from the Berlin institute for population and development shows that half of the 3 million population of Turkish descent in Germany were born there.

In response to question 23, "How good is your German?" 38% replied "Good", implying they are happy with their German language ability. Competency in German is a key facilitating factor of integration. More respondents indicated their ability was better than "good" (39%) than lesser (23%) and the total percentage replying good or better (77%) is a strong indication of a general ability to communicate in German. The "guest worker" generation found their ability to integrate limited by their poor knowledge of German and language teaching provision was weak in the 1960s and 1970s. German politicians have identified a lack of ability in German as the most significant factor in unemployment and social exclusion among immigrant communities and the 2007 immigration law sets new requirements for partners moving to Germany for family reunification to prove their proficiency in German.

Question 24, investigating which school system respondents attended found 26% went to school in Turkey and 44% in Germany while 26% attended schools in other countries. Attending school in Germany provides an early introduction to the country's cultural and social life and exposes young people to ideas in a German context, facilitating their integration.

Question 25 investigates the education level of persons of Turkish origin and the effect on their integration in Germany as it is a significant affecting factor. German scholars point out that 'Contemporary integration of immigrants can be achieved only through education'. Kenan Kolat President for Turco-German Society in Frankfurt argues that "the Turkish parents should participate in the German education system",[526] and Prof. Ingrid Ditrich argued that "German education system is discriminatory".[527] The survey results show that 84 respondents or 28% replied 'Public school' (8-9 years); 108 respondents or 36.3% 'Vocational school' or (secondary); 48 respondents or 16% 'Technical school' (and high school); 26 respondents or 8.7% responded 'High school'; 36 respondents or 12% said that they have a University Degree.

---

[526] Kenan Kolat, President for Turco-German Society, Frankfurt, 28.8.2006
[527] An article by Yalcin Doğan: *Fighting on identity issue of Turks* 18 October, 2007 [Author's translation from Turkish Daily Hürriyet, 18 October, 2007].

Question 26, "Are you interested in sports here?", explores the findings of common interests with host country members which is one of the most motivating factors of immigrants' integration and participating in sports , cultural , and political activities in the host country is a natural way of achieving this. In this way, the interaction creates a common interest and contact especially between youth of the immigrant and native-German communities leading to opportunities for more integration in the country. The survey shows that 36 respondents or 12% replied 'yes, professionally'; 63 respondents or 21% said 'not professionally'; 86 respondents or 29% said 'as hobby'; 37 respondents or 12% said that they 'sometimes' play in their leisure time; 79 respondents or 26% said they 'just watch' sports programmes. The survey results indicate that almost 12% of respondents to this survey are professional sports people (footballers, basketball players, wrestlers, boxers and from other sport branches) both at German national and local level. This number is significantly increasing year by year.

.   Question 27 "Where do you want to live in future?" investigates whether persons of Turkish origin intend to live in Germany permanently, plan to migrate to another country or will return to Turkey. The 2007 survey, shows that 35 respondents or 11.7% answered 'in Germany'; 63 respondents or 21% said 'in Turkey'; 86 respondents or 28.7% said 'Other European' countries; 37 respondents or 12.3% said that they want to live in 'Australia'; 79 respondents or 26.3% answered 'other' countries, possibly indicating as yet an unplanned desire to leave Germany.

The first and third responses show, respectively 36% answered 'want to live in Germany and 4% answered 'want to live in both Germany and Turkey', giving a total of 40 % of respondents wanting to live in Germany. Comparing this 40% survey result with the previous research from 1993 where 43 % of Turkish immigrants expressed a wish to live in Germany shows long-term consistency in the proportion of those of Turkish origin wishing to live in Germany continues.

As a result, almost half of the Turkish immigrants want to stay in Germany. In another calculation, more than over half of the respondents 100% - 40% = 60% do not wish to live in Germany. Although 60% respondents wish to live outside of Germany or consider seeking opportunity for emigration to another country from Germany, but are still living in Germany for different reasons.

Findings

This study found that survey respondents' experience of issues linked to integration, as expressed in answers to the survey questions are dependent on key facilitating factors of integration as identified here, especially individuals' Citizenship and German language ability. Other studies indicate that politicians and others with an interest in the integration process have identified these issues, evidenced by recent legal changes to facilitate naturalisation and German language teaching. Nevertheless the survey results show there is still progress to be made.

Chapter 5

5.1 Chapter Introduction

Chapter five analyses the effect of closely related variables on integration of Turkish immigrants into Germany by the aid of bar-chart graphs. Before presenting results of the bivariate analysis, the closely related variables which have similar effects can helpfully be supplemented. To consider the specific grouped questions in a comparative way, a series of bar-charts were prepared to measure similar factors' effect on integration. The first grouped questions 1, and 2 and its graph indicates Turkish immigrants' inner feeling of integration. In the same way, second group question 5 and 12 measure similar social factors' effect on integration from different relevant aspects.

The sixteen survey questions are grouped into eight major groups in accordance with their closeness and inter-relations with the research question which is 'Have Turkish immigrants integrated into Germany between years 1961-2007 and has their integration any impact on Turco-German relations?' The reasons for these groupings is that each group is inter-linked with each other more closely than other groups and each group yields parallel outcome concerning the integration factors of Turkish immigrants into German society.

As mentioned earlier in the methodology chapter, descriptive and inferential statistics were used in this survey to summarize the questionnaire results. The survey data were quantified (or turned into numbers) to generalize from the sample a 300 Turkish immigrants group (to obtain the findings) to wider group estimates 2.4 million Turkish decent populations. Inferential statistics were used as a basis for making predictions in order to make inferences about findings what is more likely to happen in relation to integration problems of Turkish immigrants in the future of Germany.

In this chapter, bar graphs are preferable to compare the size of one category with that of another. Bar-charts seem clearer to compare one category with another (height of the column or percentages). A comparative analysis is employed for the chapter and specific grouped bar-charts (questions) are considered to treat each in a comparative way with others in relation to their inter-action and closeness.

The first eight affecting factors of integration are connected to the below scheme such as survival and motivating factors (in Figure 5.1) which are also interrelated with each other. The survival factors are considered as primary conditions to be integrated. Motivating factors are those that encourage an immigrant's full potentiality to establish him or her into host society. If the survival factors are not satisfied, the motivating factors will not work properly.

The following table gives insight into the whole argument of the composite-rating during this chapter as an essential part of the thesis.

Figure 5.1, Affecting Factors of Immigrants' Integration:

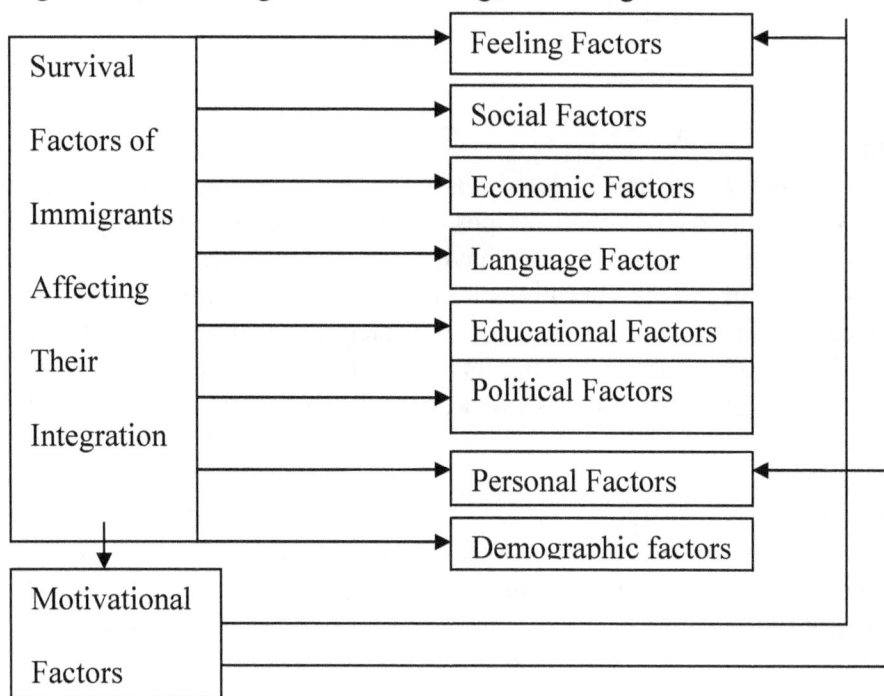

Source: Author
The idea of this figure is adapted from Abraham Maslow's pyramid-shaped diagram to express biological, spiritual or existential needs of immigrants.

Two broad categories of integration are outlined as survival and motivating factors. The survival factors are considered as primary conditions to be integrated. Although, survival factors are sufficient for an immigrant's full integration, without motivating factors the process will not be speedy. Moreover, the survival factors are also associated with access to basic human rights and benefiting from the EU integration policy quoted as follows:

"The EU integration policy is recognized by the first common basic principle in the Council conclusions emphasizing that integration is a dynamic, two way process of mutual accommodation by all immigrants and residents of member states." The principles also impose further requirements on immigrants, "the EU basic values are to be respected; basic knowledge of the host society's language, history and institutions is viewed as 'indispensable' to integration, and while practices of diverse cultures and religions must be safeguarded, they should not conflict with European human rights or national law, which includes the prevention of 'individual migrants from exercising other fundamental rights or from participating in the host society".[528]

---

[528] Ryszard Cholewinski, 2005: Migrants as Minorities, Integration and Inclusion in the Enlarged EU, p.713; JCMS 2005 Volume 43. Number 4, pp. 695-716

The first grouped questions one and two are related to feeling factors and first bar chart graph indicates Turkish immigrants' inner feeling of integration to explain relationships which have similar effect on their integration in Germany.

The second group is (survey questions 5 and 12) related to social factors, which impacts social integration of Turkish immigrants into German society.

Group three, survey questions 13, 14 are related to economic factors and graph three indicates their economic adaptation into German society from economic aspect.

Group four, which consists of questions 3 and 23 are related to language factors and graph four indicates Turkish immigrants' German language level and how much they use German language as a tool or a facilitating factor for their integration into German society and way of life.

Group five, questions 15, 25 are related to education factors and Graph 5 indicate their educational achievement as depth of integration process.

The sixth group, questions 16, 17 are related to political factors and graph six shows their political interests and German citizenship level and its impact on their integration

Group seven, questions 19, 29 are related to personal factors and graph seven examines the effect of intermarriage or marital status of Turkish immigrants on their integration into German society. This facilitates the measuring of their inter-marriage rates to Germans and the number of Turkish immigrants with German citizenship, which gives them voting rights as German in local, national and European parliament elections.

Group eight, questions 28, 30 are related to their demographic factors such as gender and age structure and graph eight explores their gender distribution and age structure which are closely related to their integration process into German society and way of life.

5.1.1 Feeling factors of Turkish immigrants as European and German

Questions 1 and 2 are used to analyse their effects on integration of Turkish immigrants. Demographic and quantitative analyses are applied to investigate the relationship of immigrants' integration as follows.

These two questions are used to analyse connections between similar categories of survey questions. Cross-comparison provides an opportunity to measure the impact of Turkish immigrants' feeling as European or German on their integration into German society.

Meanwhile, the President of European commission, Romano Prodi defines the prospective 'European identity' in his speech to the European Parliament in 1999 as "the EU institutions must build up 'a shared feeling of belonging to Europe...mutual trust, increased reliance on majority rule – a shared European-wide national identity."

The first grouped survey questions one and two are related to feeling factors in the following Graph 5.1.1 which indicates Turkish immigrants' inner feeling or state of mind to explain two variables' similar effect on their integration in Germany.

Graph 5.1.1: Turkish immigrants' feeling factor as European and German

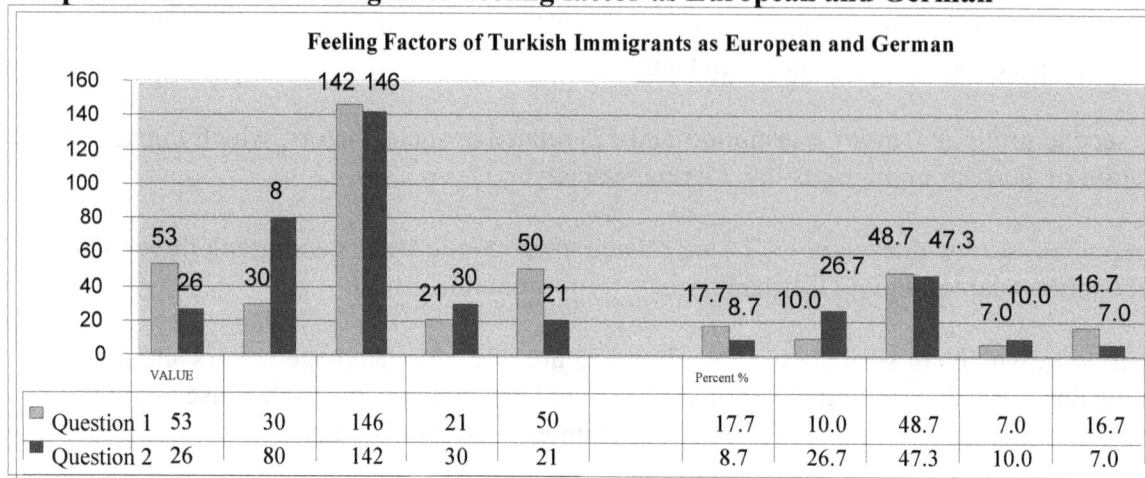

Feeling Factors of Turkish Immigrants as European and German

	VALUE					Percent %				
Question 1	53	30	146	21	50	17.7	10.0	48.7	7.0	16.7
Question 2	26	80	142	30	21	8.7	26.7	47.3	10.0	7.0

Q1. How European do you feel? (1)Not European at all (2) A little European (3) Ordinary European (4) Quite European (5) Very European
Q2. How German do you feel? (1) Not German at all (2) A little German (3) Ordinary German (4) Quite German (5) Very German

Source: Author

Graph 5.1.1 shows salient figures in the first row [1] **17.7%** of respondents answered that they feel 'Not European at all'. [2] **10%** feel 'A little European. Since, the first generation and a part of the second generation's German language and education level were very low compared to German born younger generation. The aspect of education level of Turkish immigrants will be further discussed in question fifteen, where the comparison is mainly related to how the education level affects their integration. In the mid-column [3] of the questionnaire **48.7%** of immigrants feel European. 21 responded [4] they feel 'Quite European' this group constitutes **7%** of Turkish immigrants. 50 respondents [5] **16.7%** replied they feel 'very European' it means that they are most likely to be well integrated into any European society including the German.[529]

Comparing these two closely related questions' silent figures of mid-point scores according to Bar-chart graph 5.1.1, the percentages of question one and question two are almost the same. **48.7%** feel European and German and **47.3%** percent feel 'German', which means these two groups' scores have similar effect on integration of Turkish immigrants in Germany. Findings of two rows suggest quite a high level of integration at least on the joint measure of feeling as European/German **49%/47%** consider themselves 'normally' European/German and a further **17.7%/7%** feel very European/German. If they feel integrated into any European society, they feel also integrated into German society. In general, most of the respondents feel more European than German. For example, while only 7% feel German, 17.7% feel European.

---

[529] Graph 5.1.1 displays Turkish immigrants' feeling as European and German two rows' rating respectively from category 1 (low level) to (high level) 5 (scale) [1] **17.7%** of respondents answered that they feel 'Not European at all' / the second row[1st column] **8.7%** of respondents feel 'Not German at all'; [2] **10%** feel 'A little European/ the second category [2nd column] **26.7%** of them feel 'A little German'; in the mid-column [3] of the questionnaire **48.7%** of immigrants feel 'Ordinary European'/ [3] **47.3%** of Turkish immigrants feel as 'Ordinary German'; [4] **7%** of them feel 'Quite European' /[4th column], thirty respondents **10%** replied that they feel 'Quite German' ; 50 respondents [5] **16.7%** replied they feel 'Very European/ [5] 21 respondents **7%** feel 'Very German' while living in Germany.

A similar survey was conducted on Germans about their feeling as European by Sven Gareis and Paul Klein in 2004 demonstrates the following results.[530]

Table 5.1.1: "Do you feel yourself European?" (Answers in per cent)

Very European	29.4
Quite European	42.1
A little European	19.0
Not European at all	8.0
No opinion	1.5

Source: German or European? Attitudes Towards Political or Territorial Affiliation, Sozialwissenschaftliches Institut Der Bundeswehr, Strausberg, Forum, Volume 26, 2004, p. 40-41

Table 5.1.1 above has shown that 29.4% of Germans feel very European, while **42.1%** of Germans considered themselves quite European. 27% of Germans indicate that they feel little or not at all European. Comparing of these (to Graph 5.1.1 the first row of mid-point figure) which indicates 48.7% of Turks feel European. It means that **48.7% - 42.1% = 6.6%** of the Turks in Germany feel more European than Germans (42.1%) themselves. An interesting point about feeling European related to German people in the *Neue Länder* is only 20% of former East Germans feel very European compared to 33% among West German respondents. By the collapse of the Ottoman Empire, Europeans attitude towards the Turks was expressed as 'Sick Man of Europe' – of Europe' but sick' Above figures means also that European will give up soon calling Turkey as 'the sick man of Europe' as they did towards the end of the Ottoman Empire collapse in 1918. Turkey, legacy of the Ottoman Empire, is still trying to recover and join to the EU fully.[531]

Table 5.1.2 shows the difficulty of feeling German and European at the same time (Answers in %)

Very easy	21.8
Rather easy	44.4
Rather difficult	21.0
Very difficult	7.0
No opinion	5.9

Source: German or European? Attitudes Towards Political or Territorial Affiliation, Sozialwissenschaftliches Institut Der Bundeswehr, Strausberg, Forum, Volume 26, 2004, p. 40-41)

Previous studies, on German attitudes towards European identity and feeling as European, indicates that there is a strong relationship between birthplace (with childhood memories) and feeling home *(Heimat)*.[532] A representative survey conducted by WOWI in 1995 demonstrated

---

[530] Gareis, Sven Bernhard and Klein, Paul: German or European? Attitudes Towards Political or Territorial Affiliation,
Sozialwissenschaftliches Institut Der Bundeswehr, Europe's Common Security Attitudes in France, Germany and Italy, Strausberg, Forum, Volume 26, 2004, p. 40-1)
[531] Burrows, Bernard: Turkey and the European Community, Federal Trust for Education and Research, Working Paper 3, London, 1987, p. 4.
[532] Spangenberg, Stefan and Klein, Paul: Heimat und Verteidigung. SOWI-Arbeitspapier No. 102, Strausberg 1997.

a level of emphasis on the birthplace and the current place of residence.[533] The following table explains national feelings and national pride. Tom W. Smith and Seokko Kim argue "National pride is the positive affect that the public feels towards their country, resulting from national identity. National pride is related to feelings of patriotism and nationalism, both co-exists, but feeling national pride is not equivalent to being nationalistic."[534]

Table 5.1.2a: Ranking of countries on general and domain-specific national pride for 2003/04

	General National pride	Domain-specific national pride	Average ranking
United States	17.7	4.0	1 (tied)
Australia	17.5	2.9	3
Japan	15.9	1.8	18
Great Britain	15.1	2.2	19
Germany West	14.5	1.0	28 (tied)
Germany-East	14.2	0.7	33

Source: International journal of Public Opinion Research, Vol. 18, No. 1 Spring 2006, World Opinion National Pride in Comparative Perspective; 1995/6 and 2003/4 by Tom W. Smith and Seokko Kim, National Identity Studies, Ranking of National Pride, p. 127-9

Table 1 shows the rankings on general and domain-specific national pride. The USA scores first while the former East Germany places at the bottom in 33rd place among 33 countries (counting the east and the West German regions separately. The bottom rank reflects the depressed status of national pride in ex-Socialist states. The former West Germany's finish tied for the 28th position indicates that the war guilt that has been shown to repress German national pride in the past is still effective.[535]

Table 5.1.3: "Where do you consider as your home (*Heimat*)?" (Answers in per cent)

The city where I was born	21.0
The city where I live	32.2
The region where I was born	9.9
The region where I live	18.4
Germany	13.7
Europe	2.9
World	1.7
Others	0.2

Source: Spangenberg, Stefan and Klein, Paul: Heimat und Verteidigung. SOWI-Arbeitspapier No. 102, Strausberg 1997, p. 40

Comparing the Germans' and the Turks' feeling home and attitudes towards European identity, the Table above 5.1.3 shows that less than half of the Germans (32.2%) consider their birthplace as a home where they lived since their childhood. Only minimal percentages such as 2.9% and 0.2% see their home in Europe and the World. Among the interviewers over 25 year

---

[533] Ibid., p. 38

[534] Smith, Tom W. and Kim, Seokko: International journal of Public Opinion Research, Vol. 18, No. 1 Spring 2006, World Opinion National Pride in Comparative Perspective; 1995/6 and 2003/4 by Tom W. Smith and Seokko Kim, National Identity Studies, Ranking of National Pride, p. 127-9

[535] Smith, Tom W. and Kim, Seokko: International journal of Public Opinion Research, Vol. 18, No. 1 Spring 2006, World Opinion National Pride in Comparative Perspective; 1995/6 and 2003/4 by Tom W. Smith and Seokko Kim, National Identity Studies, Ranking of National Pride, p. 127-9

olds, 83% consider their birth and childhood place as a home. This proportion decreases to 74% under the 25 years old. Furthermore, only 18% among the younger Germans acknowledge Germany as their home against 13% among the elder Germans. There are also relationships between their education levels: 16% of Germans with high school education identify Germany as their home, 5% consider it in Europe and 6% the world. While the comparable answer ratios among the respondents without high school education were only 12, 3, and 1% respectively.[536]

According to a survey was conducted on Turkish workers' children or second generation Turks in Stuttgart in 1980 shows that only one in four second generation Turks' birth place is in Germany.[537]

Table 5.1.4: Birth-place of Turkish workers' children in 1980

Country of birth-place	Number of children	Percentages (%)
Born in Turkey	76 respondents	74.5
Born in Germany	26 respondents	25.5
Total	102 respondents	100.0

Source: Orhan Türkdoğan, Turkish workers' children in Europe, Drama of the second generation, Orkun Yayinevi, Istanbul, 1984, p. 65

Table 5.1.4 has shown that **74.5%** of Turkish workers' children were born in Turkey in 1980, while only **25.5%** of them have indicated their birth place as Germany.

Table 5.1.5: Turkish immigrants' birth place, according to the 2007 Survey in Germany

Countries		Percentages (%)
Born in Turkey	191 respondents	64
Born in Germany	78 respondents	26
Born in other European country	22 respondents	7
Born in America	3 respondents	1
Born in other countries	6 respondents	2
Total	300 respondents	100

Source: Author, adapted from the results of the 2007 Survey question 22 Where were you born?

Comparing the Germans' (Table 5.1.3) and the Turks' (Table 5.1.5) feeling about their birthplace as home, 26% of the Turkish immigrants replied that they were born 'in Germany and consider Germany as their home, while 32.2% of Germans consider their birthplace as a home where they lived since their childhood. These similar responses can be interpreted that there is a strong relationship between people's birthplaces and feeling home which ties them emotionally. Calculating the non-German born Turkish immigrants, total 100% – 64% Turkish born = 36% were born out of Turkey with a western (European) background, language and education meaning they are more likely to be integrated into (the Western countries including) German life

---

[536] Ibid., p.40

[537] Türkdoğan, Orhan: Turkish workers' children in Europe, Drama of the second generation Turkish immigrants, Orkun Yayinevi, Istanbul, 1984, p. 65

than those who were Turkish-born and subsequently migrated to Germany. 53% of Turkish immigrants came to Germany through family reunification. Then 17% of Turks who live in Germany were born in the country. 54.2% of Turkish immigrants in Germany are male and 45.8% are female. [538]

As a conclusion of this section, younger generation of German and European-born (**36%**) Turks create their own distinct identity as 'Euro-Turks'. They find their own place in German European society by establishing their own businesses. There are more than 120,000 German Turks own companies only in Germany such as restaurants, fast food stalls across Europe and Germany, *döner kebab* has become a German national dish.[539]

Chris Morris argues "Despite their nomadic roots, the Turks had never been a migrant nation. Historically, it was to be a self-reliant nation, beholden to no one, and travel abroad was virtually unheard of. All of a sudden in the 1960s tens of thousands of the least-educated workers in the country pitched up in Germany."[540]

Turkish labour migration to Germany is a unique event in the long-standing Turco-German relations' history, hoping that not happens again.

5.1.2 Social factors affecting integration of Turkish immigrants

The purpose of grouping two closely related questions (5 and 12) is to investigate, to what extent; Turkish immigrants' participate in locally interaction. It is known also as social interpretive in ontological approach opposite of positivism from anthropology school of Franz Boas (German-American anthropologist) as social, cultural, political and sportive activities of the host and how their participation in those activities affects their integration.[541] These questions have also similar impact on integration as if asking two questions but getting one answer. Since an immigrant's social relation level with natives is also an affecting factor of their integration. Therefore, measuring an individual's social relation level with natives is contributing to measure his/her level of social integration too. For example, life comfort does not only affect their integration but also their decision whether they stay in Germany or emigrate from Germany to somewhere else with hope of a better future (broadly discussed The Survey question 27 in the fourth chapter). As argued earlier, 'comfortability' or immigrants' perception of Germany's life-standards is an indicator of Turkish immigrants' integration which helps to be integrated immigrants into their host country.

The second group (questions 5 and 12) and the following graph **5.1.2** are related to impact of social factors on the social integration of Turkish immigrants into German society.

---

[538] Statistisches_Bundesamt_2009_loc.3D51-0 Dezember 5 2010
[539] Morris, Chris: The New Turkey, *A Quiet Revolution on the edge of Europe*, Granda Books, London, 2006, p.186.
[540] Ibid., p. 187
[541] Franz Boas German-American anthropologist, MIS Quarterly Vol. 28 No. 1/March 2004

Graph 5.1.2 Factors related to Turkish immigrants' social life affect their social integration

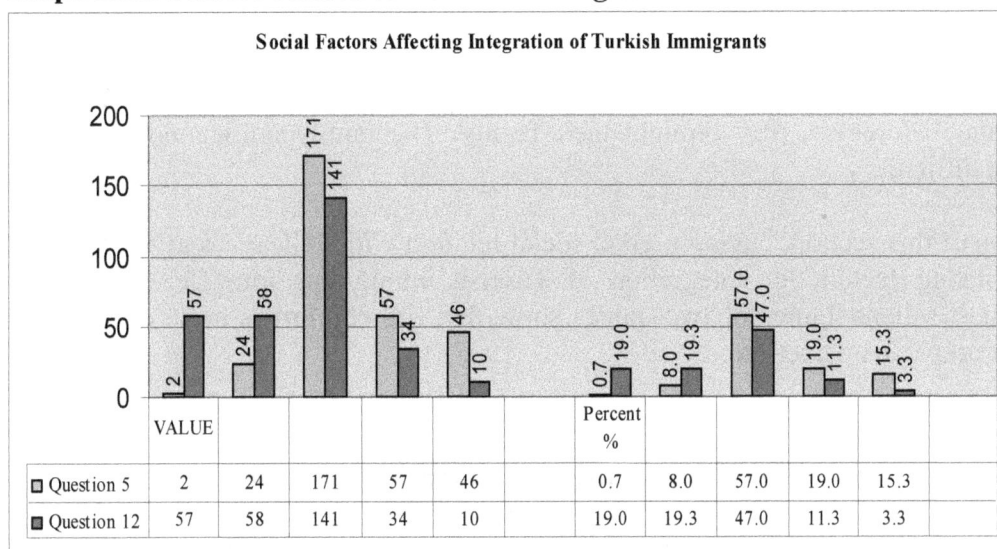

Social Factors Affecting Integration of Turkish Immigrants

	VALUE					Percent %				
Question 5	2	24	171	57	46	0.7	8.0	57.0	19.0	15.3
Question 12	57	58	141	34	10	19.0	19.3	47.0	11.3	3.3

5. How are your relations with people at work? (1) Not good (2) Not bad (3) Normal (4) very good (5) Too good
Q12. Is life comfortable here, socially? (1)Not comfortable at all (2) A little comfortable (3) Normal (4) Comfortable (5) Very comfortable

In the above graph 5.1.4, a comparison of the two mid-points of the above graph values **57%** of respondents expressed that they have had good social relations with people at work place. A survey from 2003 related to workplace interaction and friendship circles shows that this figure was 78% in the work place and 75% in friendship circles.[542] For to question 12 'life comfortability' or their perception of 'life standards' of Germany, **47%** of respondents consider that their life is comfortable in Germany. In other words, **53%** of respondents or majority feel that they do not have a comfortable life in Germany. The second row of the first column indicates **19%** of respondents feel 'not comfortable at all'. This is likely to be belonging to the first and second generation Turks. Comparing this percentage to the Survey (2007) question 29 shows the age group of respondents' are **18%** 41-50 years old and over 50 **5%**, and only **3%** of Turks in Germany are retired. They are less likely to be integrated into German society than the third and fourth generation immigrant youths. Contrast to the second row, category four **11.3%** of the respondents consider life standard is good in Germany. The second row category five **3.3%** of respondents feel that Germany's life standard is the best. They are likely to be belonging to German-born younger generation; their German language and education level are likely to be higher than their grandparents. Birgit Schultze argues that

> "Many parents want higher education for their children. If we consider that most Turkish families in Germany come from a working class background, the number of children who go to university is surprisingly high. Socially, the Turkish are well integrated into German society, participate politically and in the entertainment sector." [543]

---

[542] Article by Ayça Kılıçlı: 'Turkish Migrants in Germany, Prospects of Integration', The Research Centre for Studies on Turkey', 2003

[543] Schulze, Birgit and Königseder, Angelika: Türkische Minderheit in Deutschland, published in: Vorurteile, Informationen zur politischen Bildung (Heft 271), http://www.bpb.de/publikationen/IN6RK6,0,0,Vorurteile.html. September 7 2006

Meanwhile, the first generation and second generation's German language and education level are still low compared to German born younger generation. The first generation Turkish guest workers' intention was not to stay in Germany permanently, they came to work temporarily. When they saved enough money they would return home. Due to worsening circumstances they prolonged their stay. Moreover, they brought their family. The family unification made their return home more difficult.

As a conclusion of this section, having a good social relation with colleagues at workplace is one of the facilitating factors for integration of Turkish immigrants into German society. Comparing the most salient figures of two values show that life comfort is more effective for integration than workplace interaction.

5.1.3 Economic conditions of Turkish immigrants affecting the integration

The aim of grouping two questions (13 and 14) is to explain how Turkish immigrants' housing conditions and job availability affect their integration into German society.

Integration in labour market or employment is the desired outcome which is identified as access to job, measured as parity of employment rates with national average. The longer term goal is parity in rates of under-employment: the job should match the individual's qualifications, skills and earning potential. For example, question 13 explores the effect of their employment facilities on their integration process. The EU Conclusion 11 on immigrant integration policy Annex, Point 2 encourages immigrants receive equal job opportunities with natives through integration quoted as below:

> "Employment is 'a key part of the integration process' if such immigrants do not have access to employment on equal terms with nationals and is central to the participation of immigrant to the contribution immigrants make to the host country. The EU Member States feel more comfortable referring to immigrants and using the language of integration rather than minority protection." [544]

Similarly, Survey question 14 aims to investigate the effect of their housing conditions on their integration in the following section. This group of questions will also help to find out the EU integration policy's effect on German integration policy. Germany as an EU member state has some obligation to assist its immigrants' integration in accordance to the EU integration law which quoted as follows:

> "The dominant conception of integration in EU law and policy is that a secure residence status and equality of treatment with nationals clearly assist integration and thus contribute to the greater social cohesion, security and stability in the country." [545]

---

[544] The EC Conclusions on immigrant integration policy, Conclusion 11; Eiko R Thielemann,2004 European Journal of Migration and Law, Volume 6,No 1,pp.43-61.
[545] Ryszard Cholewinski, 2005: Migrants as Minorities, Integration and Inclusion in the Enlarged EU, p. 713; JCMS 2005 Volume 43. Number 4, pp. 695-716

Previous studies show that poverty is one of the influencing factors the migration of Turks to Germany. It has both been an affecting factors their migration to Germany in the 1960s and later their integration into German society in the time of German unification in the 1989. The following table 5.1.6 shows their situation by comparing with native Germans and other immigrant groups

Table 5.1.6: Poverty among Germans, Non-Germans and the Turks, 1984-1989 (in %)

Groups Affected by Poverty	1984	1989
Non- German Poor	21	24
Non German Poor in Employment	15	22
Turkish Poor	30	38

Source: W. Seifert, 'Am Rande der Gesellschaft? In Informationsdienst zur Auslanderarbeit, No. 3/4, 1994, p.19.

In 1989, poverty in Germany affected the Turkish immigrants more than others. Poverty is defined in comparison with average income of the host country. The above table 5.5 indicates that an income is below **50%** of Germans' and **14%** of non-Germans, but **30%** of Turks were living in poverty in 1984. By 1989, poverty among Germans had decreased to **11%** but had risen to **17%** among all non-Germans and to **38%** among Turks. Employment has not proved an effective protection against poverty. For Germans, employment normally means a decreased risk of poverty. For non-Germans, however, employment has offered only limited protection. In the course of the 1960s, the proportion of non-German poor in employment increased from **15%** to **22%** while that of Germans fell from **9%** to **8%**. Although poverty has become widespread throughout Germany, non-Germans have been three times more likely to be affected by it than Germans. In 1984, **11.8%** Germans and **25%** of non-Germans lived in poverty. With some instability during the course of the 1980s, poverty in 1992 affected 8.9 percent of Germans but 24.5 percent of non-Germans, i.e. among the former risk of poverty decreased, among the latter it remained inactive at its higher level.[546]

As discussed earlier, first males from poor village background arrived to post industrial German society, after family unification they put down unsure roots in Munich, Berlin and Cologne with a divided future plans. For example, Kemal Şahin a well educated Turk, came to Germany as a student, he has now the largest Turkish run business outside Turkey, '*Şahinler Holding*' trades in textiles, clothing and tour. It is as Vural Öğer as doing.[547]

---

[546] F. Hamburger: Migration and Armut,' in Informationsdienst Auslanderarbeit, No. 3/4, 1994
[547] Morris, Chris: The New Turkey, *A Quiet Revolution on the edge of Europe*, Granda Books, London, 2006, p.192

Graph 5.1.3 Factors related to Turkish immigrants' economic life affect their economic integration

Economic Factors Affecting Integration of Turkish Immigrants

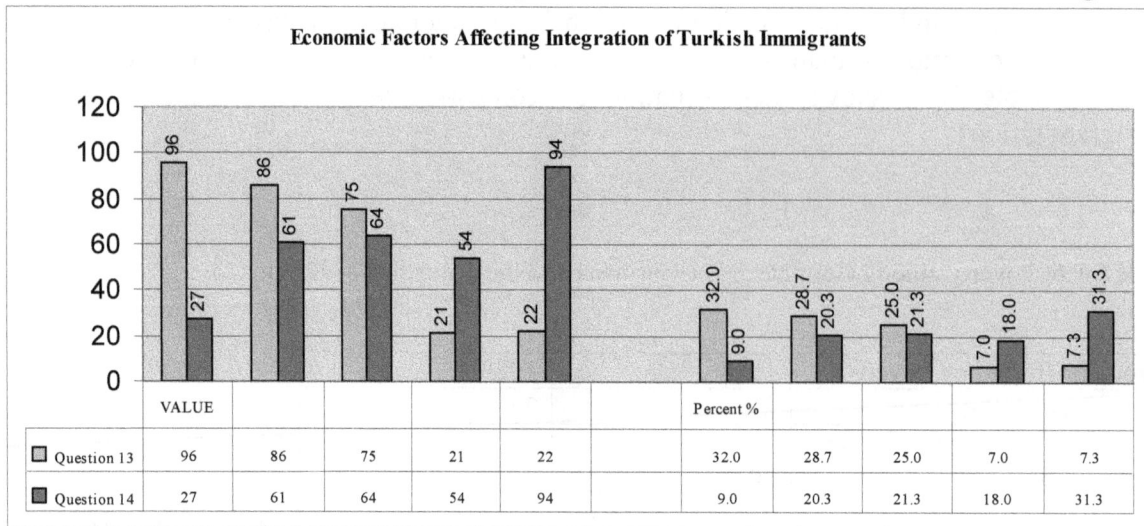

	VALUE						Percent %				
☐ Question 13	96	86	75	21	22		32.0	28.7	25.0	7.0	7.3
■ Question 14	27	61	64	54	94		9.0	20.3	21.3	18.0	31.3

Q13. Is it hard to find a job, economically? (1)Very hard (2) Hard (3) But possible (4) Sometimes (4) More opportunities here
  Q14. Is it hard to find house here? (1)Very hard (2) Hard (3) But possible (4) Sometimes (4) More opportunities here

Housing conditions of Turkish immigrants was an important influencing factor for their integration until German unification in 1990. 1/3 of respondents of Turkish origin in Germany expressed that their housing conditions have been improved since unification and 220,000 properties and houses owned by Turkish origin immigrants in Germany. On the other hand, only 14% Germans are interested in purchasing real estate's from Turkey. According Turkish Housing Minister Faruk Nafiz Özak immigrants of Turkish origin own 220,000 properties in Germany; however, the number of properties sold to (mainly Germans) foreigners was 65,000 in Turkey.[548]

On the other hand, in the 1990s, a growing number of Euro-Turks started to establish their own small businesses to avoid become unemployed and dependent on social welfare. German local governments encouraged those who wanted to form their companies by giving credit them for their investment. Their small-scale family owned and run businesses turned into entrepreneurships across Europe as well as Germany. There are 68,300 Turkish descent entrepreneurs in Germany, including Bulgaria and Romania these numbers increase to 107,000.
[549]

---

[548] Turkish Ministry of Housing and Public Affairs' Report, Ankara, 16 June 2008

[549] Şen, Faruk: Experience of Euro-Turks, *Turkey Research Centre Association*, Essen, October 2007, 26th Issue

Table 5.1.7: Development of Turkish Entrepreneurs in the EU-15

Indicator	1996	2001	2006
Entrepreneurs	56.500	81.000	101.000
Average Investment for Each Operation (€)	99.500	109.000	108.000
Total Investment Capacity (billion €)	5,6	8,8	10,9
Average Income for Each Operation (€)	386.500	430.800	435.000
Annual Total Income (billion €)	21,8	34,9	43,9
Average Number of Employees for each operation	4,1	5,0	4,7
Total Employees	232.000	405.000	474.000

Source: Turkey Research Centre Association / Essen, October 2007, 26th Issue

As a result, Turks with a good educational background integrated into their host societies, gained the country's citizenship, and established their own businesses. Those who have poor educational background are still encountering integration problems.

5.1.4: Language factor affecting integration of immigrants

The aim of grouping the two German language related questions 3 and 23 in one is to explain the role of German language's impact on their integration in Germany. Since German language is a basis or a tool for their education and career through integration into German society and way of life. Simultaneously, their German skill will add economic, politic and cultural contributions to contemporary German society.

Proficiency in host country language is one of the key facilitating factors which enable immigrants' access to social and legal institutions of the host country as well as their integration into the host country. Social and cultural integration is also dependent on German language knowledge and education level of immigrants. An immigrant's capability of host language is main contributor to his/her integration into host country socially, politically and culturally.

Table 5.1.8: German Language level of Turkish guest workers in 1981-1982

German Language Level	Number of Turkish workers
Very well	3
Good	28
Speak German a little	85
Can't speak German	2
No response	1
Total	119

Source: Ayhan Koç, Children of Turkish workers in Germany, Drama of the second generation, Orkun Yayinevi, Istanbul, 1984, p. 187

Table 5.1.8 shows only **2.5%** of the second generation Turks expressed that they speak German fluently in 1982. This meant that many second generation Turks have very little contact with Germans in the early 1980s. **71.5%** of respondents answered that they speak a little German. **1.6%** of respondents said that they do not speak German at all. In addition, **16.8%** of respondents indicated that they speak Turkish at workplace. **34.7%** indicated that they speak both German and Turkish at their workplace. **42.2%** indicated that they speak only German at their workplace.

Comparing the table 5.1.8 figures from the early 1980s to graph 5.1.4 (the 2007 Survey questionnaire) results, although there is some positive progress in their language level since 1980s, there is still a long way to reach the expected German level yet.

The following graph 5.1.4 reveals results of the language proficiency of Turkish immigrants and its effect on their integration into German society.

Graph 5.1.4: Factors related to German language affect their personal integration

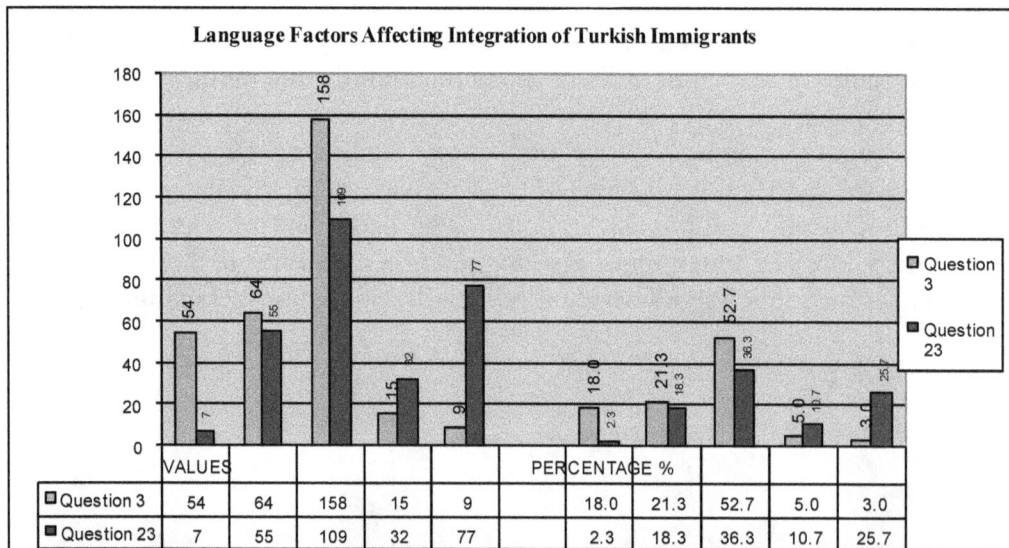

Language Factors Affecting Integration of Turkish Immigrants

	VALUES					PERCENTAGE %				
Question 3	54	64	158	15	9		18.0	21.3	52.7	5.0	3.0
Question 23	7	55	109	32	77		2.3	18.3	36.3	10.7	25.7

Source: Author
Q3. Which language do you speak at home? (1) Only Turkish (2) Mostly Turkish (3) Both German and Turkish (4) Mostly German (5) Only German Q23. How is your German? (1)Not good at all (2) Not good (3) Good (4) Very good (5) Fluent

216

As a result, comparing similar percentages of two question results reveal that question 3-midpoint scores show that **52.7%** of Turkish immigrants speak both German and Turkish at their home; and to question 23 **36.3 %** of Turkish immigrants answer that their German is good. From linguistic aspect their integration level should be significantly **50%**, but **36.3%** is under the significant level as a percentage.

Keeping in mind, the first generation's German language and education level were very low compared to German born younger generation. Then, first generation Turkish guest workers' intention was not to stay in Germany permanently, they came to work temporarily. When they saved enough money they would return home. Due to worsening circumstances they prolonged their stay. However, when they brought their family, their family unification made their return home not only difficult but also impossible, since their children attend to schools in Germany.

In the following graph 5.1.4a, four questions 3, 5, 23, 24 are grouped together (three of them are related to German language) to explain the role of German language and their attitude towards their colleagues at work place on their integration in Germany. Since German language is a basis for their integration into German society and the way of life

Graph 5.1.4a: Measuring language proficiency of T. immigrants and their integration

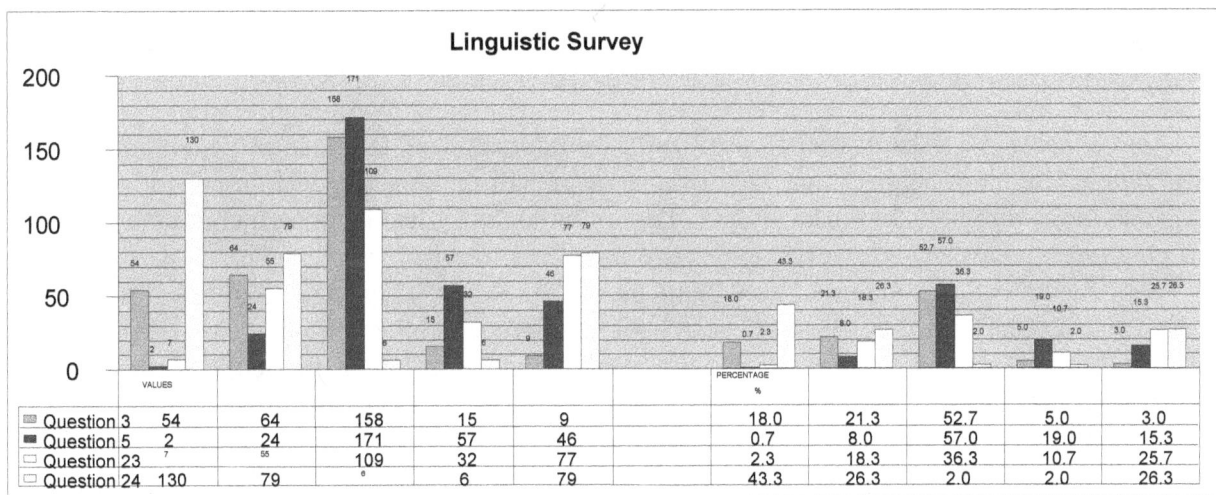

Linguistic Survey

	VALUES					PERCENTAGE %				
Question 3	54	64	158	15	9	18.0	21.3	52.7	5.0	3.0
Question 5	2	24	171	57	46	0.7	8.0	57.0	19.0	15.3
Question 23	7	55	109	32	77	2.3	18.3	36.3	10.7	25.7
Question 24	130	79	8	6	79	43.3	26.3	2.0	2.0	26.3

Q3. Which language do you speak at home? (1) Only Turkish (2) Mostly Turkish (3) Both German and Turkish (4) Mostly German (5) Only
German Q5. How are your relations with people at work? (1) Not good (2) Not bad (3) Normal (4) very good (5) Too good
Q23. How is your German? (1)Not good at all (2) Not good (3) Good (4) Very good (5) Fluent
Q24. Where did you go to school? (1) In Germany (2) in Turkey (3) in both country (4) Other European country (4) Other

As a result, comparing similar percentages of four question results in the above **Graph 5.1.4a** reveals that question three 3-midpoint indicates **52.7 %** Turkish immigrants speak at their home both languages; and mid-point of the question five shows that **57%** of Turkish immigrants have good relations at workplace. As response to question 23 only **36 .3 %** of Turks consider that their German is good; which means also they have a poor school attendance with a level of (question 24 indicates) **43.3%**. Although 43.3% of the respondents said that they attended school in Germany, but only 12% of the Turks graduated from university in Germany which means that only one out four succeeded educationally. As a result, as their German improved they obtain a better educational achievement in German school system.

5.1.5 Factors affecting Turkish immigrants' Educational Achievement

The purpose of grouping the two educational related survey questions 15 and 25 is to find out the role of education on integration of Turkish immigrants in Germany.

Table 5.1.9 Which country do you wish your children complete their education in Germany or Turkey?

Expressions	Number of (Samples) the Turkish workers
Wish their children complete it in Turkey	92
Wish their children complete it in Germany	16
No response	11
Total	119

Source: Children of Turkish workers, Drama of the second generation, Orkun Yayinevi, Istanbul, 1984, p. 183

Above Table 5.1.9 from a survey in 1982 on education of the second generation Turkish workers in Germany suggests that **77%** of respondents or the second generation Turkish workers wish children complete their education in Turkey. Since, they had a concern about the education of children in Germany. However, they were unwilling to return Turkey. This is partly because of political unrest due to military coup in the 1980. Partly, they were foreigners to German education system and they did not want their children continue the guest worker status like themselves in Germany. They were also afraid of losing control over their children in Germany. Therefore, they wished the children complete their education in Turkey. But, their wish did not become a reality, because they did not return to Turkey. The same survey suggest that **67%** of respondents or the second generation Turks wish their return Turkey after completing their careers. **26.9%** of participants or 32 respondents did not answer this question.[550]

---

[550] Türkdoğan, Orhan: Avrupa'da ki İşçilerimiz ve Çocukları, *Ikinci Neslin Dramı*, the Turkish workers and their children in Europe, Drama of the second generation, Orkun Yayınevi, Istanbul, 1984, p. 183-4

Table 5.2.1 Which behaviours of your children do you most concern in the 1980s' German society?

The second generation workers' concerns about their children in German society	Number of workers
Consuming alcohol	31
Becoming friends with German women in discos, bars and night clubs	31
Neglecting their religious duties	59
Wasting time in cinemas and guesthouses (*Gasthaus*)	21
Becoming as Germans from the aspect of mannerism	25
Getting away from Turkish customs and traditions	64
No response	13
Total respondents	260

Source: Children of Turkish workers, Drama of the second generation, Orkun Yayinevi, Istanbul, 1984, p. 184

Table 5.2.1 suggests that **54%** of second generation Turkish (parents) workers are afraid of their children get away from Turkish customs and traditions. **49.5%** have concerns that their children do not practise their religious rituals. **45%** are afraid that their children adapt German culture and behaviours by getting away from Turkish traditions as a consequence of staying in Germany too long. **10%** of respondents did not answer the earlier question.[551]

A survey from 1994 shows those of all Turkish Pupils in German Schools in 1991, only **0.8%** of students in at German Universities were Turkish with German educational qualifications. In l994, **25%** young non-Germans and only **6%** of young Germans failed to gain a school leavers' certificate. In l994, **5%** of German applicants but **1.5%** non-Germans applicants (1.829 individuals) were accepted for public sector employment.[552]

Education equips immigrants to build capacity not only to get a better paid job but also to better adapt into their host society. For Turkish immigrants in Germany technical education is more demanding and it helps them to get suitable employment. It also enables them to create a comfortable life and upward social status in Germany. This helps immigrants to educate the younger generation. Since they are working and paying taxes to the German state and the German government is benefiting from immigrants. The immigrants are also benefiting from their skilled services.

Education is a key facilitating factor in the integration of immigrants into the host society, is largely a function of the level of skills and education of immigrants entering into the host society. Availability of language tuition and language support services is also one of the key factors affecting integration of immigrants in host country.

In contrast to above figures, educational data from 1997 shows Turkish girls are doing better than boys in Germany. In addition, the number of Turkish students who attend university is also rising. Further evidence shows gender differences are evident and women and girls are doing significantly better. For example, in 1980, the proportion of Turkish female students was **12.4%**;

---

[551] Ibid, p. 184-185

[552] W., Seifert: 'Am Rande der Gesellschaft? In Informationsdienst zur Auslanderarbeit, No. 3/4, 1994, p. 19.

in 1997 this increased to **36%**. According to the 2007 survey questionnaire, gender distribution of the Turkish immigrant population in Germany is **57%** male and **43%** female. Data from 1997 indicates that Turkish immigrant students' first preference is law, economy and social sciences with **42.2%**, language and history follows this with **53%**. Their third preference is engineering departments with **78%**. Another interesting point: Turkish female students' number is doubled. For example, Turkish female students consist of **9.7%** of medical students, and male are only **4.9%** of those in German universities. The total numbers of the students of Turkish origin were 15.442 in 1997.[553]

Journalist Yalçin Doğan argues the Turks in Germany are concern about Turkish identity because German chancellor Angela Merkel's coalition government wants to abolish their identity through assimilation under the name of integration.[554]

German ambassador Eckhart Kuntz in Turkey argues that "Education is essential for Turks in Germany; German language is a key factor in resolving many problems. A part of Turkish population in Germany has not fully enjoyed the same opportunities from our education system, our labour market and many other fields."[555]

Graph 5.1.5 Factors related to educational achievement affect school integration and status

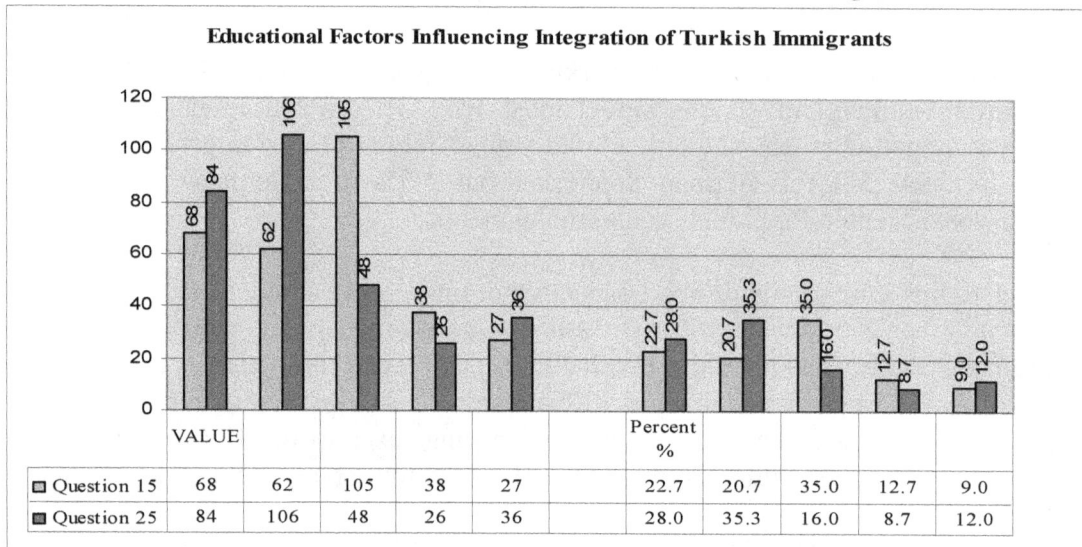

Educational Factors Influencing Integration of Turkish Immigrants

	VALUE					Percent %				
Question 15	68	62	105	38	27	22.7	20.7	35.0	12.7	9.0
Question 25	84	106	48	26	36	28.0	35.3	16.0	8.7	12.0

Q15. How are the facilities for children's education here? (1)Not good (2) Not bad (3) Good (4) More facility here (5) Very good
Q25. What is your last education degree? (1)Public school (2) Vocational school (3) Technique school (4) High school (5) University

Graph 5.1.5 indicates that only **10%** of Turkish immigrants were technically educated. **12%** of Turkish descent students were in German universities or had university degree. Comparing this **12%** with a previous survey from 1991 which showed only **0.8%** of Turks had German university degree. There is an **11.2% (12% - 0.8%)** increase in the number of Turks with German university degree. It is still low but the number of students with Turkish origin is

[553] Source: Statistische Bundesamt, Wiesbaden, 1998
[554] Article by Yalçin Doğan: 'Fighting on identity issue of Turks' October 18 2007
[555] Hürriyet Daily News, Ankara, 14 /12/2010 Interviewed by Zeynep Dereli from Skyturk TV Chanel

increasing year by year. Immigrants with high educational background are generally contributors by availability of suitable jobs. It is indeed difficult for them to educate their children given that there is no government financial assistant. As a result, the 2007 survey study suggests that among Turkish immigrants, who are more educated they are also integrated into their host country. Fluency in the host language is a key goal of the integration process, aiming for parity in outcomes at each stage of education, including pre-school take-up plays also a part for integration.

Graph 5.1.5a: Measuring of education achievement and integration of Turkish immigrants

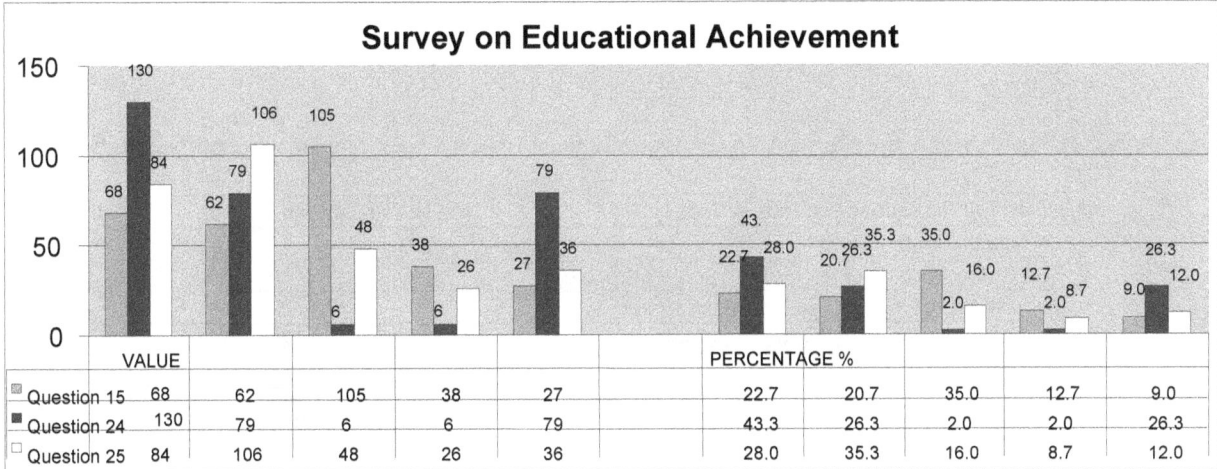

Survey on Educational Achievement

	VALUE					PERCENTAGE %				
Question 15	68	62	105	38	27	22.7	20.7	35.0	12.7	9.0
Question 24	130	79	6	6	79	43.3	26.3	2.0	2.0	26.3
Question 25	84	106	48	26	36	28.0	35.3	16.0	8.7	12.0

15. How are the facilities for children's education here? (1)Not good (2) Not bad (3) Good (4) More facility here (5) Very good
24. Where did you go to school? (1) Not much (2) Yes (3) A little (4) Sometimes (5) No
25. What is your last education degree? (1)Public school (2) Vocational school (3) Technique school (4) High school (5) University

Graph 5.1.5a indicates responses to the above questions *How are facilities for a child education here*? **35%** of Turkish immigrants expressed that they are satisfied with educational achievement in Germany; question *Where did you go to school*? Nearly double the number of Turkish immigrants attended school in Germany **43.3%** than attended school in Turkey **26.3%.** As to question 25 *What is your last education degree?* This result indicates that most of Turkish immigrants **35.3%** attended 'Vocational School education' to others. **26%** of Turkish immigrants have a primary school education and only **12%** received a university degree in Germany. Each year the Turkish Ministry of Education sends about 200 Turkish teachers.[556]

If we put into consideration the satisfaction level of their children's education, their school attendance in Germany and their last school degree by summing up the positive results of the graph 5.1.5a: **35% + 43.3% + (35.3%+12%) = 125.6: 3 = 41.8%** of respondents feel integrated from the aspect of educational achievement of their children, this is still under the significant level.

---

[556] The Turkish Republic, Ministry of National Education sent 515 teachers to Europe in 2008, 400 German-speaking, 100 French-speaking and 10 English-speaking and finally 2 music teachers. The Turkish Republic, National Ministry of Education Report, January 20 2008

5.1.6 Political factors affecting integration of Turkish immigrants

These two closely related questions deal with Turkish immigrants' interest, participation level in German politics in the framework of Germany's citizenship policy, and the number of the naturalised Turkish immigrants with gaining of voting rights in German elections.
A survey conducted on the second generation Turkish workers' interest in politics and German citizenship in the early 1980s reveals interesting results in the following table 5.2.2

Table 5.2.2: Which rights do you want to be granted the Germans have? The survey conducted in 1982

Desires of the second generation Turks	Number of Turkish workers
To vote and to be elected	71
To become partner of the factory and workplace	16
To have representatives in the trade unions	29
To have right for establishing trade unions	29
No response	28
Total	173

Source: Children of Turkish workers, Drama of the second generation, Orkun Yayinevi, Istanbul, 1984, p. 182

Table 5.2.2 indicates that **60%** of respondents wish to have voting rights and being elected if these rights were granted them by the German government in the early 1980s. **24%** of respondents or the second generation Turkish workers wish to establish trade unions and become members of it. **13.5%** of respondents or the second generation Turks wish to become partner/owner of the factory or workplaces where they work. All these expressions of the second generation Turkish workers living in Germany mean that they are willing to be integrated into German society in the early 1980s if they are given German citizenships. Since **60%** of the second generation Turkish workers wish to participate in political activities in Germany. Moreover, **71%** of them wish to have a proper house, to obtain kindergarten for their children, a fair tax system and having good relations with their German employers. In the early 1980s, this statement of the second generation Turks is a sign that they will stay in Germany permanently. These expressions also account for the German attitudes towards Turkish workers in the early 1980s which seem more friendly than today. The military coup in the 1980 and political instability in Turkey has also had an impact on their above statements which **71%** of the Turks preferred to stay in Germany in the early 1980s rather than returning to Turkey.[557]

---

[557] Türkdoğan, Orhan: Avrupa'da ki Iscilerimiz ve Cocuklari, *Ikinci Neslin Drami*, the Turkish workers and their children in Europe, Drama of the second generation, Orkun Yayinevi, Istanbul, 1984, p. 182

German political parties' integration policies play an important role in this issue, for example; If host country's ruling and opposition political parties agree on (a common and) favourable integration policy for the immigrants. This will ease integration process of the immigrants. However, so far the German political parties have not been agreed on a common integration policy.

If host country's ruling party is in favour of integration of the immigrants and the opposition is not in favour, this situation will make less likely to ease the integration of immigrants. During the time of Schröder's Red-Green coalition government from 1999 to 2005 in Germany, the government tried to change German integration policy. However, main opposition party CDU blocked government's constructive integration and citizenship law in the *Bundestag*. The Conservatives collected one million signatures to cancel the new German dual citizenship law during their election campaign in the Rein-Westphalia. The CDU succeeded to cancel the law by appealing to the High Court, but it lost the election in the Rein-Westphalia.

The EU and German integration and citizenship policy are also interrelated. For immigrants gaining citizenship of the host means that they obtain more access to the rights of the host country. Thus, citizenship of the host requires that immigrants to be integrated into the host society at a certain level.

Graph 5.1.6 Factors related to German politics affect political participation and citizenship rights

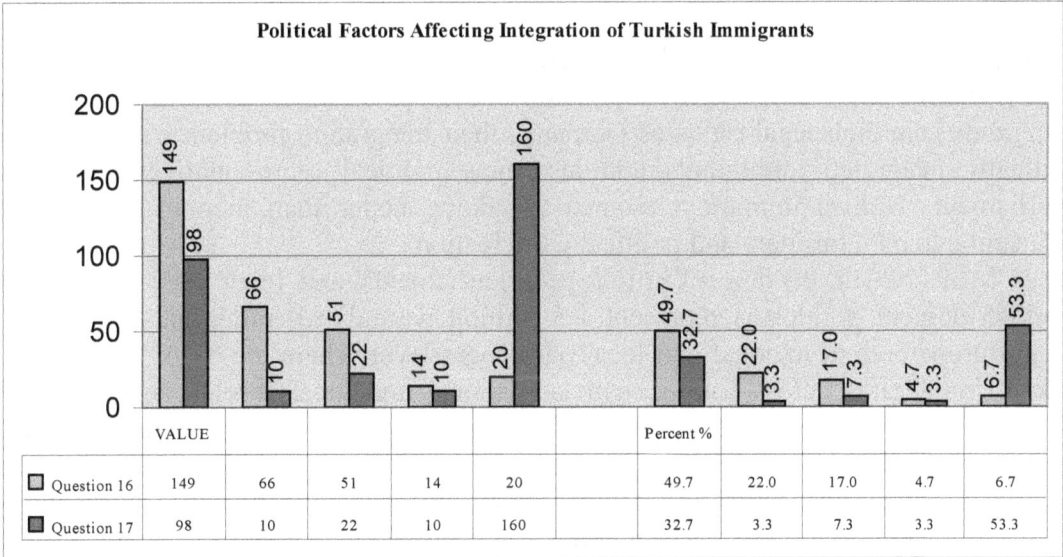

	VALUE					Percent %				
☐ Question 16	149	66	51	14	20	49.7	22.0	17.0	4.7	6.7
■ Question 17	98	10	22	10	160	32.7	3.3	7.3	3.3	53.3

16. Are you interested in politics, here? (1) Not much (2) Yes (3) A little (4) Sometimes (5) No
17. Are you German citizen? (1) Yes (2) Applied for (3) Application accepted (4) Application declined (5)
Source: Author

Graph **5.1.6** response to question 16 shows that only **17%** respondents of Turkish origin are interested in politics in Germany. Even **100%** said that they are interested in political activities in Germany; this score has no meaning unless they have not obtained German nationality because they have no voting right without gaining German citizenship. As to question 17 **32.7%** of the Turkish population in Germany gained the host country's citizenship which means they

223

have political rights (including voting rights and participation in political activities). Although the table **5.1.6** shows that **32.7%** of the Turks are German citizens, only half of them are able to vote in German election, because the other half is under voting age. In the Netherlands, the percentage of Turks voting was almost as high as the percentage of Dutch in 1987. In Sweden, the electoral participation of Turkish immigrants was equal to Swedish turn-outs in 1985.

If given figures compared with Turkish immigrants' participation in the other European welfare countries such as the Netherlands, Sweden, Denmark, and the UK, these figures are higher than in Germany. The Netherlands and Sweden have the highest ratios of naturalisation to their resident non-national population of the Turkish origin. For example, most naturalisations in the EU in 1993 were Turkish, with 43,000 Turks naturalising across the Europe. Of the Turkish citizens in the EU, almost three-quarters are resident in Germany. In 1993, more Turks have acquired Dutch citizenship **42%** than German **28%**.[558] In 2005, there were 840,000 naturalized German citizens of Turkish origin. The official number of Turks with Turkish citizenship in Germany is constantly declining, because many Turks became naturalized, and since the year 2000, children born in Germany are entitled to adopt German citizenship. In 2008, these decreased to 1,688,370 Turkish citizens (889,003 males and 799,367 females) in Germany.[559] In Germany, non-national residents are not entitled to vote, but naturalised Turks tend to favour the Social Democratic SPD and Greens (*Die Grünen*). This political behaviour of Turkish origin immigrants is also the same in the Netherlands, Sweden and Denmark.

As a consequence, naturalized Turkish immigrants have been affecting electoral politics across Europe (including Germany) as growing members of populations are ready to vote. When Turkish immigrants gain their legal rights as Germans, their integration problem will mainly be solved. Politically integrated immigrants add also new political representatives to a host country's parliament. Turkish immigrant women are doing better than men in the field of university education in both business and political participation.

There are 23 MEPs of Turkish descent in European Parliaments, and 16 of those are women. Only 28 Turkish descent politicians represent 1.5 million naturalised immigrants of Turkish descent across Europe both at national and local parliament level. There are 51 of MPs for 5.2 million Turkish immigrants across Europe both at national and local level. Those Turkish immigrants are politically active at the level of parliamentary and local government. Other European countries like the Netherlands, Sweden and UK have had more flexible integration and citizenship policies than Germany has. The naturalisations of Turks have increased substantially in certain countries. Naturalisation of Turkish citizens was limited until 1990 and then increased mainly in the Netherlands, Sweden and Germany more than in Austria, Belgium, Switzerland and France.[560]

As immigrants' socio-economic position improved and they became more integrated, their attitudes and behaviour also changed. This can be accounted for by the political behaviour of immigrants and host country's integration policy as identifying factors of immigrants' turn-outs and voting patterns. During the Red-Green coalition government in Germany every year

---

[558] Euro-stat 1995, Statistics in Focus, Population and social conditions, p.3

[559] Statistisches_Bundesamt_2009_loc.3D51-0 December 5 2010

[560] Euro-stat 1995

160,000 Turkish descents gained German citizenship in the late 1990s. An opinion poll in the late 1998 suggests that dual citizenship in Germany is not desirable and if naturalization process and dual citizenship of resident immigrants continue at this level, those immigrants would constitute a fifth of the German population by the year 2020.[561]

Only integrated immigrants can gain host country's citizenship, and only citizens of the host country can vote in election and stand as candidate in the host country's elections. This means gaining the citizenship of the host country (and participation in political and sportive activities in the host country for example, playing in the national team of the host country requires its nationality) is the last step of the integration process of immigrants.

The following Graph 5.1.6a aims to investigate Turkish immigrants' socio-politic integration with questions 12, 16, 18, 20, 26 as a ratio level of the Turkish immigrants participate in local social, cultural, political and sportive activities of the host and how their participation in those activities affects their integration.

As argued earlier, comfortability or feeling at home helps immigrants to be integrated into their host society.

Graph 5.1.6a: Measuring Socio-politics integration and status of Turkish immigrants

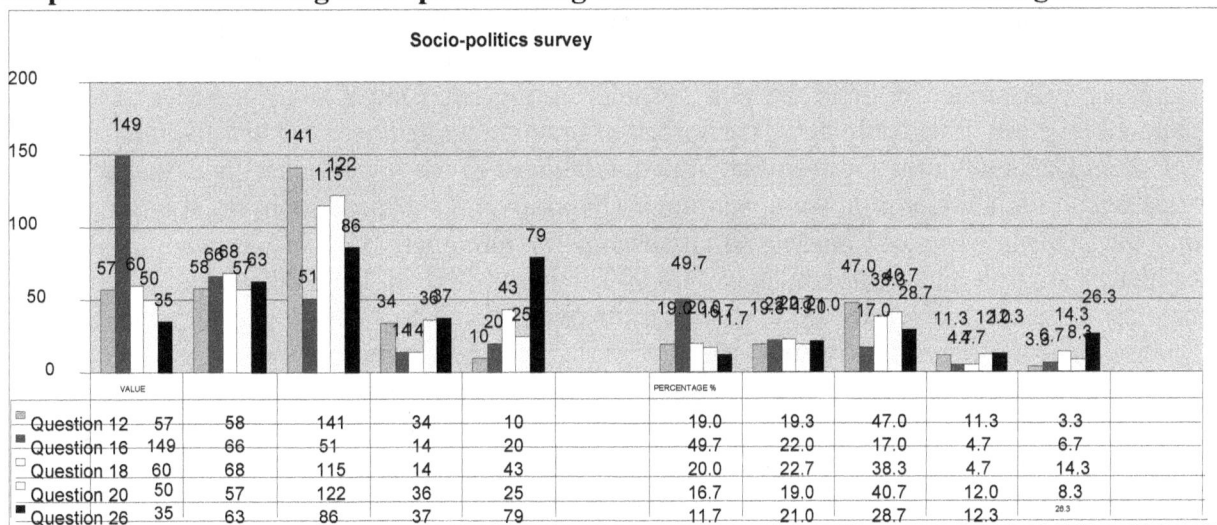

Socio-politics survey

	VALUE					PERCENTAGE %				
Question 12	57	58	141	34	10	19.0	19.3	47.0	11.3	3.3
Question 16	149	66	51	14	20	49.7	22.0	17.0	4.7	6.7
Question 18	60	68	115	14	43	20.0	22.7	38.3	4.7	14.3
Question 20	50	57	122	36	25	16.7	19.0	40.7	12.0	8.3
Question 26	35	63	86	37	79	11.7	21.0	28.7	12.3	26.3

Q12. Is life comfortable here, socially? (1)Not at all (2) Not much (3) Normal (4) Comfortable (5)Very comfortable
Q16. Are you interested in politics here? (1)Not much (2) A little (3) Yes (4) Sometimes (5) No
Q18. Do you feel culturally integrated? (1) No   (2) A Little   (3) Yes (4) Very well   (5) Totally
Q20. Are you satisfied with your status here? (1) Disappointed (2) Not much (3) Yes (4) Not bad (5) Very satisfied
Q26. Are you interested in sports here? (1) Yes, professional (2) Not professionally (3) as hobby (4) sometimes (5) Just watching

Graph 5.1.6a question 12 shows that **47%** of respondents or Turkish immigrants find life normal in German society. In other words, **53%** majority of Turkish immigrants do not feel comfortable life in German society. As argued earlier, 'comfortability' is an indicator of

---

[561] Statistisches_Bundesamt_2009_loc.3D51-0 Dezember 5 2010

Turkish immigrants' integration which helps to integrate immigrants into German society and the way of life.

Question 16 deals with Turkish immigrants' integration level of political interest in host country's politics; and Germany's citizenship policy, and the number of the naturalised Turkish immigrants with gaining of voting rights in German elections. German political parties' integration policies play an important role in this issue, for example; If host country's ruling and opposition political parties agree on (a common and) favourable integration policy for the immigrants. This will ease integration process of the immigrants. If host country's ruling party is in favour of integration of the immigrants and the opposition is not in favour, this situation will make less likely to ease the integration of immigrants. Graph 5.1.6a, results of the question 16 shows only **17%** of Turks are interested in politics in Germany.

Question18. *Do you feel culturally integrated in Germany*? **38.3%** feel culturally integrated in Germany. Turkish immigrants, who are culturally integrated, feel that they have dual identity both as Turkish and as Germans. Question 20.*Are you satisfied with your status here?* **40.7%** feel satisfied with their status in Germany. Question 26.*Are you interested in sports in Germany*? **28.7%** feel interested in sports in Germany. **11.7%** are interested in sports professionally.

If we sum up positive results of the graph: **47%+17%+38.3%+40.7%+ (28.7% + 11.7%) 40.4% = 183.4: 5 =** only **36.7%** of respondents feel integrated from the socio-political aspect.

Political representation of the Turkish community shows that their representation in Germany was limited prior to the new German immigration law (2000) – at the states and national level. In 1993, only two Turkish origin immigrants had been elected the Green Party MP Cem Özdemir in the German Parliament, (*Bundestag*) the lower house, and Berlin Green state senator Ismail Koşan in the upper house (*Bundesret*). Özdemir's lobbying was successful and the 2000 law reduced barriers to citizenship for foreigners born in Germany. Statistical estimates suggest that approximately 500.000 Turks voted in the 2002 national election, helping to re-elect Schröder by a slim margin over CDU-CSU challenger Edmund Stober. Studies indicate that approximately 160,000 Turks become German citizen every year in the late 1990s. If Turks continue to gain German citizenship with this pace, 2 million Turks will be on the voting rolls by the year 2020. Two million new voters are enough to swing an election.

As a result the survey shows that an average of **36.7%** is poor progress for their integration and immigrants' participation in host countries politic and gaining its citizenship is very important for their children and Germany's future.

5.1.7 Personal factors of Turkish immigrants such as intermarriage and their changing status which impacts on their integration level

Intermarriage is also a key affecting factor of immigrants' integration into their host country. It helps to interaction of immigrants with their host society members. A slow integration process is characterised by low intermarriage rates among the first and second generation Turks, limited upward social mobility and the persistence of trans-national ties. Many first and second generation Turks tended to choose a partner from their country of origin. Partly for linguistic, cultural and religious differences they tend to be opposed to intermarriage.

Although there is a belief among Germans that Turkish immigrants have a preference for marrying within their own group, the percentage of young Turks who choose a German partner

226

has been increasing since the 1990s. This increase may have been because of the growing numbers of naturalised Turks. In 1980 only about **28%** of unmarried Turks could imagine marrying a German. Within two decades this had doubled with men being slightly more positive than women about intermarriages. At the same time, negative opinions about intermarriage decreased from **45%** to **28%**. It is a well-known fact that intermarriage is a remarkable indicator of progressive integration.

Table 5.1.7 Number of the Turkish German Marriages in 1996

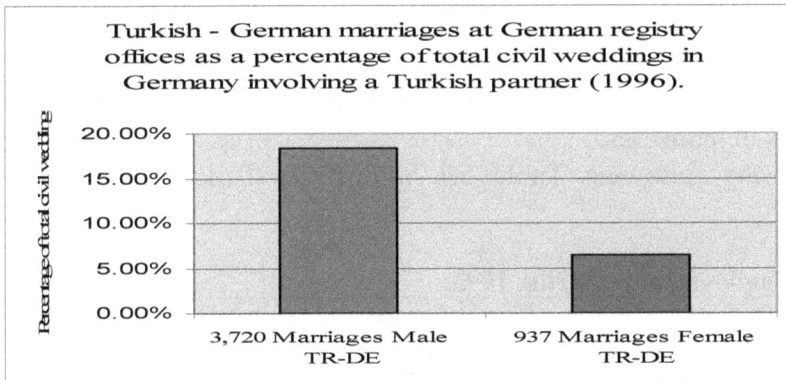

Turkish - German marriages at German registry offices as a percentage of total civil weddings in Germany involving a Turkish partner (1996).

Source: German Registry Office, 1996

Table 5.1.7 suggests that Turkish-German marriages **18.3%** were male TR-DE (3,720), **6.5%** were female TR-DE (937) at German registry offices as a percentage of total civil weddings in Germany involving a Turkish partner in 1996. Total marriages male were 20335, total female marriages 14405 in 1996.

Graph 5.1.7 Personal factors related to intermarriage and status affect integration

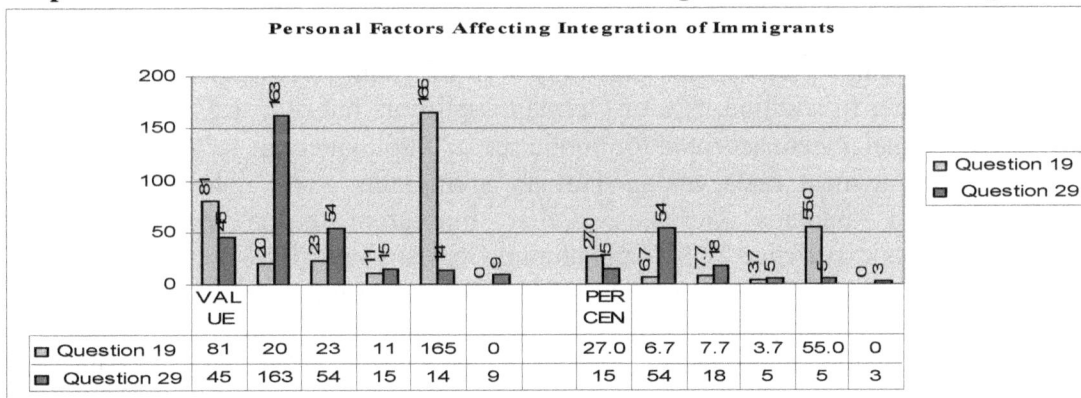

Personal Factors Affecting Integration of Immigrants

	VALUE						PERCEN					
Question 19	81	20	23	11	165	0	27.0	6.7	7.7	3.7	55.0	0
Question 29	45	163	54	15	14	9	15	54	18	5	5	3

19. Are you married to a native? (1)Yes (2) have been (3) live together (4) divorced (5) No
29. Professional classification: Student (1), Worker (2), Unemployed (3), Business-men/women (4), Academics/Actor/actress (5), Retired (6)

Graph 5.1.7 question 19 *Are you married to a native?* **27%** of Turkish immigrants are either married to German or are co-habiting with Germans. These two figures indicate that there is strong relationship between intermarriage and integration of immigrants. If we sum up positive aspects of intermarriage 27% + 6.7% + 7.7% = 41.4% of respondents' integration are positively affected from their marriage or co-habiting.

227

The survey results indicate that an immigrant who is married to native or is cohabiting with a native is integrated more and easily than non-native married. And almost all of the native married immigrants gained host country's citizenship.

This section also aims to explain Turkish immigrants' changing status regardless whether they came to Germany as guest worker, their children or they were born in Germany. In 1960s, the first generation Turks had come to Germany with the intention to earn money and achieve an upward social and economic status. So this section explains to what extent they achieved their goal by comparing previous studies with this survey results. Turks are mostly labour migrants with a largely agricultural background. They are primarily recruited for unskilled or semi-skilled work in German industries like metallurgy, mining and textiles, and although some of the Turks were skilled labourers, they have had to accept dangerous and tiring job, since their contracts may have tied them to specific jobs in industries.

Graph 5.1.7 question 29 and the following Table 5.1.7a displays Turkish immigrants' changing status in Germany.

Table 5.1.7a: Employment and Unemployment in Berlin, 1993

Status	Non-Germans in West Berlin	Non-Germans in East Berlin	Non-Germans in Berlin (all)	Germans in West Berlin	Germans in East Berlin	Germans in Berlin (all)
Employed	73	72	73	89	86	88
Unemployed	27	28	27	11	14	12
Population overall (in 1000)	328.6	44.2	372.8	867.7.3	595.3.	1461.0

Source: *Statistisches Jahrbuch*, 1994, p.92

Table 5.1.7a shows that, unemployment has affected immigrants more than Germans in the early 1990s. By unification, **14%** of Berliners, **18%** of immigrants were unemployed. After unification, unemployment rates of immigrants increased to **27%**, but among Germans it remained **12%**.

In 1994, **21%** young non-Germans and only **6%** of young Germans failed to gain a school leavers' certificate. In addition, **5%** of German applicants but only **1.5%** non Germans applicants (1.829 individuals) were accepted for public sector employment in 1994.[562]

In 1996, unemployment rates among Turkish immigrants were higher than in other immigrant groups and amongst Germans. Other immigrant group experience **19%** unemployment, the Turks experience **22.5%** and among Germans only **10%** are unemployed.[563] According to the 2002 census, in Germany, **11%** of Turks were unemployed compared to a national average of **4%**. Unemployment rates of both men and women are higher than for the general population, especially among those between the ages of 16 and 24. The following graph 5.1.7a: is used to compare Turkish immigrants' Professional Status and Job distribution.

---

[562] W. Seifert: Am Rande der Gesellschaft? In Informationsdienst zur Auslanderarbeit, No. 2/4, 1994, p. 19.
[563] Sozio-Ökonomisches Panel, Welle 1-6, 1996

Graph 5.1.7a: Comparing Turkish immigrants' Professional Status and Job distribution

Question 29: Profession (status) distribution

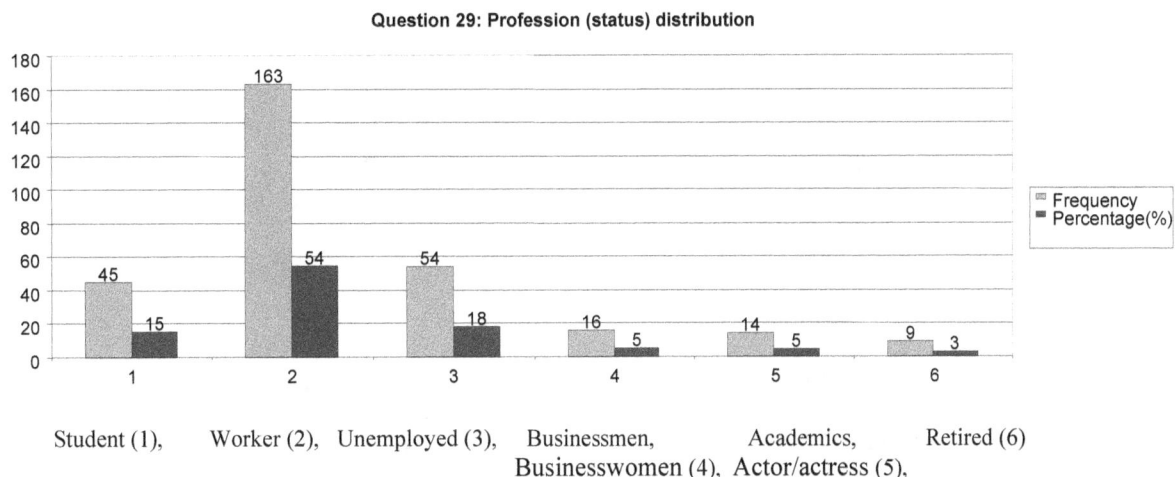

Student (1),   Worker (2),   Unemployed (3),   Businessmen,   Academics,   Retired (6)
                                              Businesswomen (4), Actor/actress (5),

Graph 5.1.7a displays Turkish immigrants' changing status in Germany as **15%** of respondents are at school age or students; **54%** of Turkish population is still workers. Only **10%** of Turkish immigrants in Germany have established their small and medium scale self-employed businesses in 47 areas such as travel agencies, food stores, and bakeries etc. Just **5%** of Turkish descent people achieved white collar status as academics and movie-stars. **3%** of respondents are retired; it means they are over 65. The survey results show that the unemployment rates among Turkish immigrants are still higher with **18%.** Summing **15%+10%+5%+3%= 33%**

Unemployment plays an effective role in increasing criminality against immigrants including Turkish in Germany. Thus previous studies suggest that hostile public attitudes, and lack of information about immigrants in the host society by media, can create a climate of fear and violence in which immigrants can hesitate to walk in the streets, to access health services or provide personal information. Particularly, in the period of economic recession immigrants have been seen as unwanted and as a danger to the national homogeneity of the German society by some neo-Nazis or extremists. This is just a perception of a tiny group, formed especially when immigrants decide to settle down permanently; there is no evidence to support this hypothesis.

A lack of integration policies in the host country generates non-integrated immigrant youths, who are more likely to commit crime because of isolation, nostalgia, and identity crises. A report from 2007 by the Research Centre for Turkish minorities at the University of Essen in Germany has shown that Turkish immigrants in Europe face discrimination in jobs, education, and housing, and this gives rise to feelings of hopelessness, exclusion and resentment. The report suggests that Turks face discrimination when the issue becomes employment, education and housing. Unemployment plays a role in discrimination, even more so than religious differences, as it leads jobless German youths to depression and desperate action against immigrants, and these unemployed youths look for a scapegoat for economic downturn and crises.

According to a survey by the Allensbach Institute in 1982 which is old but meaningful, **39%** of Germans believed that Turks took jobs from Germans (Jager and Link, 1987:198.9).

Especially, young people with a low level of education were particularly susceptible to these opinions and perceived competition by immigrants for jobs and housing; they engaged in violence against elements weaker than themselves. In Germany in 1991, especially after the unification, a number of opinion surveys showed a clear decrease in anti-foreigner attitudes (Esser, 1999; 35). However, arson (the crime of intentionally setting property on fire) on the houses of Turkish families in Mölln (November, 1992) and Solingen (May, 1993) are examples of right-wing crimes and violence against immigrants. From 1994 there was a decline in these crime rates. More recently is an arson attack 9 Turkish immigrants (5 of them children) lost their lives in Ludwigshafen.[564] Police suspect that a racist person or group set fire to the building where mostly Turkish immigrants lived (February 10, 2008). A number of right-wing extremist organisations (such as Neo-Nazis and skinheads) were banned and tough sentences were imposed on criminals.[565]

Survey *question 6* related to local people's attitude against Turkish immigrants. The survey result suggests that only *5 percent* of those have been exposed to bad behaviour.

Graph 5.1.7b: Measuring Political Attitudes and Intermarriage rates of Turkish immigrants

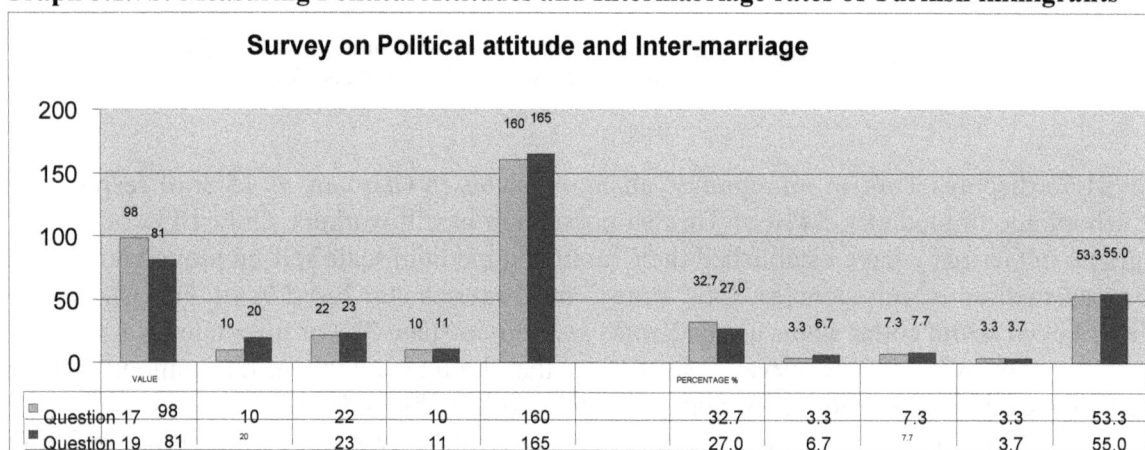

	VALUE					PERCENTAGE %				
Question 17	98	10	22	10	160	32.7	3.3	7.3	3.3	53.3
Question 19	81	20	23	11	165	27.0	6.7	7.7	3.7	55.0

17. Are you a German citizen? (1) Yes (2) Applied for (3) Application accepted (4) Application declined (5)
19. Are you married to a native? (1)Yes (2) have been (3) live together (4) divorced (5) No
Source: Author

Graph **5.1.8,** survey questions 17 *Are you German citizen?* **32.7%** of respondents or more than one in three of Turkish immigrants have become German citizens. Question 19 *Are you married to German?* **27%** of Turkish immigrants are either married to German or are co-habiting with Germans. **27% + 6.7% + 7.7% = 41.4%** summed percentage of intermarriage shows that it is a key facilitating factor for integration of immigrants.

The survey results indicate that an immigrant who is married to native or is cohabiting with a native, is likely to be integrated more and easily than non-native married. And almost all of the

---

[564] Hürriyet, February 10, 2008

[565] According to the German Ministry of the Interior, there have been 35.150 criminal cases of actions against immigrants from 1991 to 2008 on an average 3.156 annually. This includes recent fire-raids, the use of explosive, violent attacks on immigrants' properties, and in these 13 cases, acts led to death (17 of 20 were Turkish immigrants who lost their lives). This kind of violent behaviour by criminals provoked the German public to react, caused to participating in one of the largest demonstrations of the post war period in Germany (Dresden, February 18, 2008).

native married immigrants gained host country's citizenship and gained upgrade socio-economic and socio-cultural status in German society.

5.1.8 Factors related to gender and age structure affect the integration process

Demographic characteristics of Turkish immigrants such as age structure and gender distribution (Survey questions 28 and 30) are closely related to their integration process into German society and way of life.

Table 5.2.3: Distribution of Turkish-born children's birth-places in Turkey, 1971

Birth-place in Turkey	Number of children	Percentages (%)
Born in village	34 respondents	49
Born in city	32 respondents	38
Born in county	10 respondents	10
Total	78 respondents	100

Source: Suzanne Paine, Exporting workers; The Turkish case, 1974 p. 187. Turkish workers' children in Europe, Drama of the second generation, Orkun Yayinevi, Istanbul, 1984, p. 66

Table 5.2.3 (the first survey on the second generation's birth place in 1971, chapter five pages 10) suggests that **74.5%** of the second generation Turkish workers children's birth-place is in Turkey. While only **24.5%** indicated their birth-place is Germany in 1971.

This survey suggests also data on returned workers and the number of their children stayed in Germany in the late 1970s. The second generation Turkish guest workers from Anatolian villages had on average 3-6 children. In other words, **71.5%** of Turkish farmer families with village background indicated that they have 5 children. **35%** of Turkish parents who worked in service sector with city background had only 2 or 3 children in 1979. [566]

Table 5.2.4 Gender distribution of Turkish guest workers children in 1971

Gender distribution of Turkish children	Number of child
Boys	57
Girls	45
Total respondents	102

Source: Turkish workers' children in Europe, Drama of the second generation, Orkun Yayinevi, Istanbul, 1984, p. 67

Table 5.2.4 suggests that **44%** of Turkish children represent girls attending to school in Germany. While **56%** represents boys attending to school.

---

[566] Yasa, Ibrahim: Yurda Dönen İşçiler ve Toplumsal Değişme, p. 55, 1979. In Turkish workers and their children in Europe, Drama of the second generation, Orkun Yayinevi, Istanbul, 1984, p. 66

Table 5.2.5 Age distribution of guest workers children in 1974

	Majority German Population	Turkish-German Population
Age ranges	(in %)	(in %)
60 years Plus	25	50
30-59 years	50	50
Under 30 years	25	45

Source: Turkish workers' children in Europe, Drama of the second generation, Orkun Yayinevi, Istanbul, 1984, p. 67

As seen above in the table 5.2.5, 95 respondents or **93%** of the children are between 9-20 age groups. Rest of the respondents are 21-25 age groups which consist of only **7%** of the total children in 1974.

Table 5.2.6 Comparison of Turks' age structure with native Germans in Germany (in thousands)

Age group of the second generation Turkish children	Number of Turkish children
9-10 years old	43
11-15 years old	44
16-20 years old	8
21-25 years old	7
Total	102

Source: Erdem, Kutay and Schmidt, Ruth Ä. :Ethnic Marketing for Turks in Germany, Journal of Retail & Distribution Management, Vol. 36, No. 3, 2008, pp. 212-223

Above Table 5.2.6 demonstrates the age structure of the Turkish immigrant population in Germany significantly differs from that of the majority German population. **45%** of the Turkish population is under 30 years old in contrast to the majority German population which is **25%** under 30 years old. Moreover, **50%** of Turkish population in Germany is between 15 and 55 years old.[567]

A 2003 survey related to German publics' ageing concerns suggests that in 2013 42 million Germans will be working, and 24 million will be retired out of a total German population of 82 million.[568] Then **17%** of Turks who live in Germany were born in the country. **54.2%** of Turkish immigrants in Germany are male and **45.8%** are female.[569] Therefore, German authorities are trying to rise the retirement age from 65 to 75 years old. The same survey shows that will be 36 million working people, and 28 million retired Germans in Germany in 2013.

---

[567] Erdem, Kutay and Schmidt, Ruth Ä. :Ethnic Marketing for Turks in Germany, International Journal of Retail & Distribution Management Vol. 36, No. 3, 2008, pp. 212-223 www.emeraldinsight.co/0959-0552.htm accessed: 21/12/2010

[568] Observatory of European Foreign Policy EUTR 16/2003

[569] http://www.thelocal.de/national/20101012-30425.html

Furthermore, an age comparison between the Turks and Germans shows that **15.7%** of Turkish population are 50 years old while the proportion is **43%** among the German population, which accounts for **50.5%** and **33.8%** respectively for the age range 14-29 and 39-49. [570]

Graph 5.1.8 Factors related to gender and age structure affect the integration process

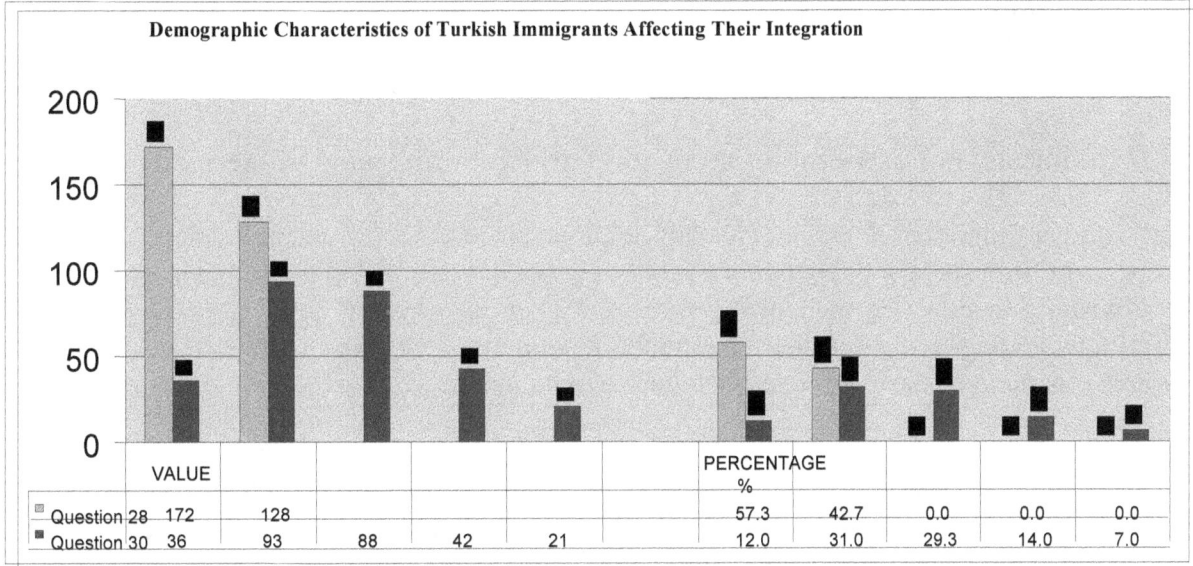

Demographic Characteristics of Turkish Immigrants Affecting Their Integration

	VALUE					PERCENTAGE %				
Question 28	172	128				57.3	42.7	0.0	0.0	0.0
Question 30	36	93	88	42	21	12.0	31.0	29.3	14.0	7.0

28. Gender: Male   Female
30. Age Structure: 15-21, 21-30, 31-40, 41-50, 51-60

Graph 5.1.8 concerning Turkish immigrants' gender and age structure in Germany suggests that **57.3%** are male; while **43.7%** are female. Then Turkish community consists of younger generation of total German population. Thus, only **3%** of Turkish immigrants are retired, **5%** over 50 years old and **18%** are between 41-50 age groups, which mean that 3% + 5% + 18% = 36% 100% - 36% = 64% are under 40 years. Obviously, Turkish population in Germany is younger than general Germany population. Although they constituted younger population in German society, the survey findings related to their gender and age structure indicates that older immigrants with low education level and poor German language skills made little integration into German society. Reasons for insufficient integration of older generation Turkish immigrants can be explained with their backgrounds such as their intention, expectation, changing circumstances and emerged integration problems as a consequence of the last 50 years coexistence within German society.

As a result, young Turks are going to stay in Germany are also willing to be integrated and. wish for better security, increased acceptance by the German people and the possibility to keep their own culture to some extent. Turkish families began to build new lives in Germany; they bought houses, their children attended schools, they established businesses etc. Therefore, co-

---

[570] Statistisches_Bundesamt_2009_loc.3D51-0 Dezember 5 2010

existence is important. No one should expect another to leave aside or ignore his/her culture. The two sides have to compromise on fundamental values.

Although the Turks lived in Germany over 50 years, many Germans know little about Turkish immigrants' original positions (cultural values, natural talents, religious beliefs and individual goals). Therefore, Germans have naturally difficulty to accept Turkish immigrants as members of their host society? A Turkish proverb says "Man is enemy of his unknown."

5.1.9 Importance of self-employment for Turkish immigrants in Germany

The Turkish immigrants prefer the self-employment to avoid unemployment and to be independent from social welfares. In addition, German states (*Länder*) grant financial supports to those wishing to establish their own businesses. They also benefit from German government facilities by getting credits for their investment. *Kreditanstalt fur Wiederaufbau* (Kalkinma Kredi Kurumu) encouraged those who establish businesses since 2002.[571]

Table 5.2.7 indicates that while **19%** of respondents consider buying a house in Turkey with the money they earn in Germany. In reality, **55%** of the Turkish workers had already possessed houses in Turkey in the early 1980s. While **18%** of respondents wished to become a partner of factories or workplaces in Germany. In fact, **22%** of the second generation Turkish workers have already become shareholders/partners of the factory or workplaces where they worked in Germany. **23.5%** of them said that they want to send Turkey as foreign currency. **6.5%** of the respondents said that they want to put money in bank for interest rates in Germany.[572]

The Turkish community in Europe as well as Germany is made up of a significant younger population when compared to the EU population and one which needs to work. Self-employment path for many first-generation redundant guest workers but it also a significant response by second generation youth, often assisted by parents who had in mind securing the future livelihoods of their children. An increasing number of self-employed immigrants come from the ranks of the second generation.

---

[571] Deutschland, Politics,Culture,Economy and Science, No. 1, February/March 2003, p.7, 26, 27,28,29 www.magazine-deutschland.de

[572] Türkdoğan, Orhan: Avrupa'da ki İşçilerimiz ve Çocukları, *Ikinci Neslin Dramı*, the Turkish workers and their children in Europe, Drama of the second generation, Orkun Yayınevi, Istanbul, 1984, p. 178

Types of investments the Turkish workers consider   Number of workers (respondents)

To purchase real estate (houses)	23
To purchase building grounds	10
To become a partner of factories or workplaces	21
To establish businesses	13
Breeding cattle	10
To run a shop and become a shopkeeper	8
To operate intercity buses	8
To put money in bank for interest rates	8
To send Turkey as foreign currency	28
No response	39
Total respondents	180
To purchase real estate (houses)	23
To purchase building grounds	10
To become a partner of factories or workplaces	21
To establish businesses	13
Breeding cattle	10
To run a shop and become a shopkeeper	8
To operate intercity buses	8
To put money in bank for interest rates	8
To send Turkey as foreign currency	28
No response	39
Total respondents	180

Table 5.2.7 Do you have any plan for investment in Turkey? A survey from the early 1980s

Source: Türkdoğan, Orhan: Avrupa'da ki İşçilerimiz ve Çocukları, *Ikinci Neslin Dramı*, the Turkish workers and their children in Europe, Drama of the second generation, Orkun Yayınevi, Istanbul, 1984, p. 178

Table 5.2.8: Occupational Status of the second generation Turks and Germans 1984-1992 (%)

Occupational Status	Turks 1984	Turks 1992	Germans 1984	Germans 1992
Unskilled workers	37	21	8	2
Semi-skilled workers	42	42	12	10
Skilled workers	13	22	22	30
Basic white collar	4	3	17	4
White collar: higher	2	4	29	44
Self-employed	2	8	3	4

Source: Eva Kolinsky, Non-German Minorities in German society, 1994, p. 95

Table 5.2.8 shows that there is a significant change from blue-collar to white-collar employees in employment of the Turks in Germany, **4%** of the Turks compared with **37%** of the Germans is still a big gap between the Turks and the Germans. But in the establishment of self-businesses the Turks have overtaken the Germans in the early 1990s, number the Turks increased from **2%** to **8%;** the number of the Germans increased only **1%** from **3%** to **4%**.[573]

In 2003, the overall proportion of Turks who are self-employed in the EU lies at **4.8%**, which is significantly below the EU average of **12.3%**. Nearly 70 per cent of all Turkish businessmen in the EU are in Germany, of which four fifths are in only three sectors: (1) retail; (2) restaurant and takeaways; and (3) the service sector. Over one third or **39.7%** of the Turkish immigrant businessmen have been living in Germany for 11-30 years (TAM-Türkiye Araştırmaları Merkezi or TRC-Turkish Research Centre, 2003). In one study of Turkish self-employed businessmen in Germany found that only **15%** were German citizens in 2003 and that **41%**, whilst born in Germany, had their parents' (Turkish) nationality.

Turkish self-employed businessmen represent a significant and growing economic force in Europe. According to Manco (2004, pp. 6-70 during 1996 an estimated 58.000 businessmen employed a total of 186,000 workers throughout Europe. The vast bulk of the firms (42,000) were in Germany, with The Netherlands, France and Austria making up the reminder. Recent data on self-employed Turkish immigrants from the Turkish Research Centre (TRC) at the University of Essen suggest that during 2002 an estimated 82,300 firms employed 411,000 people. As the above indicates, during the five-year period 1996-2002 nearly 25,000 more self-employed businesses were added to the total, representing a **41.8%** per cent rate of increase. Employment during the same period increased by 225,000, a rate of increase of 82.6 per cent TRC, 2003). According to Tumbas (2003, p. 4-5) something like **77%** per cent of Turkish businessmen in Germany have German suppliers and an increasing number are relying on German consumers. About **17%** per cent of employees in firms are Germans and **9%** per cent are from other nationalities. One estimate of the total contribution made by Turkish immigrant entrepreneurs to the European economy is that it is equivalent to one fifth of Denmark's GDP-gross domestic product and **51%** equivalent to **51%** of Greek GDP (TRC, 2000, p.3).

Mehrländer argues that "for many Germans integration means adopting German customs and traditions, but now German attitudes are much more positive and immigrants' presence is considered an enrichment of our society."[574] The social health and security systems like compulsory health and pension insurance have profited greatly from the contributions of immigrant workers. For example, in 1989 immigrant workers contributed 12.8 billion DM to the state pensions fund, **7.8%** of the total payments (164 billion DM); but only 3.43 billion DM (**1.9 %**) of the total pension volume was paid out to immigrant workers in 1992).[575]

In Germany, the economic argument has been stressed since the 1950s to gain acceptance for foreigners as net contributors to the welfare state.[576] Germany has become one of the Europe's economic giants by the aid of foreign manpower through migration. Germans have been especially proud of their economic achievement.

---

[573] Horrocks, David and Kolinsky, Eva (Eds.): Migrants or Citizens? Turks in Germany between Exclusion and Acceptance, Berghahn Books, 1996, p. 95

[574] Sarah Spencer (Ed.): Immigration as an Economic Asset, Trentham Books, 1994; in Ch.1 Ursula Mehrländer: The Development of Post War Migration and Refugee Policy, (p. 11-13).

[575] Hof,B.,1992:Arbeitskraftebedarft der Wirtschaft. Arbeitsmarktchancen fur Zuwandrer,in:Friedrich-Ebert-Stiftung(Hrsg.),Zuwanderungspolitik der Zukunft ,Reihe Gesprachskreis Arbeit und Soziales,Nr.3,S.7-22,Bonn.

[576] Horrocks, David and Kolinsky, Eva (Eds.): Migrants or Citizens? Turks in Germany between Exclusion and Acceptance, Berghahn Books, 1996, p. 99-101

As a result, even with high unemployment rates and difficulties to find a proper job in German society, most of the Turkish immigrants established their own businesses. Most of the Turkish youths are trying to get a vocational training in Germany and experiencing how to establish their self-employed businesses and participating in sportive, cultural and political activities in the host country. In this way they create an interaction and a common interest with host's youths. This is one the key factors, which develops a successful integration. In addition, the increasing number of self-employed Turkish immigrants is a good indicator for their integration into German society which means that their economic and social status is also rising significantly. They prefer the self-employed small businesses to in the factories and to avoid becoming unemployed. German Federal States encourage small entrepreneurs by financial aids. While they are doing businesses they are contributors to German economy, too. Economically well-being gives them an upward economic status in the German society which affects comfortability. Previous studies suggest that Germany will be even more dependent on immigrants in the future and indicate that immigrants will continue to be a positive economic factor for German labour market as in the past.[577]

Social attitude and an immigrant's feeling are factors which affect integration of immigrants; they are also related to comfortability, political interest, cultural feelings, satisfactory status and sport interest of immigrants. According to Walter Hanesch, socio-economic conditions "poverty (or affluence) is determined by a number of factors which contribute to the subjective well-being, and material life-chances and opportunities of a person."[578]

Table 5.2.9: Comparing the socio-economic conditions of Germans and immigrants including Turks in Germany, 1992

	Income	Housing	Education (Schools)	Vocational Training	Employment	Social Exclusion
East	13	16	1	10	21	10
West	7	11	4	24	6	7
All Germans	8	12	3	21	10	8
Immigrants (inc. Turks)	17	44	27	58	11	37

Source: Walter Hanesch et al, *Armut in Deutschland*, Reinbek, Rowohlt, 1994, p. 173

Table 5.2.9 demonstrates that in the early 1990s, **85%** of young immigrants have attended school in Germany with the lowest level (*Hauptschule*). Regardless of ethnic group, Germany produced its own social exclusion, which is defined as the gap between reality and expectation.[579]

As low-status jobs were taken up by Turkish immigrants, they were free to move from blue-collar low-paid employment to white-collar and well-paid employment by job-training and educational achievement.

---

[577] Zimmermann Klaus F.: Tackling the European Migration Problem, Journal of Economic Perspectives 9 (2) 1995, p. 45-62
[578] Horrocks, David and Kolinsky Eva (Eds.): Migrants or Citizens? Turks in Germany between Exclusion and Acceptance, Berghahn Books, 1996, p. 100
[579] Ibid., p. 95

Graph 5.1.9 Measuring Socio-economic status and integration of Turkish immigrants

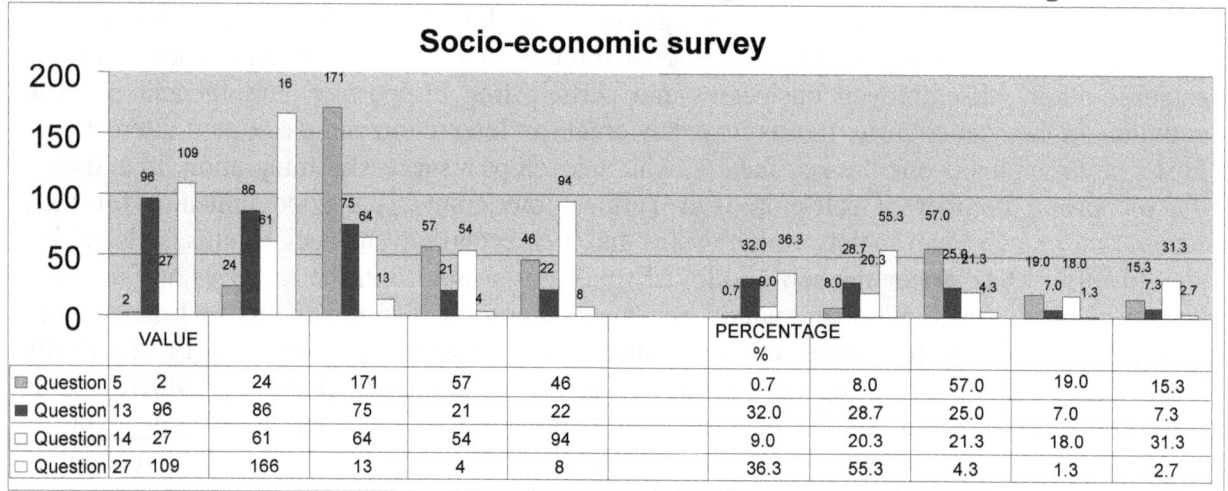

Socio-economic survey

	VALUE						PERCENTAGE %				
Question 5	2	24	171	57	46		0.7	8.0	57.0	19.0	15.3
Question 13	96	86	75	21	22		32.0	28.7	25.0	7.0	7.3
Question 14	27	61	64	54	94		9.0	20.3	21.3	18.0	31.3
Question 27	109	166	13	4	8		36.3	55.3	4.3	1.3	2.7

Q5. How are your relations with people at work? (1)Not good (2)Not bad (3)Normal (4)Very good (5)Too good
Q13. Is it hard to find a job, economically? (1)Very hard (2) Hard (3) But possible (4)Sometimes (4)More opportunities here
Q14. Is it hard to find house here? (1)Very hard (2) Hard (3) But possible (4)Sometimes (4)More opportunities here
Q27. Where do you want to live in future? (1) In Germany (2) In Turkey (3)In both country (4) In other European (5) Other
Source: Author

Graph 5.1.9 shows results of Turkish immigrants' Socio-economic status and degree of their integration in German social and economic life as percentage. For example, question 5 *How is your relation with people at work?* **57%** express their relations with friends at work are being good. Question 13 *Is it hard to find a job in Germany?* **32%** say that it is hard to find a job in Germany. Question 14 *Is it hard to find a house in Germany?* **31.3%** say that it is not difficult to find a house in Germany. Question 27 *Where do you want to live in the future?* Only **36%** want to live in Germany in the future. **55.3%** still want to return and live in Turkey in the future. This means more than half of the Turkish population in Germany do not want to live in Germany in the future, if they have a choice.

On the other hand, a lot of Germans go on holiday to Turkey and they discover Turkish society first hand. They try to learn the Turkish language and many buy a summer house or flat on the Turkish Mediterranean coast (especially in towns of Alanya, Manavgat, and Side), where there are more than 20.000 German residents, and the Aegean coast towns of Fethiye, Bodrum, Çeşme, Didim, and Marmaris.[580]

---

[580] The Turkish Ministry of Housing and Public Works Report, Ankara; 16 June 2008. *Turkish parliament allows property sales to foreigners,* **14%** Middle-class Germans are interested in purchasing real estates from Turkey. Hürriyet, 16 June 2008

5.2 Chapter Conclusion

The Turks living in Germany play a major role in creating a bridge between Turkey and Germany and between the two societies, contributing to the development of these relationships.

The aim of this paper was to measure the process or level of integration of Turkish immigrants to their new country, new way of life and the new environment after staying in Europe some years; an immigrant has already overcome some of his/her difficulties of integration, the process of integration of the given group of immigrants, the most striking features have appeared such as 'isolation', 'integration' or 'assimilation'.

The results of this research indicate not only their integration level of Turkish immigrants but also their new identities as bilingual or bicultural Germans of Turkish origin as well as the impact of their integration on bilateral relations.

At first glance, Germany may not seem an obvious model from which other European countries can learn positive lessons about integration of immigrants from German experience. However, there are a lot of positive (conceptual and structural) changes in Germany's immigration and integration policy since reunification. One of the most important changes is German politicians' attitude change towards their immigrants was the *declaration* itself as an *'immigration country'* (August 1st, 2001). For years German denied being an immigration country stressing the necessity of its immigrants' integration into Germany economically, politically, socially and culturally. Other changes are criteria for entrance, integration and naturalisation policies and the most important change is self-understanding of its national traditional, political and cultural community. The idea that Germany is not a country of immigration must be seen as part of a traditional *perception* of German as nation united by language and culture.

German experience shows that although German society wishes to preserve its social, political, and cultural values unchanged, it is inevitable that it will be exposed to changes when it is mixed with immigrants. Immigrants also wish to preserve their cultural, social, political, and linguistic values to some extent. At the same time they hope to be integrated into their host nations and accepted as equal members of their host societies. This means that, despite the inevitable dominance of the majority, a compromise is necessary on both sides to create a well-integrated German society.

Chapter 6

6.1 Chapter introduction

In this chapter a comparative bivariate analysis is employed to examine two variables' effect on the integration process of Turkish immigrants into German society such as the relationship between Turkish immigrants' birth place and feeling German, level of education and feeling German, age structure and feeling German, German citizenship and gender (females and males), gender and political interest, inter-(German)-marriage and feeling integrated, education level of Turkish immigrants and intermarriage, and gender distribution and employment facilities. As argued in chapters four and five some variables have a single effect; and some variables have a joint effect on the integration of immigrants. Since the single factor's effect or single variable analysis is limited, it needs also two factors' analyses to achieve the objectives targeted in the main research question. This can be two factors' simultaneous effect on integration which requires a joint variable analysis such as bivariate analysis to measure the joint effect of dependent variables which is 'Have Turkish immigrants integrated into Germany between years 1961-2007, and has their integration any impact on Turco-German relations? on their integration or independent variable.

A questionnaire data was used as an instrument to measure the impact of dependent variable on the independent variable and simultaneously data related to survey validity and reliability such as content, construct, concurrent and predictive validity. For example, content validity was determined by judgement concerning how well the samples represent the correct proportion.

Chapter six is also testing the relationship between two variables in the integration process of Turkish immigrants into German life, economically, socially, politically, culturally and from other relevant aspects. [581] As mentioned earlier, descriptive and inferential statistics were used in this survey. (1) Descriptive statistic was employed to summarize the questionnaire results. Then, quantifying was carried out the findings to generalize from a sample group to wider group (the population). (2) Inferential statistics were used as a basis for making inferences about finding out what is more likely to happen in relation with integration problems of Turkish immigrants in the future of Germany. Demographic and quantitative analyses are applied to measure the relationship of immigrants' subjective feelings and joint (dependent) variables' effect on independent variable or their integration. In the chapter six, a series of statistical models such as chi-square (bivariate), Pearson's correlation, linear regression and the ordered logit were applied to test and analyse.

---

[581] Buttolph Johnson, Janet and Reynolds, H. T: 'Political Science Research Methods', 5[h] Edition, 2005 by CQ Press, Washington D.C., p. 50-53, 406-412, 451

6.1.1 Impact of feeling German and birth place on integration of Turkish immigrants' into German society

According to a survey conducted on Turkish workers' children or second generation Turks in Stuttgart in 1980 shows that only one in four second generation Turks' birth place is in Germany.[582]

Frequency tables were often used in chapter three; pie-charts throughout chapter four, and bar-charts were used in chapter five.[583] Although frequency tables are useful, they often do not give adequate information.[584] When variables have a lot of categories, it can be difficult to find out whether a relationship exists or not.[585]

Tabular bivariate analysis is a simultaneous analysis of two variables, which is undertaken to see if one variable, for instance such as gender, is related to another variable, educational achievement.

Bivariate analysis starts by means of constructing table. Tables can be used to show bivariate relations with any variables, whether the variables are measured at the nominal, ordinals, intervals or ratio levels. Also, variables measured at each of these levels can be analysed by means of statistical tests of significance. The simplest form of bivariate analysis is the analysis of two variables measured at the nominal level.[586] Constructing a bivariate table is the first step to put these percentages into a properly constructed bivariate table. The percentages derived from the two-way categorization of the survey questionnaire data 2007. This table is also known as a cross classification or contingency table because the two variables are crossed with one another in the form of columns and rows of a table.

Bivariate analysis aims to find out the relationship between two different variables such as education and age, birthplace and education, gender distribution and education as well as gender and citizenship's joint effect on their integration which yields the outcome.

The following Table 6.1.1 shows the relationship between feeling German and birth place of Turkish origin immigrants.

[582] Türkdoğan, Orhan: Turkish workers' children in Europe, Drama of the second generation Turkish immigrants, Orkun Yayinevi, Istanbul, 1984, p. 65

[583] Burnham, Peter; Gilland, Karin; Wyn Grant and Layton-Henry, Zig: Research Methods in Politics, Palgrave, Macmillan, Basingstoke, 2004 (p. 132)

[584] Kranzler, J.: *Statistics for the Terrified,* Englefield Cliffs, NJ, Prentice Hall, 2003, p.49

[585] Sapsford, R.: Extracting and Presenting Statistics, in R. Sapsford and V. Jupp (Eds.), *Data Collection and analysis,* Sage, London, 1996, pp. 201-212

[586]Buttolph Johnson, Janet and Reynolds, H. T: 'Political Science Research Methods', 5h Edition, 2005 by CQ Press, Washington D.C., p. 50-53, 406-412, 451

Table 6.1.1 Relationship between feeling German and birth place immigrants of Turkish origin

Category of feeling	Germany	Turkey	Other	Total
not/little	25	58	16	99
	25.25%	58.59%	16.16%	100%
ordinary	38	83	22	143
	26.57%	58.04%	15.38%	100%
quite/very	26	16	14	56
	46.43%	28.57%	25.00%	100%
Total	89	157	52	298
	29.87%	52.68%	17.45%	100%

Source: Author adapted from the 2007 survey questionnaire data

Chi-square value=16.2551 p-value=0.003

As expected, the table shows that being born in Germany is associated with feeling German, as **46%** of respondents who feel either German or very German were born in Germany, compared with about **28.6%** and **25%** of respondents born in Turkey or elsewhere, respectively. This association is statistically significant at the **1%** level, since p-value=0.003 is less than the chosen level of statistical significance testing (Chi-square with 4 degrees of freedom = 16.25, p-value=0.003).

6.1.2 Gender distribution and education level of Turkish immigrants

There is a positive relationship between education and integration level of Turkish immigrants into German society and way of life. The well educated are better integrated. Even the well educated first generation is better integrated than the poorly educated German born fourth generation of Turkish descent.

The public belief that the younger generation immigrants are more likely to be integrated than the older is not always true. The survey result shows that more educated Turkish immigrants are better integrated even than German born and poor educated younger generation.

As a result, the survey indicates that education plays a more important role than age structure in the integration of Turkish immigrants into German society.

In contrast to above figures, educational data from 1997 shows Turkish girls are doing better than boys in Germany. In addition, the number of Turkish students who attend university is also rising. Further evidence shows gender differences are obvious and women and girls are doing significantly better. For example, in 1980, the proportion of Turkish female students was **12.4%**; in 1997 this increased to **36%**. According to the 2007 survey questionnaire, gender distribution of the Turkish immigrant population in Germany is 57% male and 43% female. Data from 1997 indicates that Turkish immigrant students' first preference is law, economy and social sciences with 42.2%, language and history follows this with 53%. Their third preference is engineering departments with 78%. Another interesting point: Turkish female students' number is doubled. For example, Turkish female students consist of **9.7%** of medical students, and male are only

242

4.9% of those in German universities. The total numbers of the students of Turkish origin were 15,442 in 1997.[587]

Frequency Table 6.1.2 Turkish immigrants' education level in Germany, 2007

Public schools	84 respondents	28%
Vocational secondary school	108 respondents	36%
Technique school	48 respondents	16%
High school	26 respondents	9%
College education	36 respondents	12%
Total	300 respondents	100%

Source: Author, adapted from the 2007 Survey

In the following Table 6.1.2, gender is designated as an independent variable and education as the dependent variable for this analysis. On this basis, a hypothesis can be established in the following way. Gender distribution of Turkish immigrants is related to survey question 29 and educational achievement is related to survey question 25. The hypothesis, 'Turkish females are doing better than males in case of educational achievement in Germany'.[588]

Table 6.1.2 Association between feeling German and education level of Turkish origin immigrants in Germany

	Primary	Secondary	University	Total
not/little	27	63	9	99
	27.27%	63.64%	9.09%	100%
ordinary	26	98	19	143
	18.18%	68.53%	13.29%	100%
quite/very	7	41	8	56
	12.5%	73.21%	14.29%	100%
Total	60	202	36	298
	20.13%	67.79%	12.08%	100%

Chi-square value=6.0341 p-value=0.197

Source: Author

There exists an association between feeling German and education level of Turkish origin immigrants as shown in Table 6.1.2. For example, a higher percentage of respondents with secondary or university education feel more German compared to those with only primary education. However, the chi-square value shows that this association is not statistically

---

[587] Source: Statistische Bundesamt, Wiesbaden, 1998
[588] Note: Secondary school education level has been taken as criteria for cross tabulation which is equivalent to Turkish Lise and German gymnasium

243

significant different from zero even at the 10% level (Chi-square with 4 degrees of freedom = 6.0341, *P-value* = 0.197).

6.1.3 Feeling German and age structure of Turkish descent immigrants in Germany

In the table 6.1.3, Turkish immigrants' age structure (comparing two contrast age groups 15-20 and over 40 years) and feeling German or integrated into German society are compared. The hypothesis can be formulated as follows: 'German born Turkish origin younger generation is likely to be better integrated than the older generation'.

German experience shows successful integration is not dependent on immigrants' age structure and birth place, but their education level (take Vural Öger as an example for well integrated first generation Turk). One of the most successful businessmen and politicians of Turkish descent Vural Öger migrated to Germany as number 31 immigrant in 1960 at the age of 18. He graduated from the University of Berlin as an engineer. He established Öger Travel Agency in Hamburg in the late 1960s which has carried more than 1 million passengers every year. The Öger Tour is one of the six largest travel agencies in Germany. He also entered into politics and is one of the German MEPs. He is called a Prussian Turk in the German Press.[589]

Assuming the first age group has not started their high school education yet. Comparing third categories of two contrast age groups shows that even 1st generation with high skills and education are better integrated than German born fourth generation. It means that the hypothesis that 'German born younger generation is better integrated than older generation' is not always true. In other words, the language skills and education level of immigrants are more significant factor for integration than age structure. Vural Öger argues that only one who commands the host language can be successfully integrated into host society.

Survey question 29 related to age structure of Turkish immigrants shows only **3%** of Turks in Germany are retired and **5%** of them are 60 years and over. General public assumptions that older immigrants are less likely to be integrated into German society, is supported by Table 6.1.3.

---

[589] German Magazine for Politics, Culture, Economy and Scientific Forum Number 1, February/March 2003, Vural Öger and other successful entrepreneurs in Germany with immigrant background, p. 26-30 www.magazine-deutschland.de

Table 6.1.3 Relationship between feeling German and age structure of Turkish descent immigrants

	15-30	31=40	above 40	Total
not/little	42	24	33	99
	42.42%	24.24%	33.33%	100%
ordinary	64	40	39	143
	44.76%	27.97%	27.27%	100%
quite/very	28	24	6	58
	48.28%	41.38%	10.34%	100%
Total	134	88	78	300
	44.67%	29.33%	26%	100%

Chi-square value= 11.7191 p-value= 0.020

Source: Author

Table 6.1.3 shows that there is an association between feeling German and age structure of Turkish descent immigrants living in Germany, about 45% and 48% of younger generation (of age between 15-30) feel German compared with 28% and 41% for middle age older generation of age between 31-40 and over 40 years. This relationship is statistically significant at the 5% level. Chi-square with 4 degrees of freedom = 11.7191, p-value = 0.020 is less than the chosen level of 5%, is statistically significance testing. [590]

Previous studies show that in the 1960s, the first Turkish guest workers to Germany were males under 30 years old, who were contract workers according to the bilateral labour force agreement between the two countries. In the late 1970s, females and children followed them though German family unification law. Although females came to Germany 15 to 20 years later than the men, they are doing better in terms of their emancipation and educational aspects.

As discussed earlier, according to German Statistics Office (*Statistische Bundesamt, Wiesbaden*, 1998), in 1980, the proportion of Turkish female students was 12.4%; in 1997 this increased to 36%. Another interesting point is that Turkish female students' number is doubled. For example, Turkish female students consist of 9.7% of medical students, and male are only 4.9% of those in German universities. Emine Altiok points out her experience in Germany as following: "Turkish women have become emancipated in Germany; they earn their own living and won't accept the usual role of a Turkish wife."[591]

---

[590] We usually test 1%, 5% or 10% level.

[591] Ardagh, John: Germany and the Germans, The United Germany in the Mid-1990s, 3rd Ed., in Ch. 5 Turkish Guest Workers and other immigrants: A Painful Path towards acceptance, Penguin Books, England, 1995 (p. 273-297).

Table 6.1.4 Gender distribution of Turkish people with immigrant background and feeling German

	female	male	Total
not/little	32	67	99
	32.32%	67.68%	100%
ordinary	43	100	143
	30.07%	69.93%	100%
quite/very	19	39	58
	32.76%	67.24%	100%
Total	94	206	300
	31.33%	68.67%	100%

Chi-square value= 0.2059 p-value= 0.902

Source: Author

Table 6.1.4 shows that there is a relationship between gender and feeling German. Feeling German means that they are integrated and consider Germany as their home country. However, this study finds no statistically significant different between gender and educational attainment.

A survey of 2000 shows Turkish-origin girls have overtaken boys, the percentage of Turkish-origin women with a diploma from the more prestigious levels of schooling (Abitur or Fachhochschulreife) is rising in Germany. About 1 in 5 Turkish women aged 18-30 at the time of the research had a diploma on this level, a clear improvement compared with the micro-census data of 1995. German micro-census data 2002 shows that Turkish-origin girls in German preparatory tracks for higher education more than doubled compared with a 1988 survey, which means that females first closed the gap with the males and have overtaken males even with better school results.[592]

The following figure shows the proportion of Turkish gender distribution with university degree and over in 1993, Turkey.

---

[592] German micro-census data from 1995 to 2002

Figure 6.1, from 1993, demonstrates Turkish women's academic status in Turkish universities; they will also have overtaken men soon. There is only 8% difference between them. [593]

Figure 6.1: The academic career pattern from a Cross-sectional Perspective in Turkey, 1993

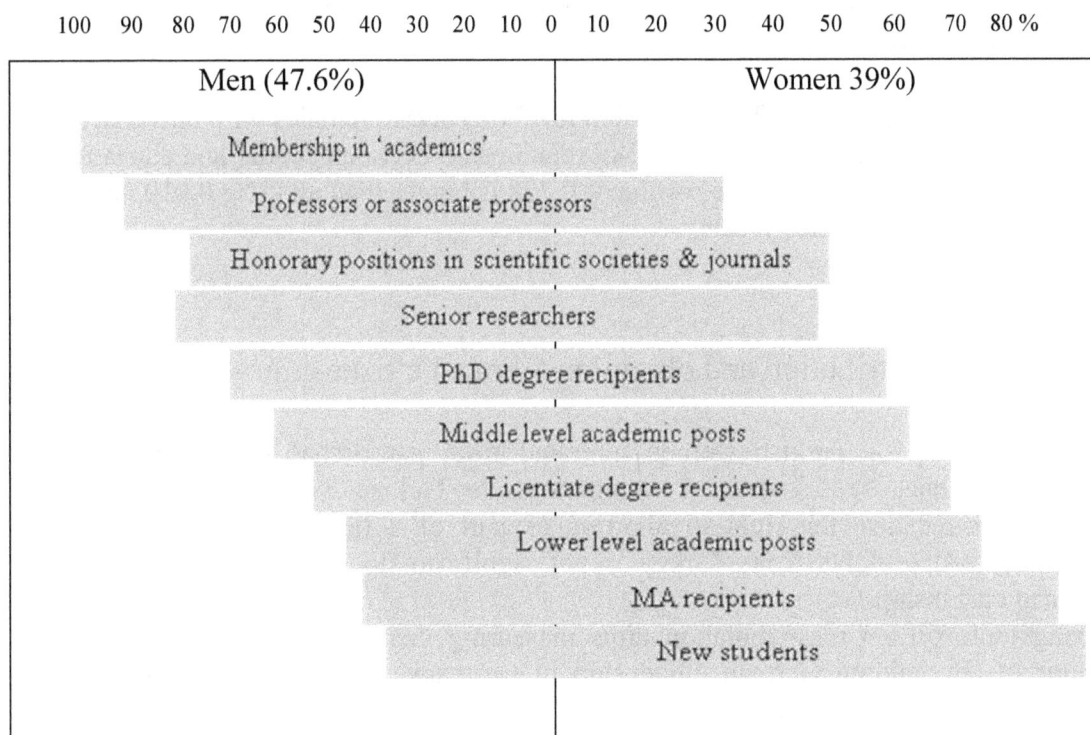

```
100  90  80  70  60  50  40  30  20  10  0  10  20  30  40  50  60  70  80 %
```

| Men (47.6%) | Women 39%) |

Membership in 'academics'

Professors or associate professors

Honorary positions in scientific societies & journals

Senior researchers

PhD degree recipients

Middle level academic posts

Licentiate degree recipients

Lower level academic posts

MA recipients

New students

Source: Adapted from Higher Education in Europe, Careers for Women at European Universities, Obstacles and Opportunities, Vol. XVIII, No. 4, 1993 p. 33

---

[593] Higher Education in Europe, Careers for Women at European Universities, Obstacles and   Opportunities, Vol. XVIII, No. 4, 1993 p. 33

Table 6.1.5 Gender distribution of Turkish people with immigrant background and education level

	Primary	Secondary	University	Total
female	17	64	13	94
	18.09%	68.09%	13.83%	100%
male	43	138	23	204
	21.08%	67.65%	11.27%	100%
Total	60	202	36	298
	20.13%	67.79%	12.08%	100%

Chi-square value= 0.6360 p-value= 0.728

Source: Author

According to previous studies Turkish origin females are doing better in German schools and are more educated than men of Turkish origin.[594]

Although the Table 6.1.5 suggests that education level of Turkish females with university degree (almost **14%**) **3%** higher than men (**11%**), relationship between gender and education level is not statistically significant. Since p-value = 0.728 is bigger than all (1%=0.010, 5% = 0.50 and 10% =0.100) above tested levels.

Table 6.1.6 Gender distribution and obtaining German citizenship

Although the majority of Turkish women migrated from patriarchal society of Turkey, founder of the Republic, Atatürk granted voting rights to Turkish women by 1935.[595] The government recognized also the right to abortion as part of a family planning policy.[596] However, having voting rights from Turkey is not significant to vote in Germany before gaining German citizenship.
The following table 6.1.6 Cross-tabulation aims measuring Gender distribution of Turkish origin immigrants by gaining German citizenship in Germany. Table 6.1.6 shows 31% of Turkish women have German citizenship as well as voting rights in Germany.

---

[594] Ibid.
[595] Arat, Yeşim: Obstacles to Political Careers, 'Perception of Turkish Women', International Political Science Review, Women in Politics, Sage Publications, Vol. 6 No. 3, 1985 pp. 355-366
[596] Ibid., p. 355

Table 6.1.6 Gender distribution and obtaining German citizenship

	no	yes	Total
female	65	29	94
	69.15%	30.85%	100%
male	147	59	206
	71.36%	28.64%	100%
Total	212	88	300
	70.67%	29.33%	100%

Chi-square value= 0.1521   *p*-value= 0.697

Source: Author

According to table 6.1.6, although citizenship percentages of female respondents (**31%**) are 2% higher than Turkish origin males (**29%**), the study reveals that an association between gender distribution of Turkish immigrants and naturalization number of German citizenship figures do not exist and it is not statistically significant level.

6.1.7 Gender distribution of Turkish immigrants by German citizenships and political interest

As mentioned earlier, bivariate descriptive statistics involves simultaneously analysing (comparing) two variables to determine if there is a relationship between the variables. The following

Table 6.1.7 shows Turkish women in Germany are likely to be interested in politics as men.

Table 6.1.7 Political interest and Gender distribution of Turkish descent immigrants

	yes	no	little/st	Total
female	15	61	18	94
	15.96%	64.89%	19.15%	100%
male	51	118	35	204
	25%	57.84%	17.16%	100%
Total	66	179	53	298
	22.15%	60.07%	17.79%	100%

Chi-square value= 3.0518 *p*-value= 0.217

Source: Author

249

Although political interest has no meaning without obtaining German citizenship, Turkish women show less interest (**16%**) in politics than Turkish men (**22%**). Table 6.1.7 suggests a relationship between political interest and gender distribution of Turkish descent immigrants does not exist. Level of relationship p-value= 0.217 is bigger than any of statistically significant testing level at 1%, 5% or 10%.

6.1.8 Intermarriage rates and integration level of Turkish origin immigrants in Germany

Federal Statistical office from 2007-8 demonstrates that there were 373,681 new marriages in 2006, 46,719 of them (12.5%) were intermarriages. 57.7% of intermarriages related to German men and 42.3% related to German women. As of 2008, people from German-speaking countries such as Austrian nationals (41.1%), nationals from Russian Federation (57.8%) were the high rates of marriage to German citizens. Polish nationals had also high intermarriage rates (37.3%). Intermarriage rates of Turkish nationals were 9.7%. Greek nationals were only 6.7%.[597]

Comparison of intermarriage rates of Turkish with other ethnic groups shows that decreasing of social boundaries and taboos over time make intermarriages are more likely between immigrant and native young groups. Sociologist Matthijs Kalmija argues those immigrants with high level of education are more likely to intermarry to different ethnic groups.[598] Their interpersonal relationships in schools and workplaces where they meet and interacted facilitate them to associate mutually. Also economists Delia Furtado and Nicolas Theodoropoulos found immigrants with high education are more likely to intermarry since they better integrate into the host country' s school system and lifestyle.[599] Although the number of marriages between German citizens has decreased since 1991, the annual numbers of intermarriages have an increasing trend from 1991 (See also intermarriage table page 213-284).

Table 6.1.8a Impact of intermarriage factor on integration of immigrants (including) Turks (in %)

Citizenship(selected groups)	Married	Married to German citizen	Intermarriage share (%)
Russian Federation	107,955	62,391	57.8
Austria	82,210	35,396	43.1
Turkey	838,502	83,208	9.7
Greece	287,187	8,529	6.7
Total	3,123,050	781,741	25.0

Source: Central Register of Foreigners (AZR), 2008

Table 6.1.8a indicates there were 43,955 or 9.7% new marriages until 2002. They peaked at 62,468 (15.9%) in the same year. In 2006, there were 373,681 new marriages, 46,719 of which (12.5%) were intermarriages. 57% of new intermarriages related to German men and 42.3% to

---

[597] Migration Policy Institute, 2009 source@migrationpolicy.org Accessed on 12/10/2009

[598] Kalmijn, Matthijs. 1998. Intermarriage and Homogamy: Causes, Patterns, Trends. *Annual Review of Sociology* 24:395-421

[599] Furtado, Delia. 2006. Human Capital and Interethnic Marriage Decisions; IZA – Institute for the Study of Labour, Discussion Paper Series No., 1989, Bonn.

German women. Having a look at the whole marriages as of 2008, individuals from a German speaking country Austria were 43.1% from Russia 57.8%. Intermarriage rates among Polish were 37.3%, Turkish **9.7%** and Greek **6.7%**. Polish females had high rates of intermarriage 28.7%, women of Romanian 26.6%, and Ukrainian origin women 21.7%. Female of Turkish origin intermarriage rate were only 3%. [600]

Previous intermarriage data by generation for different ethnic groups suggest that second generation were less likely to be married compared to the first. Because the second generation is quite younger with average age is only 15 compared to 43 for the first generation immigrant backgrounds.[601]

German Micro census data from 2007 shows second generation men who were married are more likely to be intermarried (29.6%) than first generation married men (17.2%). This supports the hypothesis that the younger generations are more likely to be integrated (feeling the host country as home and loyal to the state where they live) into their host country than the first generation. This is specific for Turkish origin immigrant group; the rate of intermarriage among the first generation Turkish men was **7.1%**, for the second generation **12.1%**. Intermarriage rates the first-generation Turkish origin female were **2.6%**. [602]

Table 6.1.8b Intermarriage rates and integration level of Turkish origin immigrants in Germany

	not	little	Feeling (integrated)	Total
yes	10	16	52	78
	12.82%	20.51%	66.67%	100%
live together	8	3	30	41
	19.51%	7.32%	73.17%	100%
no	31	50	100	181
	17.13%	27.62%	55.25%	100%
Total	49	69	182	300
	16.33%	23%	60.67%	100%

Chi-square value= 9.5851 p-value= 0.048
Source: Author

Table 6.1.8 shows 26% immigrants of Turkish origin are married to native Germans. Those who married to German natives feel integrated into German society. Also those who are living with Germans, 73% of them feel also integrated and those married to Germans, 66% of them feel integrated, compared to non-German married and not living together Turkish descent immigrants. This relationship is statistically significant at 5% level.

---

[600] Migration Policy Institute, <source@migrationpolicy.org> accessed on 12/10/2009 17:24
[601] German Microcensus data from 2007
[602] Ibid.

251

Table 6.1.9 German Turkish intermarriage rates and Education level of Turkish immigrants

Germany's ageing population and younger age structure of Turkish origin immigrants' rate makes integration of immigrants urgent in order to stabilize its system.
German Chancellor Angela Merkel at the 'Guest workers' reform' symposium on October 17th 2007 in Berlin said that one of the most important facilitating factors which are affecting the integration of immigrants is the education level of immigrants.[603]

A previous study shows those immigrants of Turkish origin, who have low intermarriage rates, also had lower graduation rates from all three school levels. For example, only 53.6% had completed schooling and only 9.2% of men and 7.6% of women held the Abitur or a comparable degree. The share of those of Turkish origin with vocational training was also exceptionally small compared to all other groups. [604]

As argued earlier, education level of immigrants is considered to be key factor for their integration from all aspects as well as choosing a partner. Germany's education system consists of three phases or levels: *Hauptschule* or primary education; *Realschule* or secondary and *Gymnasium*, all these three have a leaving exam. Diplomas from *Hauptschule* allow for apprenticeships. Graduates from secondary schools apply for *Fochoberschulen* (technical colleges). *Fochoberschulreifle* enable students to attend universities, or HF. Here, 'educated' is defined as completed 'schooling' the secondary school and *Gymnasium* and hold *Abitur* means individual can start to universities. 'Highly educated' is defined as who holds the *Abitur* or the *Fachhochschulreife*. University degree in Germany means at least for years graduation and *Habilitation* (postdoctoral degree). Vocational training means completed secondary schooling. In 2007, 83.7% of Germans, 63.7% of immigrants with migration origin completed secondary schooling. The rate of males with *Abitur* or *Fochoberschulreifle* was 23.5% among native Germans, 18.8% among immigrants with ethnic origin. It is interesting that the share of immigrant women with *Abitur* or *Fochoberschulreifle* was 19.7% and higher than German females 18.2%. Another interesting point intermarriage data from 2007 indicates first-generation women from Eastern European countries are most likely to intermarry.

As education data by migration origin shows migrant women of Polish origin, Ukrainian, and Romanian origin are highly educated in terms of schooling and vocational training. [605]

---

[603] 'Guest workers' reform' on October 17th, 2007 Berlin in German society, German Chancellor Angela Merkel said that "Guest workers from southern Europe, who migrated to Germany in 1960s, gave the German society a new face. Speaking at a two-day symposium on 'Integration through education in the 21st century' in Berlin, Merkel said "the Turks now living in Germany for the last four generations contribute a great deal to the country's economy". "Integration of immigrants will be successful but only by education". Now many German companies grant scholarships to immigrants' children for their training and education which aim at helping their integration.
[604] German Micro census 2007 and Central Register of Foreigners (AZR), 2008
Note: Numbers refer to percentage share of the group's population. Observations below 5,000 are not reported, therefore allowing only for estimates.
[605] Ibid.

Immigrants compared to other ethnic groups, have lower intermarriage rates in general, because they also had lower education rates from the aspects of all three German education levels. 53.6% of immigrants of different ethnic origin had completed schooling; 9.2% of males and 7.6% of females of Turkish origin.

As a consequence, the education data from German Microcensus 2007 support the hypothesis or assumption that more educated immigrants are more likely to be intermarried and eventually to be integrated into German society than the lower educated. This correlation is true for immigrants of Turkish origin. Those of immigrants who less education, have less intermarriage rates and less integrated than other ethnic groups with higher education in Germany.

Table 6.1.9 German Turkish intermarriage rates and Education level of Turkish immigrants

	Primary	Secondary	University	Total
yes	14	54	10	78
	17.95%	69.23%	12.82%	100%
live together	6	28	7	41
	14.63%	68.29%	17.07%	100%
no	40	120	19	179
	22.35%	67.04%	10.61%	100%
Total	60	202	36	298
	20.13%	67.79%	12.08%	100%

Chi-square value= 2.4762 p-value= 0.649

Source: Author

Table 6.1.9 shows there is a relationship between German-Turkish intermarriage rates and education level of Turkish immigrants. Thus, as the number of educated immigrants increases the number German married and cohabiting immigrants also increases. Living together has the same effect on integration as intermarriage; even the number of couple living together with university degree (17%) is higher than intermarried with university degree (13%). However, the chi-square indicates that this relationship is not statistically significant from zero even at the 10% level. Turkish women are more interested in obtaining education and emancipating in Germany, but less in marrying (to German or other ethnic groups).[606]

6.2.1 Correlation Coefficient Testing Procedures

The correlation coefficient is a suitable statistical model to test the survey data which corresponds to specific Turkish origin immigrant groups in Germany. The Spearman rho (s) correlation measures the variance in Y shared by X. When the correlation coefficient approaches ± 1.0, it means that variance in Y is shared by the variance in X.

---

[606] Intermarriages of Women with Migration Background by country of origin, 2007, Central Register of Foreigners (AZR), 2008

6.2.1 Correlation Table

	DEPENDENT VARIABLES	Education level Ind.Variable	
Q1	Level of feeling European	0.1652	*
Q2	Level of feeling German	0.102	
Q3	Language spoken at home	0.0171	
Q4	Religious affiliation	0.1412	*
Q5	Workplace interaction	0.0867	
Q6	Local people's attitude	0.1186	*
Q7	Equal treatment	0.0502	
Q8	Food consumption	-0.0271	
Q9	Lifestyle in Germany	0.1067	
Q10	Feeling part of Germany	0.0749	
Q11	Level of ties with Turkey	-0.0358	
Q12	Feeling at home in Germany	0.044	
Q13	Job availability	0.1149	*
Q14	Housing conditions	-0.071	
Q15	Education facilities	-0.0497	
Q16	Political interest	0.0278	
Q17	Acquiring German citizenship	-0.1845	*
Q18	Cultural adaptation	0.0997	
Q19	Intermarriage/cohabiting	-0.0747	*
Q20	Legal status in German society	0.0626	
Q21	Inclusion/acceptance or exclusion	0.0502	
Q22	Birth place	0.0076	
Q23	Proficiency in German language	0.1422	*
Q24	School attendance	0.2095	*
Q26	Participation in sportive activities	-0.1938	*
Q27	Preference of a country to live	0.0227	
Q29	Personal status	-0.0160	
Q30	Age structure	-0.3266	*

denotes statistical significance at 5% level

Education (Survey question 25) is correlated with all those above, for example, correlation with Question 1 shows us that educated immigrants with Turkish background feel European. The more educated immigrants feel more European. According to above (Pearson) correlation table, this positive relationship is statistically significant (p<0.1652).

Question 4 is also correlated with education which means more educated people feel less religious or have a moderate attitude towards religion.

There is a relationship between the education variable and independent variable (Q6 Local people's attitude) towards educated Turks which is statistically significant (p< 0.1186).

254

The table shows that a correlation exists between the education level of Turkish immigrants and employment facilities which means that for well educated Turkish immigrants finding a job is not so difficult in Germany. The statistical significance level is $p < 0.1149$.

Acquiring German citizenship (Q17) and education level is correlated but the relationship is a negative association at the level of -0.1845. The table indicates that more educated immigrants are more interested in gaining German citizenship and feel integrated into German society.

Q23 Proficiency in German language and education level of immigrants is also strongly associated. The relationship shows that those immigrants with a high level of education speak better than the poorly educated.

School attendance Q24 and education level of immigrants are closely related, the correlation table suggests that those who attended school in Germany and in Europe are better educated than those who attended in Turkey and other countries.

Q26 Participation in sportive activities and the education level of Turkish immigrants are correlated. Immigrants with higher education are also interested in the sportive activities of the host country. This interaction creates a common interest which is the basis for successful integration.

Q30 Age structure and education has a strong relationship, the correlation table shows 40 years compared with 15-30 years and 31-40 years compared with 15-30 years. The younger generation with better education are better integrated than older generation.

6.2.2 Linear regression analysis

The aim of the linear regression analysis is to find the effect of joint variables' on the integration level of Turkish immigrants into German society. With this objective, the linear regression analysis is used which is a common method to show the correlation of multiple variables. There are two independent variables - feeling German and feeling a part of Germany; the dependent variables are language spoken, interaction, age structure, gender, job availability, political participation, intermarriages, strength of relations with Turkey, proficiency in German language and level of education.

6.2.2 Linear regression analysis

VARIABLES	(1) Feeling German	(2) Feeling part of Germany
Languages spoken at home		
Both German & Turkish compared with Turkish only	0.273**	0.248**
	(2.142)	(2.269)
German compared with Turkish only	0.536**	0.490**
	(2.298)	(2.454)
Work place interaction	0.262***	0.0765
	(3.966)	(1.351)
Gender	0.0671	-0.0501
	(0.556)	(-0.481)
Age structure		
31-40 years compared with 15-30 years	0.117	0.0397
	(0.866)	(0.341)
Above 40 years compared with 15-30 years	-0.116	0.169
	(-0.770)	(1.307)
Ties with Turkey	0.109*	0.138***
	(1.904)	(2.822)
Job availability	0.0394	0.0804*
	(0.763)	(1.818)
Political interest	0.0559	0.0216
	(1.250)	(0.560)
Married/cohabitation	0.0861	-0.0177
	(0.744)	(-0.178)
Proficiency in German language	0.0333	0.0869*
	(0.586)	(1.772)
Level of education	0.108	0.0880
	(1.016)	(0.963)
Constant	0.843**	1.165***
	(2.026)	(3.257)
No. of observations	294	292
R-squared	0.148	0.136
Degrees of freedom	12	12
F-statistic	4.061	3.662

T-statistics in parentheses *** p<0.01, ** p<0.05, * p<0.1

Results of the Linear Regression analysis are presented in Table 6.2.2. Several variables show a significant association (p<0.05) with feeling German and feeling a part of German society. People with Turkish origin who speak both languages at home feel German and a part of German society at the same time. This relationship is statistically significant at the level of p<0.05.

Workplace interaction is associated with Turkish people's feeling German and a part of German society. Strong interaction means feeling more German. This association is statistically significant at the level of *** p<0.01.

Ties with Turkey are associated with feeling German and a part of Germany. Weak ties with Turkey make them feel a part of German society. This relationship is strongly associated with feeling a part of the host country and it is statistically significant at the level of *** p<0.01.

Immigrant people with Turkish origin who feel a part of the host society have more opportunities to find a job in Germany. In other words, job availability is for people who feel a part of German society. This association is statistically significant at the level of * p<0.1.

As to German language capability, persons of Turkish descent living in Germany who speak German fluently feel a part of German society. This correlation is statistically significant at the level of * p<0.1.

6.2.3 Ordered Logit Model Analysis

The following Ordered Logit Model analysis is employed when the dependent variable is *categorical* and consists of more than two categories.

Categories of dependent variables

Categories	Freq.	Percent
(1) ISOLATION	99	33
(2) INTEGRATION	143	47.67
(3) ASSIMILATION	58	19.33
Total	300	100

VARIABLES	
Language spoken at home	
Both	0.773***
	(0.272)
German	1.607***
	(0.508)
Workplace interaction	0.492***
	(0.146)
Gender	0.0222
Age structure	(0.257)
Age category 2 (15-30 years)	0.307
	(0.291)
Age category 3 (31-50 years)	-0.225
	(0.307)
Ties with Turkey	0.279**
	(0.123)
Employment facilities	0.0218
	(0.111)
Political participation	0.107
	(0.0931)
German married/cohabiting	-0.0458
	(0.242)
German language proficiency	0.110
	(0.119)
Education level	0.391*
	(0.223)
Estimated cutpoints	
cut1	3.590***
	(0.916)
cut2	6.034***
	(0.963)
Observations	294

6.2.3 Ordered Logit Model Table

Standard errors in parentheses *** $p<0.01$, ** $p<0.05$, * $p<0.1$

The Ordered Logit Model analysis was employed for selected dependent variables (isolation, integration and assimilation) and key dependent variables such as language spoken at home, work place interaction, age structure, ties with Turkey, employment facilities and the education level of Turkish origin immigrants in Germany. [607]

6.2.3 The Ordered Logit Model Table shows that Turkish descent people who speak both languages at home they feel more integrated and less assimilated. These correlations are statistically significant at the level of *** $p<0.01$.

Persons of Turkish origin who speak only German at home feel assimilated into German society and the German way of life. This relationship is statistically significant at the level of *** $p<0.01$.

Turkish immigrants who have a good relationship with their friends and workmates feel highly integrated. Strong interactions with natives are statistically significant at the level of *** $p<0.01$.

Ties with Turkey make them feel integrated and less assimilated. These correlations are statistically significant at the level of ** $p<0.05$.
Turkish immigrants with more education feel more integrated than those who are poorly educated. This relationship is statistically significant at the level of * $p<0.1$.

---

[607] Steven G. Heeringa; Brady T. West and Patricia A. Berlung: Applied Survey Data Analysis; CRC Press, 2010, p. 149, 164-174

Chapter 7

Chapter 7.1 Introduction: Comparative Analyses of primary and secondary data

This chapter deals with comparing German public opinion data from 2006 to 2010 with the 2007 survey results of Turkish immigrants on their self-perception. In this chapter secondary data comes from previous studies on German public perception of Turkish immigrants' presence and integration process, and primary data derives from the 2007 survey questionnaire conducted by the author in Berlin, Cologne and Munich on Turkish immigrants' self perception of German attitudes towards them; these are compared to obtain new findings in order to draw a final conclusion.

When integration is considered as a two-way process, both sides – German public perception of Turkish immigrants (data from previous studies) and Turkish immigrants' self-perception of German attitudes towards them (2007 Survey questionnaire data) need to be put into consideration together. Therefore, this thesis investigates both sides' points of view, feelings and attitudes towards each other by comparing these factual data to obtain new findings.

Table 7.1.1 A Comparative Analysis of primary and secondary data

Affecting factors of interaction	2007 survey results of Turkish immigrants on their self-perception of integration level	German Public Opinion Data on integration level of Turkish immigrants 1960s to2010
7.1.1 Feeling member of host society	47% feel member of host society	Berlin Institute Data from 2009 suggests only 31% Turks integrated
7.1.2 Feeling comfortable in Germany	48% feel comfortable in Germany	German Public opinion poll of Der Spiegel (May 2008) suggest 42% Turks feel unhap in Germany
7.1.3 To find a job in Germany	32% say it is hard to find job	Berlin Institute for Population Data from 2009 show 31% Turks hard to find job
7.1.4 To find a proper house in Germany	36% say hard to find house	Berlin Institute for Population Data of 2009 31% Turks think hard to find house
7.1.5 Educational Achievement of Turkish Immigrant children in education German schools	35% satisfied with German from 2009 suggests only 24% are satisfied	Berlin Institute for Population Data
7.1.6 School attendance of T. children	43. 3 % attended in Germany	Barometer Data 2008 indicates only 37% Turkish children attend properly
7.1.7 Last education degree they received	28% Public school; 35 % Voc. 16% Technical; 9% High school; 12% have 'University' Degree.	German Ministry of Education data 1999 show 44% managed the basic; 41% German, 27% immig. GCSE level; 26% German, 9.5% immigrant. A-level
7.1.8 Usage of German at home	52. 7 % of Turkish immigrants speak both language at home	No previous data available on it
7.1.9 German language level of Turkish	36 % indicate their German immigrants 'good'	No previous data available on it
7.2.1 Social status of Turk. immigrants	41% satisfied with their status	No previous data available on it
7.2.2 Participation in sportive activities	28. 7 interested in sports in Ger. 11. 7 % of them are professional T.	No previous data on the issue but in G. origin licensed players 250,000 in T is higher than those (225, 000) in T
7.2.3 Political interests of Turks in Ger.	17% of Turkish immigrants interested in politics	5 of the Bundestag's 613 m. T. descent Eurobarometer indicates 32% Turkish descent representatives in EP
7.2.4 Citizenship rates of Turkish origin	32.7 % of Turks gained German Citizenship	Eurostat 2006 indicates only 1/3 of Turkish

	till December 2007	immigrants (800,000) naturalised
7.2.5 Self-employment	18% are self employed	Berlin Institute Data from 2009 suggests 31% Turks self-employed
7.2.6 Number of people visit Turkey From Germany annually	No previous data available on it	DIE-Devlet Istatistik Enstitusu (*State Statistic Institute*) Data from 1999 show 2.233.740 (22.9%) Germans visited Turkey as tourists in 1998

Source: Adapted from the 2007 Survey and the existing data from German and Turkish sources, and Euro-stat/barometer

7.1.1 Comparing integration level of Turkish immigrants from primary and secondary data

The 2007 Survey data on Turkish self-perception of their integration into German society suggests **47%** feel integrated; this is fairly positive and is close to **50%** which is considered a significant integration level.

According to a Euro-barometer survey in 1996, about **51%** of residents of the European Union felt 'European'.[608] However, a recent survey from Berlin Institute 2009 on German public perception of Turkish integration shows that Turkish immigrants are a lesser integrated migrant group into German society. Turks in particular are poorly integrated into German society. Even the ethnic Germans which came decades later than the Turks, they have done relatively well. Compared with those from Italy, Greece, Spain, and Portugal and with ethnic German immigrants from Eastern Europe, the Turks come last in the Berlin Institute's integration ranking with **31%**.[609]

The Berlin Institute's study is based on the annual official census of 800,000 citizens in Germany – one percent of the 80 million total populations – in which people are asked about what kind of accommodation they have, their jobs, education, income and their citizenship. Since 2005 people have been asked to state what country their parent came from. This means that for the first time it is possible to identify trends for people who have obtained German citizenship but also have an immigrant background; a similar approach to British immigration policy. Previously, there was no way to identify naturalised Germans. For instance, immigrants from Turkey can be compared with other groups.[610]

Worldwide famous GEO journal ordered TAM (Türkiye Araştırmaları Merkezi) Turkish Research Centre a computer aided telephone questionnaire to find out German and Turkish communities' attitude and feelings towards each other. The question was "*What do Germans and Turks think about each other?*" The questionnaire was conducted on 600 people from each country in 1999. Although they have seen each other in different places they have sympathy towards each other bilaterally. But they considered that they were quite different from each other from the characteristic aspect. The survey suggested an interesting view almost all of German

---

[608] From **http:/ Pan-European identity**, European identity: Dirk Jacobs and Robert Maier, Netherlands Utrecht University. Accessed on 14.06.2009
[609] http://spiegel.de/international/Germany/0,1518,561969,00.html Access 22/06/2009
[610] Marshall, Barbara: Europe in Change, The new Germany and migration in Europe, Manchester University Press, 2000, (p. 38, 47)

respondents think Turkey is economically dependent on Germany. But half of the Turkish respondents disagree with this German view. [611]

In the framework of historic cultural relations between two countries, Germany opened a Turkish chamber (*Turkische Kammer*) in Dresden Royal Palace in March 5 2010. Andrew Curry wrote that "Saxon kings both feared and admired the Ottoman Empire; Germany has had a long fascination with Turkish art, culture and military prowess."[612] The exhibition curator Holger Schuckeit expresses that "European rulers in the beginning of 1500 were deeply impresses by Turkish culture, art and the Ottoman Empire's military prowess and a little bit jealous of the sultan's unbridled power."[613] Museum officials hope that the exhibition can contribute to the long history of Turco-German relations from cultural aspect.

A survey conducted by The Bertelsmann Foundation in 2009 showed that **69%** of those interviewed felt comfortable in their adopted country, Germany. The same study finds half of the German immigrants feel themselves like outsiders in German society, and their contribution to Germany finds lesser acknowledgements than those of Germans, according to the same survey. [614]

7.1.2 Satisfaction level of Turkish origin young immigrants about life in Germany

The 2007 survey suggests that 48% of Turks feel comfortable in Germany; there is no previous data related to feeling comfortable in German society.

Der Spiegel articles from 2008 as "Unhappy Turkish young academics emigrate to English speaking countries" suggest that considerable number of Turkish origin youths in Germany feel uncomfortable and ungrateful. Therefore, they consider emigrating to Australia and New Zealand, Canada or America from Germany. They have a feeling as if they are unwelcome in Germany. The same poll suggests that 38% of Turkish descent youths believe that they will be given more chance there if they return to Turkey or emigrate to English speaking countries. 42% of them feel that they have been deprived from feeling at home in Germany. In addition, every 4 in 5 academics believe that Germany does not have serious integration policy for its immigrants.[615]

7.1.3 Employment facilities and unemployment rates

According to the 2007 Survey 32% express that it is hard to find a job. The survey results show that the unemployment rates among Turkish immigrants are still higher with 18%. For example, in Germany, according to the 2002 census, 11% of Turks were unemployed compared to a

---

[611] Şen, Faruk: On the eve of year 2000 Europe and Turkey (*2000 yilinin esiginde Avrupa ve Türkiye*), published by Çağ Yayinevi, Istanbul, 1999, (p. 165)

[612] Dresden opens chamber of Turkish delights http://www.thelocal.de/society/20100305-25691.html

[613] Ibid., p.2

[614] 'Study finds half of German immigrants feel like outsiders' -The Local. Published: 15 June 09 17:30 CET On line: http://www.thelocal.de/society/2009/06/15-19945.html

[615] Source: Der Spiegel, May 19, 2008 [AUTHOR'S TRANSLATION]

national average of 4%. Unemployment rates of both men and women are higher than for the general population, especially among those between the ages of 16 and 24.

In 1996, unemployment rates among Turkish immigrants were higher than in other immigrant groups and amongst Germans. Other immigrant groups experience 19% unemployment respectively France 8%, Italy 4% in 1996. It was particularly high among Turks with 22%, and among Germans only 10% were unemployed. [616]

Data from 2009 show 31% Turks believe that it is hard to find a job in Germany.

Zimmermann argues that the impact of migration on the labour market, based on the economic situation of the 1960s and 1970s and the function of guest workers in it, seemed to indicate that the greatest gain for the national economy was from migration derived unskilled migrants.[617]

According to a survey by the Allensbach Institute in 1982 which is old but important, 39% of Germans believed that Turks took jobs from Germans. Especially, young Germans with a low level of educational were particularly susceptible to these opinions and perceived competition by immigrants for jobs and housing. [618]

According to the RWI there were clear beneficial effects in the 1990s (Gieseck, Heilemann and von Löffelholz, 1994): the employment of 1.4 million immigrants in 1992 created an additional 90.000 jobs. In fact, ethnic Germans take jobs from natives and represented a burden on the public budget in the form of housing, work and social benefits, which in early 1990 amounted to 7.4 billion. Moreover, their integration into the German labour market has become more difficult.[619]

In theory higher unemployment should have led to a reduction of in-migration. In reality, instead of increased out-migration in the period of economic downturn, there was higher unemployment in the areas of large in-migration. Immigrants of high skilled labour in a situation of high employment would be beneficial as it would be lower wage levels, allowing employment to grow, leading to an overall gain for the national budget of 4%.[620]

Previous studies suggest there is a relationship between migration and employment. Demographic (age, gender, education, marital status), geographical and economic factors (scarce, poverty and unemployment) affect migration. A study in 2009 has shown educated, single men, between 20-24 aged are more likely to migrate.[621]

The principle of 'dispatchment' in EU legislation meant that EU nationals could work in another state for a wage negotiated in their country of origin if they were sent abroad by their employers. In 1994 this meant in practice that a Portuguese rate (c.DM 1.130 a month whereas a German would receive a wage negotiated by the unions in the region of DM 3.450 a month. There was thus little incentive for German employers to retain German workers. The situation was eventually remedied in 1996 with the so called Arbeitnehmer-Eintsendegesets (Dispatched Workers Act). This exclusion of EU workers showed results in that since 1996 the number of

---

[616] Zimmermann Klaus F.: European Migration, Push-pull theories, Proceeding of the World Bank Annual Conference on Development Economics, Munich, 1998 (p. 8).

[617] Ibid.

[618] Ibid.

[619] Ibid., p.374

[620] Ibid., p. 10

[621] Evcil, Ayşe Nilay: An internal Conference on Globalism and Urban Change "People's Propensities on the Internal Migration: The Case of Turkey", City Futures 2009, PhD Thesis, Beykent University, Istanbul., 2009, p. 1-4

illegally employed EU workers has decreased from 17 to 14%; as unemployment has continued to rise ever since. Structural problems and the employment were seen as the main reasons for this development.[622] Illegal labour was regarded as one of the reasons for raising unemployment in Germany.

7.1.4 Comparing Housing conditions of Turkish immigrants and Germans

The 2007 survey indicates 36% Turks believe it is still hard to find a house and Berlin Institute for Population Data from 2009 suggests 31% Turks think that it is hard to find a house in Germany.

One of the main spheres of life to be influenced by low income is housing. At the time when Turks first settled in Germany, a shortage of low cost rental accommodation forced most to live in conditions which were considerably worse in terms of size and quality than those of Germans. Segregation and the emergence of districts with a high concentration of foreigners has increased rather than decreased. In 1980, 41% of non-Germans lived in areas where more than 12% of the inhabitants was foreigners. By the mid-1980s, their share rose to 45% for non-Germans generally and 49% for Turks.[623]

The most comprehensive study of the housing conditions of Turks in Germany was conducted in 1985 among 43,343 Germans and 9,676 Turkish members of the workforce at Ruhrkohle AG in the Ruhr industrial region.[624] .The average income of Turkish workers at Ruhrkohle, many of whom worked at the coal-face was 9% above that of Germans, and 59% were even willing to pay higher rents in order to improve the quality of their housing. One in three Turks (30%), but only one in six Germans (16%) lived in flats without a bathroom. 93% of Turks compared to 48% of Germans wished to have a larger home. In addition to the discrepancies in housing quality, various studies have revealed that Turks have to pay 20% more rent than Germans for prosperity of the same standards.

In the housing market, in 1989, Germans lived in accommodation with on average, 1.9 rooms per person. Taking this level as the norm, a definition of poor housing would imply that one person has one room or less to live in. in 1989, poor housing among Germans had declined to 34% but remained at 80% for Turks. By the housing standards familiar in German society, one in the three Germans, but four out of every five Turks live in over-crowded conditions.[625]

So, ghettoisation and isolation of immigrants is a barrier for them to associate with natives and other ethnic groups, those ghettos should be dispersed into other districts of the cities where fewer immigrants are residing.

---

[622] Şen, Faruk: On the eve of year 2000 Europe and Turkey (*2000 yilinin esiginde Avrupa ve Türkiye*), published by Çağ Yayinevi, Istanbul, 1999, (p. 165-168)

[623] Forschungsbericht im Auftrag des Bundesministers für Arbeit und Socialordnung,Bonn,1986,p.345.

[624] H.Korte,V.Eichene relationship between both states as well, G.Koch and K.Schmidt,Die Wohnsituation der auslandischeen Mitarbeiter der Ruhrkohle AG.Forschungsbeicht,Bochum-Essen,1981-Schrift-enreihe Landes-und statentwicknungsforschung des Landes Northrhein-

[625] Die situation der auslandischen Arbeitnehmer und ihrer Familiengehoringen in der Bundesrepublik, Represantativuntersuchnung, 1985, (Eds.) Bundesminister für Arbeit und Socialordnung, Bonn, 1986.

In 1990, low income is not the only cause of poor housing. There is little evidence for claims, repeatedly made in the literature, that the housing conditions of Turks are determined by their unwillingness to pay more rent, rather than invest in better housing and live a Turkish neighbourhood. On the contrary, recent evidence indicates that Turks are more willing to invest and improve their poor housing conditions in German society. In the late 1990s more Turks started buying houses although predominantly in those parts of town where they already lived.

In 2004, a study of housing conditions among the Ruhrkohle workforce also showed that most Turks were interested in developing social contact with Germans. Only **13%** preferred to live in a segregated neighbourhood, **53%** in a mixed neighbourhood, while **33%** even expressed a preference for neighbours who were solely German.[626]

7.1.5 Comparison of Educational Achievement of Turkish immigrant children and Germans

2007 survey suggests 35% Turkish immigrants are satisfied with education in German schools.[627] Berlin Institute for Population data from 2009 suggests only 24% are satisfied.

In the long run, young immigrants' integration will only be improved by raising their educational attainment and this in turn will determine their contribution to the welfare state. In 1994, 20% of immigrant pupils left school without any qualification as against 8% of German pupils. Ministry of Federal Education data from 1998-1999 on educational achievement of migrant children show that 44% of immigrant peoples managed only the basic qualification *(Hauptschulabschluss)* 41% of German but 27% of immigrant children achieved a medium (GCSE) level; 26% of German but 9,5% of immigrant students obtained A-level equivalents (Beauftragte, 1997: 112).

Berlin Institute for Population and Development data from 2009 show 30% of students of Turkish origin do not have a school leaving certificate and only 14% pass their final secondary school examinations.

Immigration issues have become a hot topic, and a recent survey by the Friedrich Ebert Foundation think-tank indicated more than 30% of Germans believe the country is "overrun by foreigners." On the other hand, 40% of Turks with university education, who were born in Germany, choose to leave Germany because they never felt like it's their home in Germany, where they were born and raised. They claim that if the society is supposed to be truly democratic, then Germany has to respect the opinions of the citizens.[628]

---

[626] Ibid.

[627] **German school system**: Preschool classes (*Vorklassen*), Schulkindergarten (*preparatory classes*), and Primary school (*Grundschulen*), Secondary school (*Hauptsschulen*), Multi aimed schools (*Schularten mit mehreren Bildungsgangen*), Preparatory for vocational schools (*Realschulen*), High schools (*Gymnasium*), mixed school (*Gesamtschulen/Freie Waldorfschulen*), Evening schools and colleges (*Abenschulen und Kollegs*), Special classes (*Sonderschulen*), Vocational Technique schools (*Berufschulen*), Universities (*Universität*).

[628] http://www.cbc.ca/world/story/2010/10/16/germany-merkel immigrationmulticulturalism.html#socialcomments#ixzz131eSPv4Z

Concurrently, a 40-year immigration trend is now reversing itself: Some 40,000 people left Germany for Turkey in 2009, while only 30,000 emigrated from Turkey to Germany, according to the.[629] Second-generation Turks who leave Germany tend to be well educated.

7.1.6 Measuring level of school attendance of Turkish children

The 2007 Survey indicates that 43% Turkish children attend German schools; 26% attended in Turkey; 2% replied in 'both countries'; 2% in other European countries; 26% attended in non-EU countries.

Euro Barometer Data 2008 indicates only 37% Turkish children attend German schools properly. A comparative research by Maurice Crul and Jens Schneider (2009) exhibits that 14% of Turkish immigrants aged 25-35 finished a preparatory track that would provide direct access to a university.[630] Dropout rates of Turkish immigrants in Germany were 18% of aged 25-35 in 2006, (Konsortium Bildungsberichterstattung, 2006); the overall educational situation of the second generation is significantly better as compared with the first generation. The total percentage of the first-generation individuals between 20 and 26 years of age not working and not studying is 18, 6 %, whereas this is the case only for 8, 5% of the second generation (Konsortium Bildungsberichterstattung, 2006).

7.1.7 Gauging Education level of Turkish immigrant children and Germans

According to the 2007 Survey the last education degree that 28% Turks received was Public school; 35 % have Vocational School or secondary (8-9 years); 16% 'Technical school'; 9% 'High school'; 12% have a 'University' Degree.

2009 German interior ministry report suggests around 30% immigrants have no school leaving qualification and just 14% have passed university entrance level exams, less than half the average of their German counterparts with 30%. [631].

Previous data on educational achievement indicates that a successful integration of immigrants can only be achieved by raising their educational attainment and this in turn will determine their contribution to the welfare state. Here the picture looks gloomy, in 1991 only 0.8% of students in German universities were of Turkish-origin with German educational qualifications. In 1994, one in four secondary school pupils of non-German origin failed to gain a school leavers' certificate but only six percent of those of German origin. Also in 1994, 5% of German-origin applicants but only 1.5% of non-German origin applicants (1,829 individuals) were accepted for public sector employment. Anyone with limited educational achievements is highly disadvantaged in the current German labour market.

In 1994 20% of foreign pupils still left school without any qualification (as against 8% of German pupils). 44% of German but 27% of foreign children achieved a medium (GCSE) level; 26% of

---

[629] Federal Statistics Bureau (2009)
[630] Micro-Census Data from 2005 in Germany
[631] http://www.dw-world.de/popopus/popup-lupe/0..399414_ind-1,00html Society Accessed on 02 022009

German but 9.5% of foreign students obtained A-level equivalents (Beauftragte, 1997: 15). The same picture emerges from post-school apprenticeships, as mentioned above.

A survey conducted in 1998 shows that only 8% of the German youngsters, 33% of all foreign youth and 40% of the youth of Turkish do not even start vocational training. In 1999 the number of Turkish origin pupils in Germany was 503,000. About 91,000 of them attended trade schools. 194,000 of them attended kindergarten and primary schools, while 22,400 pupils attended grammar schools. Furthermore, 19,000 studied in the same year at a university.[632]

A Study from Berlin Institute for Population and Development - 2009 shows Turkish immigrants least integrated in Germany and they are failing in education, integration and employment areas. [633] On a sliding scale of one (poorly integrated) to eight (well integrated), the Turks are the least integrated group of immigrants in German society and are also less successful than immigrants from other countries in securing a job in Germany.

A study by the Berlin Institute for Population and Development 2009 shows that Turkish immigrants came last with a score of 2.4 despite being the second most numerous immigrant groups in the country. Turks finished bottom of the table behind immigrants from the former Yugoslavia and Africa (3.2), the Middle East (4.1), southern Europe (4.4) and the Far East (4.6). The most integrated group in Germany, according to the Berlin institute, is immigrants from other EU countries who score 5.5 on the institute's index.[634]

The report's assessment is based on results from several criteria including education, assimilation into society and employment to make up its index.

In the area of education, the study shows that 30% of students of Turkish origin do not have a school leaving certificate and only 14% pass their final secondary school examinations. In the state of Saarland, 45% of Turkish immigrants have failed to complete their high school education.

In terms of integration into society, Turkish immigrants are marked down due to the fact that less than a third of Turks born in Germany have chosen to obtain German citizenship and 93% have married within the Turkish community.

7.1.8 German language usage level of Turkish immigrants at home and in public

According to the 2007 survey **53%** Turkish immigrants use both languages at home. A recent international survey has shown that children from families with a poor educational background and weak language skills have particularly bad prospects in the German school system.

---

[632] Eryilmaz, Aytaç (2002) *40 years in Germany - At Home Abroad*: DOMIT –Documentation Centre and Museum of the Migration from Turkey, Cologne (p. 6) [Translation from Turkish: Bengü Kocatürk – Schuster]

[633] http://www.dw-world.de/popus/popup-lupe/0,,3975683,00.html 26.01.2009

[634] Ibid.

Proficiency in the German language is one of the key facilitating factors which enable [635] immigrants' access to social and legal institutions of the German state as well as their integration into German society and German life standards. Their social and cultural integration is dependent on German language knowledge and education level of immigrants. Not only for immigrants' integration into German society but also to live in the society, requires a certain level of German language proficiency to interact with German society members. Therefore, German language is the main contributor for immigrants to economically, socially, culturally and politically amalgamate in society.

From linguistic aspect, Faruk Şen argues that "Most of the French immigrants are French citizens and they speak French fluently, but speaking host country's language and gaining its passport is not sufficient for integration regarding French immigrants' protests in the suburbs of Paris in 2005. Şen stresses that language factor is important but economic and psychological factors play also a part as well as host language for a successful integration of immigrants.[636] He suggests that German language education should be started at the age 4 and Turkish language should be taught as a foreign language in schools beside English and French. Because, there are 70,000 Turkish descent entrepreneurs in Germany, they also need to employ Turkish speaking German experts and academics.[637]

7.1.9 Evaluating Self-employment facilities of Turkish origin immigrants

The 2007 survey suggests **18%** Turks are self employed (**10%** men **8%** women) in Germany. Berlin Institute Data from 2009 suggests **31%** Turks have established their small and medium scale self-employed businesses in 47 areas such as travel agencies, food stores, bakeries etc.

There were 150,000 foreigner-owned businesses by 1992, including 33,000 owned by Turks. The Turkish-owned businesses generated 700,000 jobs in 1991 and recorded sales of DM 25 billion (about US $ 17 billion) and invested DM 6 million in Germany[638].

By 1993, employment in manufacturing had declined to 42% for non-German workers generally; among Turks it still constituted over 53%. Conversely, service sector employment had increased from 7% in the 1980s to almost 19% in 1993.[639]

In 1993, 35,000 Turks ran their own businesses and had created 13, 000 jobs between them. Overall, just over 200,000 immigrants were self-employed. The emergence of an entrepreneurial middle class, including a small Turkish sector, had begun, although most of these businesses were only small scale and frequently employed family members. In many cases, unemployment

---

[635] http://spiegel.de/international/Germany/0,1518,561969,00.html   Access 22/06/2009 (p.3)
[636] 'Paris Like Revolution' , 1260 cars burned down by African rebels, Vatan Gazetesi, November 5 2005
[637] Varlı, Ali: Article by Ali Varlı, 'Turkish language should be obligatory in German schools', Berlin, February 18 2008, Hürriyet.de – Gündem – Faruk Şen   Research Centre for Turkey in Essen, *Türkiye Araştırmaları Merkezi-TAM*
[638] This Week in Germany, 18 September, 1992:4.
[639] Bundesanstalt für Arbeits and Socialstatistik-Hauptergebnisse, 1993, Nuremberg, 1993 shows that in 1993, 38 percent of Germans worked in manufacturing, 22% in service sector, while white-collar employment had displaced manufacturing as the largest employment sector among Germans but not among immigrants.

had led to people setting up in business in order to reduce economic insecurity. Some Turkish businessmen, however, also stressed that their key motivation had been to achieve independence 73%, higher income 60%, higher status 62% and more security for their families.

Today, the motivations of persons of Turkish origin in pursuing self-employment can be explained as follows. The Turkish community in Europe as well as Germany is made up of a significant younger population when compared to the average of the EU population, motivated to work in order to become established. Self-employment is an option for many unemployed first-generation former guest workers but it is also increasingly an option for second generation youth, often assisted by parents who had in mind securing the future livelihoods of their children. The overall proportion of Turks who are self-employed in the EU lies at 4.8%, which is significantly below the EU average of 12.3%. Nearly 70% of all Turkish-origin business owners in the EU are in Germany, of which four fifths is in only three sectors: (1) retail; (2) restaurants and takeaways; and (3) the service sector. Over one third (39.7%) of the Turkish immigrant businessmen have lived in Germany for 11-30 years.[640] One study of Turkish self-employed businessmen in Germany found that only **15%** were German citizens in 2003 and that 41%, whilst born in Germany, had Turkish nationality.

Turkish Business World in Berlin, where the population of Turkish emigrants living outside of Turkey is most dense, also has the oldest Turkish society for businessmen in Germany. The society, which was founded by 28 Turkish businessmen in April 1996 under the name of the Berlin Brandenburg Society of Turkish-German Businessmen, today has 380 members. It is the voice of approximately 9000 Turkish business establishments in and around Berlin. The number of German members constitutes about **10%** of the whole.

In 2004, Germany's 64,600 entrepreneurs were of Turkish descent, many of whom became German citizens and had sales of 29.5 billion Euros in 2004, according to Cologne – based chamber of commerce.

As a result, Turks' establishing businesses, gaining German nationality and finally integration has had a positive impact on Turco-German relations. For example, in 2004, bilateral trade between Germany and Turkey rose to 19.6 billion, an increase of **34.1%** over 2003.[641]

In 2006, the number of Turkish business establishments in Berlin, small and large, was around 6800. According to data gathered by the Berlin Chamber of Commerce (IHK), the annual revenues of these establishments amounted to a total of 3.5 billion and they provided employment for over 29,000 people. Friday, 29 August 2008.

Turkish-Germans run some 80,000 businesses that employ, on average, five people. Still, they're only about half as likely as Germans to start companies, according to the Turkish Community in Germany, an advocacy group.

They prefer the self-employed small businesses to in the factories and to avoid becoming unemployed. German Federal States encourage small entrepreneurs by financial aids. While they are doing businesses they are contributors to German economy, too. Economic well-being gives them an upward economic status in German society which affects their integration, too.

Successful integration has been achieved only economically. Since many Turkish descent businesses have been established, Turco-German relations turned into commercial relations and an economic bridge between two communities.

---

[640] TAM-Türkiye Araştirmalari Merkezi or TRC-Turkish Research Centre, Essen, 2003
[641] http://www.iht.com/articles/2005/11/14/news/turks.php

As explained in the chapter one systematically main reason for Turkish labour migration to Germany is unemployment and poverty in poor regions of Turkey. Consequence of prolonged migration is emerged as integration problems for non-returned Turkish people in German society. [642]

7.2.1 Impact of Tourism and purchasing properties of Germans in Turkey

Impact of Tourism and purchasing properties on Turco-German relations – Turks buy from Germany, Germans buy from Turkey. Turco-German relations and tourism is a chain facilitating factor for integration of Turkish immigrants into Germany

Germany is the top country in the ranking list in the world and the relationship between the two countries affects Turkish immigrants' integration into German society. More than 9 million tourists visit Turkey every year; 2 million of them are Germans. Number of Germans as tourists visited Turkey previously between years 1995-1997 [643] respectively as follows:

Table 7.1.2 Number of Germans visiting Turkey 1995-1997

Year	Number of Germans visiting Turkey	Proportion (%)
1995	1.656.310	
1996	2.141.778	
1997	2.338.529	
1998	2.233.740	**22.9**

Source: T.C. Frankfurt Başkonsolosluğu Turizm ve Enformasyon Dairesi (T.R. Turkish Embassy, Frankfurt), 1999

According to the Turkish Statistic Institute (DIE) **9.752.697** tourists visited Turkey in 1998 (**2.338.529** of them were Germans).[644] Germans visiting Turkey does not only contribute to the Turkish economy but also changes their attitude towards their Turkish neighbours in Germany. Germans put aside their prejudices and try to understand the Turkish workers background after visiting Turkey. Their visits to Turkey make easy their co-existence and living together door to door. Germans leaving Turkey with positive impression will help Turks' integration into German society. Tourism creates a bilateral understanding between two communities in Germany.[645]

As to purchasing properties by Germans in Turkey, according to TAM, "As of April 2005, of the 49,567 immovable properties owned by foreigners, 41,413 belonged to German nationals".[646]

In return for this, according to Turkish Housing Minister Faruk Nafiz Özak's statement 'Turkish immigrants own 220,000 properties in Germany; however, the number of properties sold to foreigners mainly Germans was 65,000 in 2008.from Turkey'. [647]

---

[642] Kentleşme, Göç ve Yoksulluk (Urbanisation, migration and poverty) Ed. Ahmet Alpay Dikmen (2002): Imaj Yayinevi, Ankara, 2002 (p. 57, 62, 75)

[643] Şen, Faruk, Akkaya, Çiğdem and Güntürk, Reyhan: On the eve of year 2000 Europe and Turkey (*2000 yilinin esiginde Avrupa ve Türkiye*), published by Çağ Yayinevi, Istanbul, 1999, (p. 73)

[644] Ibid., (p. 88)

[645] Ibid., (p. 141)

[646] Turkish Research Centre-Essen University Publication ,October 2007, 26th Issue

It has been argued that if present demographic trends within Europe continue, the EU will, in future, once again welcome Turkish labour. Moreover, the Turkish economy has done quite well in recent years.[648]

7.2.2 Turkish participation in German sportive activities and their integration

2007 survey suggests **29%** Turks interested in sports in Germany.   **12%** of them are professional. Although there is no available existing data on the issue, Mahmut Özgener (2006), head of Turkish Football Association, claims that increasing number of Turkish origin players is an important factor which creates social interaction with majority youths and contributes to integration of Turkish immigrants into German sport life. He points out interesting figures such as "there are 6 million licensed professional football players in Germany, only **225, 000** in Turkey. "The number of Turkish origin licensed professional players reached **250, 000** is even higher than those Turkey." For example, German National Football Team player Mehmet Scholl, Patrick Malik, Yildiray Baştürk, twins Hamit and Mesut Altintop (Golden Ball) brothers. Mithat Demirel is also Turkish origin German National Basketball player. They are either German born or from mixed/German marriages or both. [649]

Today, Germans of Turkish descent are making it to the top in politics, the arts, sports, and academia. When soccer player Mesut Özil scored for Germany at the 2010 World Cup in South Africa, fans back home didn't care where his parents were from.

Most immigrants in Germany are integrated! The problem is the 15-20% who thinks that their tradition and religion is more important than the German constitution. If you move into another country you have to respect the constitution of the host country. [650]

7.2.3 Impact of Intermarriage Factor and Education on integration level

Even as the number of new marriages in Germany has decreased, the share of intermarriages in 2006 remained well above the share in the early 1990s though a downward trend in intermarriages is evident.

---

[647] Turkish Ministry of Housing and Public Works' Report, Ankara, 16 June 2008.

[648] G.I., Lewis: 'Turkey, The Fit Man of Europe', in Turkey and Europe in Cultural Context, proceedings of a Symposium held on 7 June 1988, Centre of Middle East Studies, University of Cambridge, England, p.19.

Wilhelm, Hummen: The Economic Future of the EC and Turkey's Membership; in Erol Manisali, ed. Turkey's place in Europe, (Istanbul, Logos, 1988) pp70-3,4.

Bernard Burrows: Turkey and the European Community, Federal Trust for Education and Research, Working Paper 3, London, 1987, p. 4

[649] Author's Translation from Turkish Daily Hürriyet, 22.6.2006

Accessed on January 17 2009 Turkish Daily Hürriyet Website www.**hurriyet**.com.tr

[650] http://www.cbc.ca/world/story/2010/10/16/germany-merkel-immigration-multiculturalism.html#socialcomments#ixzz131v3ZlPG

In 2007, 83.7% of Germany's population without migration background completed schooling compared to 63.7% among those with a migration background.

The share of male graduates with Abitur or Fachhochschulreife was also higher among natives (23.5%) compared to men with migration background (18.8%). In contrast, the share of immigrant women with Abitur or Fachhochschulreife was 19.7%, slightly higher than among natives (18.2%). In contrast, those of Turkish origin, who have low intermarriage rates, also had lower graduation rates from all three school levels.

Only 53.6% had completed schooling and only 9.2% of men and 7.6% of women held the Abitur or a comparable degree. The share of those of Turkish origin with vocational training was also exceptionally small compared to all other groups. [651]

Thus, educational data are in line with the assumption that more educated immigrants are more likely to be intermarried. However, this correlation does not imply causality and is probably related to other factors that also affect marriage choice.

Examining intermarriage by nationality and migration background reveals that intermarriage rates have generally increased from the first to the second generation, as would be expected. Also, some of the country's groups, particularly Italian men and Polish immigrants, have significantly higher intermarriage rates than others.

First- and second-generation, male and female Turkish immigrants, by far the largest group in Germany, are least likely to marry a native German — not surprising given that group size and concentration influence intermarriage rates.

Yet, intermarriage rates for men of Turkish background increased from the first to the second generation. This indicates the second generation's greater commitment to and integration into German society.

Furthermore, data support the idea that intermarriage rates and education level correlated. However, it is important to keep in mind that in addition to education, intermarriage rates are also related to residential patterns, religious beliefs, and third-party considerations, including legal restrictions and additional factors not explored here.

---

[651] *Source*: German Micro census 2007 and Central Register of Foreigners (AZR), 2008.
Note: Numbers refer to percentage share of the group's population. Observations below 5,000 are not reported, therefore allowing only for estimates.

7.2.4 Political interest and representations of immigrant origin at local, national and the EU level

The 2007 Survey suggests that only 17% of Turkish immigrants are interested and willing to participate in German politics. They are already involved politics in Germany at local (*Länder*) and national level.

Previous studies from German sources showed that there are only 82 Turkish descent political representatives throughout Germany at all levels of local, state, national (Bundestag 613 members) and European parliament (so far only five Cem Özdemir and Vural Öğer) have been elected. There are 23 MEPs of Turkish descent in European Parliaments, and 16 of those are women. Only 28 Turkish descent politicians represent 1.5 million naturalised Turkish immigrants in Europe both in national and local parliaments. There is a total of 51 MPs for 5.2 million Turkish immigrants across Europe. Those Turkish immigrants are politically active at the level of parliamentary and local government.

Of the 82 million people living in Germany, the 2.4 million ethnic Turks form the largest minority. Since first arriving as guest workers in the 1960s, however, they have remained distinguished from majority society. They are just five (Lale Akgün, Özcan Mutlu, Kenan Polat, Cem Özdemir and Vural Öğer) of the Bundestag's 613 members maintain Turkish legacy and the number of Turks holding elected office throughout all levels of government including local, state and national are about 80.[652]

Cem Özdemir, whose Turkish-born mother once worked as a seamstress in southern Germany, became the nation's first federal lawmaker from an immigrant family in 1994 and now heads the opposition Green Party, which is polling at a record high.

7.2.5 Impact of Political leaders' statements on integration of Turkish immigrants

Chancellor Angela Merkel argues that "Germany should put the job potential of migrants to better use. We can't waste any talent. Whoever lives among us also has to be ready to integrate into society, learn the language, and participate in school. There's a lot to do in that respect."[653]

Turkish community leaders argue that Germans need to be more welcoming. Only a decade ago politicians were still debating whether Germany was an "immigration country" at all.

In 2000, after the Social Democratic government of Gerhard Schröder changed the country's citizenship law to reflect the growing diversity, a leader of Merkel's Christian Democrats called for a "guiding culture" of Germanness. Another complicating factor is Europe's relationship with Turkey, a secular Muslim country that faces German and French objections to its bid to join the European Union.

Germany's denial of being an immigration country made a negative effect on the integration of Turkish immigrants. Many Turks have not felt that they are a part of German society until the official declaration of Interior Minister Otto Schilly in 2001.

---

[652] **GERMAN POLL BAROMETER 10/15/2008**
[653] Die Welt, August 20 2010

Integration issues concerning Turkish immigrants in Germany has always had an effect on Germany's bilateral relations. When a German politician visits Turkey he speaks proudly of the contribution of Turkish guest workers to Germany not only economically but also socio-culturally.

As for Turks' integration problems, in the framework of bilateral relations the German president Christian Wulff visited Ankara and he made a speech in Turkish Parliament. He admitted Germany's past immigration and integration policy ended up in failure. [654]

In this context, studies of integration from German sources suggest that Turks are a less integrated immigrant group than others. Turkish Politicians encourage Turks to resist against the German assimilation program rather than encouraging interacting with Germans. For example, during a 2008 visit to Germany, Turkish Prime Minister Recep Tayyip Erdogan told a Turkish audience, "Nobody can expect you to submit to assimilation. Assimilation is a crime against humanity." [655]

Not only bilateral relations have been affected by Turkish immigrants' integration, but also Turkey's EU membership. According to the Bild's report (October 19 2010), a German public opinion poll on the issue of Turkey's EU membership suggests 73% Germans are against Turkey's EU membership, only 13.5% support its EU membership.[656]

Economic downturns may lead to the scapegoating of ethnic minorities, because of accusation that immigrants take jobs away from native. Turkish immigrants' decision to return home depends on the Turkish economy and unemployment rates in Turkey. As discussed earlier, the Turks are not called "guests" but 'foreigners' by some Germans. In the 1960s Germans called the Turkish labour migrants 'guest workers'. (Because, when ethnic Germans fled from the Nazis to Turkey, are called 'Guests' by the Turkish authorities). Another reason for that has that the Turks did not show any reaction to being called 'guest workers, even if they had lived in Germany over 50 years. The Turks are perceived by Germans as having their political and cultural home in Turkey. In the term of economic crises, the Turks feel they are unwelcome in Germany and some of the Germans think the Turks take jobs from them. Either they want to stay in Germany full-heartedly or return to Turkey. Meanwhile, there is a German saying: "Guests are like fish. After three days, they start smelling."[657]

Since Turks have different culture and tradition which seem an obstacle for Turks' integration within European continent unlike USA.[658]

Main reason why the Turks have less integrated migrant group into German society can be explained as following:

---

[654]Turkish immigrants must learn German: presidents (October 19, 2010) from The Associated Press
http://www.cbc.ca/world/story/2010/10/19/turkey-germany-president.html#ixzz131CUp0Bh

[655] Article by Tony Czuczka - Sep 30, 2010 : Turks in Germany Bridge Two Worlds as Anti-Immigrant Voices Spark Debate, To contact the reporter on this story: Tony Czuczka in Berlin at aczuczka@bloomberg.net. To contact the editor responsible for this story: James Hertling at jhertling@bloomberg.net

[656] Vatan Gazetesi, October 19 2010

[657] Güney, Irem (Columnist): Journal of Turkish Weekly (JTW), Turks in Germany, 'Integration and Exclusion', December 30 2009

[658] Maalouf, Amin: Çivisi Çıkmış Dünya – Uygarlıklarımız Tükendiğinde, Yapı Kredi Yayınları - YKY Publication İstanbul , 2009 (Turkish version translated by Orçun Türkay) Originally Le dereglement du monde, Editins Grasset & Fasquella, 2009 (p. 17-18)

Their aim has never been to stay in Germany permanently, just to earn and save money rather than staying and living a comfortable life in Germany permanently. They were not interested in participation of social and political activities in Germany. They did not learn German and improve their German skills. Moreover, Germans had no immigration and integration policy, since they expected Turks should return. They only encouraged Turks to return home. Turks postponed returning home every year. Germany's encouraging return policy and restriction of family unification, residential and work permit caused Turks to feel unwelcome in Germany and gave them a status as permanent temporariness under the name of foreign residents.[659]

In spite of economic recession and losing the title of the World's most exporting country; Germany has still the world's fourth-largest economy. As to Turkey, the Turkish textile sector is the world's second largest textile investor after China.[660]

7.2.6 Unemployment and Employment facilities of immigrants with Turkish background

Prodromos Ioannous Panayiotopoulos points out that Turkish Diasporas is becoming an economic power in Europe, 2008.[661]In the last decade Turkish immigrants tend to establish self-employment to overcome their economic difficulties which is an effective factor for their integration.[662]

Establishing their small-scale family owned and run businesses turned into entrepreneurships across Europe as well as Germany. There are 68,300 Turkish descent entrepreneurs in Germany, including Bulgaria and Romania these numbers increase to 107,000.[663]

As a conclusion of this section, younger generation of German and European-born (**36%**) Turks create their own distinct identity as 'Euro-Turks'. They find their own place in German European society by establishing their own businesses. There are more than 120,000 German Turks own companies only in Germany such as restaurants, fast food stalls across Europe and Germany, *döner kebab* has become a German national dish.[664]

7.2.7 Conclusion and recommendations

The 2007 Survey suggests that Turks have not been integrated fully from socio-cultural and political aspects into German society since they have distinctive socio-cultural background and political system but they are willing to be integrated. Then, they are aware that integration will

---

[659] Şen, Faruk, Akkaya, Çiğdem and Güntürk, Reyhan: On the eve of year 2000 Europe and Turkey (*2000 yilinin esiginde Avrupa ve Türkiye*), published by Çağ Yayinevi, Istanbul, 1999, (p. 16-20)

[660] Turkish Textile Employers' Association (TTSIS), Accessed on 2009-01-05

[661] Panayiotopoulos, Prodromos Ioannous: Turkish Immigrant entrepreneurs in the EU; Journal of Entrepreneurial Research, 2008, Volume 14, Issue 6, pages: 395-413.

[662] Pecoud Antoine (July 2003): "Self-employment and Immigrants' incorporation (2-3): 247-261.

[663] Şen, Faruk: Experience of Euro-Turks, *Turkey Research Centre Association*, Essen, October 2007, 26th Issue

[664] Morris, Chris: The New Turkey, *A Quiet Revolution on the edge of Europe*, Granda Books, London, 2006, p.186.

give them a better access to participation in legal, social and political rights and those activities in their host country.

German public opinion suggests that Turks are a less integrated immigrant group than others. There are also some misperceptions by German public such as that Turks resist against being integrated and tend to create a parallel society in Germany. Furthermore, they do not bother to learn the German language.

The comparative analysis suggested that until mid-1980s Turkish presence in Germany was positively associated with bilateral relations between the two countries. However, in the early 1990s this relationship began to deteriorate due to a number of reasons: (i) the collapse of Soviet Block and the following German unification and a mass inflow of Ethnic Germans to West Germany, (ii) the completion of Germany's industrial revolution, and it's becoming a post industrial country lead to less demand for low skilled labour workers, (iii) the unwillingness of Turkish immigrants to return home because of poor life standards, high unemployment rates and economic and political instability (including military coup in 1980) in Turkey which lead to their need to become permanent residents in Germany.

As to commercial relations between the two countries, Turkey has always been the greatest trading partner of Germany.[665] As the biggest trade partner, Germany should encourage Turkish immigrants' integration. Although bilateral relations had been affected negatively by integration problems of Turkish immigrants, Germany continued to be the greatest trade partner of Turkey. As German chancellor Angela Merkel offered Turkey a privileged membership to the EU rather than a full membership, her idea was supported by French President Nicolay Sarkozy. Therefore, in recent years, Turkey has strengthened its commercial relations with Japan, South Korea and China which seem more trustworthy than west European states.

Philip H. Gordon argues "Turkey has been a close Western partner for so long, fading hopes for EU accession, civil-military tension, and a secular-religious divide threaten its partnership with West."[666] As Gordon pointed out Turkish immigrants' integration into Germany will also revive Turkey's fading relationship with Europe. Furthermore, "improving relationships with Turkey will keep it in the Western orbit and prevent it from slipping into either authoritoritarian or fundamentalist rule."[667] Therefore, Europe and Turkey should improve bilateral relations by renewing their commitments mutually to promote Turkey's EU membership.

As to the two countries' contribution to the integration of Turks, both presidents admitted neither country had done enough to help integrate Turkish immigrants into German society; nor both agreed that Turks living in Germany must learn to speak German at German president's visit to Turkey on October 19, 2010. German president praised the Turkish 'guest workers' efforts to rebuild postwar Germany. "Nobody is expected to give up their cultural identity or deny their roots,"[668] he said. He also urged co-operation to overcome the problems of integration. Consequently, Turkish labor migration to Germany began in the 1960s has contributed to German economy considerably. Majority of Turkish guest workers stayed in Germany. Then their integration problems emerged. The research question is 'Have Turkish immigrants

---

[665] Article by Sevil Küçükkoşum: Hürriyet Daily News, June 20 2010
[666] Gordon, Philip H. and Taşpınar, Ömer: Winning Turkey, 'How America, Europe, Turkey can revive a fading partnership', Brookings Institution Press, 2008, p. 1-3
[667] Ibid.
[668] German President Christian Wulff visits Turkey, Hurriyet, and October 19 2010.

integrated into Germany between years 1961-2007, and has their integration any impact on Turco-German relations?' To answer the question a univariate and bivariate analyses are carried out separately. Then comparative analyses of primary and secondary data have been performed to draw a final conclusion.

The conclusion to be drawn is that Turkish immigrants have not integrated into German society significantly. This is partly due to German denial of being an immigration country, subsequently lack of an integration policy more than 30 years and accepting Turkish immigrants as a part of German society. Partly due to Turks' undecided attitudes whether to return Turkey or stay in Germany permanently played a role for their unsuccessful integration process. In addition, political leaders of the both countries worsened the situation of immigrants by their inconvenient statements rather than encouraging and supporting their integration process. Then their poor integration level has not contributed fully to bilateral relations between the two countries. Therefore, until 1973 oil crisis Turkish workers were welcome and were like a bridge between two countries, as economic downturn outbreaks and unemployment raises they become a breach or a barrier for the bilateral relations, too.

The treatment of Turkish immigrants by Germans not only affects the Turks themselves but also the whole Turco-German relations indeed. A survey in the late 1981 showed 49 % of Germans have a latent hostility towards foreigners.[669] According to a survey by the Allensbach Institute at the beginning of 1982, 39% of the population believed that Turks took jobs from Germans. Young people with a low level of educational attainment were particularly susceptible to these opinions.[670]

Although according to the 2007 Survey Turkish immigrants seem that they are willing to be more integrated into German society. The survey reflects only their self-perception on their integration level. Moreover, it indicates positive figure with very close to significant level of 50% significance.[671] However, many Germans are not happy concerning Turkish immigrants' integration level. A 2009 survey of the Berlin Institute for Population and Development, 2009: Untapped potential. The state of integration in Germany on German public perception of Turkish integration shows that Turkish immigrants are less integrated immigrant among other ethnic groups into German society.[672] Furthermore, Germany has not a reasonable integration policy and many Germans do not know what they really want from Turks, integration, assimilation or sending them back. A 1992 survey showed that 78 per cent of German people want indiscriminately the all foreigners return their home country.[673]

In addition, integration of Turkish immigrants does not only influence bilateral relations but also EU-Turkey relations. A well-integrated Turkish society in Europe and Germany is always a benefit for both sides. From historical perspective, Stephen F. Larrabee argues "although the Ottoman Empire and its successor Turkey has been part of the European state system since the

---

[669] Marshall, Barbara: Europe in Change, The new Germany and migration in Europe, Manchester university Press, 2000, (p.70-75)

[670] Ibid.

[671] Outcome of the 2007 Survey on Turkish perception of their integration into German society at 50 % level is considered statistically significant.

[672] http://spiegel.de/international/Germany/0,1518,561969,00.html Access 22/06/2009

[673] Şen, Faruk, Akkaya, Çiğdem and Güntürk, Reyhan: On the eve of year 2000 Europe and Turkey (*2000 yilinin esiginde Avrupa ve Türkiye*), published by Çağ Yayinevi, Istanbul, 1999, (p. 283)

Paris Peace Conference in 1856, it was never regarded as an equal member of it. At its root, Europe was Christian."[674]

Both studies (the 2007 survey and German public opinion polls) suggest that majority of Turkish immigrants are poorly integrated into German society. Reasons to that outcome are lack of low interaction between two communities, their relationships and attitudes are like mutual misunderstanding rather than trying to understand each other better. Deep rooted good historical relations between two countries have also been affected negatively by the impact of poor integration of Turkish origin immigrants into German society. Their poor integration level is not only their fault. It is partly because of German denial of being an immigration country. Partly because of absence of German integration policy until year 2000 also played a role in Turks' poor integration.

Reiner Klingholz, the head of the Berlin Institute for Population and Development admits that they have done nothing for Turks' integration. "We invited the guest workers and thought they would leave again soon." He also thinks, Islam is not a continuous obstacle for Turks' integration. "50 years ago in Germany no one could have imagined that Catholic could marry Protestants, but these days no one talks about it anymore," he says.[675]

Integration of Turkish immigrants is considered a challenge for Germany. Germany has concerns that Turks tend to establish parallel societies in Germany and live in isolation rather than integrating into German society. Baron Bodissey writes "Gates of Vienna, at the siege of Vienna in 1683 Islam seemed to overrun Christian Europe. We are in a new phase of a very old war, A Parallel Society in Germany."[676] In contrast to this article, a research on the issue by sociology professor Jürgen Friedrichs suggests that Germans live in an isolated way in Cologne rather than Turks. "German welfare recipients are in a particularly bad situation. They are isolated, have unhealthy eating habits, have fewer visitors, live in homes that are not nearly as clean as those of their Turkish neighbours – even when those Turkish neighbours also depend on welfare payments."[677] Sociologist's findings continue such as "We noticed in other social focal points that Turks condemn vandalism, the beating of their own children, teenage pregnancies and shoplifting more strongly – that is the reason for the preliminary differentiation between Germans and Turks."[678]

Ursula Günter, a lecturer on religion at the University of Hamburg explains general Turkish attitudes towards religion as follows: "The broad majority of Germans has the false impression that all Turks are orthodox Muslims. Most religious Turks, though, do not listen to fundamentalist..."[679]

Participation in sportive activities of host country is a contributing factor for interaction and creates a common goal between immigrants and native youths which lead them to successful

---

[674] Larrabee, F. Stephen and Lesser O. Ian: Turkish Foreign Policy in an Age of Uncertainty, Published by RAND (National Security Research Division), 2003, p. 45

[675] http://Spiegel.de/international/Germany/0,1518,561969,00.html Access 22/06/2009

[676] Ibid.

[677] Gates of Vienna, A Parallel Society in Germany, January 5 2009 FreedomBloggers.ca or Pro-Köln website Accessed on October 13 2009

[678] Ibid.

[679] http://Spiegel.de/international/Germany/0,1518,561969,00.html Access 22/06/2009

integration. Establishing their own businesses is also an integrative factor and helps them avoid unemployment.

Nature of bilateral relations between two countries varies from trade, economic, military, and socio-cultural and to diplomatic relations. Most of the multinational German companies were established in Turkey such as Bosch, Siemens, Mercedes Benz, Man and Volkswagen operates in the framework of the bilateral agreement. Those companies employ Germans in their management but workers are Turks.[680]

On one hand, German politicians stress on integration of Turkish youths into German society. On the other hand, German defence minister proposed citizenship to German-born Turkish descent youths living in Germany, if they serve their military duty in the German army instead of the Turkish in 1998. So citizenship does not mean anything whether immigrants have been integrated or not. The idea was refused by his Turkish counterpart. [681]

Although German unification made a positive impact on housing conditions it affected the integration of Turkish immigrants negatively. When ethnic Germans came back West German authorities ignored the integration of other ethnic groups including Turkish.[682] The unification did not change Germans; they did not give up their traditional tendencies. A small Nazi group attacked on Turkish immigrants' properties in two small German villages in Mölln, 1992; Solingen in 1993. In 2008, The Nazi group burned down a house in Ludwigshafen where 8 Turks died, 60 people injured.[683]

Lack of modernization in Islamic religion and misinterpretation of Islam by stereotype, poorly educated religious leaders causes hesitations in immigrant youths in their integration process into German society.[684] Unemployment also plays a role in discrimination which deepens the problem of youth unemployment. Those desperate youths look for a scapegoat for their discriminative attitude. If politicians don't take any measures, the issue of integration will be at stake.[685]

---

[680] Şentürk, Cem: Article by Cem Şentürk, 'The Germans in Turkey' Türkiye Araştırmaları Merkezi-TAM, October 15 2007 (p. 2)

[681] Geddes, Andrew and Favell, Adrian: Politics of Belonging, Ashgate, 1999, p. 176-191

[682] Fumus, Norman and Başgöz, Ilhan: Turkish immigrants in Europe, An interdisciplinary Study, Indiana University Turkish Studies,1985, p. 3-22

[683] Hurriyet: Five Turkish immigrant children burned down by Skin heads in Solingen in 1993; 9 Turks burned in Ludwigshafen in 2008. Hurriyet.de – Gündem Berlin, February 18 2008

[684] Tavernise, Sabrina: "In Turkey, a Sign of a Rising Islamic Middle Class," *New York Times*, July 23 2007

[685] Wallraff, Günter: Article by Günter Wallraff, "In these days, due to economic crisis not only Turks but also many Germans are at the bottom of socio-economic ladder'', Turkish Daily Hürriyet, November 11 2006

Bibliography

Abadan-Unat, Nermin: Unending Migration: from Guest-worker to Transnational Citizen (Bitmeyen Goc: Konuk iscilikten Ulus-otesi Yurttasliga), Istanbul Bilgi University Press on Migration Studies, 2002

Akçam Dursun. Deutsches Heim- Glück allein (Alaman Ocağı), Göttingen 1982.

Alba, Richard and Victor, Nee: Rethinking Assimilation Theory for a New era of Immigration, in: International Migration Review 31, 1997 p. 226-274

Aleinikoff, T. Alexander and Douglas Klusmeyer (Eds.): Citizenship Today: Global Perspectives and Practices. Washington, DC: Brookings Institution Press, 2001

Atabay, I.: Zwischen Tradition und Assimilation, Lambertus-Verlag, Berlin, 1998
Aygün, T. (2005), Deutschtürkisches Konsumentenverhalten, EUL Verlag, Cologne, .
Bade, Klaus J.: Germans abroad – foreigners in Germany. Migration in Geschichte und Gegenwart, Munich, 1992

Banks, M.: Ethnicity: Anthropological Constructions, Routhledge, London, 1996

Barbalet, J.M.: Citizenship Rights, Struggle and Class Inequality, Open University Press, 1988.
Bauböck, R.: Migration and Citizenship, New Community, 18 (1 October 1991), pp.27-48.
BBC News, "Turkey must have secular leader" April 24 2007
Bentz, U. (2006), "Umworbene Minderheiten", Extradienst, available at: www.extradienst.at (accessed March 26 2006
Bergstrom, H.: Sweden Learns to be Less Stable, More Normal', The European, 17-20 June 1993.
Boos-Nünning, Ursula: Quotierung und Gerechtigkeit, Selbstverlag, Düsseldorf, 1999
Borjas, George J.: The Economics of Immigration, Journal of Economic Literature 32, 1994, 1667–1717.

Borjas, George. Friends or Strangers: the impact of immigration on the U.S. Economy, New York: Basic Books, 1990
Brubaker, Rogers, 'Immigration, Citizenship, and the Nation-State in France and Germany': Shafir, Gershon ed., the Citizenship Debates; Minneapolis; University of Minnesota Press, 1998 (pp.131-167)

Brubaker, Roger: Citizenship and Nationhood in Franc and in Germany, Cambridge: Harvard University Press, 1992, p. 174

Brubaker, Rogers: 'Immigration, Citizenship, and the Nation-State in France and Germany,' pp. 131-167 in Shafir, Gershon ed., the Citizenship Debates. Minneapolis, University of Minnesota Press, 1998

Brzezinski, Zbigniew: Out of Control, Global Turmoil on the Eva of Twenty-first Century. New York: Touchstone Books, 1993.
Dahredorf, R.: 'The Erosion of Citizenship and its Consequences for all', New Statesman and Society, 12 June 1987.

Buchel, F. and Frick, J.R.: Panel data from SOEP (German Socio-economic Panel Study) and BHP (the British Household Survey), Immigrants' economic performance across Europe, Journal Population Research and Policy Review (2005) 24, p.193

Carmon, Naomi (Ed.): Immigration and Integration in Post-Industrial Societies: Theoretical Analysis and Policy-Related Research: Centre for Research in Ethnic Relations, Warwick, 1996.

Castles, Stephen, Heather Booth and Tina Wallace: Here for Good: Western Europe's New Ethnic Minorities. London, DATE

Çinar, M. (2002), "Ethno-Marketing für Deutschtürken", Direkt-Marketing, available at: www.im-marketing-forum.de/zeitschriften (accessed 12 February 2006), No.38

Şentürk, Cem: Article by Cem Şentürk, 'The Germans in Turkey' Türkiye Araştırmaları Merkezi-TAM, October 15 2007 (p. 2)

Close, Paul: Children's Rights, Labour and Citizenship', ESRC Seminar Series 1993-4 on Childhood and Society, University of Keely, 1993

Close, Paul: Children's Rights, Labour and Citizenship', ESRC Seminar Series 1993-4 on Childhood and Society, University of Keely, 1993

Commissary for Foreign Affairs (2002), Daten und Fakten zur Auslandssituation, 20th ed., available at: www.tcberlinbe.de (accessed 1 February 2006)

Constant, A., Shachmurove, Y., Zimmermann, Klaus F. (2004), What Makes and Entrepreneur and Does It Pay? Native Men, Turks, and Other Migrants in Germany, Institute for the Study of Labour, Bonn, IZA DP, No. 940, D i s c u s s i o n - p a p e r s e r i e s, 1999 (p. 3, 6, 32)

Dahredorf, R.: 'The Erosion of Citizenship and its Consequences for all', New Statesman and Society, 1987

Eder, Klaus & Bernhard Giesen, Bernhard (eds.): National Identity and Citizenship, The Cases of Germany and France, European Citizenship between National legacies and Postnational Projects. Oxford, New York: Oxford University Press, 2001, pp. 36-61

Ehrkamp, Patricia, "We Turks are no Germans": assimilation discourses and the dialectical construction of identities in Germany, *Environment and Planning, A* 2006, volume 38, pages 1673-1692

Ekin, Nusret: "The Problem on the Agenda: Turkish Migrant Workers"; *Economic and Touristic Bazaar International*; 1982; Vol. 1; No: 2; p. 3-4.

Ekin, Nusret: "Turkey's and the World's Most Pressing Problem: Unemployment"; Article by Nusret Ekin, *Anka Review*; Dec. 20, 1983

Eriksen, Erik Oddvar and Jarle Weigård, 2000. 'The End of Citizenship? New Roles Challenging the Political Order,' pp.13-34 in Catriona McKinnon & Lain Hamper Monk eds., The Demand of Citizenship.

Eryilmaz, Aytaç/Jamin, Mathilde (Eds.): Fremde Heimat, Die Geschichte der Einwanderung aus Türkei; Essen, Klartext, 1998p. 93-123)

Esser H, 2003, ``Does the new immigration require a new theory of intergenerational integration?", WP 71, Mannheimer" Generation und Identität" Edited by H. Esser and J. Friedrichs. Opladen, Westdeutscher Verlag. 2007 (p. 2)

Esser, H. (1990b) Familienmigration und Schulkarriere ausländischer Kinder und Jugendlicher. Pp.127–146 in Esser, H.: Aspects of migration sociology, Darmstadt and Neuwied, 1980

Federal Statistical Office (2005), "Einbürgerungen nach ausgewählten bisherigen Staatsangehörigkeiten", available at: www.destatis.de (Access 5 June 2006),
Federal Statistical Office (2006), "Ausländische Bevölkerung am 31 December 2005 nach, Durchschnittsalter und-Aufenthaltsdauer", available at: www.destatis.de (Access 5 June 2006),

Fijalkowski, Jürgen: 'Conditions of Ethnic Mobilisation: The German Case' in John Rex and Beatrice Drudy (Eds.) *Ethnic Mobilisation in a Multi-cultural Europe*. Aldershot and Brookfield, VE: Averbury, 1994

280

Firat, I. (1990), Nirgends zu Hause!? Türkische Schüler zwischen Integration in der BRD und Remigration in die Türkei, Verlag für Interkulturelle Kommunikation, Frankfurt/M, 1990

Frassmann, Heinz, and Rainier Münz. (Hg.): Migration: Europe, Frankfurt: Campus 1996.

Frassmann, Heinz, and Rainier Münz: (Eds.) European Migration in the Late Twentieth Century: Historical Patterns, Actual Trends and Social Implications, Luxemburg, Austria, International Institute for Applied Systems Analysis, 1994.

Fumus, Norman and Başgöz, Ilhan: Turkish immigrants in Europe, An interdisciplinary Study, Indiana University Turkish Studies, 1985, p. 3-22

Greve, M., Cinar, T. (1998), Das türkische Berlin. Ausländerbeauftrage des Senats für Berlin, Springer, Berlin,

Greve, Martin und Orhan, Kalbiye Nur: Berlin deutsch – türkische in die neue Vielfalt, Stadt der Vielfalt – Das Guardian, 3 June, 1993, Webster, P., 'Pasqual Aims for "Zero" Migration'

Heckmann, F. (1992), Ethnische Minderheiten. Volk und Nation. Soziologie interethnischer Beziehungen, Lucius & Lucius, Stuttgart

Hof, B.: Arbeitskraftebedarft der Wirtschaft. Arbeitsmarktchancen für Zuwandrer,in:Friedrich-Ebert-Stiftung(Hrsg.),Zuwanderungspolitik der Zukunft ,Reihe Gesprachskreis Arbeit und Soziales,Nr.3,S.7-22,Bonn, l992

Joppke, Christian: Immigration and the Nation-state, the United States, Germany, and the Great Britain, 1999, (p. 200)
Hof, B.: Arbeitskraftebedarft der Wirtschaft. Arbeitsmarktchancen für Zuwandrer,in:Friedrich-Ebert-Stiftung(Hrsg.),Zuwanderungspolitik der Zukunft ,Reihe Gesprachskreis Arbeit und Soziales,Nr.3,S.7-22,Bonn, l992
Gang, Ira and Klaus F. Zimmermann: Is Child like Parent? Educational Attainment and Ethnic Origin, Bonn, Germany: Institute for the Study of Labour, 1999.

Gardner, J.P., What Lawyers Mean by Citizenship', Encouraging Citizenship: Report of the Commission on Citizenship, London: HMSO, 1990

Geddes, Andrew and Adrian Favell (eds.): The Politics of Belonging: Migrants and Minorities in Contemporary Europe, Ashgate, 1999, p. 176-191

Geddes, Andrew: Immigration and European Integration: Towards Fortress Europe? New York: St. Martin's Press, 2000.
Gogolin, I., Nauck, B. (2000), Migration, gesellschaftliche Differenzierung und Bildung, Leske und Budrich, Opladen,

Gordon, Milton: Assimilation in American Society. New York, Oxford University Press, 1964 Gordon, Milton: Assimilation in American Society. New York, Oxford University Press, 1964

Güntürk, R. (1999), "Mediennutzung der Migranten – mediale Isolation?", in Butterwegge, F. (Eds), Medien und multikulturelle Gesellschaft, Leske und Budrich, Opladen,

Habermas, Jürgen: the European Nation State: On the Past and Future of Citizenship, *Public Culture,* Vol. 18, No. 2, 1998, 409

Hafez, K. (2002), Türkische Mediennutzung in Deutschland: Hemmnis oder Chance der gesellschaftlichen Integration? Eine qualitative Studie im Auftrag des Presse- und Informationsamtes der Bundesregierung, Federal Public Relations and Information Office, Hamburg, available at: www.mediacultureonline.de (Access 16 June 2006)

Halfmann, J.: Two Discourse of Citizenship in Germany: The Difference between Public Debate and Administrative Practice, *Citizenship Studies,* Volume 1 No. 3, 1997, p.316

Hallbronner, K.: Citizenship and Nationhood in Germany, in *Immigration and the Politics of Citizenship in Europe and North America,* William Rogers Brubaker Ed.), New York: University Press of America, 1989, p. 67

Heitmeyer, W., Dollase, R. (1996), Die bedrängte Toleranz, 2nd Eds., Suhrkamp, Frankfurt

Horrocks, David, and Eva Kolinsky (eds.): Turkish Culture in German Society Today, Providence, R.I. Berghahn 1994
Hunter, Shireen T.: The Future of Islam and the west: Clash of Civilisations or Peaceful Coexistence? Westport, Conn, Praeger, 1998.

Kraus-Weysser, F., Uğurdemir-Brincks, B.N. (2002), Ethno-Marketing: Türkische Zielgruppen verstehen und gewinnen, Redline Wirtschaft bei Verlag Moderne Industrie, München,

Kastoryano, Riva: *Negotiating Identities. States and immigrants in France and Germany,* Princeton, N. J.: Princeton, University Press, 2001

Katharina G. Abraham and Susan N. Houseman: Lessons from Germany and Job Security in America, 'Labour Market Performance in Germany and the US, Univ. of Maryland, 1987 (p. 47-50), and General Anzeiger, 23.3.l992

Katharina G. Abraham and Susan N. Houseman: Lessons from Germany and Job Security in America, 'Labor Market Performance in Germany and the US, Univ. of Maryland, 1987 and General Anzeiger, l992 (p. 47-50)

Kaya Ayhan and Kentel Ferhat: (2005): *Euro-Türkler Türkiye ile Avrupa Birliği Arasında Köprü mü Engel mi?*(Euro- Turks: A Bridge or a A Breach Between Turkey and European Union) Istanbul Bilgi Üniversitesi Press, Migration Studies, Istanbul.

Kritz, Mary M., Elizabeth m. Petras, Charles B. Keely and Silvano M. Tomasi (eds.) Global Trends in Migration: Theory and Research on International population Movements. Staten Island, NY: Centre for Migration Studies, 1981.

Klusmeyer, D.: 'A guiding culture' for immigrants? Integration and diversity in Germany, *Journal of Ethnic and Migration Studies,* 27/3: 519-32, 2001,

Küçükcan, Talip: Turks in Germany; Between Inclusion and Exclusion, *Islam Araştırmaları Dergisi*, Sayı 7, 2009, pp 97-118

Manz, Stefan: *Journal of Multilingual and Multicultural Development* (Guiding culture-*Leitkultur*) Debate in Germany. In Chapter, 'Constructing a Normative National Identity: The *Leitkultur* Debate in Germany, 2000-2001', Vol. 25: 586, Special Issue, 2004, (p. 481-489, 494-495)

Marshall, Barbara: Europe in Change: the New Germany and Migration in Europe, Manchester University Press, 2000
Martin Greve und Kalbiye Nur Orhan: Berlin deutsch – türkische in die neue Vielfalt, April 2008

Mayer, Jochen, and Regina T. Riphahn: Fertility Assimilation of Immigrants: Evidence from Count Data Models. Bonn, Germany: Institute for the Study of Labour, 1999.

Modood, Tariq, and Pnina, Werbner (eds.): The Politics of Multiculturalism in the New Europe; Racism, Identity and Community. New York: Zed Books Ltd., 1997.

282

Myrdal, Gunnar, 'Immigration as an economic asset', in Sarah Spencer (ed.), Rivers Oram Press, l994, p. 34

Myrdal, Gunnar: Rich Lands and Poor. New York: Harper and Row, 1957.

Nieke, W. (1991), "Situation ausländischer Kinder und Jugendlicher in der Bundesrepublik Deutschland: Vorschule, Schule, Berufsausbildung, Freizeit, Kriminalität", in Laijos, K. (Eds),Die zweite und dritte Ausländergeneration. Ihre Situation und Zukunft in der Bundesrepublik Deutschland, Leske und Budrich, Opladen,

Norman Fumes and Ilhan Başgöz: Turkish immigrants in Europe, An interdisciplinary Study, Indiana University Turkish Studies, 1985, p. 3-22

Ogan, Christine and Marisca Milikowski: 'Boundaries Crossed and Maintained: Turkish Migrants' Culture, Religion and Use of Satellite Television' Paper presented to the Intercultural and Development Division of the International Communication Association Conference, Jerusalem, 1998

Otyakmaz, Berrin Özlem: Auffallen Stühlen, Türkischer Migrantinnen in Deutschland, Köln: ISP,1995. Pagenstecher, C. Dr. (1996), "Die Illusion der Rückkehr. Zur Mentalitätsgeschichte von Gastarbeit und Einwanderung", Soziale Welt, available at: www.cord-pagenstecher.de (Access 15 May 2006), Vol. 47 No.2, pp.149-79.

Panayiotopoulos, Prodromos Ioannous: Turkish Immigrant Entrepreneurs in the European Union: International Journal of Entrepreneural Behaviorist & Research Vol. 14 No. 6, 2008, (pp. 399)

Park, R. E.: The Urban Community as a Spatial Pattern and a Moral Order. Pp. 3–18 in The Urban Community, edited Park, Robert E.: Race and Culture, Glencoe, Ill., the Free Press, 1950

People on the move, New migration flows in Europe (European Issues), Council of Europe Pres, 1992 (.9-14, 66-75, 100-101

Polat, Ü.: Soziale und kulturelle Identität türkischer Migranten der zweiten Generation in Deutschland, Verlag Dr. Kovac, Hamburg, 1998

Prakash Shah and Werner F. Menski: Migration Diasporas and Legal Systems in Europe: 2006 by Routhledge-Cavendish London and New York

Preuss, Ulrich K.: 'Problems of a Concept of European Citizenship', 1995, pp. 267-281 in European Law Journal. Vol. 1, no. 3. Prodromos Ioannous Panayiotopoulos:"Turkish immigrant entrepreneurs in the European Union: a political-institutional approach", International Journal of Entrepreneurial Behaviour & Research, Vol. 14 Issue: 6, 2008, pp. 395 – 413

Richter Michael (2005): *Geldiler ve Kaldılar...Almanya Türklerinin Yaşam Öyküleri (They came and stayed ...Life Stories of Turks in Germany)* translated by Mutlu Çomak Özbatır, Istanbul Bilgi Üniversitesi Press, Migration Studies, Istanbul.

Sauer, M. (2003), "Kulturelle Integration, Deprivation und Segregationstendenzen türkischer Migranten in Nordrhein-Westfalen", in Goldberg, A. (Eds), Migrationsbericht der Stiftung Zentrum für Türkeistudien, Lit-Verlag, Münster, available at: www.anschub.de (Access 28 March 2007), .

Sauer, M. and Goldberg, A.: Lebenssituation und Partizipation türkischer Migranten in Nordrhein-Westfalen, Lit-Verlag, Münster, 2001

Schültze, Günter: 'The Importance of Associations and Clubs for the Identities of Young Turks in Germany' in John Rex and Beatrice Drudy (eds.) Ethnic Mobilisation in a Multi-cultural Europe. Aldershot and Brookfield, VE: Averbury, 1994

Seibel-Erdt, R., Söhret, A.: Nicht ganz hier und nicht mehr zu Hause: Gespräche mit Türkinnen und Türken der ersten Generation, Waxmann, Münster, 1999

Seifert, Wolfgang, 1997. 'Admission policy, patterns of migration and integration: the German and French case compared' pp. 441-460 in New Community, Vol. 23, no 4.

Sen, F. and Goldberg, A. (1994), Türken in Deutschland: Leben zwischen zwei Kulturen, C.H. Beck, München

Sen, F., Sauer, M., Halm, D. (2001), "Intergeneratives Verhalten und (Selbst-) Ethnitisierung von türkischen Zuwanderern", Gutachten des Zft für die Unabhängige Kommission 'Zuwanderung', Zentrums für Türkeistudien, Lit-Verlag, München, .

Sen, F.: Türkische Minderheit in Deutschland. Bundeszentrale für politische Bildung, Informationen zur politischen Bildung, Franzis Print & Media, München, Issue 277, 2002

Sen, Faruk: Forty Years Later, Turkish Immigrants in Germany, Private View, Essen, 2002.

Sen, Faruk: Turks in Federal Republic of Germany; Achievements, problems and Expectations, *Turkish Studies Quarterly `Digest,* Vol. 13 No. 17, 1989, p. 41

Soysal, Yasemin, 1998. 'Toward a Postnational Model of Membership' pp. 198-221 in Shafir, Gershon ed., The Citizenship Debates, Minneapolis: University of Minnesota Press.

Soysal, Yasemin: 'Participation of Immigrants in European Public Spheres' in H. Entzinger et al. Political and Social Participation of Immigrants through consultative Bodies. Strasbourg: Council of Europe, 1999

Soysal, Yasemin: Limits of Citizenship: Migrants and Postnational Membership in Europe. Chicago: University of Chicago Press, 1994.

Spencer, Sarah : 'Immigration as an Economic Asset'; German Experience, A positive Approach to Migrants, River Oram Press, 1994, (p.11-13) In Sarah Spencer (Ed.),"A Positive Approach to Migrants" Rivers Oram Press 1994, Chapter 5, (p. 93-103)

Stark, Oded: The Migration of Labour; Basil Blackwell, Oxford, 1991 (pp. 406)
.

Steven G. Heeringa; Brady T. West and Patricia A. Berlung: Applied Survey Data Analysis; CRC Press, 2010, p. 149, 164-174

Tavernise, Sabrina: "In Turkey, a Sign of a Rising Islamic Middle Class," New York Times, July 23 2007

Ulrich, Ralf: German Socio-economic Panel Study,"A Positive Approach to Migrants", in: Sarah Spencer (Ed.), Rivers Oram Press, 1994. Chapter 4, p.65.

Ulusoy, Y. (2003), "Sozioökonomische Lage, Spar und Investitionsverhalten türkischer Migranten in Deutschland – Ergebnisse einer repräsentativen Telefonanfragung", in Goldberg, A. (Eds),Migrationsbericht der Stiftung Zentrum für Türkeistudien, Lit-Verlag, Münster, available at: www.anschub.de (Access 28 March 2007), .

Uzun, E. (1993), "Gastarbeiter – Immigration – Minderheit. Vom Identitätswandel der Türken in Deutschland", in Leggewie, C., Senocak, Z. (Eds),Deutsche Türken. Das Ende der Geduld, Rowohlt, Reinbek, Hamburg, .

Varlı, Ali: Article by Ali Varlı, Five Turkish immigrant children burned down by Skin heads in Solingen in 1993; 9 Turks burned in Ludwigshafen in 2008. Hurriyet.de – Gündem Berlin, February 18 2008

284

Verheyen, Dirk: The German Question, A Cultural, Historical, and Geo-political Exploration. Colorado: Westview Press, 1999.

Wallraff, Günter: Article by Günter Wallraff, "In these days, due to economic crisis not only Turks but also many Germans are at the bottom of socio-economic ladder'', Turkish Daily Hürriyet, November 11 2006

Weber, C. (1989), Selbstkonzept, Identität und Integration. Eine empirische Untersuchung türkischer, griechischer und deutscher Jugendlicher in der Bundesrepublik Deutschland, VWB-Verlag, Berlin,

Weidacher, A.: "Migrationsspezifische Bedingungen und soziokulturelle Orientierungen", Deutschland zu Hause. Politische Orientierungen griechischer, italienischer, türkischer und deutscher junger Erwachsener im Vergleich, Leske und Budrich, Opladen, 2000

Weiß, H.-J., Trebbe, J.: Mediennutzung und Integration der türkischen Bevölkerung in Deutschland. Ergebnisse einer Umfrage des Presse- und Informationsamtes der Bundesregierung, Nomos Verlag, Baden, available at: www.media-culture.de Access on 29 March 2007

Wodak, Ruth & Michael Meyer: Methods of Critical Discourse Analysis, Stage, London, 2001

Yildiz, Erol: Die halbierte Gesellschaft der Postmoderne, Probleme des Minderheitendiskurses unter Berücksichtigung alternativer Ansätze in den Niederlanden, Opladen: Westdeutsche Verlag 1997.

Varlı, Ali: Article by Ali Varlı, 'Turkish language should be obligatory in German schools', Berlin, February 18 2008, Hürriyet.de – Gündem – Faruk Şen
Books, 1996.

Wiener, Antje: 'European' Citizenship Practice – Building Institutions of a Non-state. Boulder/Oxford: Westview Press, 1998.

Zimmermann, Klaus F.: Ethnic German Migration since 1989, Results and Perspectives IZA DP No. 50, D i s c u ssi o n p a p e r s e r i e s, 1999 (p. 3, 6, 32)

Zimmermann, Klaus F.: European Migration, Proceeding of the World Bank Annual Conference on Development Economics, University of Munich, 1994 (p. 313).

Zimmermann, Klaus F.: European Migration, Proceeding of the World Bank Annual Conference on Development Economics, University of Munich, 1994 (p.313).